The Other Sides of Paradise

Houses and graves in Cairo's Northern Cemetery, as seen from a Mamluk tomb.

THE OTHER SIDES OF PARADISE

Explorations into the Religious Meanings of Domestic Space in Islam

Juan Eduardo Campo

University of South Carolina Press

Published in Columbia, South Carolina, by the
University of South Carolina Press

Manufactured in the United States of America

Library of Congress Cataloging-in-Publication Data

Campo, Juan Eduardo, 1950–
The other sides of paradise : explorations into the religious meanings of domestic space in Islam / Juan Eduardo Campo.
p. cm.—(Studies in comparative religion)
Includes bibliographical references (p.) and index.
ISBN 0–87249–738–0 (hard cover : acid-free)
1. Islam—Egypt. 2. Egypt—Religious life and customs. 3. Dwellings—Egypt. 4. Dwellings—Religious aspects—Islam. I. Title. II. Series: Studies in comparative religion (Columbia, S.C.)
BP63.E3C36 1991
297′.0962—dc20 90-26356

Para mis padres, Kathryn Ruth y Julio Hernan Campo.
Que en sus migraciones me han enseñado los senderos
que conducen al corazón del hogar.

Studies in Comparative Religion

Frederick M. Denny, Editor

The Holy Book in Comparative Perspective
Edited by Frederick M. Denny and Rodney L. Taylor

Dr. Strangegod: On the Symbolic Meaning of Nuclear Weapons
By Ira Chernus

Native American Religious Action: A Performance Approach to Religion
By Sam Gill

The Confucian Way of Contemplation: Okada Takehiko and the Tradition of Quiet-Sitting
By Rodney L. Taylor

Human Rights and the Conflict of Cultures: Western and Islamic Perspectives on Religious Liberty
By David Little, John Kelsay, and Abdulaziz A. Sachedina

The Munshidin of Egypt: Their World and Their Song
By Earle H. Waugh

The Buddhist Revival in Sri Lanka: Religious Tradition, Reinterpretation and Response
By George D. Bond

A History of the Jews of Arabia: From Ancient Times to Their Eclipse Under Islam
By Gordon Darnell Newby

Arjuna in the Mahabharata: Where Krishna Is, There Is Victory
By Ruth Cecily Katz

Ethics, Wealth, and Salvation: A Study in Buddhist Social Ethics
Edited by Russell F. Sizemore and Donald K. Swearer

Ritual Criticism: Case Studies in Its Practice, Essays on Its Theory
By Ronald L. Grimes

The Dragons of Tiananmen: Beijing as a Sacred City
By Jeffrey F. Meyer

The Other Sides of Paradise: Explorations into the Religious Meanings of Domestic Space in Islam
By Juan Eduardo Campo

Contents

Figures ix
Tables ix
Series Editor's Preface x
Preface and Acknowledgments xi
Transliteration and Other Technical Matters xv

Introduction 1

1. **Images of Domestic Space in the Quran** 7
   - Quranic House Terms 8
   - God's House 9
   - Sacred History 14
   - House Rules 19
   - The Hereafter 24

2. **The Houses of the Hadiths** 28
   - House Terms 29
   - God's House 30
   - House Rules 32
   - The Hereafter 41
   - Parables 44
   - Conclusions 46

3. **The Birth of the House of Submission** 48
   - The Prophet's House 50
   - Kufa and Baghdad, Houses of Conquest and Empire 56
   - The House of Islam 63
   - Alternative Houses 67

4. **Muslim Dwellings in Urban Egypt, Past and Present** 74
Domestications of Islam in Premodern Cairo 75
Domestic Space and Urban Society in Egypt Today 87
House Terms in Modern Egyptian Discourse 91
Appropriating Meaning for the House: Action, Speech, and Interior Display 94

5. **Domestications of Islam in Modern Egypt: A Cultural Analysis** 98
The Components of Sacrality in Egyptian Muslim Homes 98
"Building a House": Foundation and Marriage Ceremonies 103
"Death and the Destruction of Houses" 113
Internal Arrangements 124
Estrangements 130
Conclusion 137

6. **The Metamorphosis of Domestic Space in the Pilgrimage Murals of Egypt** 139
Pragmatic Description 140
Curiosities and Congeries: The History of Interpretation 143
Semiotic Analysis 146
Semantic Analyses and Transformations 149
Comparisons, Contexts, Explanations 158

Epilogue 166

Appendix A. Epigraphic Formulae Used in Hajj Murals: Index and Commentary 170

Appendix B. Iconic Figures Used in Hajj Murals: Index and Commentary 181

Notes 192

Select Bibliography 231

Subject Index 237

Index of Quran Citations 243

Index of Hadith Citations 245

Figures

Frontispiece. Houses and graves in Cairo's Northern Cemetery, as seen from a Mamluk tomb.

Figure 1. Layouts of the Prophet's house-mosque in Medina during the first year of the Hijra and after Caliph ᶜUthman's expansions, c. 30/650. 52

Figure 2. The Round Medina of Baghdad, founded by the Caliph Mansur in 145/762. 61

Figure 3. Hasan Kashif mansion, Cairo (twelfth/eighteenth century). 81

Figure 4. Qasim Bey mansion, southern Cairo (twelfth/eighteenth century). 82

Figure 5. Quranic inscription in the *qāᶜa* of Jamal al-Din al-Dhahabi's house, inner Cairo (c. eleventh/seventeenth century). 85

Figure 6. *Baladi* apartments in southern Cairo, still overshadowed by the religious college-tomb complex of Sultan Hasan and Muhammad ᶜAli's citadel mosque. 89

Figure 7. Cemetery dwellers. 124

Figure 8. Hajj mural on house in Imbaba, western edge of modern Cairo. 148

Figure 9. Hajj mural on house in al-Ballas, Upper Egypt. 152

Figure 10. Hajj mural on front of house near Qurna, Upper Egypt. 155

Tables

1. Thematic Classification of Quranic House Terms. 10
2. Index of Semantic Categories and Epigraphic Formulae Used in Egyptian Hajj Murals. 170
3. Inventory of Epigraphic Formulae Used in Egyptian Hajj Murals. 179
4. Index of Iconic Figures Used in Egyptian Hajj Murals. 181

Series Editor's Preface

Islam specialists have long charged that the academic study of religion has neglected the study of Islam. This neglect has extended to areas of research such as myth, ritual, and symbolism—areas that are so prominent in the study of other traditions. Recently, however, the situation has begun to improve as demonstrated by the appearance of imaginative new approaches to Islamic topics.

The study of the religious meanings of space has been, especially under the influence of Mircea Eliade, a prominent topic in comparative religion. Research has generally focused on civic and public ritual spaces, environments, and structures. Recent books in this vein include Jeffrey Meyer's important study of a classic ceremonial urban center, *The Dragons of Tiananmen: Beijing as a Sacred City,* also published in this series. However, there has been little study of the religious meanings of domestic space, particularly with reference to Islam. Juan Eduardo Campo's *The Other Sides of Paradise: Explorations into the Religious Meanings of Domestic Space in Islam* is therefore a groundbreaking work; one that offers a new way of understanding Islam, not only as a great symbol and action system in time and space but also as a human phenomenon anchored in domestic structures and loyalties. While increasing our understanding of Islam, the author has also provided a model for the study of the religious meanings of domestic space in other traditions.

Frederick Mathewson Denny

Preface and Acknowledgments

This is a book about the houses many Muslims have imagined and in which they have lived. In writing about this subject, I have employed both textual and ethnographic modes of analysis. I view these as complementary, not antagonistic, undertakings. What we learn from the study of texts allows us to compose our histories, but it ought to inform us about human values and dilemmas in present contexts, also. Ethnography at its best yields knowledge about the living institutions and symbolic worlds of different peoples, and it has the potential for imbuing historical inquiries with a deeper appreciation for the complexities of social and cultural life outside the confines of palaces and academies.

The textual analysis, which prevails in the book's first chapters, systematically examines Islamic configurations of domestic space contained in the Quran, the canonical hadith collections, and early Islamic historical literature. The Arabic version of the Quran that I use is the Royal Edition of Cairo, first printed in 1337/1919, now widely available in the Muslim world. There are few standard editions of canonical Islamic texts and historical literature other than the Quran. Whenever possible, I prefer Arabic editions printed in Egypt and Lebanon over European ones. After all, these are the versions that Arab Muslims themselves have chosen to publish, read, and study in the modern period (often with the help of European scholarship).

For the book's ethnographic sections, I have drawn together information from previously published accounts and from the field work I conducted while living in Egypt in 1976–1977, 1978–79, and in the summer of 1985. During these visits I enjoyed the hospitality of Egyptians at their homes, mosques, churches, and public places. I learned much from these encounters about Egyptian Muslim values, beliefs, and practices in a rapidly changing religious, social, economic, and political environment. For an American these were exciting times to live in the country, but for many Egyptians life was perhaps more difficult and uncertain than it had been formerly, during the years of military confrontation with Israel.

As I became more familiar with the people and conditions there, I found that my perspective on Egyptian life was torn between seeing it as a comfortable outsider and trying to comprehend it as an Egyptian might. This struggle was instructive, but not resolved. To many of the Egyptians I know, I am a paradox: a foreigner acquiring fluency in literary and colloquial Arabic, an American who was born in Latin America of Colombian and Irish-American parents, a California student from the University of Chicago, a non-Muslim interested in and knowledgeable of Islam. As a stranger, rather than finding closed doors, I was allowed access to areas of domestic life that are inaccessible to most outsiders. The fact that my wife, Magda, an Egyptian, accompanied me on many of my visits, that we lived with her family in Cairo, and that our first son was born in a Cairene maternity clinic facilitated my research at times and strengthened the bonds of familiarity and friendship within a wide circle of people.

Writers' egos commonly lead them to believe that the words they put on paper are uniquely theirs. Like other people, they must accept both credit and responsibility for their work. From another perspective, however, writing is situated within spheres of human discourse. For most scholarly writers, the matrix of their labors is the university—that peculiar institution where they are nurtured, weaned, and socialized into family circles of knowledge and discourse.

I am responsible for this book, but writing it would not have been possible without the inspiration, support, and prodding of many individuals and institutions. At the University of Chicago, where the work first came to fruition as a doctoral dissertation, I am indebted to Jonathan Z. Smith. He introduced me to the challenges entailed by the critical study of religions as complex human phenomena; in *ghayba* he has continued to provoke new thoughts about old things. Professors Robert Biggs, Paul Wheatley, and the late Fazlur Rahman, each in his special ways, contributed greatly to my scholarly growth. I must also acknowledge the generosity of the Divinity School, and especially of Deans Larry Greenfield and James Lewis, both of whom came to my rescue at critical moments.

My Arabic teachers at the University of Chicago, particularly Carolyn Killean, and at the Center for Arabic Studies Abroad Program in Cairo provided the requisite language skills for pursuing questions about Islam in the everyday world and in Arabic texts. The field research upon which the second half of the book is based was funded by a generous Fulbright-Hayes Dissertation Fellowship (1978–1979). Without the opportunity to go to Egypt that this fellowship afforded me, and without the kind hospitality of many Egyptians, this book would not have been possible.

A good deal of my rethinking about Islam, domestic space, and the history of religions in recent years has been inspired by discussions with Professors Bruce Lawrence, Charles Long, Richard Martin, Marilyn Waldman, and Mark Woodward during meetings in Chicago and Tempe. Professor Gordon Newby was kind enough to provide me with the proofs for his *The Making of the Last Prophet* (1989), which were helpful in writing several sections of this book. Moreover, I owe a great debt of gratitude to Professor Frederick M. Denny, who supported the project from its infancy, and who invited me to discuss my ideas with colleagues in the humanities and social sciences at the University of Colorado at Boulder. During the last stages of writing, the readers' comments had a salutary effect upon the book's contents and organization. I also have Ken Scott, my editor, to thank for his attention to the manuscript as it made its way to press.

The University of California Regents, the Academic Senate, and my colleagues in the Department of Religious Studies at the University of California at Santa Barbara have been most generous with their support. Professors Catherine Albanese, W. Randall Garr, Richard Hecht, and Birger A. Pearson gave their thoughtful attention to sections from earlier drafts of the manuscript. Professor Allan Grapard and Erin H. Addison donated their artistic gifts to make careful line drawings of two Hajj murals (figures 8 and 9 respectively) from my photographs. The department staff—Jean Burrey, Kimberly Labor, and Doris Scoltock-Smeltz—has also been of inestimable help during the last two years.

Above all, the contributions of Magda Malouf Campo, my wife, have been immeasurable. Co-worker, critic, informant, and go-between, she remained a font of encouragement as the book was being researched and composed. And thanks also go to Andrés and Federico, our sons, who have persistently reminded Magda and me of what really matters in this life.

Transliteration and Other Technical Matters

TRANSLITERATION

For classical Arabic, I use the system recommended by the *International Journal of Middle East Studies.* Initial *hamza*s (ʾ) are deleted, but all *ʿayn*s (ʿ) are kept. For important Arabic words and titles of books written in Arabic, I provide full diacritics. Except for *ʿayn* and the non-initial *hamza,* I have chosen not to use diacritics for Arabic personal names, place names, and Arabic loanwords occurring in the English language. For place names and loanwords, I rely on the spellings that appear in *The Random House Dictionary of the English Language,* second unabridged edition (1987). Chapters 4, 5, and 6, together with Appendixes A and B, include transliterations from the modern Egyptian colloquial dialect spoken in Cairo. For colloquial terms, I transliterate the classical Arabic *jīm* with a hard "g" (as in "guitar") instead of a "j," and I use *il-* (and its assimilated forms) for the definite article instead of the classical *al-*. Otherwise, transliterations from colloquial Arabic are consistent with those used for classical Arabic.

TRANSLATION AND CITATION

Unless otherwise indicated, all translations from Arabic and modern European languages are my own. For this book, the following editorial signs are used in translated passages and statements:

( ) with italics denote words in the text's original language; parentheses without italics circumscribe interpolations added by the translator–editor.
[ ] denote restorations from parallel sources.
⟨ ⟩ denote corrections made in a text by the translator–editor.

The numerical method for citing chapters and verses in the Quran is a convention employed mainly by Euramerican scholars, but it is not familiar to most Muslims. In order to make Quran citations more accessible to Muslim and non-Muslim readers alike, I have devised my own citation method. This involves providing the chapter number, its Arabic name in italics without the definite article, and the verse number. For example, instead of the citation 2: 255, I use 2 *Baqara* 255. My method for citing from hadith collections is explained at the beginning of the notes for chapter 2. Although I worked from the Cairo edition of al-Tabari's *Taʾrikh,* my citations are based on de Goeje's edition. This is the form of citation used in its English translation, now in publication. Complete publication data on all Arabic sources used in this book is provided in the notes and in the bibliography.

DATES

In discussions requiring reference to dates in Islamic history, especially before the modern era, I follow the style employed by the *Encyclopaedia of Islam.* This means that the Hijra year or century is cited first, followed by a slash (/) and then the Common Era (C.E.; Euramerican) date.

APPENDIXES

The appendixes have two purposes: they help readers follow my analysis of Hajj murals in chapter 6 and contribute to the study of popular Islamic iconography by providing an itemized discussion of each type of inscription and figure occurring in the murals. My classifications of inscriptions and figures are listed in tables 2 and 4. Commentary on inscriptions and figures follows each table.

ABBREVIATIONS

b. "son of" *(ibn)* in Muslim personal names
C.E. Common Era
d. year of death
pl. plural form of word
PN. personal name, used generically instead of actual name
v. verse
vv. verses

The Other Sides of Paradise

Introduction

Inquiry into the religious meanings of domestic space is an important part of the study of sacred space. The modern study of religion, however, has often sidestepped the challenging task of illuminating the place of religion in houses, and the place of houses in the history of religions. Instead, its central concerns have been with church histories, theology, sacred scriptures, esoteric symbols, and doctrines, or the exotica of religious thought and practice in "archaic" and "oriental" cultures. For many scholars of religion, houses appear to be outside the field of subjects defined by sacred texts, mysticism, and holy places. It is as if houses were too much within the mundane sphere of human existence.

This is not to say that the topic has been completely neglected. More than a century ago, Fustel de Coulanges saw in the domestic cult of the family hearth the origins of ancient Greco-Roman religion and civilization.[1] Early in this century the phenomenologist of religion, Gerardus van der Leeuw, considered the houses of premodern man to be "enclosures of power," enclaves wherein the human being could encounter the Absolute. Such houses were essentially temples.[2] Mircea Eliade, who can be regarded as the leading sage in the modern study of sacred space, elaborated upon van der Leeuw's work. Like van der Leeuw, Eliade did not write extensively on houses, but he did place the dwellings of "religious man" within a group of homologous places (e.g., mountains, cities, temples, palaces, huts, and the human body) that replicated the cosmic order, and filled profane space with meaning.[3]

These early studies had their limitations, however. Fustel de Coulanges did not recognize that household religious practices and beliefs continued be a part of domestic and civil life after the rise of the classical city and Christian Europe. Van der Leeuw and Eliade were more concerned with discovering the archetypal totalities of the sacred than they were with investigating the variety of ways different groups and cultures have attributed religious significance to their houses. It should be of no surprise, therefore, that they were inclined to disregard questions relating to the causes and directions of historical change indomestic religious symbolisms and practices, unless it was to bemoan the general deterioration of the sacred with the onset of modernity. Only recently have scholars of religious studies begun to ground research of domestic space in specific historical and cultural contexts.[4]

Post-colonial structuralist anthropology has advanced the study of traditional houses by examining the ways they encode mythico-ritual systems, and mediate among indigenous social and natural categories.[5] As a rule, however, these studies avoid questions of synchronic and diachronic variation among house forms, and whether there might be conflicting notions about the mythico-ritual order of the house, nature, and culture. For example, Pierre Bourdieu's essay on the Kabyle Berber house devises a static male-oriented model of domestic space.[6] Just how representative Bourdieu's Kabyle house actually is, where it is located in the settlement, how it compares with Berber houses elsewhere in north Africa, or how it is related to other forms of domestic architecture in the region, including non-Berber ones, are serious questions that are left unanswered. Even more curious is the fact that Bourdieu does not discuss the Islamic aspects of Berber domestic order. It is as if "the" house exists in a vacuum. There have been more thorough anthropological studies of house symbolisms in premodern cultures. Perhaps the most outstanding among these, one that takes the question of variation quite seriously, is Lebeuf's study of Fali houses in Cameroon.[7]

As with the study of the religious dimensions of houses, the critical study of Islam as a religion also has been a neglected topic until quite recently. Islam is not readily amenable to analysis in terms of church history; for centuries it has been the target of church polemics. In the eyes of many contemporary historians of religions, it is not esoteric or exotic enough to deserve sustained attention. Only two Islamic topics have been taken up seriously in religious studies with any regularity, the Quran and Islamic mysticism. Perhaps this lack of attention is because people hold that Islam is neither oriental nor occidental enough; it is not completely "theirs," nor is it completely "ours." Another reason may be that, like houses, Islam is judged to be too mundane, too embedded in society and history (and politics) to allow scholars free rein to imagine religion as they wish. Consequently the study of Islam has been largely relegated to area studies specialists, such as Middle East historians, political scientists, anthropologists, and sociologists. One of the objectives of this book is to fix the study of Islam squarely within the history of religions, thereby introducing new areas of inquiry to both the history of religions and Islamic studies.

Few Middle East scholars have yet looked carefully at the relation between houses and religious configurations of meaning. The richly detailed volumes published in recent years by the Institut Français d'Archéologie Orientale and the Centre National de la Recherche Scientifique on the medieval and Ottoman houses of Egypt and Tunisia describe the social environments of domestic architecture and allude to isomorphisms between grand houses and religious architecture, but they eschew symbolic analysis.[8] Like art historian Oleg Grabar, who has considerably advanced our knowledge of the religious and cultural symbolisms of mosques, most area specialists regard houses as a form of "secular" Islamic architecture, thus circumventing inquiry into their religious aspects.[9] Some Arab and Muslim scholars, nonetheless, have conducted studies that touch upon the issue either as an aspect of local folk culture, or Islamic property laws.[10]

Even though the question of the relations between religion and houses has not yet found a prominent place in conventional scholarly discourse, it is not a trifling question. This is because the topic lies at the heart of how people develop profound attachments to the places in which they reside, or in which they imagine themselves to reside. It is also related to the history of premodern cosmological thought, spatial symbolisms, and concepts of afterlife.

In the case of Islam, we find that actual human dwellings and verbal images of houses have obtained rich and complex valuations in different contexts since this religion's appearance in seventh-century C.E. Arabia. These valuations are expressed in the Quran and hadith, in medieval Islamic literature, and in the design and decoration of the palaces of Muslim elites in centuries past. Moreover, ethnographic research suggests that Muslims widely attribute religious significance to their houses today, even when their dwellings happen to be apartments designed according to European and American prototypes.

The fabric of Muslim domestic valuations extends beyond ordinary habitations to include the principal holy sites of Mecca and Medina, notions about life in the hereafter, and ritual practices such as prayer and pilgrimage. This fabric embodies the aspirations and concerns of Muslim collectivities, and it informs the attitudes and behavior of individual Muslims toward each other, toward non-Muslims, and toward the world at large. Because of the historical richness of its valuations of domestic space and its cross-cultural diversity, Islam provides a promising point of departure for inquiring into the relations between religion and houses.

One would normally expect that a study of the symbolisms of domestic space is a study of locative or place-related symbolisms. Islam presents an intriguing problem in this regard: it has made a virtue of movement. Emigration, going in the "way of God," jihad, pilgrimage, resurrection, and gathering for final judgment are key features of Islamic thought, practice, and history. Movement is inscribed, therefore, in Muslim houses. It must be accounted for in any study of the religious significance Muslims attribute to their houses.

The book is concerned with two sets of problems in particular. The first focuses on how houses are construed within Islamic canonical discourse, namely the Quran and the hadith literature. The Quran, regarded by Muslims as a book of revelations from God, and the hadith, regarded as a body of authoritative statements from or about the Prophet Muhammad, both embody Islamic discourses about domestic space that emerged during the historical formation of the religion; that is, between the seventh and ninth centuries of the Common Era. As canonical works, they are first constructed, and then they instruct. Hence, by undertaking an analysis of the religious meanings attributed to houses in the Quran and hadith, we will not only learn about how the first generations of Muslims thought about their houses, but we will also become familiar with the domestic metaphors that have affected Muslim practices, self-understandings, and discourses about the world long after the era in which they were first produced.

The Islamic canon was promulgated by the leadership of an Arabian religious reform movement that had succeeded in founding new settlements and establishing an empire in a region once dominated by Byzantium and Persia. Therefore, if canonical Islamic figurations of domestic space are to be understood historically, it is necessary to situate them within this imperial milieu. To what extent did they embody domination? Did Islamic definitions of domestic space affect the definition of sacred space and the organization of the first Muslim settlements? Did they contribute to the formulation of an Islamic imperial ideology? The answers to these questions turn in large measure on the paradigmatic status of the Prophet's house-mosque in Medina and the significance of the concept of the House of Islam.

If the first set of inquiries taken up by the book is concerned with figurations of domestic space in the Islamic canon and their relation to the beginnings of an Islamic empire, the second set is concerned with how Muslims attribute religious meaning to the dwellings in which they actually reside. In other words, how do ordinary Muslims domesticate Islam? There is no written canon to instruct them on precisely how to construct, orient, and ritualize their houses. Nor is there a guild of ritual priests to do this for them. In the absence of a formal ritual code, we must learn how Muslims appropriate Islamic practices and symbols in the improvisation of a domestic order that has religious meaning.

Islam has a history of some thirteen centuries; it has established itself in many different natural and cultural environments, from west Africa to east Asia, and, in recent decades, the United States and Canada. It would be imperious of me to pretend to impart a complete picture of how millions of people in the past and present have sought to domesticate Islam, or Islamize their houses. A more practical alternative is to focus on a particular Islamic society. Because of the extent of documentation available, the number of extant premodern houses still standing, and its relative openness to foreign researchers, I have made Egypt the focus for the second half of the book. Egyptian society, too, is sizeable, so I will concentrate on discussing the domestication of Islam among modern Cairene townsfolk, the *ahl al-balad,* and, to a lesser extent, the rural populace.

This is a book about houses, but not as we are accustomed to think of them. Houses as physical creations wrought by human hands from natural materials for storage and shelter are but one part of a heterogeneous framework of images, ideas, practices, and institutions. Houses are constructions of our minds, our speech and writing, and our actions as members of human groups, as well as products of our manual labors. Harboring us against chaos and meaninglessness, they embody representations of relations between social and natural worlds, and they often furnish us representations for these worlds.

In order to describe houses as abstractions, figures of speech, and physical dwelling places, I use the term "domestic space" in this book. Unlike "house," this is a patently etic term, exterior to the forms and meanings houses can have within specific social or textual environments. No one is likely to feel "at home" in "domestic space." Although there are few cultural contexts (outside the university) wherein "domestic space" per se serves as an intrinsic category of meaning or discourse, I regard it as a working concept to facilitate inquiry into the different functions and provinces of meaning houses acquire in culture.

By contrast, the term "house" itself, or its analogues in other languages, helps us become familiar with dwellings and their meanings as they are construed within particular cultural environments.[11] For example, in American English, we use it in referring to dwellings for humans, animals, and God. Sometimes we use it when talking about our natal families, our places of entertainment, and hotels and motels. We even use it to designate our prisons and centers of political power—the White

House, the House of Representatives, and the State House. The word can assume different functions in our utterances; in addition to being a noun, it can be a verb or an adjective (e.g., "house arrest," "house call," and "housewife").

Of course, such a lexical sampling must be matched by careful relational analyses and comparisons of individual architectures and discourses, as well as their histories. It is precisely in this set of undertakings that the working concept of "domestic space" can be most helpful. It allows us to assess the continuities and discontinuities, parallels and antimonies among culturally embedded formulations of what houses are and what they represent.

In the pages to follow, my discussion will employ the terms "house" and "domestic space" jointly so as to determine the semantic range of religious meanings dwellings can acquire in Islamic contexts, and then to enframe my findings within the discourses of the human sciences. Moreover, to the extent that Muslim houses are representations of and for worlds fashioned by human imagination, to the extent that Muslims imbue them with complex and overlapping meanings, they are varieties of sacred space, and fall especially within the purview of the would-be discipline of the history of religions.[12]

1

Images of Domestic Space in the Quran

How important are figurations of domestic space in early Islamic discourse? Are houses key metaphors that link together major components of belief and practice, or are they isolated images of little symbolic value? If they are key metaphors, how are they used? What meanings do they convey? To answer these questions, we must define the parameters of domestic discourse in the body of canonical texts constructed in the first two centuries of Islamic history, namely, the Quran and the hadith.

Much of the analysis in this and the following chapter rests upon careful consideration of domestic lexemes and their meanings within a narrow, but exceedingly important range of material. I do not intend this to be a strictly lexicographic inquiry, however. I am instead more interested in using lexemes to map the development of varieties of early Islamic discourse about houses, as well as identifying the discourses in which houses play a role in the formulation of Islam as a distinctive variety of religion.

The Quran and authoritative hadith collections occupy a position of primary importance here for several reasons. First, they contain the earliest surviving statements of Islamic ideas about God, humans, and the nature of existence in this world and in the world to come. Second, Muslims regard the Quran as the fundamental revelation of the word of God, and the hadith as statements containing the divinely inspired words and actions of his last prophet, Muhammad. These texts have acquired normative status in Islam; in fact, they comprise the two principal sources of Islamic law, the Shariᶜa. Third, because Muslims believe the Quran and hadith express timeless truths that should inform human thought and action, they have promulgated them, studied them, wrangled over them, and resorted to them for guidance through the centuries.

The Quran as a document of history is a compilation of prophetical orations in the Arabic language conveyed by Muhammad to an assortment of groups residing in and adjacent to a region of western Arabia, known as the Hejaz, between 610 and 11/632. It reflects the concerns of a local religious reform movement struggling for integrity and autonomy through a radical criticism of the prevailing values and manners of Arab elites in Mecca (the Quraysh), Jews, and Christians. These orations were committed to memory and reportedly written down during Muhammad's lifetime by his companions. After the Prophet's death, when the movement dominated the region, his companions and their followers carried recensions of the Quran with them as they moved into Syria, Iraq, Egypt, and Persia by successive waves of conquest and migration. The canonical consonantal text of the Quran was a result of orders issued by the early Muslim rulers, particularly the third caliph (a caliph is a "successor" of the Prophet and God's vicegerent), ʿUthman b. ʿAffan (reigned 23/644–35/656).[1]

The meanings attributed to domestic space by the Quran, therefore, emerged from a milieu wherein Muslims were a religio-political minority that moved from marginal to dominant status in a very short period of time. As we discuss the quranic discourses of domestic space, therefore, it is advisable to regard them as a set of statements grounded in marginality, but which, with each success of the Prophet and his movement, increasingly became part of a discourse of superordination and control.

QURANIC HOUSE TERMS

The Quran uses six key Arabic words to refer to a house or a dwelling place. Not unexpectedly, the most prominent of these are *bayt* (pl. *buyūt*) and *dār* (pl. *diyār*). As straightforward lexical items, both can refer to a dwelling place and to a kin group. They tend to differ from each other, however, for *dār* conveys the idea of a large, enclosed compound, and *bayt* denotes a smaller dwelling place, or a subdivision within a *dār*. These words also differ in gender; *dār* takes feminine agreement, and *bayt* masculine. Yet a third term used by the Quran in connection with houses is *ghurfa*. This word denotes the upper story of a domestic compound, but it is not used to classify kin groups.

In addition to these primary house terms, the Quran employs three others that are nouns of place derived from verbal stems. These include *maʾwā* "shelter, refuge," from *āwā; mathwā* "dwelling" from *thawā;* and *maskin* "dwelling" from *sakana*.

Half of these words, *bayt, dār,* and *maskin,* are etymologically linked to domestic terms in ancient Akkadian, biblical Hebrew, and Aramaic. All six words occur a total of 164 times in the Quran, mainly in the longer Medinan suras. In fact, they turn up in about two-thirds of the Medinan suras, and in about one-third of the Meccan ones. Altogether, they are found in 42 percent of the Quran's 114 chapters.[2]

These six house terms are not synonymous in the Quran. Moreover, no single mythic, ritual, or cosmological paradigm governs their use. Instead, quranic house terminology is deployed in four different narrative contexts: verses concerned with God's house, sacred history, rules of behavior, and the hereafter (see table 1).[3]

God's house and the hereafter are two of the most important places in quranic cosmology. The former, which Muslims traditionally identify with the Kaᶜba in Mecca, is regarded as the ontological center of this world, a point of origins. In contrast, the hereafter is the polarized space of paradise and hell, the realms of ultimate human destiny.[4]

Narratives of sacred history seek to draw a set of parallels between significant events in the lives of previous prophets and peoples and the experiences of Muhammad and his listeners, especially when they were in Medina. Such narratives are meant to guide people's actions and attitudes among themselves and with outsiders. Lastly, rules of behavior are expressed as commands. They address such matters as ritual, family life, inheritance, contracts, punishments, and social etiquette. Although it will shortly become apparent that these narrative contexts can overlap, they do not constitute a highly integrated system of symbolic discourse.

GOD'S HOUSE

The Quran uses the term *bayt* to describe God's house fifteen times. No other domestic term is used with reference to this place. Besides being designated as simply "the house," it is also called "the first house," "the ancient house,"[5] "the sacred house" *(al-bayt al-ḥarām)*, "your forbidden *(muḥarram)* house," "the flourishing *(maᶜmūr)* house," and "my house." In twelve instances, the Quran mentions God's house in the context of sacred history, especially in connection with the figure of Ibrahim (Abraham). It is identified with Kaᶜba in only one verse (5 *Māʾida* 97), and once with Mecca, albeit indirectly (3 *Al ᶜImrān* 96). The Quran associates God's house with the "sacred mosque" in two places (5 *Māʾida* 2; 8 *Anfāl* 34–35).

The earliest reference to God's house occurs in 106 *Quraysh:* "For the joining together of the Quraysh to form groups for the winter and summer journeys, let them worship the lord of this house who gives them food against hunger and security against fear."[6] Here God is represented as a powerful householder who looks after the needs of his people, expecting service and obedience—synonyms for worship—in return.

Table 1. Thematic Classification of Quranic House Terms

House Term	God's House	Sacred History		Rules	Hereafter	
		Pre-Medinan	Medinan		Hell	Paradise
bayt	2:125–27* 2:158* 3:96–97 5:2, 97* 8:35*; 14:37* 22:26, 29, 33* 52:4; 106:3*	2:125–27* 3:96–97* 7:74; 10:87 11:73 12:23 14:37* 15:82; 16:80 22:26, 29* 26:149 27:52; 28:12 51:36; 66:11* 71:28 106:3*	3:154; 4:100 8:5, 35* 17:93 33:13, 33* 43:33–34 59:2	2:158*, 189 3:96–97* 4:15 5:3, 97* 22:26, 29, 33* 24:27–29, 36, 61 33:33–34*, 53 65:1		66:11*
dār		2:84–85, 243, 246 7:78, 91, 145* 11:94; 17:5 28:37, 77, 81–83; 29:37 38:46*	3:195; 4:66 8:47; 13:31 22:40; 33:27 59:2, 8–9* 60:8–9*	59:8–9* 60:8–9*	7:145* 13:25 14:28 40:52 41:28	2:94 3:22–24, 42 6:32, 127, 135; 7:169 10:25; 12:109 16:30; 28:37, 77, 83* 29:64; 35:35 40:39 44:2[illegible]

maʾwā	29:25*			3:151,162, 197 4:97, 121 5:75; 8:16 9:73, 95; 10:8 13:18; 17:97 24:57 29:25* 32:20; 45:34 57:15; 66:9 79:39	32:19 53:15 79:41
mathwā	12:21, 23	47:19		3:151; 6:128 16:29; 29:68 39:32, 60, 72 40:76; 41:24 47:12	
maskin	14:45; 20:128 21:13 27:18 28:58; 29:38 32:26; 34:15 46:25		9:24		9:72; 61:12
ghurfa					25:75; 29:58 34:37; 39:20

Note: Citations are according to chapter:verse
*Indicates classification under more than one category.

The most elaborate discourses about God's house, however, occur in Medinan suras.

> Truly the first house founded for people is that which is in Bakka, blessed and a guidance for created things. In it are clear signs—the station of Ibrahim. Whoever enters it is secure. God requires all people to perform a Hajj to the house if they are able to do so. If anyone denies (it), God can do without created things. (3 *Al ᶜImrān* 96–97)

> Previously we made the house a meeting place for people, and a place of security. Take for yourselves a prayer place from the station of Ibrahim. We made a pact with Ibrahim and Ismaᶜil (Ishmael): "Purify my house for those who circumambulate it, and who go into retreat there, for bowings and prostrations!"
>
> Then Ibrahim said, "Lord, make this a secure land, and bestow (your) fruits in abundance upon its people—those who believe in God and the last day." (God says), "If anyone denies (this), I will let him enjoy life for a little while, then I will oblige him to suffer the fire. What a wretched fate!"
>
> And then Ibrahim and Ismaᶜil raised the foundations of the house.
>
> "Our lord, accept (this) from us, for indeed you are all-hearing and all-knowing. Our lord, make us *muslims* unto you, and make of our offspring a *muslim* community unto you. Show us our rites and turn towards us. Truly you are oft-turning and all-compassionate." (2 *Baqara* 125–28)

> God made the Kaᶜba the sacred house—as a support for people; also the sacred month, the offerings and necklaces. This is so you will know that God knows what is in the heavens and on earth, and that God is in every matter all-knowing. (5 *Māʾida* 97)

Each of these passages portrays the origin of God's house in laconic terms and relates the house to the history and ritual practices of the people who submit. In the last two selections, the Quran states that God himself made the house. The second passage adds that Ibrahim and Ismaᶜil purified it at God's command, and raised its foundations. This passage also conjoins the narrative of building God's house with the creation of a *muslim* community, that is, a community of submitters. These submitters will obtain blessing, guidance, and security in contrast to those who deny God and the last day. The deniers will eventually be consigned to the anti-domestic space of hell. Through such a narrative, a linkage is being forged between ancestral times (the time of Ibrahim), the present audience (ostensibly that of Muhammad and the "people"), and future times.

The selection above from 3 *Al ᶜImrān* contains an interesting ambiguity. Does the phrase "the first house founded for people" refer to a dwelling place, or only to a house of worship? Most Muslim commentators have agreed that it means a place of worship. Nevertheless, it is ambiguous enough to allow some people to see in God's house the prototype for all human dwellings. Even today, artists use this verse in Egyptian Hajj murals to establish a symbolic linkage between the pilgrim's house and God's house in Mecca.[7]

Quranic discourses about the origin of God's house include statements about the ritual observances conducted there. These include purification, prayer, retreat, circumambulation, and animal sacrifice. Pilgrimage rites receive the most attention in this regard. The Quran states that performing them entails blessing and prosperity for the people and the land. Avoiding or denying them *(kufr)* results in divine punishment. I will have more to say about these quranic rules for ritual behavior at God's house shortly.

If most of the Quran's references to God's house do in fact derive from the time after Muhammad and his followers had settled in Medina, it is likely that such statements are being construed in a setting in which the righteous community either does not actually have access to the divine sanctuary, or it does not have complete control of it. Mecca did not fall to the Prophet until eight years after the Hijra, or emigration (622 C.E.). This skews the interpretation of the passages quoted above in an intriguing manner. Statements about God's house being a place of security for the "people," about purifying it, and the importance of making a pilgrimage and praying there form a polemical discourse against non-Muslims, that is the people who actually have control of God's house. This orientation is expressed most clearly in the following attack against God's (and the Prophet's) opponents:

> They deserve nothing better than for God to torment them. They debar (the pious) from the sacred mosque. They were not its protectors. Its protectors can only be the pious, but most of them do not know it. When they prayed at the house, they only whistled and clapped. So taste the torment for what you have denied! Those who denied spend their wealth in order to debar (the pious) from the way of God. So they spend, but then (their wealth) will become a source of grief for them, and then they will be defeated. Those who denied will be assembled in hell! (8 *Anfāl* 34–36)

From a Medinan perspective, God's house appears to be in the hands of the wrong people, who are practicing its rites incorrectly. It should really be in the hands of the pious. Ultimately the deniers *(kāfirūn)* will be overcome and will fall victim to God's wrath. Such is the polemic of the righteous minority when they discover themselves alienated from

God's house. It is analogous to views contained in the Hebrew Bible, the Qumran texts, and the Pseudepigrapha with reference to the status of the Jerusalem temple. In the end, the true Muslims expect to gain full control of the holy sites, and purify them of their despoilers, the polytheists.

> It was not for polytheists to visit God's mosques, giving witness against themselves through denial. Those are the ones whose works have failed them. They shall dwell eternally in the fire. It is for those who believe in God and the last day, who pray and give alms, fearing none but God, to visit God's mosques. . . . O you who believe! The polytheists are unclean, they shall not come near the sacred mosque after this year of theirs. (9 *Tawba* 17, 18, 28)

Quranic discourses about the house of God are based upon the ancient temple language native to the east Mediterranean and southwest Asian regions. They cannot be attributed to uniquely Arabian roots, because first-/seventh-century Arabian societies had already been involved with all the major empires, social groups and religious communities in the region for several centuries. We should, however, recognize the ways in which the Quran transformed the old house-temple of God. Gone is the propaganda on behalf of an elite sacrificial priesthood and a royal household. Cultic duties are to be shared by all believers. If there is divine kingship, it is strictly that of God. The cult of idols in the sanctuary is conclusively rejected. The prophet himself, as portrayed in the Quran, is likened more to figures like Abraham and Moses than priestly and royal figures such as Aaron, David, and Solomon. In other words, he inspires the community to reform its temple worship. He does not seek to officiate in that worship as a priest or king.

SACRED HISTORY

According to the Quran, human habitations, like God's house, have been created by God.

> God made a dwelling place *(sakan)* for you from among your houses *(buyūt)*. He made houses for you from animal skins, so you will find them light when you travel and when you camp. (He made) furnishings and conveniences (for you) out of their wool, fur, and hair for a time. . . . Thus does he bring his grace upon you to completion so that you enter into *islām*. . . . They know God's grace, but then they repudiate it. Most of them are the deniers. (16 *Naḥl* 80–83)

This quranic statement maintains that houses and domestic furnishings are more than material acquisitions. They are actually provided to humans by God. Recognizing this leads to *islām*, submission. To this extent, all houses can have religious significance; however, the verse also indicates that failing to acknowledge God's grace in such mundane matters places people in the dangerous condition of denial *(kufr)*. Contrary to Eliade's views of domestic symbolism in the history of religions, therefore, the Quran does not attribute the sacrality of houses to grand cosmological or cosmogonic schemes.

The quranic conception of the origin of human houses can be viewed in relation to a wider set of discourses about the sacred histories of the ancestors and the fates of their houses. These discourses are built upon the topoi of divine blessings and curses. According to the Quran, having houses and wealth is not always a sign of blessing, nor is lacking them a sign of God's ire. The crux of the matter rests on how householders conduct themselves and the sincerity of their faith.

If the people of former times possessed houses and were prosperous, but failed to heed God and his messengers; if they committed injustices against one another, or inclined too favorably to the pleasures of living in this world—God destroyed them and left their ruined houses as a sign for succeeding generations.

> Remember when (God) appointed you (Thamud) the successors of ʿAd, and settled you in the land. You take palaces for yourselves on the plains and houses in the mountains. Remember God's benefits, and do not act evilly in the land, spreading disorder. . . . (But now) those houses of theirs stand empty as a result of their wrongdoing. Truly in that there is a sign from which a people should learn.[8]

Besides Thamud and ʿAd (46 *Aḥqāf* 25), the Quran states that God destroyed the people and houses of Sheba (34 *Saba* 15) and Midyan (e.g., 7 *Aʿrāf* 91 and 11 *Hūd* 94–95). A strand from biblical tradition can also be found in this type of narrative. Korah (Qarun) was given great wealth by God, but he and his house were swallowed up by the earth for treating his people immorally and leading them to desiring material wealth instead of following God's way (28 *Qaṣaṣ* 79–82).[9] The Quran, in one of the last suras revealed before the Hijra to Medina, states "(Polytheists) before them acted with deceit, so God destroyed their building *(bunyān)* from the foundations. The ceiling collapsed upon their heads, and torment came unto them from whence they knew not" (16 *Naḥl* 26). This discourse goes on to say that such polytheists will enter the doors of hell on Resurrection Day, and find their dwelling *(mathwā)* there for ever.

How do these discourses about the destruction of houses of former times compare with discourses about domestic space set within the time frame of Muhammad and his people? Since I have defined narratives of sacred history as stories of the past that serve as commentaries and guides for action and belief in the present, it is reasonable to expect that there will be a relatively close parallel between these two groups of discourse in the Quran.

In a passage revealed before the Hijra, the Quran states

> Were it not that people would be one community (loving wordly riches) we would have made for those who deny (God) the all-merciful roofs of silver for their houses, stairs for climbing, doors for their houses, couches for reclining, and gold ornaments. Surely all this is but the enjoyment of the present life. The hereafter with your lord is for the pious. (43 *Zukhruf* 33–35)

This statement acknowledges that grand houses and prosperity come from God, just as the modest houses and furnishings mentioned in 16 *Naḥl* 80–83 come from him. It also seeks to drive a wedge between deniers and the pious, but it does this in terms of connecting the former with the proclivity for worldly luxury, and the latter with the yearning for life in the hereafter. The statement recognizes differences in the distribution of wealth, and implies that poverty is a virtue. Real riches, the Quran proclaims later in the sura, await the faithful in the gardens of paradise (43 *Zukhruf* 68–73).

Nothing is said in these verses, however, about the fate of the houses of the deniers in Muhammad's time. This subject is addressed in Medinan revelations, at a time when the stature and power of Muhammad and the believers waxed against their opponents and critics. These passages state that the deniers are responsible for the destruction of their own houses, and that they can be expelled from them by God and his believers.

> It is (God) who expelled the deniers among the people of the book from their houses *(diyār)* at the first assembly. You did not think that they would depart. They thought that their fortresses would defend them from God. But God came from where they did not expect, and cast terror into their hearts. They are destroying their houses *(buyūt)* with their own hands and the hands of the believers.
>
> Consider this, you who have vision! If God had not established in writing that they be exiled, he would have caused them to suffer in the world. In the hereafter they will suffer the fire. That is because they made a breach with God and his messenger. Whosoever makes a breach with God, God is severe in punishment. (59 *Ḥashr* 2–4)

Muslim historians and commentators associate these verses with the expulsion of a Jewish tribe, the Banu Nadir, from Medina for plotting to assassinate Muhammad during the fourth year of the Hijra. The typological elements contained in these verses are more interesting, however. For example, here the Quran applies the name "denier" to a group that has a scripture, and it sets a precedent for the destruction or seizure of their properties. Such acts are sanctioned by God and are correlated with the fate awaiting deniers in the hereafter. Moreover, according to subsequent statements in this sura (vv. 7–8), the houses and properties of the deniers are not destroyed wantonly. Instead, they are to be given over to the Prophet so that he might redistribute them among needy followers, especially to poor emigrants who have been driven from their houses by the faithless (vv. 8–9; cf. 33 *Aḥzāb* 27).[10]

In respect to being expelled from or abandoning houses, the Quran views believers and deniers differently. Possessing a house is not necessarily a sign of divine favor, nor is homelessness a sign of divine disfavor. If a believer has left his or her home to follow God's path, or is expelled from it by the deniers, then blessing is promised. Of course, the Quran threatens a miserable end for anyone who drives the faithful from their homes, but as a general principle, it makes virtues of emigration and fighting on behalf of God.

> Believers who sit (at home)—unless they have an injury—are not the equals of those who strive in the path of God with their possessions and their selves. God has preferred those who strive with their possessions and their selves to those who sit (at home) by a degree, though he has promised both the best. God has preferred with a magnificent reward those who strive over those who sit (at home).
>
> Truly those whom the angels take in death—those who do wrong against themselves—are asked, "In what circumstances were you?" They say, "We were oppressed on the earth." (The angels) say, "Was not God's earth sufficiently wide that you might have emigrated in it?" Those are the ones whose shelter *(maʾwā)* is hell. What an evil fate! Unless the oppressed include men, women, and children who are unable to find a way out—these God may find a way to forgive. . . .
>
> Whoever emigrates in God's way will find many a road and open opportunity in the land. Whoever leaves his house, emigrating to God and his messenger, and then is overtaken by death, his reward is incumbent upon God. God is most forgiving and merciful. (4 *Nisāʾ* 95–100)

This is a somewhat complex discourse. It is mainly addressed to people within Muhammad's community; deniers and polytheists are not explicitly mentioned. Instead, it seeks to distinguish activists from passivists. The former are promised great rewards, especially if they give up their houses and die, while the latter are subtly threatened with perdition. Exceptions are made for people who are injured, and those too poor or weak to fight and emigrate to God and his messenger.

By making a virtue of abandoning one's home, the Quran reverses an important topos in the literatures of ancient Mesopotamia and Israel where to abandon or be driven from the home was considered as a catastrophic event that entails divine punishment.[11] The quranic attitude to this subject is closer to that expressed in the Exodus theme of the Hebrew Bible, and in the gospel rules for Jesus's disciples which urge them to renounce family life and seek out "the lost sheep of the house of Israel."[12] The positive value the Quran assigns to emigration most likely has some basis in nomadic modes of subsistence indigenous to the Arabian Peninsula, but because of its theological significance, it is perhaps more congruent with the on-going cosmological revaluations that had been occurring in the religious life of towns and cities in the hellenistic and late-antique worlds.

An interweaving of specifically Judaic and Islamic discourses on houses and emigration is evident in the quranic rendition of the story of Moses, where the life of the ancient prophet of Israel serves as an allegory for the life of the prophet of Arabia. In one passage, Moses and Aaron, having bested Pharoah's sorcerers in a contest of magic, receive a revelation that commands them to "seek lodging for your people in houses *(buyūt)* in Egypt, and make your houses into a *qibla* (i.e., orient them for prayer). Perform prayers, and bring news to the believers" (10 *Yūnus* 87). Moses and his brother thus receive authorization for housing their followers in the land of the corrupt Pharaoh, and for making houses places of prayer, like mosques.[13]

In a subsequent verse, however, Moses mentions to God that Pharaoh and his subjects have been using their worldly treasures to mislead people, so he calls for their destruction. Once the Israelites have been led across the sea, and Pharaoh's forces have perished, the Quran declares, "We have lodged the children of Israel in a lodging *(mubawwaʾ)* of righteousness,[14] and we have bestowed good things upon them" (10 *Yūnus* 93).

Taken together, these verses contain a double movement: one involves taking up residence among unbelieving opponents, the second entails emigration from corruption to righteousness and blessing. These movements are set in the context of the sacred history of Moses and the Israelites, but they may well have been construed to define the status of Muhammad and his people at the moment of their Hijra.[15]

A different variety of domestic discourse in quranic narratives about sacred history concerns "the people of the house" (*ahl al-bayt*, or *ahl bayt*). The phrase occurs only three times in the Quran. In each instance, it is connected with the household of a major prophet, and it involves reference to female members of that household. The Quran uses it in a discourse about the blessings bestowed on Ibrahim's household in 11 *Hūd* 73. In 28 *Qaṣaṣ* 12, the phrase denotes the family in which Moses was born and raised. Finally, in the Medinan passage 33 *Aḥzāb* 33, the Quran uses it in the context of rulings addressed to Muhammad's wives. A subtle correspondence is made thereby between Muhammad's life and the lives of previous prophets through the application of the phrase *ahl al-bayt* to his household as well as theirs.[16]

The most important aspect of the "people of the house" phrase is not its use in the Quran per se, however, but what Muslims later made of it. After Muhammad's death it came to designate not only the Prophet and his immediate family, but also his noble descendents. Its genealogical connotations actually superceded its spatial ones, as different sectors of the Islamic community vied with each other for dominance in the new empire. Shiᶜite groups and the ᶜAbbasid rulers alike sought to legitimate their claims to leadership by claiming the heritage of the "people of the house" of the Prophet as their own.[17]

HOUSE RULES

Houses are also the objects of regulatory discourse in the Quran. All such rules are held to have been revealed after the Hijra, which conforms to the widely held view that quranic rules were promulgated during the years of Muhammad's residence in Medina, not in Mecca. Basically two kinds of houses are subject to regulatory discourse, the house of God and the human dwelling.

Visiting the house of God on the Hajj and the ᶜUmra (lesser pilgrimage) should be done in conformance to ritual rules. These rules are stated in greatest detail in 2 *Baqara* 196–203, but additional ones are stated elsewhere in the Quran. They do not constitute anything close to a comprehensive ritual code of the sort found in Leviticus, the Talmud, or in later Muslim juridical literature for that matter. *Baqara* 196–203 takes up questions concerning substitute pilgrimages, the time and location of the rites, prescribed behavior, and the remembrance of God during the rites. Elsewhere, the Quran makes Hajj an obligation for all able believers (3 *Al ᶜImrān* 97); and it makes passing mention of procedures for purification, circumambulation, sacrifice, and prayer while in the *ḥaram* of God's house (22 *Ḥajj* 26 and 2 *Baqara* 125–27). The Quran prohibits the hunting of animals in the sacred precincts, but it upholds animal sacrifice, together with acts of charity on behalf of the destitute during the pilgrimage (5 *Mā'ida* 94–96). One set of instructions about visiting the Kaʿba states,

> O you who believe! Do not desecrate God's waymarks, nor the sacred month; neither the sacrificial offering, nor the necklaces, nor those going to the sacred house who are seeking benefit and approval from their lord. Hunt wild game (only when) you have desacralized yourselves.
>
> Let not detestation for a people who have barred you from the sacred mosque move you to commit aggression. Cooperate on behalf of righteousness and piety, and do not cooperate on behalf of crime and aggression. Fear God. Truly God is severe in punishment. (5 *Mā'ida* 2)

With the exception of 5 *Mā'ida* 2, which is later, all of these rulings appear to come from a time when Muslims were barred from pilgrimage to the house of God. It is as if the Quran was reformulating rules with which Muhammad's followers were already familiar in preparation for the eventuality of being allowed to return. The verses just quoted reflect a stage when believers were obliged to tolerate the presence of others at the pilgrimage site. The last stage in this process, as I mentioned earlier, entailed the actual expulsion of polytheists from the sacred precincts (9 *Tawba* 17, 18, 28). In the end, the criteria of belief in one God and of ritual purity became the basic ones for gaining admission to the sacred precincts. These criteria, however, did not restrict access on the basis of genealogy, caste affiliation, or gender.

Quranic rules governing human dwelling places comprise two groups: rules for the houses of all believers and rules for the house of the Prophet. The most general rules are stated as follows:

> O you who believe! Do not enter houses *(buyūt)* other than your own until you have asked permission and greeted the family within. That is a good thing for you, that you might remember. If you do not find anyone within, do not enter until given permission. If you are told, "Return," then return. It is of greater purity *(azkā)* for you. God is all-knowing in what you do. It is no sin on your part to enter unoccupied houses—in these there is convenience for you. God knows what you do openly and in secret. (24 *Nūr* 27–29)

> (O you who believe!) There is no wrong in the blind, lame, sick, or in yourselves if you consume from your houses *(buyūt)*, or from (the houses) of your fathers, mothers, brothers, sisters, paternal uncles and aunts, maternal uncles and aunts; or from (houses) whereof you possess the keys, or from your friends. There is no wrong for you in eating together or individually. When you enter houses, greet each other with a salutation from God for

> blessing and goodness. Thus God makes the signs clear to you, so that you might comprehend. (24 *Nūr* 61)

Both of these passages treat matters of everyday social life as religious practices. Ideas about God, right and wrong, purity, and blessing are connected with visitation customs, eating, and exchanging greetings. The rules for visitation suggest that the houses of believers were seen to have a certain degree of inviolability. They were to be entered only under certain conditions. Permission to do so had to be obtained first, and special greetings were to be expressed upon entering, although the Quran does not indicate precisely what was to be said. Eating rules appear to have been concerned with broadening the circle of people with whom believers could share their food. A person was allowed to eat alone, with family and friends, and with the weak and disabled.[18]

Verses 27 to 29 occur within a quranic context that has had an important effect on life within Muslim houses. They are preceded by verses concerned with adultery and denouncing slander against virtuous men and women (vv. 2–26), and are followed with rulings that urge men and women to lower their gaze and cover their genitals (vv. 30–31). Women especially are urged to cover their bodies in front of men with whom marriage is permitted. The ensuing verses set guidelines for marriage.

Discourses on adultery, visitation, the body, and marriage are thereby conjoined within a single relatively short section of the Quran. This conjunction suggests that rules governing access to domestic space are regarded as similar to rules governing exposure of and access to the human body. The very presence of these rules in the Quran, together in one place, lends itself to the creation of a perduring linkage between the house, the human—especially female—body, and sexual relations. Following the rules entails purity, goodness, and blessing in the eyes of God. To violate them is as good as following in "the footsteps of Satan" (v. 21).

The Quran appends to these regulations the famous Light Verse:

> God is the light of the heavens and the earth. The likeness of his light is as a niche wherein is a lamp. The lamp is in a glass, the glass as if a glittering star. . . . Light upon light, God guides to his light whom he will. . . . In houses *(buyūt)* that God has allowed to be raised up, therein is his name remembered, therein is he glorified mornings and evenings by men whom neither commerce nor selling can divert from remembering God, performing prayers and giving alms. (24 *Nūr* 35–37)

There is a long history of interpretation concerning this verse, especially in esoteric Sufism, but if viewed narrowly within its quranic context alone, it looks as if it is a statement about the relation between God and the houses of believers. Through similes based on the idea of light, it identifies the visible presence of God in the universe with the presence of a lantern in the house, that is, a house where he is worshiped regularly. Some commentators say that "houses" actually means "mosques." This is an anachronistic view, because there was no absolutely clear distinction between the two places in the early stages of Islam's historical development. Instead, the Light Verse is best understood in relation to the regulations that precede it, which are concerned with defining the house as a moral center for believers.[19]

A more puzzling house rule is one that states, "It is not proper for you to approach houses from the rear. It is proper, however, to be pious. So approach houses by their (front) doors, and fear God that you might prosper" (2 *Baqara* 189). Taken out of context, it appears to be another visitation rule. As with the visitation rules in 24 *Nūr,* it uses social custom as an expression of piety.

Yet in the Quran, this statement occurs amid regulations concerning fasting, combat, and pilgrimage. So instead of considering it to be a general rule for visitation, Muslim commentators such as al-Tabari (d. 311/923), al-Zamakhshari (d. 539/1144), and al-Baydawi (d. circa 685/1286) have chosen to treat it as a Hajj rule. They explain that prior to the rise of Islam, returning pilgrims would bore holes in the backs of their houses to use them as entrances instead of the front doors as long as they were still in a sacralized condition *(iḥrām).*[20] This ruling, therefore, was promulgated to put an end to this practice.

Another subgroup of house rules pertains to the status of women in cases of adultery, insolence, and divorce. According to one ruling, a legally confirmed adulteress was to be confined to her house until death, or until God provided some other way out (4 *Nisā*ʾ 15).[21] The Quran also states that a good woman is obedient towards her menfolk and keeps in secret that which God protects (i.e., her body), but if she is rebellious, her husband or male guardian is authorized to confine her to bed and beat her until she becomes obedient (4 *Nisā*ʾ 34). Confinement within domestic space thereby becomes a substitute for a woman's control of her body. It also serves as a method for obliging submission to the male.

In divorce cases, the Quran provides that the woman be obliged to remain in "her" house—or where her husband resides—for a prescribed waiting period to see whether she is with child, unless she is guilty of adultery. She should not be evicted, nor should she leave the house during this time. These are said to be God's "limits." Whoever transgresses them does wrong against themselves (65 *Ṭalāq* 1, 6) and is in danger of spending eternity in hell.

The second major group of rules pertaining to domestic space in the Quran specifically concerns the household of the Prophet in Medina. One verse states,

> O you who believe! Do not enter the houses of the Prophet *(buyūt al-nabī)*, unless you are given leave to have a bite to eat. But do not look (at the food) until it is cooked. When you are invited, enter. When you have eaten, disperse without engaging in idle talk. Truly your (idle talk) has annoyed the Prophet. He is embarrassed by you, (but) God is not embarrassed by (telling) the truth.
>
> When you ask (his women) for some convenience, ask them from behind a barrier *(ḥijāb)*. That is purer *(aṭhar)* for your hearts and for theirs. You should not annoy God's messenger. Do not ever marry his wives after him. (33 *Aḥzāb* 53)

These commands, like those in 24 *Nūr* 27–29 and 61, provide guidelines to believers in matters connected with visitation and commensality. Similarly, they suggest a connection between the notion of purity and domestic behavior. The chief difference, however, is that this second group intimates that special rules should be followed in the living quarters of Muhammad. The Quran appears to be disposed to give the Prophet's guests less access to his quarters and his women than would be the case in other households. The instruction about the "barrier" reflects this restrictiveness, although eventually it would affect the arrangement of many Muslim domestic spaces.

The Quran states the special status of the Prophet's wives and daughters more explicitly in a passage found earlier in the same sura:

> O women of the Prophet! You are not like any of the other women. If you are pious, do not be soft in your speech, for he who is diseased of heart will desire (you). Speak in the customary manner.
>
> Stay in your houses *(buyūt)*. Do not array yourselves as was done in the first time of ignorance. Pray, give alms, and obey God and his messenger. Truly God wishes to rid you of impurity, O people of the house, and to make you completely pure. Remember the verses of God and of wisdom that are recited in your houses. God is most subtle and most aware. (33 *Aḥzāb* 32–34)

These rules establish manifest associations between domestic space, ritual practices, and the submission of women to the Prophet and to God. Proper speech, including recitations from the Quran, and dress are also incorporated within this discourse. Moreover, as in other statements containing house rules, the Quran links domestic life to the idea of purity.[22] Near the end of the sura, provision for the movement of the women of the Prophet and the women of the believers outside the house is made by the command that they should wear cloaks lest they be recognized or annoyed (v. 59).

Quranic rulings concerning the houses of God, his Prophet, and ordinary believers do not constitute a complete code. They are partial attempts at ordering spatial behavior based on social practice, religious belief, and historical circumstance. Rules for the Kaᶜba and human dwellings entail making distinctions between believers and deniers, as well as between the conditions of purity and impurity. Both the Kaᶜba and human dwellings should be approached in conformity to rules of etiquette, and both provide people with a quality space for prayer and the remembrance of God. These correspondences are not elaborately developed, however, nor are they complete.

The Quran's rules for visiting the house of God appear, at least initially, to be part of an effort to appropriate a ritual space from another group. Its rules for human dwellings involve both estrangement from old houses through the positive value attached to emigration, and the appropriation of new ones. Visiting etiquette, forms of greeting, the sequestering of women, and ritual practices such as prayer and reciting verses of the Quran contribute to making houses religious places, but they also function to give members of the community of believers a corporate identity vis-à-vis other groups in Medina and elsewhere in the Hijaz. The Prophet's household is exemplary in this regard; it sets the standard that Muslims would seek to emulate for centuries to come. Domestic order therefore should be seen as a key factor in the creation of the new Islamic social order.

THE HEREAFTER

Statements about the hereafter[23] provide contexts for about one-third of the house terms in the Quran. The realm of the blessed is called simply "the house" *(al-dār),*[24] but also "the house of residence" *(dār al-muqāma),*[25] "the house of permanence" *(dār al-qarār),*[26] "the house of the pious" *(dār al-muttaqīn),*[27] and "the final house" *(al-dār al-ākhira).*[28] Another name the Quran gives this region is "house of peace" *(dār al-salām).*[29]

The use of *dār* as an appellation for the realm of the blessed occurs in suras assigned to both the Meccan and Medinan groups. The domestic character of the "house" of paradise is conveyed in the following passage:

> Those who fulfill God's covenant, without undoing the agreement; those who join together (in close family relationships) which God has commanded

> to be joined, fearing their lord and dreading the terrible reckoning; those who have dedicated themselves to earnestly seeking the face of their lord, praying and disbursing (the bounty) that we have bestowed upon them secretly and openly, and repelling evil with good—those are the ones who will have the reward of the house.
>
> Gardens of Eden—they will enter them together with whoever of their fathers, spouses, and children has acted righteously. And angels will come unto them from every door saying, "Peace be upon you for what you have patiently endured." How excellent is the reward of the house! (13 *Raʿd* 20–24)

These verses link righteous behavior in this world to attaining a domestic paradise in the hereafter. Other descriptions of paradise in the Quran emphasize garden imagery, the sumptuous banquets, and the seductive beauty of the houris who will join the blessed (e.g., 52 *Ṭūr* 17–26; 55 *Raḥmān* 46–78). In each of these descriptions, the quality of life in paradise is an idealized rendering of the best aspects of domestic life in this world. The verses quoted above indicate that families will be reunited, and that they will be visited by angels, who will address them with greetings similar to those exchanged in everyday life.

According to Colleen McDannell and Bernhard Lang, this is an example of an "anthropocentric" portrayal of the afterlife. It stresses the human qualities of eternity, as opposed to absolutely transcendent ones, shorn of mundane images. Other anthropocentric notions of the afterlife are attested in ancient Egypt, rabbinic Judaism, and recurrently in Christianity. The most distinguishing aspect of the quranic depictions is that their emphasis upon domestic and familial images has made these images a tenacious feature of subsequent Islamic discourses about paradise.[30]

In addition to *dār,* the Quran employs other house terms such as *maʾwā, ghurfa* (pl. *ghuraf*), *maskin* (pl. *masākin*), and *bayt* in its discussions about the dwellings of the blessed in the hereafter. Some verses call the paradisal gardens a "shelter" *(maʾwā)* for those who fear God (79 *Nāziʿāt* 41). Other passages proclaim,

> For those who believe and do good works, we shall house them in lofty rooms *(ghuraf)* in the garden, beneath which rivers flow. There they shall be for ever. (29 *ʿAnkabūt* 58)

> To believing men and women God has promised gardens from beneath which rivers flow, wherein they shall be for ever. And (he has promised them) good dwellings *(masākin)* in the gardens of Eden. (9 *Tawba* 72)[31]

> God has set forth as a model for those who believe the wife of Pharaoh, for she said, "O Lord! Build a house *(bayt)* for me near you in the garden! Save me from Pharaoh and his deeds! Save me from the people who do wrong!" (66 *Taḥrīm* 11)

If house language can be used to describe the realms of the blessed in the hereafter, can it also be used to describe the realms of the damned as it was in the funerary texts of ancient Egypt and in rabbinic literature?[32] Yes, in fact, the Quran uses *dār* to describe hell as "the evil house" *(sūʾ al-dār),*[33] "the house of perdition" *(dār al-bawār),*[34] and "the house of eternity" *(dār al-khuld).*[35]

Terms for "shelter" *(maʾwā)* and "dwelling" *(mathwā)* are used more frequently in quranic references to hell than is *dār.*[36]

> We shall cast terror into those who have denied God by associating partners with him, something for which no authorization has been sent. Their shelter *(maʾwā)* shall be the fire. How bad is the dwelling *(mathwā)* of the wrong-doers! (3 *Al ʿImrān* 151)

> On the day of resurrection you will see those who told lies against God, their faces blackened. Isn't there in Gehenna a dwelling *(mathwā)* for the arrogant? (39 *Zumar* 60)

In such contexts, therefore, the Quran employs domestic terms to conceptualize anti-domestic spaces, that is, places wherein the most horrendous aspects of life are to be experienced for death's eternity.

The Quran usually refers to paradise and hell as the garden and the fire respectively. The domestic or anti-domestic characteristics of these locales in quranic discourse is undeniable, as I have shown. These localities, moveover, have other house-like features. Paradise and hell are separated from each other by a barrier *(ḥijāb),*[37] across which the inhabitants of each realm converse with one another, not unlike the rule for conducting discourse between the Prophet's women and his guests across a barrier in his house. Paradise and hell each reportedly have their own doors *(abwāb).*[38] Finally, just as the blessed recline on beds or couches in paradise,[39] so do the damned find themselves on beds in hell.

> Truly those who deny our signs and scorn them, the gates of heaven will not be opened for them, nor will they enter paradise. . . . They will have a bed in hell, with covers over them. This is how we recompense the wrong-doers. (7 *Aʿrāf* 40–41)

> Do not be misled by the vicissitude in the land of those who deny. (They enjoy) some convenience, but then hell will be their shelter *(maʾwā),* and how bad their bed shall be! (3 *Al ʿImrān* 196–97)

The Quran does not construe domestic space as a comprehensive mythic, ritual, or symbolic system. Nevertheless, it does express a conjunction of part systems through the parallels, oppositions, and causal relations it draws between the four main contexts within which house terms occur. The building of God's house and recognizing the origins of human dwellings alike are situations that depend upon making a distinction between true belief—a form of submission *(islām)*—and denial *(kufr)*. Likewise, the opposition between true belief and good deeds on the one hand, and denial and wrongdoing on the other, is paralleled by the opposition between paradise as the dwelling place for the righteous and hell as the dwelling place for the damned.

According to the Quran, denial can entail both the destruction of one's house in this world and the punishment of hell in the hereafter. Emigration in the way of God and losing one's house as a consequence leads to both forgiveness and admission to paradise.

> I do not lose track of anything you have done—male or female, you are alike. Those who emigrated, were expelled from their houses *(diyār)*, were harmed (following) in my way, fought and were killed—surely I cover up for them their evil deeds. Surely I shall admit them into gardens from beneath which rivers flow. A reward from God! The fairest reward is with God! (3 *Al ʿImrān* 195)

As for house rules, they, too, are framed in terms of belief and denial, correct actions and wrongful ones. Moreover, the Quran seems to want to make of the dwelling a place for the confinement of women in order to protect them, punish them, and enhance their piety, depending on the circumstances. These statements are linked to discourses about the prison-houses of the damned and the dwellings awarded to the righteous in the hereafter, like other domestic discourses in the Quran.

In this chapter, I have shown that the Quran employs domestic figures as key metaphors for discussing important concepts: God's house, emigration, belief, and disbelief, not to mention notions about the afterlife. It also makes simple human dwellings and customs pertaining to privacy, visitation, and hospitality part of a universal pattern of order and salvation. Now I shall turn to discourses of domestic space in the hadith literature, where we expect to find a confirmation and elaboration of quranic discourses.

2

The Houses of the Hadiths

The hadith literature comprises a much more extensive corpus of statements than the Quran. As the Quran contains the eternal word of God, Muslims view hadiths as the authoritative word of Muhammad or his companions (with the exception of a small subgroup of "holy hadiths" attributed to God himself). Ideally hadiths reinforce and elaborate upon statements made in the Quran, especially in regard to the regulation of human behavior. Most of them address subjects such as the primary Islamic ritual duties, warfare, family law, commercial transactions, and social etiquette.

The history of the authoritative hadith collections differs from that of the Quran.[1] They may be based on a core of oral traditions that can be traced back to the Prophet and his companions, but they are first of all written products of the dedicated efforts of Muslim sages, especially those of non-Arab or mixed descent, living in the major post-conquest urban centers. By using reports about Muhammad's sayings and deeds to determine which Muslim practices and ideas in the far-flung empire were correct ones, these people hoped to bring to light a set of explicit Islamic norms which, in conformity with the Quran, were to be acknowledged by all members of the community wherever they lived.

Although the sages were convinced that by creating and promulgating an authoritative written canon of traditions, they were reproducing the "pristine" culture of the first Muslims in Medina,[2] in fact they were producing an ideal Islamic post-conquest *oikoumene*. Piety and a scribal desire for coherence may have been strong motivations for their efforts, but even stronger was their desire to counteract communal fragmentation and limit caliphal absolutism. By the time the canon of authoritative hadiths had been assembled in written form (third/ninth century), Muslim solidarity had already been severely strained by four civil wars and numerous local revolts. Together, the Quran and the canonical hadiths have provided stability and coherence in times of prosperity and disaster alike. This is no less true among Muslims today, living under the effects of colonialism and modernization, than it was centuries ago.[3]

Muslims acknowledge that, unlike the Quran, hadiths are susceptible to fabrication. Hence, they have developed a "science" to evaluate their authenticity for legal, doctrinal, and practical applications. On the basis of criteria for authenticity developed by this hadith science, non-Shiʿi Muslims assign the hadith collections of Muhammad b. ʿAbd Allah al-Bukhari (d. 256/870) and Muslim b. al-Hajjaj (d. 261/875) exemplary status. They refer to these books as the *ṣaḥīḥān* "the two correct (collections)." Other esteemed early collections, called the *Sunan,* are those of Abu Dawud (d. 275/888), al-Tirmidhi (d. 279/892), and al-Nasaʾi (d. 303/915). Hadith scholars have disagreed on the status of the *Sunan* of Ibn Maja (d. 273/886), because it purportedly includes too many spurious traditions. But, since the sixth/twelfth century, many traditionalists have considered it one of the six canonical hadith collections.[4] The *Muwaṭṭaʾ* of Malik b. Anas (d. 179/795) and the *Musnad* of Ahmad b. Hanbal (d. 241/855) are two other important hadith sources.

These eight books contain similar, if not identical, hadiths. Each, however, also contains hadiths and commentary unique to itself. All but one of these collections are organized by topic, a fact that facilitates the location of related hadiths in deciding legal and doctrinal issues. Ibn Hanbal's *Musnad,* as the title implies, is organized according to the names of the authorities who transmitted the hadiths, rather than by their contents.

In defining the contours of discourses about domestic space in hadiths, I shall mainly confine my remarks to these eight collections. Given their history and purpose, we can expect that the domestic spaces of hadiths are similar to those of the Quran. In accordance with the premise that hadiths in their written form are products of an imperial Islamic milieu, however, we will find the effects of domination inscribed more deeply in the domestic discourses of hadiths than they were in the Quran.

HOUSE TERMS

Within the eight leading hadith collections, *bayt* and *dār* are the most frequently used lexemes for "house."[5] *Ghurfa* and *maskin* occur less often, and they have a narrower range of meanings than *bayt* or *dār.* Rarer still are *maʾwā* and *mathwā.* A new lexeme for "house," unattested in the Quran, appears in the hadith: *manzil,* derived from a verb meaning "to occupy or sojourn in a place."[6] Usually it is synonymous with *bayt, dār,* and *maskin.* Indeed, traditional commentaries on the Quran and hadith regularly gloss one of these terms with another from the same group.

This class of lexemes occurs chiefly in three sorts of context in the hadith materials: statements about God's house; rules for domestic behavior; and visions of life in the hereafter.

GOD'S HOUSE

Mecca's surrender to Muslim forces in 8/630, and Muhammad's last Hajj two years later are the events from which most of the hadiths about the Kaᶜba, Hajj, and ᶜUmra are derived. As in the Quran, the Kaᶜba is identified with God's house. Many hadiths deal with the circumambulation of the pilgrims about "the house" *(al-bayt)*, others with rules for entering and praying within the building, or touching its corners. Some traditions are concerned with the history of the Kaᶜba, its demolitions and restorations. A subgroup of these is composed of statements intended to explain why Muhammad did not renovate the Kaᶜba after he gained control of Mecca.[7] In contrast to the Quran, however, little mention is made of the shrine's connection to Ibrahim and his son in the standard hadith collections.

Most of the hadith collections group statements that mention God's house together with others concerned with the sanctity of Mecca and the ritual practices and prohibitions pilgrims should observe when they enter its sacred precincts, or *ḥaram*. Some of these traditions allege that the Mecca and its *ḥaram* were sanctified by God himself when the world was created, and that they would remain so until the world's end. On the authority of Ibn ᶜAbbas, the Prophet said,

> The day of conquest, the conquest of Mecca: Truly God sanctified this town the day he created the heavens and the earth. So it is sacred *(ḥaram)* through God's sacrality *(ḥurma)* until resurrection day. Before me, fighting was not permitted in it to anyone. Nor was it permitted to me except for one hour on one day. So it is sacred through God's sacrality until resurrection day.
>
> Its thorny bushes shall not be cut, nor its game animals scared away. No one shall take a misplaced thing unless he has made it known. Nor shall (Mecca's) greenery be plucked [except for the *idhkhir*-reed used for their graves and houses].[8]

This hadith gives Muhammad a prominent role in the restoration of Mecca's sanctity. It joins with other hadiths about the conquest of Mecca, which describe how, when the Prophet entered the city, he kissed the black stone, circumambulated the Kaᶜba, and destroyed the 360 idols the Meccans had placed there.[9]

Other hadiths pertaining to God's house associated it not with events at the beginning, but with the signs of the hour at the end of time. One of these signs was that a man, or a defenseless tribe, would seek refuge in "the house" (i.e., the Kaᶜba), and that an army would be dispatched to besiege it. The army, which was to include members of the Prophet's community, would sink into the ground on a plain, perhaps at Medina.[10] Here we can see that the idea of violence against God's house was combined with a vision of internecine conflict to supply part of the Islamic discourse about the end of the world.

Lastly there are the hadiths mentioning *al-bayt al-maᶜmūr* "the flourishing house."[11] The Quran mentions it only once, without any descriptive details (52 *Ṭūr* 4). The authoritative collections contain hadiths that describe it as one of the remarkable things seen by the Prophet during his tour of the heavens. According to one version, when Gabriel and Muhammad reach the seventh heaven, "the flourishing house" is raised up before their eyes. The Prophet then learns "seventy thousand angels pray (in it) every day. Once they exit from it, they do not return to it again."[12] Other versions mention that they find Ibrahim there, leaning against it.

On the basis of these statements, we can surmise that "the flourishing house" was understood by late second-/eighth-century Muslims to be a heavenly temple. It is a meeting place for the angels; they pray there continuously. It is located in the purest part of heaven, in or near paradise itself. Moreover, by some accounts, it is associated with Ibrahim, a figure connected in post-biblical Jewish tradition with God's house in Jerusalem, and in Islamic tradition with the Kaᶜba.

Was the "flourishing house" originally understood as an idealized version of the Kaᶜba in Mecca? The authoritative hadith collections do not contain statements making an explicit connection between the two houses. Several of the hadiths about Muhammad's ascent mention that he was taken up from the Kaᶜba to the seventh heaven.[13] For the most part, however, the relation between God's house in Mecca and "the flourishing house" is an ambiguous one that has to be inferred from shared traits, such as their connection with Ibrahim, the idea that both are places of prayer and visitation, and that each is called a *bayt*.

But the same traits could just as well be those of the heavenly version of the Jerusalem temple, which held an important place in Judaic cosmology. According to some early Islamic ascent accounts, Muhammad was taken up from the Jerusalem temple site (called *bayt al-maqdis*) to Ibrahim and the "flourishing house."[14] To prevent people from maintaining that Muhammad had seen the heavenly temple of Jerusalem, and to enhance the status of Mecca, however, later hadiths and commentaries made a direct connection between the "flourishing house" and God's house in Mecca.[15]

HOUSE RULES

People's houses and behavior in them are regular objects of discourse in the hadiths, more so than the house of God. In this respect, too, the Quran and the hadiths are similar (see table 1). This group of hadiths is particularly concerned with houses as places for prayer, and with rules governing both access to and control over domestic space.

Prayer is said to be one of Islam's five "pillars." Obligatory prayer consists of a regularlized sequence of body postures and formulaic utterances that should be performed daily by the faithful in a condition of ritual purity. Non-Muslims often think that it has to be performed in a formal place of worship, that is, a mosque. The word "mosque," however, is derived from the Arabic *masjid,* which means simply "place for prostration." Prayer, therefore, can actually be performed almost anywhere. Although some places are considered more meritorious than others for prayer (e.g., the mosques of Mecca, Medina, and Jerusalem), the authoritative hadith collections include statements validating prayer wherever it is performed. On the authority of Abu Dharr, Muhammad said, "The earth is a mosque for you, so pray wherever you happen to be when prayer time comes." According to Jabir b. ᶜAbd Allah al-Ansari, he also declared, "the earth was made as a pleasant place, a source of purification, and a mosque for me. So if a man finds that it is time for prayer, let him pray wherever he is."[16]

Hadiths indicate that within this universal definition of mosque space, Muslim houses occupy a special position. Performing prayers at home is supposed to bring it life and goodness. There are a number of hadiths that attest to this. According to Ibn ᶜUmar, the Prophet declared, "Perform some of your prayers in your houses *(buyūt),* and don't make them into graves!" One hadith associates prayer with the act of remembering God; it says that the difference between a house where God is remembered and one where he is not is analogous to the difference between the living and the dead. Another, transmitted by Jabir, advises the pious man to reserve part of his mosque prayer for the house *(bayt),* "for God will bring goodness into his house from his prayer."[17] Other hadiths equate prayer with light, stating, "As for a man's prayer, it is light; so illuminate your houses *(buyūt)!*"[18]

There are several reports that relate how people would invite the Prophet to sup with them in their homes, then lead them in prayer, and call blessings upon the household.[19] Other hadiths recommend prayer at home under specific conditions, particularly during inclement weather.[20] This principle is set forth most elaborately in the following account:

> ʿItban b. Malik, a companion of God's Messenger . . . from among the Ansar, approached God's Messenger, saying, "O God's Messenger! I have lost my sight, and I lead my people in prayer. When the rain flooded the gorge between me and them, I was unable to go to their mosque to lead their prayers. I hope, O God's Messenger, that you will come to pray in [a part of my house *(bayt)* that you select as a prayer place *(muṣallā)*]." God's Messenger replied, "I will do it, God willing."
>
> According to ʿItban, God's Messenger went the next morning with Abu Bakr. He asked permission (to enter), and permission was given. He did not take a seat until he entered the house, then he said, "Whereabouts in your house would you like me to pray?" I pointed out to him a part of the house [where I like to pray], and God's Messenger arose and pronounced the *takbīr* (for prayer). Then we stood up and arranged ourselves into rows [behind him]. He performed two *rakʿa*s of prayer, then he concluded with the *taslīm*.
>
> (When we finished,) we detained him with an invitation to have a meat dish we had prepared for him. [Having heard that God's Messenger was in my house,] a lot of (my) kinsmen who lived in the compound *(dār)*[21] came back and assembled in the house.[22]

The inauguration of a prayer place in ʿItban's house was regarded by pious Muslims as a precedent for allowing mosques to be built in houses. The Quran contains passages that show that houses could be used as prayer places, as I indicated in the previous chapter, but authoritative hadiths give this practice more explicit support. Another of Muhammad's companions is reported to have performed congregational prayers in a mosque within his *dār*.[23] There are also hadiths that disclose that Muhammad commanded his followers to build mosques in their domestic compounds *(dūr)*, and to purify them and keep them in good repair.[24] Except for the Prophet's mosque in Medina, there is little information as to what these house-mosques looked like. They were probably modest structures erected in courtyards, comprised of a small enclosed portico made of palm trunks and dried fronds, perhaps with rugs or reed mats for ground covering.[25]

Even Abu Bakr, the first ruler (caliph) of the Muslim community after Muhammad, is reported to have built a mosque adjacent to his house prior to the Hijra to Medina. His daughter ʿAʾisha testified, "I always knew my parents to be religious people. Mornings and evenings, not a day would pass but that God's Messenger would come to (visit) us. Then Abu Bakr saw fit to build a mosque in the space *(fināʾ)* in front of his house *(dār)*. He would pray there and read the Quran.''[26] Apparently Abu Bakr's mosque was in the midst of, or adjacent to, a public thoroughfare, for polytheist women and children would stop and stare at him in wonder. This development provoked the animosity of the leaders of the Quraysh, the Muslims' most powerful opponents. Neither the authoritative hadiths nor Ibn Ishaq's *Sīra* furnish information about the outcome of this confrontation, except to suggest that it helped precipitate the Hijra to Medina.

The authorization for praying at home and building mosques there is subject to limitations. Prayer should not always be performed at home, nor should every house have a mosque. Otherwise, solidarity among members of the group would be in danger of dissipating. While performing supererogatory night prayers at home, Muhammad reportedly admonished a group of companions to pray in their own houses, ''because the best of prayers are those performed in one's home, except the required ones.''[27] This is an important exception, for it implies that the prayers of the collectivity have precedence. This idea is made explicit in hadiths that instructed Muslims that collective prayer is twenty-five times better for a man than praying at home alone or in the market place.[28]

Other hadiths point out the virtues of having to walk some distance to get to a mosque, as opposed to taking up residence next to one. Muhammad is said to have ordered the Banu Salama not to move their houses *(diyār)* next to his, for all of their steps to the Prophet's mosque are recorded as meritorious ones.[29] Another tradition, cited in Muslim's collection, states, ''Whoever purifies himself at home, then walks to one of God's houses *(buyūt)* to fulfill one of the duties imposed by God—for every two steps he takes, one will diminish a sin, the other will enhance (his merit) by a degree.''[30]

Such positive inducements to pray outside of one's own home as these are complemented by negative ones. Several hadiths curse and threaten people who miss performing prayers (especially collective ones) with the incineration of their houses *(buyūt)*, or with the loss of property and family.[31] This type of pronouncement bears some similarity to quranic statements that describe how the houses of deniers were destroyed in punishment for their failure to acknowledge God's messengers. The hadiths in question, however, are directed expressly against members of the community of believers. One subgroup of these hadiths ostensibly threatened Meccan polytheists who had prevented Muhammad from performing the ''middle'' prayer when they attacked Medina during the Battle of the

Ditch. But in his *Ṣaḥīḥ*, Muslim suggests that even these statements could be used to admonish wayward members of the community.

Threats to burn down people's houses for not praying, or not joining others in prayer, were not designed to prohibit prayer at home, but rather to prohibit its neglect and to delimit its practice on behalf of promoting collective worship. After all, even with the establishment of an Islamic empire outside the Arabian Peninsula, the majority of mosques were house-mosques.[32] Moreover, through the centuries, Muslims customarily have regarded their houses as appropriate places for prayer, remembering God, and reciting the Quran.

Indeed, the house is esteemed as the most appropriate place for the prayer of women. It is true that some hadiths sanction their right to go out to mosques for prayer, once they have obtained permission to do so.[33] The Quran, however, had already instructed the Prophet's wives to stay at home, and to worship there (33 *Aḥzāb* 33–34). Statements preserved in the compilations of Abu Dawud and Ibn Hanbal endorse the extension of this principle to include Muslim women in general. One hadith declares, "Do not forbid women from going to mosques, (but) their houses *(buyūt)* are better for them."[34] In another hadith, the Prophet tells a female follower,

> I know that you like to pray with me. Prayer in your quarters *(bayt)* is better for you than prayer in your courtyard enclosure *(ḥujra)*;[35] and prayer in your courtyard enclosure is better than prayer in your domestic compound *(dār)*; and prayer in your domestic compound is better than prayer in your clan's mosque; and prayer in your clan's mosque is better than prayer in my (communal) mosque.[36]

The woman consequently ordered that a mosque be built for her in the innermost part of her house, that is, in a place where she was least likely to be seen by strange men. Even when women prayed with men, they are obliged to do so behind them, whether at a communal mosque or at home.

When ʿItban b. Malik invited the Prophet to dedicate a prayer place in his house, the narrative takes care to note both that Muhammad asked permission to enter and that he was invited to share food with his hosts afterwards. This occasion, therefore, exemplifies the other major subject area addressed in hadiths about human dwellings: rules governing access to and control over domestic space. Neither the Quran nor hadiths make Muslim houses into isolated enclaves, closed to outsiders. Rather, they treat them as zones for social interaction between the occupants and outsiders. In this regard, social interaction represents a form of moral action.

The authoritative hadith collections contain numerous statements affirming respect among family members, and condemning the severance of kinship relations. On the other hand, they also commend acts of kindness toward coreligionists, strangers, widows, orphans, the poor, and the sick.[37] When asked which aspect of Islam was best, the Prophet reportedly said, "That you should provide food and recite the greeting 'Peace be upon you' for both those you know and those you do not know."[38] In a similar vein, on the authority of Abu Hurayra, he said, "Whoever believes in God and the Last Day should not harm his neighbor, . . . he should honor his guest . . . and let him either say good things or be quiet."[39] In the hadith about the Prophet's visit to ᶜItban's house and in the two hadiths just quoted, Islam (or submission to God) is linked unequivocally to everyday exchanges of words and of things. The human dwelling in particular constitutes an important arena for these exchanges.

When the hadiths talk about asking permission to enter a house and greeting the people within, they are elaborating upon rules stated in the Quran. Al-Bukhari, for example, begins his chapter, "Asking Permission" (*istiʾdhān*), with an account about the origination of the greeting, "Peace be upon you," in the discourse between Adam and the angels. Then he quotes the quranic verses about asking permission (24 *Nūr* 27–29), together with a commentary on the rules about lowering one's gaze and covering the genitals (vv. 30–31). As in the Quran, therefore, compilers of authoritative hadiths saw interrelationships between exchanging greetings, visitation rules, and preserving intimate parts of the body from the view of others. Baring the privates in front of strangers was something foreigners might do, but not Muslim women or men.[40]

When visitors come to a house, according to hadith rules, they should stand near the door and seek permission to enter up to three times. Requests should be accompanied by the correct greeting. Muhammad is reported to have refused entrance to a visitor until he said, "Peace be upon you."[41] If the door has no curtain (or similar barrier), they should face the entrance obliquely when they seek permission, in imitation of the Prophet.[42] When asked to identify themselves, they should respond by giving their proper name, not by saying, "It is I."

Once they are invited to enter, their hosts are obliged to treat them according to the rules of hospitality. Commentators note that this hospitality should be extended to rich and poor, Muslim and denier *(kāfir)* alike. Some hadiths recommend a three-day limit on the duration of this obligation. Muslim guests, moreover, should not be such a burden on their coreligionist hosts as to cause them to overlook other obligations; that is, taking care of the needs of parents, spouses, children and other dependents.[43]

The Quran connects rulings for salutation and seeking permission to enter a house with ideas of blessing and purity for those who adhere to them. Another side to this subject is revealed in the hadiths. There, visitation rules are concerned more with defining the house as a sacred area *(ḥaram)* that must be respected by others. Failure to do so may have dangerous consequences for violators. One of the bluntest statements on this subject is cited by Ibn Hanbal, on the authority of ʿUbada b. al-Samit: "God's Messenger said, 'The house *(dār)* is a sacred area. If anyone comes into your *ḥaram* (without your permission), kill him!' "[44] Other traditions, quoted more widely in the authoritative collections, state that people who intentionally peek into houses without permission should be blinded. Indeed, the Prophet reportedly declared that rules for asking permission were promulgated to prevent "seeing" inside the house.[45] The eye, like the genitals, can commit adultery.[46]

A great part of a house's sacrality depends on the reputation of its female occupants. Outside the Quran and authoritative hadiths, Arabic-speaking Muslims use the term *ḥaram* to denote both the forbidden character of domestic space and a person's wife. The semantic relation between the wife and the house is implied in the hadiths quoted from Ibn Hanbal above. Likewise, the term *bayt,* although it lacks the explicit idea of sacrality, can mean either the dwelling place or the wife, depending on the context. Hence, beyond recommending that visitors seek permission before entering or looking into a house, the Prophet cautioned male visitors against entering houses at all if it meant that they would be alone with a marriageable woman.[47]

What are people supposed to do when they enter their own houses? The Quran states that they should pronounce God's greeting (24 *Nūr* 61). This will bring blessing. One rare hadith expresses a similar idea in declaring that greeting the family when entering is a blessing for the person and his house.[48] According to the most authoritative hadiths on this subject, the Prophet said, "If a man goes into his house mentioning God when he enters and when he sups, Satan says (to himself), 'You have no lodging or dinner.' But if he goes in and does not mention God when he enters, Satan says, 'You have acquired lodging.' And if he does not mention God when he sups, he says, 'You have acquired lodging and dinner.' "[49] This hadith complements the other two statements by substituting the threat of evil if the rule is not followed for the promise of blessing if it is. Another group of hadiths recommends invoking God's protection against evil when leaving the house.[50]

Entering and leaving the human dwelling therefore has a bearing on the relation between humans and spiritual powers. Correct entry brings God's blessing. Incorrect entry, or violation of domestic space, can bring harm to the violator. As the hadith just quoted suggests, this can entail affliction by satanic forces.

The contents of a house and their arrangement can have an effect on the attraction and repulsion of devils and angels. The Prophet reportedly advised his companions, "(When night falls), restrain your children, for Satan comes out at that time. One hour after nightfall, let them go, close the doors, and mention God's name. Satan does not open a closed door. Tie up the tops of the water skins and mention God's name. Cover up your store jars—anything will do—and mention God's name, and extinguish your lanterns."[51] What kind of evil can Satan bring to the house? No doubt, a number of misfortunes are possible, but the hadiths mention specifically that failure to follow such procedures can result in the destruction of the house by fire, or an outbreak of the plague.

Angels can also visit people in their homes. The Prophet received them many times—even his wife ʿAʾisha is said to have been visited by the angel Gabriel, although she failed to see him.[52] Angels can be repulsed, however, for they do not enter houses that contain portraits of living things, statues, or dogs. In some contexts this might be a good thing, for as hellenistic magical texts and the apocalyptic books of John and Enoch show, angels can be just as harmful to humans as devils. Accounts of the life of Muhammad mention that he himself had been violently throttled by Gabriel during their first encounter on Mt. Hira. It is also a widely acknowledged Islamic doctrine that angels are emissaries of death.[53]

The hadiths tend to regard concourse with angels in the world of the living as a good thing. The fending off of angels from the house provoked the Prophet's anger. Dogs are a source of impurity, so they have to be removed from the house before the angels will enter. Figural images, such as those on the curtains in ʿAʾisha's house, aggravated Muhammad even more. Their creators were attempting to usurp the power of the Creator, and they would be punished in the hell for doing so.[54] As a rule, angels should be welcomed into the home; pictures and dogs should be removed from it.

One of the most peculiar groups of hadiths pertaining to houses is that which deals with the killing of snakes. The Prophet banned this practice for snakes found in houses, except two kinds, one of which causes miscarriages, the other blindness. Some traditions add that householders should give a snake until three days to leave, for it may be one of the jinn (spirits made of fire) that have become Muslims. If, after three days, it is seen again in the house, it should be killed. This is because it must be either a satan or a denier. Therefore, most kinds of snakes, also known as house jinn, are allowed a three-day stay in the house, like human visitors. It is possible, as one hadith states, that respect for snakes was motivated by a desire for being protected from their "evil," that is, from a fatal bite.[55]

The special relation between Muslim women and domestic space is indicated in several quranic passages, as I have indicated. The hadiths affirm this relationship, extending quranic rules addressed to the Prophet's women to all women. Rules governing entering and looking into houses were in part designed to protect their privacy. But do hadiths acknowledge who actually controls domestic space? If we look at the rules such as those prohibiting men from meeting with women alone, those requiring women to obtain permission from fathers or husbands before going out for prayer,[56] and the Prophet's objections to the curtains hung by ʿAʾisha, then it would appear that men have greater authority in the domestic sphere than do women.

This principle is most aptly stated in the following hadith, related on the authority of ʿAbd Allah b. ʿUmar:

> Each of you is a shepherd and each of you is responsible for his flock. A ruler who leads the people is a shepherd responsible for his flock. A man is the shepherd of the people of his house *(bayt)*, responsible for them. A woman is the shepherd of her husband's house and children, responsible for them. A servant is the shepherd of his master's property, responsible for it. Each of you is responsible for his flock.[57]

Men come after the ruler (*amīr* or *imām*) in this hierarchy, but ahead of women. A woman's responsibility is phrased in terms of her husband's house and her husband's children. As a rule, hadiths promote loving relations between husband and wife. They oblige the husband to care for his spouse and children. Nonetheless, they also urge women to please their husbands, and obey them, in conformity with quranic rules (e.g., 4 *Nisāʾ* 34). To some degree, the ideal domestic order and the ideal social order are images of each other.

In a famous sermon delivered during his last pilgrimage, the Prophet instructed men to obey God in matters concerning women. If they have taken wives for themselves in a lawful manner, then they must see to it that no wife brings someone the husband dislikes into his bedroom. This is adulterous behavior. For violating this rule, a woman is to be beaten, but not too severely.[58] Control over domestic space, therefore, appears to be a predominantly male prerogative from the point of view of the Quran and hadiths. A woman's rights are couched in obedience to men, as a man's rights are couched in obedience to rulers.

Nothing is explicitly mentioned in the authoritative hadith collections about the ability of the ruler to violate the rules of access to Muslim houses. Later traditions concerning the caliph ᶜUmar (ruled 13/634–23/644), leader at the time of the major Arab conquests and strict upholder of Islam, addressed this issue, however. According to one hadith,

> Once ᶜUmar, may God be pleased with him, was patrolling Medina at night when he heard a man's voice singing in a house. He climbed over the wall and found him with a woman and alcohol. He said, "O enemy of God, did you think that God would shield you while you were disobeying him?"
>
> (The man) replied, "O Commander of the Faithful, don't be so hasty. If I disobeyed God once, you did it three times. God Almighty said, 'Do not spy into private matters' (49 *Ḥujurāt* 12), but you spied. God Almighty said, 'It is not proper for you to approach houses from the rear' (2 *Baqara* 189), but you climbed over my wall. And God Almighty said, 'Do not enter houses other than your own' (24 *Nūr* 27), but you entered my house without permission and without greeting."
>
> ᶜUmar, may God be pleased with him, said, "If I were to forgive you, would you do good things?" He replied, "Yes. By God, O Commander of the Faithful, if you were to forgive me, I would not do anything like this ever again." So he forgave him, went (out of the house), and left.[59]

This tradition shows that even such an honored and powerful figure as ᶜUmar could be faulted for violating quranically validated rules for domestic boundaries. Note, however, that the caliph still has authority to threaten the offender with a punishment. Adhering to his duty to "command the good and forbid wrongdoing," ᶜUmar presses him to correct his ways. The common moral order does not stop at the limits of the house.[60]

The ownership and control of domestic space became concerns of Islamic jurisprudence, particularly in regard to matters of divorce, inheritance, and property rights. Although rulings on these matters refer to precedents set by the Quran and the authoritative hadith, their fullest development occurred in the hands of scholars of Islamic legal science, the *fuqahāʾ*, after the late second/eighth century. A careful examination of the complex details of their rulings pertaining to Muslim houses falls outside the purview of this book; however, I should point out that these rulings strongly affirmed domestic privacy and property rights. In regard to the mutual rights and duties of men and women relating to domestic space, jurists were inclined to uphold the rights of women to lodging and maintenance as long as they obeyed their husbands and male guardians. The abuses and injustices that have occurred in the application of this principle, and related ones, have prompted calls in many modern Muslim countries for new legislation to improve the legal status of women.[61]

Aside from hadiths dealing with the relation between houses and prayer, and with rules governing access and control, there are others which are closer to being proverbs than rules. For example, the Prophet reputedly said, "The world is the house *(dār)* of those who have no house; unto it are gathered thoughtless people."[62] A similar hadith states, "The world is a prison for believers, and paradise for deniers."[63] Being homeless is a figure of speech for people who will not reside in the heavenly paradise, and who allow their mundane desires to lead them to deny God and the Last Day.

The authoritative collections also contain hadiths stating that the house *(dār)* is one of the three evil omens, along with women and horses.[64] Some commentators on this group of hadiths explain that houses can be evil when burdened with poverty or nasty neighbors. A woman becomes inauspicious through her immoral actions; and a horse becomes so when it is stubborn. Yet, it is also possible that the evil of these three things comes from their association with *fitna;* that is, they are instruments through which God puts the faith of Muslims to the test. If they succumb to the temptations of wealth, women, or power, then they are not likely to be among the blessed in the hereafter (cf. 64 *Taghābun* 14f).[65]

THE HEREAFTER

The hadiths use house terms in discourses about the hereafter.[66] The words *dār, bayt, ghurfa,* and *maskin* occur in these discourses, just as they do in the Quran. They are much more likely, however, to be used in reference to paradisal dwellings than to infernal ones.[67] This does not mean that hadiths do not mention hell. Rather, they cease to consider it as a kind of domestic space. The hadiths also use the word *khayma* "tent" in descriptions of paradise; this is an elaboration of a single reference in the Quran to the tents of the houris (55 *Raḥmān* 72).

The Prophet was able to convey information about paradise and hell to his companions because of his night visions and heavenly tour. In one of his longest hadiths, he tells them of a dream in which two men showed him the tortures suffered by liars, neglecters of the Quran, adulterers, and usurers in hell. Then he says,

> We went on until we reached a green garden in which there was an enormous tree. At its foot was a shaykh and some children; and there was a man standing near the tree lighting a fire in front of him.
>
> The (two men) took me up into the tree, into a house *(dār)* more beautiful than I had ever seen before in my life. In it were shaykhs, youths, women, and children. Then the (two men) led me out, and took me up (further) into the tree, into a house even more beautiful and pleasant. In it were shaykhs and youths.

In explaining these sights to him, one of his guides says:

> "The shaykh at the foot of the tree is Ibrahim, peace be upon him, and the children around him are offspring of the people. The one lighting the fire is Malik, the keeper of the fire. The first house that you entered is the house of the common believers. As for this house, it is the house of the martyrs.[68] I am Gabriel and this is Michael. Now look up!"
>
> So I looked up, and, behold, above me were what seemed to be clouds. Then they said, "That is your dwelling *(manzil)*." I said, "Let me enter my dwelling." They replied, "Your life is not yet complete. If it were, you would have gone (all the way) to your dwelling."[69]

This text illustrates several important facets of early Islamic discourses about the houses of paradise: house and garden images are closely interwoven; different kinds of houses contain different ranks of people, in moral gradations from prophet to common believer; the Prophet receives a preview of his heavenly dwelling before death; and the discourse depends on portraying the condition of the blessed in contrast to that of the damned.

These facets of discourse about paradise are not unique to this text. The Quran clearly combines house and garden imagery, it assumes that Muhammad has seen paradise and hell, and it consistently juxtaposes discourses about paradise with discourses about hell. What is most notable in hadiths about the hereafter, however, is that they develop a hierarchy of houses (and people) in paradise, an economy of awards and punishments based on the quality of an individual's actions and faith, and a tradition about the Prophet's vision of the destiny of the blessed and the damned. In doing this, Islamic discourses about the hereafter assume many of the attributes of Judaic ones formulated prior to the appearance of Islam during the Hellenistic and Late-Antique eras.[70]

The idea that there are different ranks among the blessed is reinforced by a group of authoritative hadiths that takes up questions about the lofty dwellings *(ghuraf)* in paradise and their occupants.[71] These places are more elegant than others; they appear like stars on the horizon to the common people of paradise.[72] They house prophets, martyrs, Muhammad's companions, and Quran reciters. According to one tradition, God has prepared a transparent one of these dwellings for those who give food to the needy, speak kindly, fast regularly, and pray nightly.[73]

God also reportedly builds paradisal houses for people who build and care for mosques, and for those who perform supererogatory prayers.[74] The common believer, who has been transformed into a creature of great beauty and bodily purity, lives in paradise with a family *(ahl)* in one corner of a sixty-mile wide tent formed from an enormous hollow pearl. Family privacy is preserved in this tent, since one group can not see the others due to the vastness of the space in which they reside.[75] The only real barriers in paradise are the walls that inclose it and the veil *(ḥijāb)* that separates the blessed from God, but even this is lifted so that they can behold his face. God will even reward the lowest inhabitants of paradise with dwellings *(manāzil)* superior to those of the mightiest kings.[76]

The authoritative traditions also point out that God allows each man in paradise to have two wives of unsurpassed loveliness.[77] Several spurious hadiths allege that he can enjoy many more, including the wives of the damned.[78] Others indicate that in paradise a man is bestowed with the unflagging potency of a hundred mortals in order to sexually satisfy all his wives and concubines.[79] Muhammad's vision of paradise informs us that children dwell there too, but traditionists differ as to whether the blessed could actually engender them there. According to one disputed hadith, the Prophet declared, "When a believer desires a child in paradise, its conception, birth, and growth occur within an hour—whenever he so desires."[80]

The hadiths rule against burying people in houses, except in extraordinary cases such as those of the Prophet and the first caliphs (see below).[81] Indeed, wishing that a person's house become a tomb is a curse.[82] On the other hand, hadiths occasionally do apply domestic terms to the space of the dead, that is cemeteries and tombs. Passing by the graveyard in Medina, Muhammad reportedly addressed the deceased saying, "Peace be unto you, O house *(dār)* of believing people! You are ahead of us, and we are catching up."[83] Other hadiths state that the grave is a person's first dwelling *(manzil)* in the hereafter.

According to one set of traditions, the grave could even provide its inhabitant with a preview of his or her destiny.

> Every day the grave speaks. It says, "I am the house *(bayt)* of exile. I am the house of loneliness. I am the house of dust. I am the house of maggots."

> When a faithful servant is buried, the grave says to him, "Greetings! Welcome! If you were the most enamored of me among those who walk above, then you are placed under my control today. You have come to me, and you will see what I'm going to do with you." Then his power of vision is enhanced, and the door to paradise is opened for him.[84]

Despite the grave's hospitality, its desolation sets it apart from the splendorous mansions of paradise. It is, moreover, far less hospitable to sinners and deniers, whom it receives rudely and crushes savagely.[85] Hence, for the individual, the grave can serve as a conduit either to bliss or punishment. Indeed, Muhammad reportedly stated that it is both one of the gardens of paradise and one of the pits of hell.[86]

There is no precedent in the Quran for the use of house terms in discourses about the grave. This is an area where the hadiths and the Quran differ. That Muslims would apply house terms to the grave should not be surprising, however. The grave had been regarded as a kind of house for centuries in ancient Mesopotamia, Egypt, and Israel-Palestine. This notion also was held by people living in the region during the Hellenistic and Late-Antique eras. Also, given that ordinary human dwellings were objects of early Islamic discourse and rulings, and that Muslims were taught to be mindful of the resurrection and houses of the hereafter in the conduct of everyday affairs, it stands to reason that the grave would be viewed within Islamic circles as a kind of dwelling place between this world and eternity. This idea probably developed in a context where people believed that Judgment Day was no longer imminent, but where talk of bliss and punishment in the hereafter could be used to regulate behavior over a long period of time. Although it is possible that this view arose in the Prophet's lifetime, it probably began in the late first/early eighth century, when Islam became established as the religion of a territorial state outside the Arabian peninsula.

PARABLES

The semantic complexities of the figure of the house in early Islamic discourse are conveyed most succinctly in the form of the parable *(mathal)*, which is an utterance that uses simple verbal images to teach or persuade people about salient points of religious practice and belief. Proverbial statements can be found interspersed throughout the hadith literature, but al-Tirmidhi assembled several of the most pertinent ones in a chapter located at the end of his collection.

Al-Tirmidhi opens this chapter with parables concerning God's relation to "his servants." The first of these speaks of a straight path, on either side of which stands a house *(dār)* with a curtained doorway. The faithful are invited by God and his warner to follow this path, and to observe his limits (or penalties). By doing this, the curtain is lifted, and the believer is admitted into "the house of peace," which, as we know, is an epithet for paradise.

The next parable is more elaborate and is worth presenting in full. It says that one day the Prophet went out to his companions and informed them,

> In my sleep I thought I saw Gabriel at my head and Michael at my feet. One said, "Coin a parable for him." (The other) said, "The best (parable) for you and your community of which you have heard, or contemplated, is that of a king who has taken a house *(dār)*, and built a room *(bayt)* therein. Then he prepared a banquet, and sent a messenger to summon the people to his meal. Some of them responded to the messenger, but some turned away.
>
> "Now God is the king, the house is Islam *(al-dār al-islām)*, the room is paradise *(al-bayt al-janna)*, and you, O Muhammad, are the messenger. Whoever responds to you, O Muhammad, enters Islam, and whoever enters Islam enters paradise and whoever enters paradise eats whatever is in it."[87]

This hadith is an Islamized rendering of the New Testament parable of the marriage feast (*Matthew* 22.1–4; *Luke* 14.16–24), accompanied by convenient explanatory glosses.[88] It combines two ideas about houses presented in the Quran and the hadiths—namely the idea of the house as a locus for hospitality and as a paradisal habitation—in order to express the conviction that salvation comes through Islam; that is, through submission to God and his messenger. Moreover, the gloss clearly identifies Islam itself with a house governed by a king. This is the only hadith in the authoritative collections that echoes the third/ninth century legal concept of the House of Islam *(dār al-islām)*, about which I will have more to say in the next chapter.

Next, al-Tirmidhi provides a proverb about Muhammad and the other prophets, which is partly an Islamic rendering of the idea of Jesus as the cornerstone of the spiritual house of God (1 *Peter* 2.4–10). According to this tradition, Muhammad said,

> My parable and that of the prophets before me is like the man who built a house *(dār)*, and then completed and beautified it, all but for a single brick [in one corner]. Then, people began to enter it and marvel at it. They said, ["This (last) brick has not been laid. Let the building be completed!" I said, "I am (that) brick, and I am the seal of the prophets."][89]

This hadith uses the theme of house building and visitation rather than commensality. Unlike its New Testament antecedent, it does not make all the faithful an integral part of the building structure; this house is for them, but not of them. Nor does the hadith invoke the language of priesthood, sacrifice, and the rejected stone. The Prophet is represented as a "living brick" that completes and perfects the house of prophets that God has created for believers. The house is a metaphor for true religion. If we were to pay attention to details supplied by different versions of this parable, we would also discover that the house resembles the Kaᶜba. For example, some versions mention that people come to circumambulate it, as they should do when they visit the Kaᶜba. The association of Muhammad with the last brick is reminiscent of the account of the rebuilding of the Kaᶜba, and how Muhammad completed it by placing the black stone in one of its corners. The hadith implies, therefore, that the house of God is also the house of prophets towards whom the people turn for guidance.

By locating this group of parables at the end of his collection of hadiths, al-Tirmidhi intended to convey essential Islamic ideas concisely to the learned masters of tradition and to their listeners. In fact, these proverbs convey a rationale for following the rules embodied in the thousands of hadiths that he and others dedicated themselves to collecting. Rules were not to be followed for their own sake, but to achieve a blessed destiny through submission to God and his Prophet. In the hadith, as in the Quran, houses were both the objects of regulation, and key metaphors for articulating central Islamic convictions.

CONCLUSIONS

The hadith literature reflects a continuation of the domestic discourses of the Quran, but it is a continuation with changes. The Kaᶜba, the human dwelling, and the hereafter continue to be referred to in similar terms, but there is a greater elaboration of detail with respect to each of these domestic spheres. For example, information about pilgrimage rites, visiting etiquette, and the topography and demography of paradise are set forth with more precision than they are in the Quran. Some quranic house lexemes fall into disuse, and a new one, *manzil,* is introduced. The hellfire completely ceases to be designated as a house.

There is also a shift in the focus of sacred history, from the time of the former prophets and peoples to the life of the Prophet Muhammad and his followers. The paradigm of the Medina community, after all, provides the basis for distinguishing Muslims from non-Muslims in the new *oikoumene*. If Abraham, Moses, and Jesus were to serve as the central authorities for law and conduct inside and outside the home, the most likely result would have been the assimilation of Muslims into the cultures they had initially conquered.

We find the effects of imperial Islam inscribed in the hadiths in several ways. The status of God's house and the pilgrimage is tied to Muslim conquest and control of Mecca, which is sanctified when taken by Muhammad. The establishment of mosques in human dwellings is encouraged, but not to the detriment of prayer at communal mosques. Hence, the new religious order can permeate domestic life, and link it to the life of the wider community. Neglect of prayer, on the other hand, can lead to the destruction of people's houses. The extension of rules for segregation of the sexes from the Prophet's household to all Muslim dwellings also reflects the imposition of external controls on domestic life, perhaps reinforcing the dominance of the male order in new Muslim settlements. Visions of paradise portray it as a hierarchical arrangement of houses and people, but unlike the empire, it is based on moral excellence, not on power and wealth. This suggests that the hadiths do not merely sustain the imperial order. Rather, they seek to compel it to adhere to the example set by the original Medina community and the Prophet himself. Finally, the fact that hadiths concerning domestic space were collected and organized in encyclopedic compendia by non-Arab Muslims for transmission to other times and places can be seen as an effect of the successful establishment of an Islamic *oikoumene*.

3

The Birth of the House of Submission

Muslims have regarded Alexander the Great, whom they call Dhu al-Qarnayn, as a prophet and a king. According to an early Islamic rendering of Jewish and Christian versions of the Alexander Romance,[1] he was sent by God to subdue peoples living in the four corners of the earth. Beginning in the west and moving counterclockwise he called each nation he met to worship God. When a people refused his calling, Alexander attacked them with the force of darkness.[2] It enveloped them; it invaded their bodies, houses, and apartments. Fearing utter destruction, they surrendered to him and responded to his calling. Alexander then recruited soldiers for his army from among the vanquished.

According to the story, when all four world regions had been subdued in this manner, Alexander was called upon by a community of the faithful to raise a great barrier in the east against Gog and Magog, a race of demonic barbarians that threatened to overrun the civilized world. These were creatures with voracious appetites who mated with each other incessantly, until each had engendered a thousand offspring. They had no houses; instead they found shelter within the folds of their own great, furry ears. Alexander successfully blockaded them, but the barrier will not hold forever. According to the Prophet Muhammad, they will break through the barrier in the future to ravage the land. Muslims will be driven back into their cities and castles until God comes to their aid.

Alexander then encountered the antithesis of the beastly races: a community of saints. These people comprised a utopia where each member treated the other with equal justice and kindness, where there was neither strife nor disease or poverty, and where there was actually no need for rulers. They buried their dead at the entrances to their houses, which had no doors to debar visitors. When Alexander asked about these unusual domestic customs, they explained that seeing graves at their doorstep every day keeps the memory of death alive in their hearts. They had no doors because all members of the community were absolutely trustworthy.[3]

This story about Alexander's world conquests is remarkable in several ways. First, it shows conquest to be a form of superordinate moral action through which the figure of prophet-king deals with true belief, disbelief, and nonbelief. His conquests are instrumental to the creation of the believing community. They expunge disbelief, and turn its resources to the advantage of the victorious. Moreover, they protect faithful subjects from the threat of nonbelief, which is embodied by the utterly alien race of Gog and Magog.

Second, the story uses houses to illuminate the differences between the worlds it construes. The houses of the infidels are vulnerable to invasion by the just ruler, who acts as an agent of God. Invasion results in submission. The houses of the beasts are their bodies, an apt way of expressing uncontrolled obsession with carnal appetites. Such beings must be completely excluded from the human realm. The houses of the utopian community are ideal dwellings. They are open to all, free of trouble, and, through God's grace, immune from conquest. Indeed, they seem to represent the paradise of the world to come.

Third, although the narrator makes imperial soteriology the leading edge of conquest, he does not allow the ruler's power to be absolute. Rather, he wishes to show both that it ultimately originates in God, and that it is subordinate to the moral suasion of the saintly community of true believers, who, after all, have no need for an army or government. Indeed, the statements the author puts on their lips in answer to Alexander's queries could well be moral lessons intended for actual rulers.

Ibn Ishaq (d. 151/768) incorporated the story of Alexander into a larger work about the lives of the prophets, which ends with the biography of Muhammad himself, whom he portrays as the consummate prophet, conqueror, and moral ruler. An expert in religious tradition from Medina, the Prophet's city, Ibn Ishaq intended this biographical work (the *Sīra*) specifically for the instruction of the princes of the nascent ʿAbbasid dynasty.[4] The account of Alexander's life demonstrates how texts and themes from Hellenistic and Late-Antique cultures were appropriated by Muslims and reworked to conform with their vision of the world. Through their religious convictions, political skills, and successes in battle, Alexander's *oikoumene* was transformed into the *Dār al-Islām*, "the House of Islam," that is, the realm governed by the caliphate, where in principle the norms of true religious belief and practice could be most fully realized.

This chapter is about the discourses of domestic space that prevailed as a result of the creation of the first Muslim empires. In particular, the traditions concerning the house of the Prophet in Medina contained in the hadiths and early historical literature are discussed, and the paradigmatic role the image of his house played in the establishment of early Muslim settlements examined. Moreover, it traces the transformation of subordinate Muslim discourses of domestic space into a superordinate ideology of empire, the *Dār al-Islām*, which was formulated to encompass both Muslims and non-Muslims, and regulate their relations. The chapter concludes with a survey of second-order Muslim discourses of domestic space that reflect the impact of the displacements caused by the subordination of west Asian cultures by a new imperial regime.

THE PROPHET'S HOUSE

The dwelling place of the Prophet is a focal point for rules set forth in the Quran and the hadiths. We have seen that regulations concerning such varied subjects as prayer, visitation, and female privacy are typically related to events that transpired at his house. But just how important was this place within the range of Islamic discourse about domestic space? What place does it occupy in the idealized history of the life of the community? How is the Prophet's house related to God's house, and to the houses of paradise?

Answering these questions satisfactorily means that we have to consider other texts in addition to the Quran and authoritative hadith collections. These include biographies of the Prophet, such as those found in Ibn Ishaq's *Sīra* and Ibn Saᶜd's *al-Ṭabaqāt al-kubrā*; histories of the early Islamic conquests, such as al-Baladhuri's *Futūḥ al-buldān*;[5] and chronicles, such as al-Tabari's famous *Taʾrīkh al-rusul wa'l-mulūk*.[6] Later topographies, histories of Medina, and literature touting the virtues of mosques and shrines form a secondary stratum of sources for information on this subject.

The Hijra to Medina (formerly known as Yathrib) in September of 622 C.E. is a symbolic event that Muslims use to mark the beginning of their time in the world as a self-sustaining community under the leadership of the Prophet Muhammad. It represents movement across space, but it is a qualitative movement away from the disbelief and polytheism embodied by Mecca of the *Jāhiliyya* (the world of ignorance) to belief in God and his prophets in a new homeland.[7] According to Muslim accounts, Muhammad had arranged to send nearly all his seventy or so Meccan followers to Medina ahead of himself, and to have them protected and housed there by his Medinan "helpers," the Ansar. Nevertheless, it is the emigration of Muhammad himself and the construction of his house-mosque[8] compound in Medina that stand out most distinctly in Muslim descriptions of the Hijra.

The importance of this house-mosque is first signalled in traditional accounts by the divinatory method Muhammad used to select its site. When he arrived in the precincts of Medina, he turned down the hospitable invitations of his supporters there, and allowed his camel to wander among their houses instead. When it reached the quarter of the Banu Najjar clan,[9] it was "commanded" by some invisible force to settle down on a lot near the edge of town. The lot is reported to have served as a drying floor for dates and as a cemetery for polytheists. Part of it may also have been used beforehand as a mosque by some of his followers.[10] After the lot had been purchased from its owners, Muhammad ordered that it be cleared of the graves and levelled for building. This may have been simply a practical measure, but it may have been a symbolic act for publicly taking possession of the place, too. The removal of the graves conforms to the tradition of not allowing graves in houses, but it also signifies the displacement of the remnants of polytheism and disbelief by Islam. Centuries later, Ibn Khaldun (d. 808/1406) would write, "(The Prophet) settled there and built his mosque and his houses (*buyūt*) in the place God had prepared for that (purpose) and had ennobled an eternity ago. . . . The power of Islam was perfected in Medina until it gained supremacy over (all the other) powers."[11]

Muhammad's house-mosque was a modest structure at first (figure 1), closer in appearance to the vernacular adobe structures of southwest Asia and northeast Africa than to monumental mosque architecture that would appear during the next two centuries in the Islamic capitols of Syria, Iraq, Spain, and Egypt. Some hadiths suggest that Muhammad at first merely wanted to erect a small temporary shelter, "like the booth of Moses," in anticipation of the imminent arrival of Judgment Day.[12] The compound that was actually built, however, was larger and more durable. According to traditional accounts, it had adobe walls, a large squarish courtyard with porticos for shade on its north and south sides, and three doorways, one on every side except the *qibla* side. When the *qibla*, or prayer direction, was changed from the north (Jerusalem) to the south (Mecca) side during the second year of the Hijra, the south doorway was closed, and a new one was made in the north wall.

The Prophet's residential quarters (*buyūt, manāzil*), or rooms, were built next to each other on the southeast side of the courtyard. They too were made from adobe, and covered with roofs fashioned from palm trunks and branches. Each room had an area of about 239.4 square feet (about 23 square meters or 81 square cubits), and a ceiling between nine

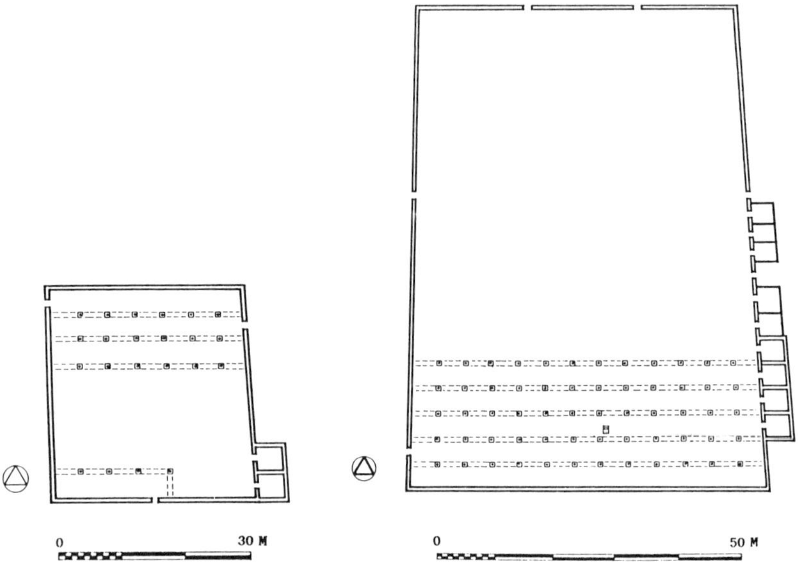

Figure 1. Layouts of the Prophet's house-mosque in Medina during the first year of the Hijra (left) and after Caliph ᶜUthman's expansions (right), c. 30/650. The quarters of his wives are the rooms on the right-hand side of the complex. (Adopted from reconstructions by Salih Lamᶜi Mustafa, in *al-Madīna al-munawwara: Taṭawwuruhā al-ᶜumrānī wa-turāthuhā al-miᶜmārī*. Beirut: Dar al-Nahda al-ᶜArabiyya, 1981.)

and twelve feet high (2.7 to 3.6 meters).[13] In the ten years Muhammad lived in Medina, the number of rooms increased from one to nine; a room was added for each new wife he acquired.[14]

Muslim accounts stress the collective significance of the Prophet's house-mosque from its foundation. The construction of the original compound, which took several months, was an occasion that united both major groups of believers: the Emigrants of Mecca (*muhājirūn*) and the Ansar of Medina. Muhammad joined with them to help carry the mud bricks, and together they all chanted, "There is no life but the life of the hereafter. God have mercy on the Ansar and the Emigrants!"[15] The collective nature of the event also is indicated by its association with the drafting of a written covenant that regulated the relations among the Emigrants, Ansar, and Jews, and that recognized the authority of God and his prophet.[16] Indeed, after describing the building of the house-mosque and recording the covenant terms, Ibn Ishaq observes,

> When God's messenger had secured himself in Medina, when the Emigrants had gathered unto him, and the question of the Ansar had been resolved, the rule (*amr*) of Islam became established. Prayer was instituted. Alms-giving

and fasting were prescribed. Punishments were prescribed. *Islam took up residence among them*. It was this group of Ansar to whom (the Quran) refers as "those who took up residence in the house (*dār*)."[17] (italics added.)

Looking back on these events, Muslims saw in the creation of the house-mosque and related events the establishment of their religion and their society. The residence of Muhammad became for them an exemplary communal gathering place, a place of worship, and a center of power. One set of traditions maintains that even the homeless were able to find shelter there; later generations looked back on these people as models of religious devotion, the forerunners of Sufism.[18] It is also reported that Abu Bakr, ᶜUmar, and ᶜUthman—the first three rulers of the Islamic community after Muhammad, and his close companions—joined him in laying the building foundations.[19] Its status is enhanced by the fact that the Prophet was buried in it, as were the Abu Bakr and ᶜUmar.

While Medina served as the capital of the nascent empire after the death of the Prophet (11/632), the house-mosque compound was expanded by the caliphs ᶜUmar and ᶜUthman in order to accommodate the growing size of crowds assembled there for communal prayer and other occasions. It was ᶜUthman who began to transform it into a monumental structure by expanding it and providing it with stone columns, a roof of imported teak, and carnelian pebbles for the courtyard (figure 1).[20]

When the political center of power shifted to Iraq and Syria, rulers continued to expend funds for its maintenance and renovation. The Umayyad caliph al-Walid ordered the demolition of the old mosque and the dwellings of the Prophet's wives in 88/707. In their place he erected a fully monumental mosque, twice the size of the original; its walls were decorated with marble, mosaics, and inscriptions from the Quran.[21] Numerous restorations and expansions of the mosque were sponsored by subsequent Muslim rulers, including the modern Saudi dynasty. Yet the monumentalization of the Prophet's house-mosque by Islamic governments stands in marked contrast to the modesty of the original compound described in the literature of the traditionists. When they reported that the Prophet said, "The most evil thing on which the wealth of Muslims is spent is building,"[22] it is as if some of them wanted to remind the caliphs that their true duty was to care for Islam and the well-being of the community of believers, not to squander revenues on lavish buildings.

What is the relation between the house-mosque of the Prophet and God's house-mosque in Mecca? This question has been debated by traditionists and legal schools since the second/eighth century. It reflects older intracommunal differences based on distinctions made between the Meccan Emigrants and the Medinan Ansar. The prevailing view among the learned is that both are sacred places, but that Mecca is superior to Medina.[23] Muhammad is reported to have said that Mecca is the dearest place on earth in God's eyes, and that he would never have left it if he had not been forced to do so. Authoritative hadiths indicate that it had precedence in regard to prayer. The Kaʿba, after all, is the *qibla*, not the Prophet's house-mosque. Prayer in the Medina mosque is reported to be a thousand times more meritorious than in any other house or mosque, except the one in Mecca. There, prayer is a hundred times more meritorious than prayer in the Prophet's house-mosque. As for pilgrimage, its required rituals, which include circumambulating God's house-mosque, are only fulfilled in the *ḥaram* of Mecca.[24]

Other authoritative hadiths, however, indicate that a state of parity was reached between the two locales in the eyes of Muslims. Muhammad declared that Medina is a *ḥaram* area, just as Ibrahim had done for Mecca. In both places, people are to observe prohibitions against hunting, violence, and uprooting trees. Likewise, they are both centers of divine blessing. Muhammad's house-mosque is said to be the last mosque, in juxtaposition to God's house-mosque in Mecca, which the Quran and the hadiths call the first mosque.[25] The Kaʿba claims the station of Ibrahim, which is usually regarded as the stone where Ibrahim and his son stood to build the shrine, or the place from which they proclaimed the pilgrimage.[26] The Prophet's mosque claims his pulpit (or throne-chair), where he delivered his sermons. In practice, Muslims can pray before each when they visit Mecca and Medina. The Hijr, a walled area adjoining the Kaʿba, contains the graves of Hajar and Ismaʿil;[27] Muhammad's body lies where ʿAʾisha's quarters (*bayt*) used to be, next to the original mosque courtyard.[28] Finally, in the last days of the world, Mecca and Medina alone are to be spared afflictions caused by the false messiah, al-Dajjal. Later traditions would endorse pilgrimage to Medina, although it would be called *ziyāra* (visitation) to distinguish it from the Hajj to Mecca.[29]

At least one group of Muslims, which included followers of the Medinan jurist Malik b. Anas, maintained that Medina was actually superior to Mecca. To do this, they invoked hadiths in support of the view that prayer was more meritorious there, and that it contained a greater degree of *baraka*. Moreover, did not the Prophet choose to live out the last years of his life in Medina, even after he had conquered his native Mecca? Unlike Mecca, Medina is the burial place of the last prophet, the first caliphs, and many of the members of the original community of

Muslims.[30] To this day, there are some Muslims who make more of their desire to visit Medina, where they can obtain the Prophet's intercession, than they do of making Hajj to Mecca.[31]

One way in which the Prophet's house-mosque in Medina gained, for some people, precedence over God's house-mosque in Mecca was its close affiliation with paradise. We have already seen that the Quran promises houses in paradise for people who emigrate in the way of God; the hadith-parable of the royal supper equates the king's house with Islam, and entry into his quarters with entry into paradise; and Muhammad and his followers sang of life in the hereafter as they built his house-mosque. Other early traditions, however, indicate that his house-mosque contained a portion of paradise within its very walls. Thus, Muhammad is reported to have said, "What is between my house (*bayt*) and my pulpit is one of the gardens of paradise."[32] Variants of this hadith add that his pulpit is on his pool, which came to be seen as a large reservoir from which the blessed will drink on their way into paradise.[33] The part of the house-mosque compound that this hadith associates with a paradisal garden, therefore, is the communal prayer area in the courtyard, which probably had a drinking trough or cistern for ablutions.[34]

God's house-mosque in Mecca, on the other hand, had a more tenuous relation to paradise. Facing it in prayer and travelling there on Hajj can bring the faithful to paradise after death. According to traditions collected by al-Tirmidhi and Ibn Hanbal, the Black Stone in the Kaᶜba was originally a white stone from paradise, but humans had sullied it with their corrupt deeds.[35] Unlike traditions about the Prophet's paradisal garden, however, these statements do not occur in the *ṣaḥīḥ* collections of al-Bukhari and Muslim. Later, however, some traditionists also took pains to connect God's house-mosque explicitly with paradise.

Accounts of al-Walid's reconstruction of the Medina house-mosque (completed by 91/710) indicate that its association with paradise was realized in architectural space. Prayer area walls bore mosaic depictions of fruit-laden trees and buildings. One of the artisans involved in making them said, "We have reproduced images that we have found of the trees and houses of paradise."[36] Unfortunately these decorations have been destroyed by fires and subsequent restorations, but we can see comparable ones on the façades of the Umayyad mosques in Jerusalem and Damascus (also built during al-Walid's reign).[37] Hellenistic and Late-Antique motifs connected with the imagery of the royal palaces, reinforced by Jewish and Christian notions of paradise, clearly influenced this art.

In short, the Prophet's house served as a focal point for communal life in his lifetime. Soon after his death it was transformed into a paradisal symbol of profound significance to rulers, the learned, and believers in general. The verses of poetry that Ibn Hisham (d. c. 218/833) added to the end of his version of Ibn Ishaq's biography of the Prophet convey the deep reverence Muslims hold for his house-mosque and tomb. They show just how closely house, mosque, Prophet, tomb, and future paradise can coalesce in Islamic discourse.

In (Medina) are the traces of the Messenger, and a luminous abode of gathering—though traces may disappear and perish.
The signs of a sacred house (*dār ḥurma*) are not effaced; in it the Guide's pulpit, which he used to ascend.
Plain are the remains and lasting the landmarks; in his quarters (*rabᶜ*) a prayer place and mosque.
In it are enclosures (*ḥujurāt*) wherein would descend God's light brilliant and bright.
Some features have not disappeared—with time, some of its signs become decayed, some of its signs become renewed.
In it I have come to recognize the traces of the Messenger, his former character, and a tomb hidden in the dirt by some grave digger. . . .

Long did I stand crying bitterly over the mound of the tomb containing Ahmad.[38]
Be blessed O tomb of the Messenger! And blessed be the land where the rightly guided one resided!
And blessed be your niche (O tomb!), wherein was placed a good man; above him a broad-stoned building, well-arranged. . . .

A glorious lord raised him from boyhood; he became perfect with the most noble qualities.
Regulation of Muslims reached its highest degree with him; knowledge was not fettered, reasoned opinion was not refuted.
I say, and none can fault what I say, unless he be completely without reason—
I have no desire to refrain from eulogizing him; perhaps in doing so I will dwell forever in paradise eternal—
With Mustafa,[39] close to whom I hope to abide thereby. To attain that day I strive steadfastly.[40]

KUFA AND BAGHDAD, HOUSES OF CONQUEST AND EMPIRE

Less than a century after Muhammad's death, Arab Islam established itself as a religion of empire in an irregular band of contiguous lands from the Atlantic shores of north Africa to the Indus River valley. This band was some 4,400 miles long (7,040 km). It was as narrow as 50 miles (80 km) along the Mediterranean shoreline of Africa, but it ballooned up to a width of about 2,400 miles (3,840 km) in the east, between the southernmost tip of Arabia and the Aral Sea. It included peoples who had formerly been governed by Hellenistic, Roman, Byzantine, and Persian rulers. Different ethnic, social, and religious populations found themselves under the sway of Arab rulers and their religion. Within this milieu Islam became a cosmopolitan religion that transformed the cultures over which it gained domination at the same time that it was itself transformed through interaction with those cultures.

With the creation of this empire, how did Muslims create new homes for themselves? How did they regard the homes of subjugated peoples? The Quran endorses giving up homes to fight and emigrate for God in the face of violent opposition. Traditions idealized the creation of the Prophet's new house in Medina as a process of the peaceful acquisition of vacant land from sympathetic local groups. Later, when Muslim forces marched into Mecca, according to tradition, they did not violently seize the property of its people. Nor did the Prophet allow his emigrant followers to reclaim their former houses. On the other hand, the Quran speaks of how God laid low the houses of deniers, which, at least in the case of the Banu Nadir, meant that Muslims could make them their own. Eventually all non-Muslims, especially Jews, were forced to abandon Medina and surrounding towns. In a like manner, Meccans were obliged by divine decree to leave their city if they chose to remain polytheists. But what happened outside of the Hijaz?

Histories of the conquest, though frustratingly reticent about this issue, suggest that Muslim settlement in conquered land was a very complex process of interactions between Arab Muslims and local populations.[41] Three of the chief ways in which settlement took place were: occupation of houses and lands abandoned after the capitulation of non-Muslim populations; occupation by force of houses and lands seized from belligerent and rebellious populations; and creation of new garrison encampments adjacent to extant non-Muslim settlements.

The first of these patterns was typical of Muslim settlement in Syria. There, they exchanged their military encampments for quarters in established towns like Damascus, Hims, and Aleppo. A portion of the Christian population in these cities had abandoned their houses to live in areas that were still under Byzantine control, so Muslims easily took possession of the deserted dwellings.[42] In other instances, the terms of surrender included a clause according to which the captured town was required to cede a portion of its houses and churches to the conquerors for their use.[43]

Both the first and the second pattern are attested in the conquest of the borderlands of eastern Iran. When Kirman fell in 29/650, the Arab victors reportedly divided the houses (*manāzil*) and lands of the fleeing populace among themselves.[44] More than half a century later, far to the north in Bukhara, the populace of this great central Asian trading city chose to hold their place, accepting nominal conversion to Islam. Three times during the caliphate of al-Walid they had to be subdued by Arab forces. The fourth time, Qutayba b. Muslim, the brilliant Arab commander of the region,

> seized the city and established Islam there after much difficulty. He instilled Islam in their hearts, and made (their religion) difficult for them in every way. They accepted Islam in appearance but in secret worshipped idols. Qutayba thought it proper to order the people of Bukhara to give one-half of their homes to the Arabs so that the Arabs might be with them [mixed together] and informed of their sentiments. *Then they would be obliged to be Muslims.* In this manner he made Islam prevail and imposed the religious laws on them. He built mosques and eradicated traces of unbelief and the precepts of the fire-worshippers. He labored a great deal and punished everyone who broke the decrees of the religious laws. He built a grand mosque, and ordered the people to perform the Friday prayer there so that God the Exalted would reward the people of Bukhara for this good (deed) on the final judgement. [They all became Muslims.] (italics added)[45]

This account portrays the settling of soldiers in conquered towns as more than simply a way of rewarding them or providing them shelter. It was a strategy for enforcing the religious submission of the vanquished, which was unmistakably part of a more general governmental strategy. Moreover, it reveals the conjunction of conquest, the establishment of a domestic space for Islam, mosque-building, and the promise of paradise in a context outside of the Quran, hadith, and *sīra* literature.

The third pattern of settlement, the creation of garrisons adjacent to populated areas, is most typical for Muslim migration into Mesopotamia, north Africa, and parts of Iran. It offered the advantage of controlling territory without dispossessing local populations and disrupting their economic life, except that tax revenues would now be directed to new Muslim rulers.[46] It also slowed the pace of acculturation. One of the most distinguished of these new garrison settlements was that of Kufa, located on the east bank of the Euphrates next to the Christian Arab city Hira. Not far away were the ruins of ancient Babylon and Nippur.

The settlement of Kufa began when the caliph ᶜUmar ordered his commander in Iraq to "select for the Muslims" a "house of emigration" (*dār hijra*) and a "dwelling place for war" (*manzil jihād*). He issued this order shortly after the Muslim army had defeated the Persians decisively at al-Qadisiyya, near Hira (c. 14/636), thus opening the way into Mesopotamia proper and lands further east.[47] When Muslim scouts discovered the site for Kufa, they reportedly prayed that God would "send blessings upon this Kufa, and make it a secure dwelling place" (*manzil*). There were already some monasteries in the vicinity, but the site itself was unoccupied.[48]

At first, Kufa was a garrison of tents and reed huts. When fire swept through it a few months after its founding, ʿUmar authorized his commander there to build a new settlement out of sun-dried bricks in its stead. The new Kufa was systematically built according to a plan devised by the caliph, his commander, a Persian planning expert, and other influential people. Its principal features were a community mosque and a government house (*dār al-imāra*) complex located in a plaza, and residential areas situated around the plaza for soldiers, their families, other migrants, and slaves.

The details of the spatial organization of this city disclose again an intimate association between mosques, houses, and authority.[49] But Kufa, unlike Mecca, Medina, Damascus, and Bukhara, was founded as a purely Islamic city. Hence, it can provide us with an idea of how first- and second-generation Muslims organized their own urban space when they had the opportunity.

The community mosque is reported to have been the first building they laid out. As in Medina, it had a square shape, with a portico on its *qibla* side. Unlike Medina, however, it was located at the physical center of the town. After its foundation lines had been traced in the ground, an archer stood in the middle and shot arrows in the four cardinal directions to determine the perimeter for the plaza that was to surround the mosque. Beyond this perimeter, people were allowed to build houses (*dūr, manāzil*) for themselves along fifteen radial thoroughfares, within lots that were allocated by tribe. As a general rule, the most influential from among the Companions of the Prophet built their houses on the immediate perimeter of the plaza. Each of the tribal quarters had its own local mosque. Market places were established in the plaza itself, to the east of the community mosque.[50]

The government house, or palace, served as the local ruler's residence and as a storehouse for tax revenues and booty. It stood adjacent to the main mosque on its *qibla* side, which made it easy for the ruler to leave his quarters and assume his station at the front of the mosque during communal prayers. Moreover, its location on the *qibla* side of the mosque meant that people had to face towards it whenever they prayed there. Facing towards God's house in Mecca entailed facing one of the most obvious symbols of control: the house of the local governor. Submitting to God coincided with submitting to mundane Muslim authorities.

Kufa's layout, as Hichem Djait has pointed out, served as a device for transcending family and tribal divisions.[51] Each group had its own domestic compounds and mosques, but the centrality of the mosque-palace complex favored social integration within a more inclusive religio-political order. Even though the mosque-palace complex resembled the temple-palace complexes of pre-Islamic urban centers in the region, it departed from previous forms to the extent that it bonded together disparate groups through a collective variety of worship that knew no priestly hierarchy, mysteries, or hidden sanctuary within precincts of worship itself.

Kufa underwent dramatic changes in the decades following its foundation. The initial Arab Muslim population of about 20,000 soldiers and dependents increased as mercenaries, Persian soldiers and gentry, and Jews who had been expelled from Arabia migrated there. By 113/750, according to some estimates, it had reached a population of some 350,000, living in 80,000 dwellings.[52] Both its government house and communal mosque assumed monumental form, and it was not long before the houses of the most powerful families started to encroach upon the plaza, blurring the lines that had formerly set this central space apart from the rest of the settlement.[53] During ᶜAli's caliphate (35/656–40/661), Kufa served as the capital of the Islamic empire, thus replacing Medina. Thereafter Kufa was a focal point for Shiᶜite opposition movements, and was even considered as a possible site for the capital of the ᶜAbbasid dynasty.

The founding of the actual ᶜAbbasid capital Baghdad in 145/762 was partly inspired by Kufa's success. It too exemplifies a conjunction of religion, the creation of domestic space, and power.[54] Muslim sources relate how the caliph al-Mansur himself took an active part in its foundation. He scouted the site, employed an architect of Buddhist ancestry to design it, collected the building materials, summoned artisans to build it, inspected the actual layout, and officiated at the foundation ceremonies. Like an ancient king, al-Mansur laid the first brick with his own hands, and asked for divine blessing, saying, "In the name of God, praise be to God! 'The earth belongs to God. He gives it as an inheritance to whomever he wishes among his servants. The reward is for the pious' (7 *Aᶜrāf* 128). Build with God's blessing!"[55]

Even if this invocation was not actually delivered by the caliph, it at least shows how closely Muslim historiographers were willing to wed quranic concepts with imperial ideology. Reports also state that al-

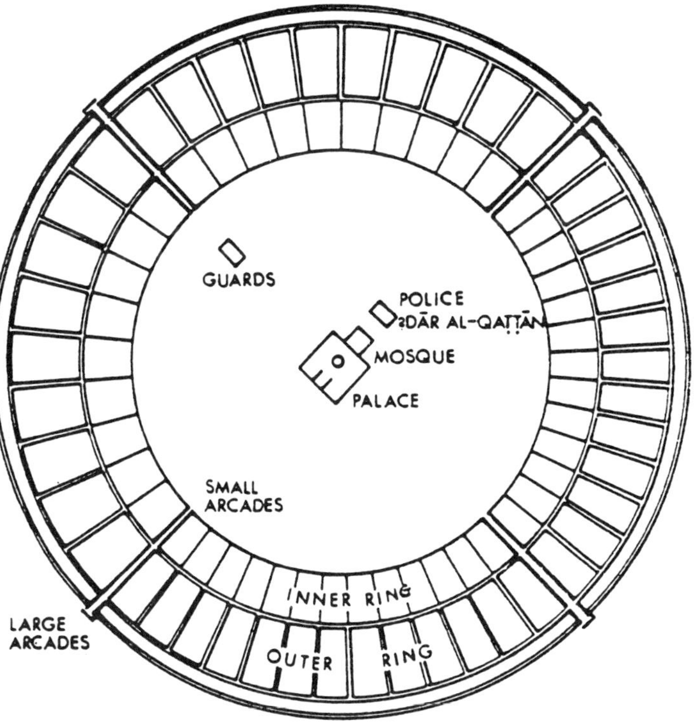

Figure 2. The Round Medina of Baghdad, founded by the Caliph Mansur in 145/762 (from Jacob Lassner, *The Shaping of Abbasid Rule*, 1980; reprinted by permission of Princeton University Press).

Mansur consulted astrologers to determine the most auspicious time for beginning the project. Because he took such a prominent role in its foundation, the original caliphal settlement of Baghdad gained epithets such as "al-Mansur's Medina" (or "city") and "Abu Jaᶜfar's Medina."

Early Baghdad was also known as "Round Medina," because of its distinctively circular ground plan (figure 2). Like the Islamic settlements that preceded it, such as Kufa, its center consisted of a large plaza containing a mosque-palace complex. Like Kufa, the *qibla* side of the communal mosque faced the palace; the two buildings may even have shared a wall at this point. According to Jacob Lassner's reconstruction based on textual sources (the site has not yet been excavated), two concentric rings of buildings intervened between the perimeter of the plaza and the outer fortifications of the city. The inner ring contained residential quarters for the caliph's children and servants, as well as government offices, the community treasury, the arsenal, and the public kitchen. The outer ring contained housing for the military, palace guards, and government officials.[56] Four monumental gateways gave access to the inner city through a series of arcades extending along radii that intersected perpendicularly with the walls of the central mosque-palace complex. The gates themselves each bore the name of the city or region to which it led: Kufa, Syria, Khurasan, and Basra.

In addition to symbolizing the "tremendous power" of the new Muslim dynasty, as Oleg Grabar has concluded,[57] Baghdad's planners also intended that it should provide the ruler with adequate security from attack. The ʿAbbasids, after all, only rose to power after a long, bloody period of factional conflict. The caliph could not afford to be caught off-guard. The layout of Round Medina, as well as the placement of a guard house and police station in its central plaza, was intended to meet this concern. The location of these buildings would have been particularly advantageous for quelling disturbances during Friday prayers and other occasions when crowds assembled in the plaza and mosque. Looking at the plan of Round Medina, however, we can hardly escape concluding that the residential quarters of the ruler were as much a monumental prison as they were a grand palace. No wonder, then, that the ʿAbbasids soon moved to palaces outside the perimeters of the Round Medina.[58]

The Arabian Medina of the Prophet, with Muhammad's house-mosque at its heart, must have served as an ideal prototype for both Kufa and al-Mansur's Medina, much as Muslim rulers struggled to assert their kinship with the Prophet himself.[59] Like the Prophet's city, Kufa was called a "house (*dār*) of emigration." Baghdad, on the other hand, laid claim to Medina's paradisal symbolism. One of its official epithets was "Medina of Peace" (*madīnat al-salām*). The learned conjectured that this name was either based on the phrase "city of God," since *al-salām* is one of the names of God; or on the quranic name for paradise: *dār al-salām* (for example, as mentioned in 6 *Anʿām* 127 and 10 *Yūnus* 25). According to yet another opinion, Baghdad was named after the Tigris, which was known by the epithet "palace/river of peace" (*qaṣr/nahr al-salām*). One of the virtues of this river according to biblical, rabbinic, and hadith traditions alike was that it was believed to be one of the rivers of paradise.[60] Baghdad's association with a paradisal river is analogous to the connection between the pool and the Prophet's mosque that I discussed earlier.

The idea of paradise informed Baghdad's toponymy as well as its etymology. Al-Mansur named the palace he built just outside the perimeter of Round Medina "Eternity" (*khuld*), one of the gardens of paradise mentioned in the Quran (25 *Furqān* 15). A palace complex on the east bank of the Tigris called "House (*dār*) of the Caliphate"—built and occupied by later Abbasids—contained royal residences with names like "Paradise Palace," "House (*dār*) of the Tree," as well as the very quranic "House of Peace."[61]

The paradisal virtues of Baghdad were also sung in poetry:

> Have you seen in the length and breadth of the earth
> A house (*dār*) like Baghdad? Truly, it is a paradise on earth.
> Life in Baghdad is pure; its wood is verdant,
> Life outside of it is impure and stale.
> One's life span in it is long, its food
> Is healthful, for some parts of the earth are more healthful than others.
> Its lord has ruled that no caliph shall die
> In it. Truly, he rules what he wishes for his creation.[62]

The poet combines here the qualities of domestic prosperity—purity, long life, good food, and health—with paradisal images to make a statement about the imperial capital. He portrays a close relationship between God and the ruler at the capital, which is reminiscent of the relation between God and the Prophet at Medina. Nevertheless, in comparing this poem with the eulogies for the Prophet found at the end of the *Sīra*, we find a remarkable difference. Medina's paradisal status hinges upon the fact that it contains the remains of the deceased Prophet. Baghdad, on the other hand, is the city of the living ruler, so it is represented as an earthly manifestation of the realm of the blessed in the hereafter. Indeed, accounts of formal visitations to the caliphal court are reminiscent of descriptions of journeys to behold the face of God in the hereafter.[63] According to one declaration, moreover, "whoever takes residence in Baghdad, lives in accordance with the Sunna and the community, and dies—*he will be transported from one paradise to another*" (italics added).[64]

THE HOUSE OF ISLAM

If, as I argue on the foregoing pages, house terms were truly key metaphors in early Islamic discourses about the Kaᶜba, the Prophet's city, major new urban centers such as Kufa and Baghdad, and paradise; then it should come as no surprise that Muslim jurists developed the idea that the entire Islamic world could be conceived as the "House of Islam," or "House of Submission."

The *dār al-islām* is not explicitly mentioned in either the Quran or the authoritative hadith collections. Nevertheless, it is safe to say that it had become a formal part of Islamic legal discourse by the early third/ninth century, when the schools of religious law were engaged in codifying norms for Muslim belief and conduct.[65] The concept actually hinges upon a classification of the human world into two opposed territorial spheres: the House of Islam and the House of War (*ḥarb*). This dichotomy echoes the quranic oppositions of faith and denial, of paradise and hell. In fact, there are fairly clear indications that living in the House of Islam, or in the House of War, is correlated both to the nature of a person's beliefs and to his or her fate in the hereafter.

In legal terms, the House of Islam normally refers to all territory under Muslim rule, where the Shariᶜa is enforced. It is where Muslims can live with greatest security. In the words of a modern Sudanese Muslim writer, "Above all, Dār al-Islām means a society whose central commitment is to uphold the ideals of Islam, to foster and persevere in God's grand design for man on this earth. Dār al-Islām is thus the home of the Muslim Umma, custodians of all humanity of the true faith."[66]

As conquered peoples, non-Muslims hold subordinate, "protected" (*dhimmī*) status there, as long as they pay their taxes to Muslim authorities, and do not put down the politically dominant religion, or disturb the social order. They are also obliged to conform to other regulations, which include lodging Muslim travelers in their houses for up to three days, abstaining from decorating their houses, and not building them higher than Muslim houses. Otherwise, their lives and property are supposed to be inviolable. In the House of Islam, therefore, Muslims and *dhimmī*s both must submit to superior powers, but the character of their submission differs in such a way that non-Muslims acquire the most inferior status.

The House of War refers to territory where Islamic law is not observed, and where Muslims are not able to follow the tenets of their religion. It is the land where they are least secure, and where the enemies of the House of Islam reside. Muslims are enjoined to fight them until they are subdued. This is the duty of jihad, a concept that is associated with emigration and doing battle on behalf of God in the Quran and hadiths. Ideally, the whole world is expected to be transformed into the House of Islam through jihad. Vanquished non-Muslims have the option either to assume "protected" minority status in the House of Islam, or convert.

Muslim legists, particularly of the Shafiᶜi school, also allowed for an intermediate territory, the House of Reconciliation (*ṣulḥ*). This refers to any non-Muslim land with which the House of Islam establishes peaceful relations through a treaty, or with which de facto they are not at war. It is also a place where Muslims are able to practice their religion, even though they are not actually in control.[67]

In theory, the House of Islam is divided internally into three regions: the *ḥaram* areas of Mecca and Medina, the Hijaz, and all other House of Islam lands. According to most schools of law, the heart of the House of Islam, region 1, is forbidden to all non-Muslims. Muslims from abroad themselves are subject to complex ritual duties and prohibitions when they enter it for pilgrimage. Non-Muslims can stay for three-day sojourns in region 2, and if any of them were to die there, the body must be transported elsewhere for burial. Otherwise, non-Muslims are as free as anyone else to move about in the House of Islam, as long as they do not intend any harm.

Non-Muslims from the House of War legally can take up residence in the House of Islam if they receive permission from any Muslim adult man, woman, or slave. Muslim rulers have the special privilege of being able to grant permission to groups of foreigners, such as merchants and ambassadors. After a year, when their permission expires, foreigners must leave the House of Islam or renew their permission. As for Muslims who find themselves living in the House of War, they are obliged to fight or emigrate to the House of Islam, just as the Prophet and his followers abandoned Mecca for Medina.

From the foregoing outline of their ideas, we can see that Muslim jurists define the House of Islam in terms of relational fields of action arising from encounters between different kinds of people. It has clear limits and internal divisions, but these are mutable with respect to physical space.

Seen this way, the House of Islam is congruent to the definition of Muslim dwellings in the Quran and hadith. After all, these places are similarly defined in terms of regulated exchanges across boundaries—hospitality, polite visitation, pilgrimage, and charity in good times, emigration and warfare in difficult times. They are not isolated or absolutely private blocs. Furthermore, if this congruency between the House of Islam and ideas about the houses of Muslims is valid, then it is reasonable to propose that even conquest and territorial appropriation might parallel certain facets of domestic life. As reflected in the heroic events of the Hijra, the building of Muhammad's house-mosque, and in the expulsion of the Jews from Medina, the establishment of Islam is intimately connected with the creation, appropriation, and expansion of Muslim domestic space.

Why does the House of Islam concept forbid all non-Muslims from entering the sacralized territory of Mecca and Medina? People nowadays are often surprised when they discover that only Muslims can travel there. The prohibition seems to contradict the relational definition of domestic space posited above. Muslims themselves validate the sanction by pointing out quranic verses that ban polytheists and deniers from the sacred mosque. The application of the ban to all non-Muslims, and to the entire *ḥaram* areas of both Mecca and Medina is a product of later jurisprudence, however.

If this is so, then the ban cannot be explained simply with reference to a quranic proof text. It relies upon the authority of a scribal, religious elite who expect that the ban can be promulgated and enforced by Muslims. In other words, the forbidden status of Mecca and Medina implies the ability to control access to the areas and to control their meaning. It is more than coincidental, therefore, that hadiths concerning the sanctified status of both places found their way into the authoritative hadith collections at the same time that the Islamic empire was at its height.

As Muslims after the late second/eighth century became more conscious of shifting power balances within their community, of the movement of their center of government from one city to another, and of the community's transformation from an Arab one into an ethnically diverse one, they increasingly looked to Mecca and Medina as eternal way marks in a new and changing world. It is as if Mecca and Medina had become for the House of Islam the analogues of the immutable, hidden heart of an ideal Muslim house. The *ḥaram* of each is a product of collective life, and it fosters group solidarity, along with the capability of Islamic society to embrace, reject, subdue, and transform the stranger.

The idea of the Kaᶜba as the center of the world especially was promoted by Muslim scholars starting when the ᶜAbbasid dynasty was at its height. For example, in the mid-third/ninth century, al-Azraqi wrote a history of Mecca in which he sought to convey its extraordinary qualities in minute detail. In the opening section of this history, he cites the following noncanonical hadith from the Prophet about God's house:

> This is the fifth of fifteen houses (*buyūt*), seven of which are in heaven until the throne and seven of which reach down to *Tukhum*, the lowest earth. The highest of them is the "flourishing house," which is adjacent to the throne. Each of these houses has a sacred precinct (*ḥaram*) like the sacred precinct of this house.
>
> If any of these houses should fall, they would all fall on top of each other down to the *Tukhum*, the lowest earth. Each house belonging to the people of heaven and the people of earth is visited just as this house is.[68]

This statement makes an explicit connection between God's house in Mecca and the "flourishing house" in heaven, an idea that was gaining great currency at the time. More than this, however, it promotes a domestic image of the universe, and indicates that God's house, the Kaᶜba, holds a pivotal place in its organization. Al-Azraqi is hardly being discreet as he details the history of caliphal building projects in the *ḥaram* area. By doing this, he is advising Muslim rulers to care for God's house, because it is essential to the maintenance of the order of the world.

Why was it so important for him to make this argument? Because he saw evidence that some of the ʿAbbasid caliphs were tempted to place their capitals on a level with Mecca, perhaps even neglect it. Al-Mansur and his entourage apparently hoped that Baghdad would become the center of the world, a paradise on earth.[69] A Shiʿite revolt in Medina and Mecca (145/762) in fact may have been fueled by suspicions that al-Mansur's project opposed God's sovereignty and belittled "the Sacred Kaʿba."[70] During al-Azraqi's own lifetime, the caliph al-Muʿtasim (r. 218/833–227/842) had a Kaʿba built on the site of his new capital, Samarra, along with replicas of other important Meccan sites. This was to allow his newly converted Turkish guard to perform the pilgrimage without ever travelling to Mecca.[71] Al-Muʿtasim's stratagem did not succeed. Thanks in part to scholars like al-Azraqi, rulers learned that it was advantageous for them to care for the most ancient Islamic holy sites, but to keep them at a distance and protect them from the turmoil and danger that beset life in the imperial capitals.

By the end of the third/ninth century, depictions of God's house began to appear on schematic maps of the world. These maps show the Kaʿba in the center of a large circle divided into eight, eleven, twelve, or more sections. Each section is oriented towards the center, and represents a different region in the House of Islam. The practical function of such maps was to indicate at a glance the *qibla* orientations for all parts of the Muslim world.[72] Perhaps the most intriguing thing about them, however, is that they bear a striking resemblance to the plan of al-Mansur's Medina, the original Baghdad, where the caliph's house occupies the center instead of God's house. It may be that some people saw these domicentric representations of the civilized world as complementary; one represented the power of God, the other the power of his caliph. It is more likely, however, that they actually represent competing ideas. Whatever may have been the case, the vision of the Kaʿba as the center of the world has consistently prevailed in Muslim eyes over that of any seat of mundane governmental power.

ALTERNATIVE HOUSES

The idea of the House of Islam is part of an imperial concept of order and significance that formed in the urban centers of southwest Asia between the first/seventh and third/ninth centuries. It was based on an appropriation of the houses of others, real and imagined, and it contributed to the formation of a new, quite remarkable civilization.

Yet, the appropriation of domestic space to form a dominant discourse of religio-political power was only accomplished through a series of displacements. By this, I do not only mean the sort of displacement represented by the Hijra of the Prophet and his followers. I also mean the displacements of populations brought about by the waves of conquest outside the Arabian Peninsula. Many groups benefitted by giving up their old homes. Others, the victims of conquest, suffered. For even though the conquerors were careful about how they handled subjects in the heartlands of Syria, Mesopotamia, Iran, and northern Egypt, they apparently treated peoples in the eastern, western, and northern borderlands harshly for not submitting to their control with alacrity. This region corresponds roughly with the land of Gog and Magog described in the Islamic version of the Alexander Romance, that is, the land of utterly alien people.

Like other conquerors, when Muslim armies encountered armed opposition from local populations, they had the option of killing the men, enslaving them, or forcing them into military service. Women and children were enslaved, dwellings and property looted or destroyed. Prisoners of war were, like booty, often transferred to the garrison cities of Iraq, particularly to Kufa, Basra, and Wasit. In Medina we know of a group of eighty hostages from among the nobles of Bukhara who, faced with servitude and fearing that they would never see their homeland again, reportedly committed suicide after killing their captor, the son of ᶜUthman, the third caliph.[73]

In sum, the rise of the House of Islam has had other sides to it. As a dominant discourse, it implies the existence of other discourses—alternative, oppositional, and suppressed—that should not be ignored, even if they might be difficult to reconstruct. Without them, the dominant discourse would not have been possible.

Because of the nature of the documentary evidence, it may be an impossible task to describe precisely and comprehensively what these other discourses of domestic space were like. The majority of Jews and Christians who did not become Muslims found ways to accommodate themselves to the new order. After all, both groups, especially the Jews, had already experienced centuries of subordination under other rulers before the arrival of the Arab Muslim forces. As a rule, while *dhimmī*s were the majority population, they prospered under Muslim domination, and contributed greatly to the establishment and operation of the caliphal government. The palaces of the rulers looked like those of the Persian and Byzantine princes that preceded them, and the dwellings of common people embodied regional rather than religious differences. Nonetheless, some people, as I have shown, fled their homes in the face of the conquest. Some found in cultural suicide a final alternative. Yet others turned to forms of asceticism, making a virtue out of homelessness. Through mystical retreat, they turned from the disappointments and uncertainties of this world to contemplate eternal truths and the bliss of the hereafter.

Of course, alternative discourses arose within the Muslim community. Some of the most politicized of these discourses were espoused by members of the Kharijite and Imami Shiᶜite movements. Both movements were able to attract followers from dissident Arabs and from subjugated native populations in Iraq, Iran, and north Africa. The most extreme factions of the Kharijites reportedly defined their own communities as the true House of Islam, its people were the "people of paradise." Muslims who refused to emigrate to them, or who violated the rule of God, were consigned to the House of War or the House of Denial; they were the "people of the fire." Moderate Kharijite groups, who dwelt among other Muslims, devised another designation: the House of Dissimulation (*taqiyya*). By this rubric, they sought to define the status of group members who were compelled to conceal their true beliefs from other Muslims. They called the realm shared by Kharijite and non-Kharijite Muslims the House of Unity (*tawḥīd*), and the House of Mixing.[74] Similarly Imami Shiᶜite jurists invented a House of Faith within the House of Islam to accommodate Muslims who believed that the Imam-messiah, a designated heir from the "people of the house" of the Prophet, was the perfect leader for humanity, not a flawed caliph or sultan.

Shiᶜite Muslims have reinterpreted quranic and hadith discourses about the houses of paradise so as to express their deep feelings about the martyrdom of Husayn, their third Imam, at the hands of the Umayyads on the plain of Karbala (60/680). According to a tradition attributed to the Imam Zayn al-ᶜAbidin,

> Whatever believer's eyes shed tears for the death of al-Husayn until they flow over his cheeks, will be provided by God, as a consequence, with rooms in paradise which he will inhabit for a long time. Whatever believer's eyes shed tears until they flow over his cheeks because of the grievous harm inflicted upon us by our enemies in this world, will be provided by God, as a consequence, with a true abode in paradise.[75]

Sufism is a mystical form of Islam based on the quest for intimate union with God, or obtaining beatific vision of him in the hereafter. Two of the most prominent stages on the Sufi path to transcendence are unselfish trust in God (*tawakkul*) and rigorous asceticism (*zuhd*). Biographical narratives about Muslim mystics are careful to note how they renounced worldly comforts and concerns to achieve their goal. They made a virtue of poverty. No less a figure than Abu Hamid al-Ghazali (d. 505/1111), a leading teacher in medieval Baghdad, gave up his position, property, family, and friends to devote himself to God. Other Sufis chose celibacy over marriage, resisting dominant Islamic norms in order to become more faithful to their lord.[76]

Sufi writers have employed domestic discourse in their literature to highlight their definitions of truth and reality, and to spur other Muslims into imagining their religion and their world in a new light. Like the Quran and canonical hadiths, their stories and teachings contain references to God's house, human habitations, and the dwellings of the hereafter. Sufis ascribed meanings to these places that sometimes put them at odds with the consensus of the community of scholars and jurists.

For example, the Kaᶜba for Sufis was a spur for deeper religious experience and contemplation. They cautioned common believers and jurists against making it the final goal of prayer and pilgrimage, for this would actually separate them from God. An early Persian mystic, Abu Yazid al-Bistami (d. 261/874), reputedly stated, "On my first pilgrimage I saw only the house, the second time I saw the house and the lord of the house, and the third time I saw the lord alone." Glossing this statement, al-Hujwiri (d.c. 465/1072) wrote,

> In short . . . the sanctuary is where contemplation is. Unless the whole universe is a man's trysting-place, where he comes nigh unto God, and a retired chamber, where he enjoys intimacy with God, he is still a stranger to divine love. When he has vision, the whole universe is his sanctuary. But when he is veiled, the sanctuary is the gloomiest universe, for the *gloomiest thing is the house of the beloved in the absence of the beloved.* (italics added)[77]

This manner of thinking led Sufis to maintain that the true house of God, even the true seat of paradise, lay within the heart of the believer, not in the heart of the Hijaz.[78] Indeed, many devotees concluded that people were free to seek God and his house everywhere, as God himself allegedly revealed to al-Niffari (d. 354/965), an Iraqi mystic. "When you see me alone in your house (*bayt*), it is the secure sanctuary that keeps you safe from that which is other than me. If you do not see me in your house, seek after me in everything. Then, when you see me, rush in; don't even ask for permission to enter.[79]

This "revelation" exemplifies the kind of language that disturbed religious conservatives. Not only does it attribute statements to God that are not attested in the Quran and the authoritative hadith, it identifies God's house first with the "house" of the visionary, and then directs him, if he cannot find his lord therein, to search for him everywhere; not just in Mecca. The divine discourse concludes with a qualified abrogation of the requirement to seek permission before entering a house.

The Persian-born mystic Mansur al-Hallaj (d. 309/922), after he had performed the Hajj for the third time, returned to his home in Baghdad and reportedly built a replica of the Kaᶜba within it. Moreover, he ruled that the Hajj obligation could be fulfilled if pilgrims acted in their houses as if they were at the Kaᶜba.

> If someone wishes to make the Hajj, but is unable to do so, let him set aside a room (*bayt*) in his house (*dār*) that is free of impurity. No one should enter it; nor should any one go near it. When the time of the Hajj arrives, he should circumambulate it as if it were the Sacred House. When he finishes this, then he should fulfill the rest of the ritual requirements as if he were in Mecca.
>
> (Thereafter) he should assemble thirty orphans and prepare for them the most wholesome meal possible. He should bring them into that (special) room to give them this meal, and serve them himself. When they finish eating and washing their hands, he should dress each one in a shirt, and pay each one seven . . . dirhems. When he does all that, it takes the place of the Hajj.[80]

From the point of view of the ᶜulama, this was a seditious pronouncement. It gave ordinary Muslims a way to make their own homes into houses of God if they chose, and a license for bypassing other ritual duties. Such developments could very well undermine the authority of conservative jurists. They could also threaten the established government, whose legitimacy depended on sponsoring the Hajj rites and maintaining the holy sites.[81]

Another set of discourses about domestic space connected with the early mystics deals with the common human dwelling. Houses and family life are portrayed as comforts the seeker must avoid or relinquish in order to obtain the true object of desire. For example, stories about the female mystic Rabiᶜa al-ᶜAdawiyya (second/eighth century) depict her as a woman who was born into poverty, sold into slavery, and who later refused opportunities to acquire the security of married life and a comfortable house in order to experience God's love more intimately. Her own house, which became a center for Sufi gatherings, reputedly was dilapidated, and possessed only the most austere furnishings.[82]

Ibrahim b. Adham, a contemporary of Rabiᶜa's, was a Buddha-like figure from Balkh in the eastern reaches of Persia. After renouncing his princely wealth and family, he reportedly embarked upon a fourteen-year trek to Mecca. There, next to the Kaᶜba, he lived a life as a carpenter in the company of other ascetics. He was a man who spurned the most opulent sort of human dwelling, the royal palace, in order to attach himself to God's house.[83] Although he and Rabiᶜa came from different social strata, and different ends of the Muslim world, both ended their lives in material poverty, but rich in their devotion to God.[84]

One of the foremost subjects of Sufi discourse, from its earliest stages of development, is mindfulness of the hereafter. Many people let their fear of hell and their dreams of paradise govern behavior in this world. Others, such as Rabiᶜa, Ibrahim, and Abu Yazid al-Bistami, criticized such anthropocentric orientations in favor of theocentric ones. For them, both hell and paradise, like the Kaᶜba, were veils that separate the blessed from God. Indeed, it was Rabiᶜa who, when asked about paradise, reputedly declared, "First the neighbor (*jār*), then the house (*dār*)" (i.e., "First God, then paradise").[85]

Factional and mystical formulations of Islamic domestic space, such as those I have just identified, are alternatives to the dominant concept of the House of Islam. Like the virtuous community in the Muslim rendering of the Alexander Romance, they challenged prevailing attitudes about the House of Islam, God's house, pilgrimage, the human dwelling, and the hereafter. One of the paradoxes of Shiᶜi and Sufi formulations of these alternative discourses is that they actually helped bridge the gap between imperial, juristic Islam and popular religiosity. In an era when conversion was making Islam the majority religion in Iraq, Iran, Syria, and Egypt, the Shiᶜa idealized the "house" of the Prophet, which they defined primarily in genealogical rather than spatial terms. To the line of Imams descended from this "house," the displaced could attach their hopes for messianic rectification of the injustices committed by illegitimate rulers. Concomitantly the Sufis formulated ways for channeling the transcendent into mundane life. Al-Hallaj and al-Niffari both expressed the propriety of identifying the ordinary human dwelling with the Kaᶜba. Rabiᶜa provided women and the poor with an example of how life in the humblest of dwellings had profound virtue. After the seventh/twelfth century, these Shiᶜi and Sufi strands of religiosity inspired widespread devotionalism for the Prophet and his family and the veneration of saints throughout the Muslim world. By regarding the holy dead as kindred, and by caring for their shrine tombs, rulers and commoners alike sought to reap material and spiritual benefits for themselves, their families, and their homes.

To obtain a more precise idea of how Muslims have ascribed religious significance to the homes in which they actually dwell, in contrast to normative ones which they verbally construct in their texts, I now turn to Egypt. In the next three chapters, I describe how Islam has been domesticated in architecture, ritual activities, arrangements of household objects, and popular iconography. This analysis links premodern varieties of Islamic discourse with those of the present, which have been affected by the processes of colonialism, nationalism, urbanization, and the proliferation of rapid modes of communication and transportation.

4

Muslim Dwellings in Urban Egypt, Past and Present

When Muslim warriors first came upon the Nile plain where modern Cairo now stands, they found a large Byzantine fortress, a few Coptic Christian farms and villages, and a number of churches and monasteries, all interspersed among cultivated fields.[1] In 21/642 (just three years after the founding of Kufa), Muslims, with the cooperation of the native Coptic Christian population, succeeded in wresting control of the region from its Byzantine defenders. They assembled their garrison settlement of Fustat next to the Byzantine fortress, and brought their dependents to live there. Fustat replaced Alexandria as the regional seat of government, and it began to attract a large immigrant population of Arabs and Copts, joined by Greek converts, Persians, Jews, and Africans.

The garrison town, with its ethnically diverse population of some thirteen thousand, increased in size during the eras of Umayyad and ᶜAbbasid rule, becoming a dominant urban center in the region. In 358/969, the rival Shiᶜi Fatimid dynasty established Cairo (al-Qahira, "The Victorious"), a walled caliphal enclave, on the vacant land situated but a short walk away from the northeastern edge of Fustat. By 390/1000, Fustat and Cairo jointly formed one of the largest and most splendid centers of commerce and culture in the medieval world, with a population of an estimated one-half million people.[2] Subsequent centuries, however, witnessed the gradual decline of Fustat, and the evolution of Cairo (under Sunni Muslim control after the sixth/twelfth century), into a modern metropolis of fourteen million inhabitants.

The history of Islam in Egypt is the longest and best-documented of all the Islamic regions. Certainly Egypt had its share of wars, famines, plagues, and earthquakes, but it did not suffer the terrible destruction of the Mongol invasions, as did the lands of Persia and Iraq. Unlike Spain and greater Syria, it was able to hold back the Crusader armies. Cairo, its capital, attracted people of differing ethnic and religious affiliations, and evolved into a locus of political, commercial, and religious power for centuries after Baghdad ceased to be a caliphal capital. It was a transregional center of Islamic learning, where scholars, jurists, mystics, and the devout kept textual traditions alive, and nurtured quranic values from century to century. Thanks to such men, it is possible today for us to obtain a detailed (though far from complete) knowledge of life and thought in a premodern Islamic society. Even now, Egypt is an active force in the arenas of politics, learning, and religious life, not only in the Arab world but in the Muslim world at large.

For these reasons, Egypt and Cairo are highly suited for discussing the history of relations between domestic space and Islamic configurations of meaning and action. Modern Egypt, furthermore, provides us with an opportunity to determine how Muslims living there ascribe religious significance to their houses, as seen against a rich and varied sociocultural history. The domestication of Islam in Egypt thus entails two sets of processes. On the one hand, it involves the effects Egypt's conversion to Islam had upon local definitions of domestic space. On the other, it involves the ways in which Egyptians select and utilize Islamic symbols and practices in their own homes and lives. I examine both of these aspects of domestication in this chapter and in those that follow.

DOMESTICATIONS OF ISLAM IN PREMODERN CAIRO

The plan of early Fustat, like that of Kufa, reveals a close association between mosques, houses, and authority. Arab Muslim tribal groups eschewed the seizure or occupation of native houses, and erected their first dwellings on lots of vacant land around the Byzantine fortress. Tribal mosques intermingled with their houses, indistinguishably at first, within each of the tracts. The residence of ᶜAmr, the Muslim military governor, stood near the banks of the Nile in the center of the garrison, adjacent to the fortress. It was part of the tract belonging to the honorable ''People of the Banner;'' that is, warriors from among the Prophet's Meccan and Medinan companions, accompanied by their dependents. Unlike Kufa (and other Iraqi garrison towns), Fustat lacked a *dār al-imāra* complex for nearly 150 years. The governor's private dwelling and the adjacent community mosque for the district of the nobles served functions analogous to those of the mosque-palace complexes in Iraq.[3]

The religious outlook of the first Muslim settlers, sustained by quranic injunctions against worldly ostentation, plus Fustat's provincial status, curtailed the erection of opulent buildings there, but did not prohibit it. As a new ruling minority, Muslims drew upon the technical skills and labor of the local population. Although there is little archaeological evidence for the architecture of early Fustat, we can reasonably infer that its first buildings looked like those of the preconquest population.

If this is the case, then Muslim houses there were of two basic types: the humble dwelling (*bayt, manzil*) with a nominal courtyard, or none at all; and the grand domestic complex (*dār*) consisting of multiple rooms arranged about a large court defined by walls and columned porticos. The first type was a continuation of the Hellenistic *oikos* and the ancient Egyptian house. The second was a continuation of the Hellenistic peristyle mansion.[4] Most houses were low-standing and joined together in neighborhood clusters. Arab Muslim adoption of these local house forms was reinforced by their affinity with the domestic architectures of the Hijaz, Syria, and Iraq. It was also supported by the Muslim acceptance of Coptic households around and amid their settlement[5] and their intermarriage with local women.

Features of pre-Islamic architectures from Arabia, the Nile Valley, Mesopotamia, and the Mediterranean basin subsequently amalgamated to engender new monumental forms for mosques and dwellings. During the Umayyad dynasty, residents and visitors to Fustat could begin to distinguish the community mosque of ᶜAmr as an Islamic building, with its porticoed courtyard, minaret towers, decorated walls and ceilings, prayer niche, governor's prayer enclosure, and *minbar*.[6] It became visibly distinct from neighboring churches and monasteries, and because of Islam's emphasis on communal prayer and rejection of priestly liturgy, it became functionally different.

The Umayyads also began to build palace-like compounds in and around the city near the end of first/seventh century. No doubt these had developed from earlier prototypes, but they reflected the presence of a new dominant class, as did Umayyad country palaces in Syria and Iraq.[7] For example, Umayyad governor ᶜAbd al-ᶜAziz b. Marwan established a residential complex south of Fustat in Helwan (c. 70/689) to avoid a plague that was sweeping the city. It contained several elegant dwellings and mosques, palm groves, vineyards, and probably a bath.[8] Later, with the creation of Egypt's first official mosque-palace complex at al-ᶜAskar—a forerunner of Fatimid Cairo—on the northern flank of the city (c. 169/785), people could discern a fully Islamic architecture of power.

By the eleventh century, the majority of Egypt's population spoke Arabic and had converted to Islam, particularly those living in the cities and towns.[9] In Fustat-Cairo, their domestic architecture, formerly comprised mostly of low-standing mud brick dwelling clusters, had evolved into towering buildings, splendid palaces, and ubiquitous collective housing complexes. When Nasir-e Khosraw, a Persian scholar, visited the city in 438/1046–441/1049, he left a description of its houses in his memoirs.

The mansions of the Fatimid quarter, he wrote, were five stories high, surrounded by gardens and open spaces. Fustat looked like a mountain from afar; its dwellings were from seven to fourteen stories high.[10] From other contemporary sources, we know that these buildings were adjoined by open spaces too, but they often contained ruined buildings instead of gardens. Walled courtyards, with fountains and gardens, usually open to the sky, constituted the heart of most houses. The vacant spaces outside offered opportunities for expansion of a dwelling as the number of its occupants increased.[11]

The palaces of the ruling elites in Cairo were designed to house cohorts of kin, clients, officials, and troops. They had many rooms, and usually possessed large courts and covered halls, known as *qāʿas*. One of the most important functions of these halls was to entertain guests. Some halls were large enough to contain 350 people for holiday festivities and weddings. Family dwellings of wealthy citizens had similar features, but on a smaller scale. Although they were busy centers of domestic and communal activity, palaces, family houses, and common apartments seldom seem to have been overcrowded. The typical household in Fustat consisted of a husband, wife, and children. The small size of most common dwellings limited the number of relatives who could be accommodated, but the ideal was to group members of the extended family within the same building or neighborhood.

Although providing some degree of privacy was an important aspect in the arrangement of domestic space, no special arrangements were made in house design for the segregation of men and women during the Fatimid era. Distinct harem quarters within houses appeared in Egypt in the palatial dwellings of the Mamluks and Ottomans; that is, after the eighth/fourteenth century.[12] Home ownership was a cherished goal for many. Nonetheless, many families leased or sold spare rooms to strangers as an additional source of income. People transferred ownership of parts of their houses as wedding gifts, or converted them into pious trusts, the rents of which accrued to the benefit of the poor, or to religious institutions and their personnel.[13] Taken together, these practices suggest that the composition of most dwelling complexes was unlikely to be homogeneous with respect to lineage, ethnicity, or even religion. Grand palaces and apartment buildings alike represented forms of shared housing. In the history of housing in Islamic societies, complete privacy has probably been more a desire of the wealthy than a reality for the common person.

The key factor in residential location was what André Raymond has called an *exclusivisme sociale*, based on a family's socioeconomic status.

For example, Fatimid Cairo contained the palaces of the ruling elite and their entourages, while Fustat, where the markets were located, contained housing for mercantile, artisanal, and laboring classes. Ethnic and religious affiliation were important secondary factors affecting residence, but they were not dominant. The Fatimids settled their troops in Cairo within districts according to their tribal and national origins, but the ethnic exclusivism of these neighborhoods diminished with time. In Fustat, Jews and Christians tended to cluster near their places of worship. This does not mean that they were residentially segregated from Fustat's Muslim populace, however, as commercial records of the period make evident.[14]

Socioeconomic status continued to determine residential patterns in Cairo after the Fatimid era, as it did in other medieval Muslim cities. During the Mamluk and Ottoman ages (seventh/thirteenth to thirteenth/nineteenth centuries), the chief markets, communal mosques, and religious colleges were concentrated in the center of the city. Wealthy merchants and Muslim religious leaders made their homes nearby. The ruling classes, immigrant Circassian and Turkish Muslims who held the choicest properties in the old Fatimid part of the city, emigrated to open land in times of prosperity—mainly southwards, and west to the Nile. This is where they could find enough room to build palaces for their families and clients, and to found new religious and commercial complexes. When Napoleon's army occupied Cairo in 1213/1798, they found some of the grandest houses of the ruling emirs and wealthy bourgeoisie in the pleasant green zone on the eastern and southern shores of Azbakiyya Pond, between Fatimid Cairo and the Nile. The poorest classes were concentrated on the peripheries of the commercial center, where the most noxious industries were located.[15]

The government's desire to control minorities, minority desire for mutual reinforcement, and their involvement in international commerce affected their patterns of residence. Hence, Christians congregated in quarters near the residences of the ruling elite in the Azbakiyya area, in the port area, and in the southern suburbs, where their oldest churches were. Most Jews lived in a quarter in the middle of the commercial center, near the currency exchanges and gold markets where many of them worked, and near their synagogues.[16]

There were numerous types of dwelling places during the ages of the Mamluks and Ottomans, but the most complete knowledge we have pertains mainly to the monumental residences of the ruling classes and wealthy bourgeoisie. Details have been preserved in historical texts and documentary archives.[17] We are also helped by the fact that several palaces and middle-class housing complexes have survived to the present day. These buildings were evolved forms of old Fatimid structures, enriched by the decorative predilections of peoples who immigrated to Egypt in the wake of the Mongol onslaughts in Persia, Iraq, and Syria during the seventh/thirteenth century, and as a result of the subsequent rise of the Ottoman empire in Anatolia.

From the outside, Cairo's early Mamluk palaces had the stark appearance of towering fortresses, reflecting defensive concerns prevailing at the time of the Mongol invasions and the Crusades. Palaces and mansions built after the ninth/fifteenth century were less massive and reveal that their builders paid attention to the aesthetics of public display. Their façades were graced with beautiful floral, geometric, and epigraphic decorations, carved in stone. Much of this external decor turned on the entryways. Windows were barred by iron grillwork, or were covered with adjustable wooden shutters. Bay windows, enclosed by delicately carved wooden screens, projected out over adjacent streets and open spaces.[18] Such embellishments helped assure domestic privacy and security, yet they also were displays of status to outsiders.

European Orientalists habitually portray life in Cairo's medieval Muslim houses as being dominated by a concern for maintaining a rigid segregation between males and females. They have asserted that the master of the house is the only man who can enter the women's quarters, known as the *ḥarīm*, and that women are never seen in the male areas. Of course, this schema tends to disregard the mediating functions of children, the elderly, and servants. It also fails to recognize that accommodations were made inside dwellings for visiting families, and that housing compounds could be shared by several different families. Indeed, Stanley Lane-Poole, the author of an oft-cited history of Cairo, asserted that only the women's quarters in a house can be considered "domestic." Given this kind of outlook, it is of little surprise to us when Lane-Poole concludes, "The inhabitants of a house . . . lead a dreary monotonous life; fortunately they are not often conscious of its emptiness."[19]

In fact, although the layouts of Cairo's grand houses reflected a desire for privacy, this was balanced against the desire for entertaining guests on important holidays and special family celebrations, and for conducting the affairs of state and commerce. The internal arrangement of spaces actually facilitated the regulation of relations between outsiders and occupants. Visitors first had to be allowed through the ornate main entrance by a doorkeeper. They then entered a narrow bent-axis corridor, which led to a large inner courtyard. The design of the entry made it impossible for passersby to be able to peer directly into the complex, and provided a defensible zone against uninvited physical intrusions, which might occur at any time. Male visitors were led to comfortable sitting rooms and verandas (figures 3 and 4) that faced the courtyard on the ground floor. These areas could also be converted into lodgings for long-term guests. When there were large gatherings, visitors walked to a spacious *qāʿa*, also known as a *mandara* (figure 3). Honored guests might be invited to join their host in a second-floor loggia.[20] Elaborately decorated façades of dressed stone, ground level gardens, water basins, and fountains helped create a pleasant atmosphere in the dwelling for residents and visitors alike.

Women crossed the courtyard and ascended special stairways to *qāʿa*s and chambers in the upper two or three levels of the house. Above, they held their own assemblies, and observed activities in the court and halls below from behind the wooden lattices without themselves being seen. Mazes of sitting rooms, corridors, stairwells, and small apartments provided suitable places for children, household servants, and intimate family gatherings. When outsiders were not present, the courtyard became a work place for men and women, and the reception rooms could be converted into bedrooms that were cooled on summer nights by breezes coming down the ventilation shafts. The physical layout of the house, therefore, allowed people to take advantage of the relatively unstructured moments of their lives, as well as the structured ones. Clearly, such houses reflected the status and wealth of their occupants. Moreover, they provided arenas for regulating the integration of family life with that of the community at large.

The particular amalgamations of design and decoration embodied by the noble dwellings of the Mamluk and Ottoman Egypt were undoubtedly a localized result of the history of Islamic civilization. But just because they were results of a specific order of history, and they were inhabited by Muslims, does not necessarily mean that such houses had an obvious religious meaning. On the other hand, there is some persuasive circumstantial evidence in support of the contention that Cairene houses could have religious significance for their occupants.

First of all, according to an economy of architectural design, religious buildings, mansions, and—to a certain degree—apartment houses looked alike; principles used in the construction of Cairene dwellings were also applied to buildings serving religious functions.[21] Most palaces, mosques, religious colleges, and the larger Sufi monasteries had similar proportions; great vaulted halls (*qāʿa*s and *iwān*s) facing onto courts with fountains; interior spaces partitioned into small apartments

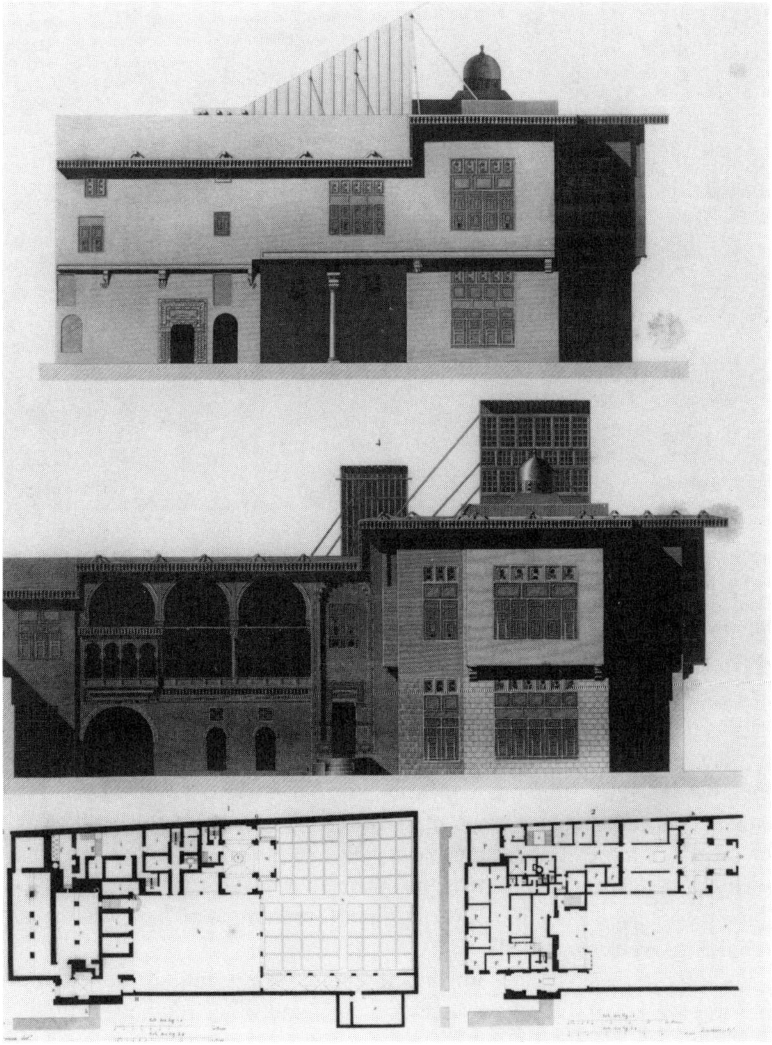

Figure 3. Hasan Kashif mansion, Cairo (twelfth/eighteenth century). Rooftop ventilators open to north. First elevation (top, south to north) shows courtyard entrance to women's quarters, ground-level veranda, and *qāʿa* façade. Second elevation (center, east to west) shows main entry, ceremonial stairway to second floor loggia, and *qāʿa* façade. Floor plans show ground level (bottom left) with courtyard, *qāʿa*, and garden; and second floor (bottom right) (from Jomard, ed., *Description de l'Egypte*).

Figure 4. Qasim Bey mansion, southern Cairo (twelfth/eighteenth century). View to south from ground level veranda showing enclosed courtyard and ceremonial entrance to second floor loggia. Mural and arabesques decorate walls (from Jomard, ed., *Description de l'Egypte*).

and annexes; intricate arabesque designs in wood, stone, and stucco—often gaily colored—; quranic inscriptions; ceremonial entrances; rooftop cupolas and ventilation shafts; and columned arcades. There was a striking isomorphism, inside and outside, between elite dwellings and buildings for worship, religious education, and mystic retreat.[22] Given their wealth and resources, patrons of Islamic architecture could have sought to create a more diverse repertoire. By conserving a set of common forms and elaborating on them, however, they created a configuration of correspondences wherein collective manifestations of power, wealth, and religiosity were conjoined.

Orientation was another important feature of this architectural isomorphism. We know, of course, that mosques and other religious buildings in Egypt were oriented to the southeast so that their prayer niches aligned with the northwest side of God's House in Mecca, the Kaᶜba. Some Cairene palaces and mansions also had prayer niches in their reception halls that faced in this direction.[23] Even when there were no such niches, however, builders attempted to make most *qāᶜa*s and loggias (that is, the ceremonial spaces and summer bedrooms of the house) either parallel to what they believed to be the northwest side of the Kaᶜba, or perpendicular to it.[24] In figure 3, the *qāᶜa* and the upstairs loggia of Hasan Kashif's mansion are perpendicular to the Kaᶜba. We can also see that the courtyard and the veranda were parallel to it. In fact all parts of the dwelling appear to have been aligned orthogonally with respect to each other and the Kaᶜba, including the gardens.[25]

A second principle followed by builders was to have house loggias and ventilators face towards the northeast or northwest. This is apparent in figure 3, and in other drawings made by Europeans who visited Cairo in the thirteenth/nineteenth century. Egyptians believed that the most propitious winds blew from the north, and that the south wind brought misfortune.[26] Therefore, by being mindful of both the *qibla* and the north wind, they seem to have been using orientation as a magical way of increasing the prosperity of their houses.

The physical and semiotic isomorphisms shared by Cairene monumental architecture were augmented by the contiguity of houses and religious places. Within the city, religious buildings often stood on old house foundations. Owners converted their houses, or segments of them, into religious structures.[27] Wealthy urban landholders could dedicate tracts of land next to their houses for religious buildings. Sometimes this necessitated the realignment of adjacent streets, or the complex formed the basis for a new neighborhood.[28] Other people built their houses next to existing mosques, restoring them in the process.

For example, Mamluk emir Ibrahim Agha (eleventh/seventeenth century) created an ensemble of buildings that stretched for 750 feet on a tract of land located south of the former limits of Fatimid Cairo. Its nucleus consisted of the principal mansion, next to which the emir attached a tomb and a public water trough (*sabīl*). South of his mansion, across a narrow alley, he usurped and renovated a spacious old Mamluk mosque-tomb (where he himself was to be buried), and built a second house next to it. The emir established a collective housing complex (*rab*ᶜ) and a third mansion on the west side of the main thoroughfare, facing these buildings.[29]

When a person invested his wealth in this manner, he stood to enhance his honor in the eyes of neighbors and associates, and obtain their loyalty. We should also recall the canonical hadith that made a virtue of mosque building by promising the builders houses in paradise.

The immense expenditure required for building and maintaining such large urban complexes was financed primarily by conversion of income-producing real estate, including housing, into charitable trusts, known as *waqf*s.[30] These trusts had several advantages: in addition to serving as a vehicle for expressing religious and civic virtue, they gave donors a legal means for making their property inalienable and for evading quranic inheritance laws that often resulted in the disintegration of private estates. As a rule, donors exercised great control over their *waqf* property, especially because they had the freedom to choose the administrators. Often the donor himself, a relative, or descendent assumed this task. It is not unusual to find that women were named as *waqf* administrators, since this allowed wives to keep control of family property when their spouses died, and receive an annual stipend for managing it.

Apart from benefits accrued to the donor and his family, charitable trusts were largely responsible for the establishment and long-term operation of the foremost public and religious institutions of medieval Islamic cities. They financed the creation of many of the finest examples of Islamic monumental architecture. Moreover, artisans, merchants, religious specialists, and the common people benefitted from *waqf* endowments, to the degree that they received income from them and enjoyed the amenities they provided.[31] Endowments, after all, paid for the services of skilled workers, and they subsidized and fed Quran reciters, mosque attendants, and religious scholars. They even furnished low-cost housing for the poor and students attending the religious colleges.

Charitable trusts transferred income from rental housing into capital for building and maintaining mosques, colleges, Sufi convents, lodges, and even tombs, as evidenced in Ibrahim Agha's complex. In one case, a leading physician in the Mamluk court built a mosque and apartments for his entourage next to his residence, which was recognized as one of the most resplendent in all Cairo. Later, with the conversion of his property into a trust, he allocated a portion of the income to the care of his own tomb, where Quran reciters would chant verses for the salvation of his soul.[32] It was not unusual, in fact, for donors to rent out rooms in their own homes to pay for their funerals and their mausoleums. Hence *waqf*s linked the houses of the living with those of the dead through long-term charitable transactions. Endowment income also supported the annual pilgrim caravan to Mecca, and paid for the cloth covering of the Kaʿba.[33]

Aside from the factors just mentioned, Cairene mansions probably also obtained religious significance from their own decoration. During the Ottoman era, many of them had murals of Mecca or Medina in their reception halls, which created a subtle visual linkage between the dwellings and the most holy Islamic sites.[34]

As we have observed, the entries, floors, ceilings, and walls of Mamluk and Ottoman mansions were decorated with gaily colored floral, astral, and geometric designs. These may well have been paradisal and magic symbols believed to be efficacious in attracting blessing and deflecting evil forces. Sculpted marble tablets, bands of wooden plaques with Arabic inscriptions (figure 5), and framed parchments also graced

Figure 5. Quranic inscription in the *qāʿa* of Jamal al-Din al-Dhahabi's house, inner Cairo (c. eleventh/seventeenth century): "In the name of God most compassionate and merciful. Blessed be he, who, if he likes, will do something better than that for you—(paradisal) gardens beneath which rivers flow" (25 *Furqān* 10).

qāʿa walls and ceilings These contained dedicatory inscriptions, Quran verses, panegyrics for the house and its owner, and lines from al-Busiri's devotional *Mantle* poem in praise of the Prophet.

Apart from their pleasing appearance, these inscriptions explicitly make the house an earthly paradise and a secure enclave against evil forces. This is exemplified by a band of epigraphs inside the grand *mandara* of the Musafirkhana, an early thirteenth-/late eighteenth-century palace that once belonged to Muhammad ʿAli, the man who initiated Egypt's modernization. It says in part:

> This pleasant spot was built in glory,
> made victorious by God over the others.
> By the names and verses of (God) Magnificent, Almighty,
> It is kept in safety.
> The garden of bliss blooms in its luxuriance,
> The nightingale of joy sings in it. . . .
> Watchful eyes guard it,
> Protecting it from the evil of envying eyes.[35]

Perhaps the Quran verse most customarily inscribed inside Cairo's elegant houses (as well as mosques, colleges, and tombs) was the Throne

Verse (2 *Baqara* 255). Ostensibly it testifies to God's uniqueness and sublime power over heaven and earth. In popular usage, however, it is believed to be an efficacious device for combating demons and other evil forces.

In the foregoing discussion, I have offered evidence to show that Muslim houses played a key role in the establishment of Islam in Egypt, similar to the one they played in Medina and in Iraq. Over time, it appears as if the houses of the Cairene elites were instrumental to the development of urban religious institutions. Palaces, mansions, mosques, religious colleges, and Sufi monasteries, if not exactly identical in appearance, nevertheless came to share a common vocabulary of architectural features and decorative embellishments. Private, family-based charitable trusts supported the creation of Islamic institutions of worship, learning, and public charity. Sometimes these acts were inspired by the example of powerful sultans, but they often filled the void resulting from the neglect or instability of the state. Consequently the landscape of medieval Cairo to a great degree came to reflect a partial transference of the world of the house into the world of the city. Nevertheless, distinctions still had to be maintained between these two worlds: houses required a degree of seclusion and security, and the city needed its public markets, community mosques, baths, thoroughfares, and parade grounds.

Cairo's elite mansions were places where people attempted to reconcile the potentially conflicting Islamic norms of privacy and hospitality. By design and custom, these dwellings could shelter the intimate aspects of family life from public view, yet provide abundant space for social intercourse. We have also seen evidence that upper echelons of Cairene society sought to affiliate their mansions with such collective Islamic symbols as Mecca, Medina, mosques, and paradise through orientation and forms of visual representation. They used Arabic epigraphs and apotropaic signs to bless their homes and protect them from misfortune. Palatial houses therefore reflected the partial transference of formal Islamic codes of behavior and symbols to the domestic sphere.

I say partial because Islamic norms were appropriated only to the degree that they were in accord with the conventional practices, values, attitudes, and feelings of the people—women and men—living in the houses, rather than with the normative consensus of Muslim jurists, the *ʿulama*. Members of the latter group lived within such domestic spaces; they probably advised other homeowners in the selection of inscriptions and symbols for their houses. We have no evidence, however, that as a body of experts they unilaterally determined the religious meanings of people's houses.

Unfortunately we still lack sufficient evidence to thoroughly assess how people used religious symbols and practices to render their homes meaningful. This is especially true for the majority of the populace, who left few if any written records, and whose fragile dwellings have long since perished.[36] To gain a more complete picture, we must look to evidence from modern Egypt.

DOMESTIC SPACE AND URBAN SOCIETY IN EGYPT TODAY

Egypt's ethnic makeup today is predominantly Arab—it calls itself the Arab Republic of Egypt—but it also includes strong African and Mediterranean elements. It has a total estimated population of fifty-five million, 91 percent of which is Muslim. This makes it the largest Muslim country of the Arabic-speaking world, and the ninth largest of the forty countries in which Muslims are a majority of the population. Its 2.9 percent population growth rate is above average, despite a sustained campaign for family planning.[37] This means that one million more people are added to its population every eight months. As we shall see shortly, this growth rate, combined with a declining mortality rate, places a severe burden upon the ability of Egyptians to acquire adequate housing, as well as upon the country's overall development.

As in centuries past, Egyptians today prefer to live in the Nile Valley and Delta. Most of them are crowded into a very small portion (about 4 percent) of the country's total area. Although more than half of them are still classified as rural, the trend in recent decades has been for Egyptians to migrate to urban areas, where population growth rates are already high. This trend corresponds to population shifts in other Arab, Islamic, and developing nations in general.[38] For Egyptians in the countryside, moreover, life today is strongly influenced by urban institutions and values. Paved roads, railways, airlines, telephones, radio, television, newspapers, magazines, schools, and government agencies link cities to all but the most remote sectors of the population. In addition, there are few rural families that do not have close relatives who have moved to one of Egypt's major cities. Hence, familial ties serve as another medium through which urban life affects life in the countryside.

Cairo is Egypt's primary city. Cairenes like to refer to it as "Mother of the World." In many respects, they are right. With its estimated fourteen million inhabitants, Greater Cairo ranks today as the largest city in both the Arab world and the Islamic world.[39] About one of every four Egyptians lives there, which makes Cairo the dominant center of government, industry, commerce, education, publication, and broadcasting in the region. Its print media, films, radio and television programs disseminate Egyptian culture and politics to all other Arabic-speaking countries in the region.

Cairo is also home to al-Azhar University, which is a leading university for the propagation of Islamic learning within the Sunni majority branch of the Islamic community. Like their predecessors in centuries past, Muslim students from other parts of Africa and Asia travel there today to acquire advanced learning in the Quran, hadiths, and religious law. In former times, al-Azhar was but one of many centers for advanced religious learning located in Cairo.[40]

The layout of modern Cairo is completely different from the Cairo of the Fatimids, Mamluks, and Ottomans. During the nineteenth century, Egypt's rulers, after eliminating the last vestiges of the country's Mamluk aristocracy, set out to remold it according to modern European prototypes. In the 1860s and 70s, the Khedive Ismaᶜil, who was born in the palace of Muhammad ᶜAli mentioned above, promoted the introduction of Parisian-style paved boulevards, lined with trees, and meeting at radial intersections. He built an opera house to entertain European dignitaries during inaugural ceremonies for the Suez Canal in 1869. He had French and Italian contractors and architects commissioned to erect European-style palaces, civic buildings, hotels, and apartments. Orientation according to the *qibla* and the north wind had no place in the Khedive's plans.

For a long time these changes affected only the lands due west and north of the thirteenth-/eighteenth-century limits of Cairo. The governmental center gradually moved closer to the banks of the Nile, in effect creating two Cairos: a European colonial one and a native Islamic one. British domination of Egyptian political and economic life between 1882 and 1956 quickened the pace of the modern city's transformation, and widened the gap separating it from the old city.[41] Since the 1950s, medieval Cairo has been engulfed by urban sprawl, and gradually infiltrated by the amenities and corrosive effects of modern urban life (figure 6).

Modernization and the rise of the nation state have severely curtailed the size and number of *waqf* properties. A special government ministry has been created to administer what remains after large familial *waqf* holdings were broken up and redistributed. Today, in addition to overseeing the upkeep of religious buildings and subsidizing imams, preachers, and other mosque personnel, the ministry has also become involved with building shops, apartments, and low-income housing.[42] Nonetheless, the quality of the built environment in the medieval city has steadily declined, a process that has been aggravated by official neglect and the long-term impact of waves of peasant immigration.

Figure 6. *Baladi* apartments in southern Cairo, still overshadowed by the religious college-tomb complex of Sultan Hasan (left) and Muhammad ʿAli's citadel mosque (upper right).

As a result of these modern changes, five types of residential areas, distinguished by social class and occupation, have become established in Cairo. Wealthy and powerful elites occupy a zone in the center of the city, along the banks of the Nile, and on the Jazira, an island in the middle of the river. Middle class professionals, bureaucrats, and merchants live adjacent to this zone, especially on Roda Island (south of the Jazira), the west bank of the Nile, and a narrow corridor extending to the northeast from downtown. Skilled workers, petite bourgeoisie, and low-income white collar workers live in neighborhoods bordering the downtown area on its north and east sides. They also occupy a strip paralleling the northern flank of the middle class zone that runs northeast of town.

The fourth type of residential area is home to artisans, peddlers, semi- and unskilled laborers, and a young generation of educated but low-salaried white-collar workers. They live in a narrow band of urban land along the east bank of the Nile, which is broken in half by the upper class downtown and governmental districts. Members of this class also inhabit what remains of the medieval city, now situated due east of the downtown elite and middle class zones.

The fifth, most impoverished, type of residential area is occupied by villagers whose lands and houses have been swallowed up by the urban sprawl, and by people who have migrated to Cairo from rural parts of upper and lower Egypt. This zone forms the periphery for most of Cairo. On the eastern edge it consists mainly of the dwellings that have been established in the Qarafa, where the city's old cemeteries are located (see frontispiece).[43]

In order to facilitate the analysis of Egyptian domestic space, it is useful to divide this five-fold residential topography of Cairene society into three positional subcultures. The *afrangi*, or western-style, subculture stands at one extreme. It is characterized by the adoption of individualistic Euramerican manners of behavior, speech, dress, cuisine, and household decor. As a subculture, it is typically found in residential areas occupied by upper class elites, and is shared by many of the best educated members of the populace. Because this group controls media, business, and investment, however, its values are widely disseminated in Egyptian society and beyond. At the opposite extreme stands the poverty-stricken *rīfi*, or rural, subculture. This is the lifestyle of the peasants, characterized by strong attachments to local custom, family honor and solidarity, and the land. In Cairo, this subculture has established itself in the peripheral districts associated with the fifth type of residential zone, and within parts of the medieval city. Its members are the ones most likely to live in the tombs and squatter housing. The *baladi*, or urban native, sub-culture occupies the gap separating *afrangi* from *rīfi* elements of the population. The most varied of the three, it typifies life in the middle- and working-class sections of Cairo, that is, in residential zones three and four.

Though these designations have somewhat fuzzy semantic boundaries, Egyptians often define themselves expressly as members of one of these groups, distinct from the other two. For example, members of the *baladi* population proudly identify themselves as *wilād il-balad* "children of the town," and make critical remarks of the manners of the *afrangi* and *rīfi* groups. They criticize the former for putting on airs, neglecting their familial duties, and abandoning their native roots. They reproach the latter for their ignorance and crude manners.[44] Influenced by their own points of view, members of the other groups engage in a similar discourse of social ranking.

A person's subculture is also connoted through association with a locality. Toponymic designations like *Ṣaʿīdi* "Upper Egyptian," or the mention that someone is from a particular Cairene district such as Zamalik, Shubra, Sayyida Zaynab, Zaynhum, Gamaliyya, Khalifa, or Imbaba carry unambiguous connotations in native discourse relating to lifestyle. Despite the large number of such toponymic designations, they can nonetheless be classified in terms of one of the three main positional designations.[45]

Do residential patterns based on social class and subculture correspond to religious divisions? The answer generally is no. Most of the Jewish population has emigrated. Masr al-Qadima and Shubra are sometimes associated with the Christian, especially Coptic Christian, community, but a closer look reveals that these areas today possess sizeable Muslim populations. Concomitantly, Copts have taken up residence in nearly all Cairene residential districts, if not in every quarter or subdistrict. Arab and Armenian Christian families cluster in the most Europeanized sections of the city, but these are not so exclusive as to form real quarters.

With the exception of several thousand Arab and Armenian Christians, Egypt's Christians and Muslims cannot be relegated to any single one of the *afrangi*, *baladi*, or *rīfi* subcultures. Muslims and Copts alike can be found in all three, perhaps with higher proportions of Copts in the first two categories. Arab and Armenian Christians, however, are all members of the *afrangi* subculture, but they share this status with Copts and Muslims.

HOUSE TERMS IN MODERN EGYPTIAN DISCOURSE

All of the key house terms that occur in the Quran (see table 1) and the hadiths are used by Egyptians in everyday discourse.[46] *Bayt* remains the most common and inclusive lexeme for "house"; as in previous centuries, it can be used to designate both a place of residence and the family unit. Egyptians also employ it as a metaphor for wife.[47]

Urban Egyptians usually employ the term *dār* for "house" when they wish to express traditional values by means of proverbs. For example, the virtue of remaining loyal to the family is sanctioned by the proverb, "Whoever leaves his house (*dār*), loses esteem." Egyptians also use this proverb to urge the resolution of domestic conflicts before one of the parties leaves in anger, as well as to criticize women who seek a living outside the domestic sphere. Disruptions caused by the loss of a loved one and burdens imposed by funerals are acknowledged in the saying, "Death and the destruction of houses" (*diyār*). A third proverb, "Buy the neighbor before the house" (*dār*), expresses the wisdom of knowing who one's neighbors will be before moving to a new place. In modern parlance, *dār* can also refer to certain kinds of business establishments, especially publishing houses.[48] Egyptians do not use the word, as Syrians and Lebanese do, to signify a courtyard or reception room.

Rural Egyptians use *dār* more often than their urban counterparts when referring to houses, in common speech and in proverbial expressions alike.

Of the remaining quranic terms, *ma'wā* and *mathwā* (also *matwā*) continue to denote shelter and refuge. A homeless person is said to be without a *matwā*.[49] The Egyptian press and urban planners use a verbal noun based on the same root from which *ma'wā* is derived, *iwā'*, to refer to the provision of shelter to the homeless. *Maskan* denotes only one kind of housing: public housing projects for the urban poor; the related term *iskān* is used by planners, bureaucrats, and the press in talking about providing this kind of housing. Indeed, the government has created a ministry for *iskān*.[50] As for the term *ghurfa*, unlike Arabs living in western Asia, Egyptians seldom use it in everyday speech.

An ubiquitous house term from the hadiths and early Islamic texts, *manzil*, also occurs in Egyptian vernacular speech. It is used in formal discourse to denote a place of residence, but Egyptians do not usually employ it when talking about their own homes.[51] It occurs occasionally in symbolic discourse, in folk songs for example. They sometimes use another early Arabic term, *ḥujra* (*ḥugra* in colloquial), to denote an ordinary room within a house, but they prefer the term *ūda*, a Turkish loanword.[52] This usage is common especially in urban contexts.

The mass reproduction of Islam through the print and broadcast media, as well as cycles of Quran recitations during Ramadan, feast days, and life-cycle events sustain the religious connotations of some domestic lexemes. Egyptians continue to know the Kaʿba as ''God's sacred house'' (*bayt*). They refer to the world of the hereafter as a *dār*, while many of them understand the bliss of paradise as a transfiguration of the best qualities and pleasures of domestic life in this world.

The majority of urban Egyptians today are renters, not home owners. When they speak of their *bayt*, they often mean a small apartment comprised of one to five rooms in a multistory western-style apartment building. The Egyptian word for this kind of house is *shaqqa*, a term that was not widely used in connection with residential space before the twentieth century. Like the English ''apartment,'' it is based upon the idea of splitting something apart from a larger whole. It is related to the word *shaqq*, which denotes an individual burial site as opposed to a family mausoleum.[53] Cognates derived from the same root (*shqq*) are used in Egyptian colloquial to denote a full brother or sister (*shaqīq, shaqīqa*) and the idea of hardship and distress (*mashaqqa*).[54] Although the words *bayt* and *shaqqa* can be synonymous, their latent significations are remarkably different. The former term connotes the idea of wholeness, both in genealogical and spatial terms. The latter implies fragmentation, hardship, even death.

If *shaqqa* is a common house term among *baladi* Egyptians, the wealthy *afrangi* subculture has appropriated special lexemes, besides *shaqqa*, for referring to its own houses, or the houses it would like to acquire for itself. By and large, they have relinquished older terms for palatial and luxurious dwellings such as *dār, qaṣr*, and the Persian *sarāya* in favor of terms such as *fīla* (or villa, an Italian loanword) and *shalēh* (a French loanword). The former signifies a Euramerican-style single family dwelling, or a spacious duplex apartment; the latter refers to a weekend or summer retreat for the wealthy. *Qaṣr* and *sarāya* today refer to large European-style architectural complexes that serve as reception halls for government officials and foreign dignitaries.

Anthropological research in Cairo's poor but relatively stable *baladi* neighborhoods has revealed another set of lexemes for domestic space. Nawal al-Messiri Nadim found that residents of an alley in "medieval Cairo" use the term *bayt* or *rabᶜ* to designate the medieval buildings that provide them with collective lodgings. Moreover, she discovered that they consider the alley, or *ḥāra*, as a kind of extended household space. Residents call their individual quarters, in which five or six members of a nuclear family usually live in one or two rooms, "places" (*maṭāriḥ*). The continuities between the space of the alley and the interior space of the individual lodgings are reflected in manners of dress, the sharing of cooking areas, the practice of sleeping on outside doorsteps in hot weather, and, contrary once again to statements made by outside observers, the fact that residents leave their front doors open for most of the day.[55]

Elsewhere in poor *baladi* areas, where strong corporate relations may be lacking, people also refer to the rooms of their houses as "places." This is a reflection of the fact that when life is difficult, and living space is limited, optimal use must be made of each part of the house. In a culture of poverty, families do not have the luxury of dedicating separate rooms to sleeping, bathing, food preparation, or receiving guests. Having rooms with special functions is more typical for the prosperous sectors of the *baladi* population, and for *afrangi* Egyptians.

Lastly, there are the dwelling places that one Egyptian housing expert calls "deformed housing."[56] These are the makeshift squatter houses—usually lacking adequate water and sewage services—found on the outskirts of Cairo, in the tombs, and in open spaces within the older sections of town. They may be canvas tents (*khiyam*), or shacks made of mud and scrap materials (*ᶜishash* or *akshāk*). To these we can add the dwelling places people have improvised on the city's rooftops, under its stairways, and in its bomb shelters. According to one estimate, as many as one million Egyptians live in such conditions.[57] Not all of them are rural immigrants; many once lived in buildings that collapsed or were condemned. They are joined by city dwellers who simply cannot afford to pay exorbitant key money for an apartment, or meet the monthly rents.

APPROPRIATING MEANING FOR THE HOUSE: ACTION, SPEECH, AND INTERIOR DISPLAY

Given the variety of house forms and shelters in which Muslims have lived from the earliest centuries to the present day, it is fair to conclude that whatever religious meanings Muslims ascribe to their homes, they are not determined a priori by house form. Admittedly the courtyard house is the most common form in many parts of the Muslim world, especially in the traditional heartlands of Islam, including Egypt. There are those, consequently, who have maintained that it is particularly Islamic, that its design has a cosmic, or archetypal, significance in Arab Muslim environments.[58] But there is as yet no strong evidence to support the validity of such an interpretation, especially because the shape is so basic. Indeed, the use of this house form in western Asia antedates the Islamic era by millennia. Furthermore, aside from the fact that it can be found in non-Muslim communities and regions of the world, the courtyard house can assume different shapes and functions even within Muslim settlements themselves.

If the shape of a Muslim house, even an Arab Muslim house, does not automatically convey religious significance, and if, on the basis of what I have said in previous chapters, there exists no normative canon for special household rituals and geomantic procedures in Islam, where do we look to find the religious meanings of the houses in which Muslims live?

In answer to this question, I recommend that we look to three aspects of life within the domestic sphere that are involved in the attribution of religious meaning to houses: social action, speech, and interior display.

By social action I mean specifically the conduct of relations between family members, men and women, hosts and visitors, as well as neighbors. It has power to create, maintain, and alter domestic space and its meanings. Speech is a verbal modality of action that links human thought to the worlds of society and nature. It has direct and indirect effects on these worlds, and on their comprehension by individuals. In other words, speech has power, just as other social actions have power. Although sociolinguists nowadays tend to see language largely as the product of society, I wish to examine the reciprocities between language and society that occur through speech in its oral and written forms.[59] With regard to Muslim houses, therefore, I ask which social situations and occasions produce (or reproduce) certain kinds of verbal statements, which statements are believed to be efficacious within the social and physical environments where they are uttered, and how they operate.

As for interior display, by this I mean the presentation within the house of the body, material artifacts, and ornamentations, and their dispositions in the physical space of a house. Architectural form sets some limits on interior display, but it does not actually determine how a person or object is presented. Nor does architecture, apart from human appropriation of it, determine the limits of places human beings choose to call home.

Action, speech, and interior display are interrelated facets of human existence. Hannah Arendt has observed that action and speech are the means by which people assert their existence in the world. When they operate together, action and speech create a "space of appearance," wherein the body and material objects, as well as society have their places.[60] Moreover, in positing that speech and action are preconditions for space and power, Arendt suggests that the private and the public worlds cannot be treated as mutually exclusive spheres, even when people declare explicitly that this is so. Instead, they are complementary. If it is true that one world is not severed from the other, then it is reasonable to propose that domestic life and public life must be complementary. Human society cannot exist for long when one excludes the other, or when one completely assimilates the other. We have already seen evidence for this complementarity reflected in the Islamic literary canon, in the history of the formation of early Islamic cities, and in layout and decoration of Cairo's medieval palaces and houses.

When we view the public and the private as complementary spheres of speech and action, the question of boundaries becomes more important, not less so. This is because under the old truth that public and private are mutually exclusive, the existence of boundaries is a preinterpretive fact. Their existence facilitates the explanation of other social phenomena in private life or in society at large, but they themselves cannot be critically examined. On the other hand, were we to view them in relational terms, we would find ourselves asking about how boundaries are defined, maintained, and crossed. Indeed, if the work of Georges Bataille, Mary Douglas, and Victor Turner is correct, then we could even postulate that boundaries exist to be crossed as well as to separate or exclude. In Lévi-Strauss's words, "Every interdiction is at the same time, and in another regard, a prescription.'' When controlled by rules, boundary crossing actions allow for intercourse between the public and private (or outside and inside), while concomitantly affirming their differences.[61]

According to an idea prevailing among Muslims today, Islam is a religion (*dīn*) that embodies values and rules for every time and place. From this point of view, there should be little question that it has a bearing on the meaning of life at home as well as in society at large. This claim may be true, but it falls short of explaining the variety of ways Muslims might seek to appropriate Islam for themselves and their houses. The *ᶜulama*, those virtuosos of Islamic law and tradition, and purist religious reformers would even consider some configurations of meaning in Muslim houses to be corrupting innovations (*bidᶜa*), hence actually un–Islamic and worthy of condemnation. Therefore, by proposing to look to social action, speech, interior display, and the definition of boundaries, I am shifting analysis from normative discourses generated by Islamic academies and by modern reformers to everyday discourse generated by Egyptian Muslims in specific domestic situations.

In the ensuing chapters, I present the essential components of the system of religious meanings a respectable number of Muslims ascribe to their houses within the context of their everyday lives, and describe under what circumstances these meanings are produced, maintained, and destroyed. Although I make comparisons with other Egyptian subcultures, my discussion turns primarily on configurations of domestic meaning formulated by Cairene *baladi* Egyptians. This has the advantage of shifting attention to the sector of the populace that is in many ways most representative of the post-colonial Egyptian Muslim identity. Like the people portrayed in the novels of Nobel laureate Naguib Mahfouz, they have been deeply involved in the events and transformations that have swept their country during this century. Though they have not been in the vanguard of modernization, they have not been isolated by traditionalism and poverty. Rather, they largely have struggled to reach a compromise between modernity and tradition.

The *afrangi* subculture, though powerful, represents a very small segment of the population. To the extent that it seeks to emulate the individualistic lifestyles of Euramerican cultures, it is unable to attribute religious significance to the house, or it is uninterested in doing so. The *rīfi* sector has been the one to suffer the negative impacts of urbanization and modernization most strongly. Though perhaps the largest sector in Egypt, we can no longer speak of a pristine peasant society in Egypt, if there ever was one. Its ways of ascribing religious significance to domestic space today tend to emulate those of the *baladi* sector.

The present and the future of Egyptian society, as well as its definition of what Islam is and will be there, now lie primarily in the hands of *baladi* Egyptians. The ways they ascribe religious significance to their dwelling places embody the past, present, and future of religion in their country.

5

Domestications of Islam in Modern Egypt: A Cultural Analysis

> The house is the first thing we own, and the last thing we sell. It is our tomb in this life.
>
> Arab Proverb

> The first school in which I learned the most important lessons in my life was my house.
>
> Ahmad Amin

Appropriating religious meaning to a house occurs within particular frames of collective discourse and action. To obtain sufficient understanding of what happens when people domesticate religious symbols and practices, not only must the particular components of meaning be identified, but the modalities of signification have to be elucidated in terms of tangible places and events. This chapter is concerned with describing the components of sacrality that Egyptians themselves attribute to their homes, and explores how this sacrality is conveyed and maintained through patterns of action, speech, and internal display. In particular, it will show that observances connected with marriage and death are of primary importance in establishing domestic sacrality. In the last part of the chapter I take up the question of what Egyptians do when faced with situations where domestic sacrality is perceived to have been violated.

THE COMPONENTS OF SACRALITY IN EGYPTIAN MUSLIM HOMES

"Every house has its own sacrality *(ḥurma)*."[1] It would be hard to find a more explicit statement in the Egyptian colloquial Arabic about the sacred, inviolable quality people attribute to their houses. As an adage, it has several levels of meaning. On one level, it indicates that entering someone's house requires a demonstration of respect *(iḥtirām)* toward the people living there. This is particularly important in regard to recognizing that the house is the domain for women in the family. To enter without permission or incorrectly, to call out a woman's personal name so that outsiders can hear it, to speak brazenly, and to look in without permission are violations of the house's *ḥurma*. They are very reprehensible forms of behavior against which there must be a defense. The intimate connection between domestic sacrality and the female is demonstrated aptly by the fact that *ḥurma*, as well as its cognate *ḥaram*, also happens to be a customary way of making respectful reference to a man's wife. She is the foremost repository of a house's sacrality, followed by the daughters. The adage implies, therefore, that not only does every house have a sacral character, but that this sacral character is dependent upon the presence of women.[2]

That houses have sacrality, and that this is connected with married women does not mean that domestic space and women must be absolutely segregated from the outside world. The *baladi* Egyptian idea of *ḥurma* normally accepts access to the house, it permits vision, it allows speech. But it sanctions these actions by setting limits on them. The same idea is evidenced by early Islamic discourses of domestic space, which prohibit unauthorized intrusions at the same time that they place positive sanctions on visitation and hospitality. This may be paradoxical, but the same can be said of *ḥurma* when identified strictly with women, for they only become fully "inviolable" through marriage to men. In a sense, inviolability is based on controlled violation.

For Egyptian Muslims, *ḥurma* is a term that can also signify the sacred quality of mosque space, from local prayer places to the precincts of the holiest sites in Mecca and Medina. Sacrality thus provides a tacit linkage between the human household, God's house(s), and the Prophet's house-mosque. When sentiments that people associate with their own dwellings are connected with such localities, these sentiments are both affirmed and objectified in terms of translocal Islamic discourse. Local mosques, Mecca, Medina, and ordinary houses are obviously not totally segregated localities. They would be of little use to anyone if they were. *Ḥurma* therefore provokes the setting of limitations on accessibility to the sacralized space that it signifies, but it cannot absolutely prevent human access.[3]

Sharaf "honor" is the masculine counterpart of *ḥurma;* they are two sides of the same coin. In spatial terms, we can consider *sharaf* as a sort of cover for *ḥurma;* providing it with its public face and its defensive mask. The word *sharaf* suggests the idea of height, and of "overseeing." Without *ḥurma*, *sharaf* loses its reason for being, however. Likewise, *ḥurma* cannot be preserved for long without its outward visage.

In terms of social status, *sharaf* is the noble quality that accrues to a family, especially its male members, as a result of looking after the *ḥurma* of its wives and dwellings, or at least for appearing to be doing so to the outside world.[4] To maintain or improve their social standing, males should observe domestic responsibilities by furnishing wives and mothers with money and goods needed for managing the household. They should also keep the rules of hospitality, and defend both the household and its females from public shame *(ʿār)* and disgrace *(faḍīḥa)*. If they consistently fail to do these things, or behave scandalously, their esteem is likely to decrease in the eyes of relatives, friends, and neighbors. Shame harms households directly if men need to rally the support of others in times of illness, discord, or financial necessity. A man's dishonorable reputation can affect a daughter's marriage prospects. It can also disrupt his commercial transactions and vital relations with people in the world of labor.

Concomitantly, the actions, dress, and speech of women can either bolster a family's *sharaf* or seriously undermine it. For example, if a woman upbraids her husband in front of his associates, or if she dresses immodestly in public, and he does not scold her, then she can damage his communal standing, and that of the family. Likewise, the immodest reputation of a daughter can limit or cripple her marriage prospects and those of her sisters. If she accepts marriage to a disreputable man as a last resort, her shameful reputation can be transmitted to her daughters.

In a society based on long-standing patriarchal values, such as Egypt's, the qualities of sacrality and honor can be understood as part of what Dale Eickelman calls a "practical ideology" for enforcing male dominance and female compliance.[5] Seldom articulated systematically, they form a partial blueprint that governs a wide range of formal and informal social relations. As a result of the operation of this ideology, women find it advantageous to keep to the domestic sphere, with limited contacts with males and institutions outside the natal family. Men have relatively more rights outside the home, but unless they are either wealthy or powerful, they, too, are subject to strict controls in their quotidian dealings with relatives, friends, associates, and governmental agencies. Sacrality and honor influence men even when they visit others in their homes.

We might be led to conclude that the only place that a man's authority is absolute is in his own house, where he is supposedly not subject to the behavioral constraints he faces on the outside. In colloquial discourse, a husband is called "lord *(rabb)* of the house," which also happens to be one of God's epithets. Despite such explicit claims, however, a man must often learn to accommodate his desires to the domestic regime skilfully implemented by female members of the family: wife, mother, sisters, and daughters. Women usually control household finances. A popular proverb declares, "He is your husband to the extent that you train him, and your son to the extent that you raise him." Such a statement would not be possible if a man's control of the domestic sphere were absolute.[6]

The ideology of male dominance based on sacrality and honor gives women the possibility of exercising a subversive power with which they can sometimes accrue respect for themselves, against or in spite of males, or undermine a man's communal status through well-timed words, actions, and bodily displays. By not providing suitable refreshments when male visitors come calling, or by publicly criticizing a man's character, sexual potency, or failure to provide adequate support for household necessities, women can try to modify the behavior of their husbands to their advantage. These are very risky strategies, however, since they can result in physical abuse, divorce, and sometimes death.

In advanced capitalist societies, the familial dwelling place is frequently regarded in economic terms as a unit for the consumption of mass-produced consumer goods and services. In other parts of the world, however, houses function as important centers of small-scale production as well as consumption. The household division of labor according to age, sex, and kinship is responsible for providing goods and services needed for the perpetuation of the family itself, as well as for the procreation and care of successive generations of family members.

In urban Egypt today we find that the domestic sphere is the primary locus for birth, raising children, food preparation, health care, support for the elderly, sewing and mending clothing. With the growing shortage of classroom space and teachers, the home also is becoming a center for study, the transmission of knowledge. In all of these activities, it is often the women of the house who play the leading role. The creation of heavy industry and commercial centers by the state has given new employment opportunities to both men and women, drawing them directly into the world economic system, but it has not overtly harmed the domestic economy. In fact, development may well have compelled Egypt's citizens to rely more than ever on domestic modes of production in order to meet their everyday needs. Women raise rabbits, chickens, pigeons, ducks, and goats on balconies, rooftops, and in courtyards to supplement the family diet and ensure food for special occasions. They sell eggs and animals for additional income, or exchange them for other goods and services. Women also contract to sew, do embroidery, or make holiday candy at home for factories and merchants.[7] Moreover, despite an increasing rate of employment outside the home and better education, Egyptian women today continue to view the fulfillment of their responsibilities as wives and mothers as their primary purpose.[8] Most males, of course, sustain this view.

In indigenous terms, the productive capacity of a household is understood symbolically in terms of *baraka*. This word often occurs in scholarly discussions about the belief systems of Arab Islamic societies, where it is treated as a miraculous blessing power possessed by saints and holy places from which common people can benefit.[9] Perhaps this is *baraka*'s most obvious characteristic. On the domestic level, however, it is the miraculous force behind mundane successes: marriage, the birth of a son, loving relations between family members, happiness, good health, and material prosperity. In other words, it is a form of luck or good fortune relative to house and family. *Khayr* "goodness" is often used in everyday speech as a synonym for *baraka*, but since it is itself not a form of power, it is more the visible manifestation of *baraka*'s operation rather than *baraka* itself. A house fraught with strife, sterility, extreme poverty, or tragic death lacks sufficient *baraka* and *khayr*.

Sharr is the term Egyptians use to designate the most general forms of evil and misfortune in everyday life. They acknowledge that it afflicts even virtuous and successful people, but the poor and the weak are its greatest victims. According to the *baladi* belief system, it usually operates through the force of envy *(ḥasad)* or the doings of malevolent spirits. The urban poor and immigrants from the countryside maintain that it can also be the result of black magic. Just as *baraka* can be transmitted easily through close physical contact and speech, evil can strike with the glance of an eye and the slip of a tongue. It brings with it family conflict, infertility, illness, untimely death, financial loss, theft, and the destruction of property. Misfortune may be the result of a divine punishment for moral evil, but evil acts do not necessarily bring misfortune in this life. In accordance with quranic notions of divine justice, evildoers might not be punished until after their deaths. Likewise, the virtuous might not realize rewards for the suffering they have endured in their earthly lives until they attain the hereafter.

There is nothing especially Islamic about a practical ideology of household sacrality and honor that functions to promote prosperity and deflect misfortune. Comparable configurations predate Islam's appearance and occur outside its historical heartlands. In Egypt (and other Muslim countries in the region), however, the language in which this ideology is phrased intersects with key aspects of Islamic discourse. I have already pointed out that *ḥurma* and *ḥaram* can be used in reference to holy places as well as the home. The hadiths even suggest that *ḥurma* is a quality of God. *Sharaf,* although lacking quranic authority, has, through its cognate *sharīf* ("high," "noble"), been used widely by

Muslims in recent centuries to characterize Mecca's sacred precincts *(al-ḥaram al-sharīf)* and to designate noble descendants of the Prophet's house. It is a quality of holy men and holy places alike that has been bestowed by God himself, although it is not one of his attributes per se. *Baraka* and *khayr* (or cognates) occur in the Quran and the hadiths. Both are often conceived as forms of God's grace.

Evil is closely associated with satanic forces against which people appeal to God and the Prophet for help. These harmful forces are mentioned explicitly in the last two chapters of the Quran:

> Say, "I seek protection through the lord of daybreak from the evil *(sharr)* of what he has created; from the evil of twilight; from the evil of the women who blow on knots; and from the evil of the envious when he envies." (113 *Falaq*)

> Say, "I seek protection from the lord of humans, king of humans, and god of humans, from the evil of the whisperer—who withdraws when God's name is mentioned, and who whispers into the hearts of humans, of the jinn and humans." (114 *Nās*)

The "whisperer" mentioned in the second chapter is widely regarded as an epithet for Satan. Egyptian Muslims usually memorize both chapters during childhood, and use them often to protect themselves, their houses, and businesses against misfortune.

To a great extent, *baladi* Egyptians appropriate Islamic ideas to reinforce local configurations of meaning. Concomitantly the local principles of domestic sacrality achieve an objective validation. The order of their houses comes to be seen in terms of universal patterns of dominance and submission, good and evil, blessing and misfortune. God has ultimate control in the cosmos, but humans assume the task of manipulating its forces of good and evil for their own benefit.[10]

"BUILDING A HOUSE": INAUGURATION AND MARRIAGE CEREMONIES

A house's sacrality consists of *ḥurma* and *sharaf,* its feminine and masculine qualities. This sacrality cannot be known in itself, but must be manifested in concrete signs communicated by social action, speech, and interior display. The successful establishment of sacrality is linked with the generation of the power of blessing and debilitation of the effects of evil. Concomitantly, were sacrality to be nonexistent, violated, or diminished, the well-being of the household would be affected negatively, and the effects of evil increase. Women and men alike are responsible for caring for the sacral character of their houses. They are also its greatest threats.

Among the most important occasions involved in the transformation of an ordinary architectural space into a sacralized place are inauguration ceremonies conducted when a house is built or when a family moves into a new dwelling and marriage ceremonies. In rural areas of northern Africa and the east Mediterranean, including Egypt, the building of new dwellings is marked by a series of ceremonial activities.[11] When house foundations are laid, builders put dates, grain, flour, salt, and perhaps even small silver or gold objects into them. When a wall, threshold, vault, but most of all when the whole building has been completed, a fowl or sheep is sacrificed and a feast is held by the builders or their patrons. At such times, the blood of the sacrificed animal is smeared on the house, usually on its door posts. Some people bury an offering under the threshold. The Quran is recited, often the *Fātiḥa* (its first chapter) or apotropaic verses (e.g., the Throne Verse, 2 *Baqara* 255; 113 *Falaq,* and 114 *Nās*). On rare occasions, a copy of the Quran is buried in the foundations or within a house wall. Before a new house is occupied, water or salt might be sprinkled on its floors, and it will be fumigated with incense.

These actions involve house builders, the prospective residents, their kin, and neighbors. But it is also clear that they are interwoven with transactions involving supernatural beings and forces. God is the highest power invoked, as reflected in the use made of the Quran, his eternal word. The offerings and sacrifices are not for him, however; they are for lesser beings, the spirits of the place—jinn and *ʿafrīt*s. Although the family may not be able to rid the place completely of spirits, gifts help deter them from afflicting it and the new house with sterility, illness, bloodshed, or loss.

Quran recitation and throwing salt have a double purpose: they ensure domestic blessing and they repel the malevolent forces of envy, the evil eye in particular. One of the formulas Egyptians use to repel the eye is "A grain of salt in the eye of him who does not bless the Prophet!" On the other hand, the word "salt" *malḥ* is a metaphor for true friendship in colloquial discourse, and is related to the word *malīḥ,* which signifies something or someone that is good or pleasant.[12] Salt therefore functions as a metaphor for solidarity, a form of blessing, and as a device for counteracting effects of hostile feelings arising in everyday situations. Burning incense, which often contains salt as one of its ingredients, also has a double purpose: it appeases local spirits and deflects the eye.

Most *baladi* Egyptians neither have a say in the design of the dwellings that they rent, nor do they build their own houses. They move into crowded collective housing complexes modeled after Euramerican buildings. Unless occupation of a new flat is part of a cycle of wedding ceremonies, it does not entail as much ritual activity as building a new house. The head of household sometimes places leaves of chard on the threshold, then enters the dwelling right foot first, followed by other members of the family. Egyptians call this the "green step" or the "good step" *(qadam khayr)*. When people come to congratulate them, they customarily say, "May God make it green chard for you!" or "You are blessed *(mabrūk)*!"[13] Like new occupants, first-time visitors are mindful of entering a house right foot first. Wives carry common staples, for example, rice and cooking fat, or bread, into their houses the first time they cross the threshold.

Each of these procedures is part of the etiquette for appropriating a new space, one that will be favorable for future domestic prosperity.[14] The items laid across the threshold and carried into the house signify ideal aspects of domestic life. Green represents both the holiness of the Prophet and bounty. The word *salq*, "chard," is etymologically related to the word for boiling, one of the most common ways of preparing vegetables and meats. It sounds like the word *salak*, which means "to pass through" a place unimpeded, "to cope" with difficulties.[15] Egyptians use rice as a simile for expressing the idea that something is available in great quantities. *Samna*, or cooking fat, suggests the ideal qualities of a husband (a good job, wealth) and wife (plumpness).[16] Moreover, unlike most other Arabic speakers, Egyptians use the word *ʿaysh* for "bread." This is also the word for "life." "Eating bread" is another way of saying "making a living." When people say, "We have eaten bread and salt together," they mean to express the closeness of their relationship to each other.[17]

The Quran, too, plays a role in the appropriation of a new dwelling place. For some *baladi* families, it is customary to carry a copy of it into the house, encased in a bright green, red, or blue velvet box. They give it a place of honor in the sitting area or family room. Posters and placards containing verses of the Quran or the names of God and the Prophet are hung on the walls in prominent parts of the dwelling also. Furthermore, moving into a new house can be an appropriate time to hold a Quran recital for family and friends. When hiring a professional reciter is beyond a family's means, playing a cassette recording of a recital, or tuning in to Egyptian radio's Quran station are acceptable alternatives.

It is often the case that acquiring a dwelling place coincides with the joining of a man and woman in marriage. Religious law makes marriage a fundamental requirement of Muslim social life; it also makes it the chief context for legitimate sexual relations between men and women.

Concomitantly, religious law places strong negative sanctions against sexual relations outside of marriage and against living in complete abstinence. For males, according to popular Egyptian precept, to get married is to "complete half of one's religion." For males and females together, it also means that they have "entered a world" *(dakhal dunyā)*.

Social norms, validated by religious requirements that give men the primary responsibility for maintenance, dictate that a marriage cannot be consummated until the male has acquired a dwelling place. In many cases, due to the influence of *rīfi* tradition and the chronic housing shortage, this may simply mean making new sleeping arrangements for the couple in the groom's parents' house.[18] If the groom's parents' quarters are already too crowded, and if he lacks the capital necessary for renting a place on his own, he can bargain with the bride's family to either reside with them, or to occupy a flat that they have set aside for their daughter. In fact, middle and upper class Egyptians use the promise of a new flat to enhance their daughter's marriageability.

Religious identity, marriage, sexual intercourse, and the appropriation of domestic space are all closely interrelated. In the Egyptian Muslim idiom, "building a house" does not simply mean to create a physical dwelling space, it means to get married, procreate, and fulfill one's religious duty. Another way of exemplifying the close rapport in Egyptian thought between domestic space, sex, and marriage is with a negative example. A man and woman who are not closely related avoid situations where they might be seen going together into a house, even that of a relative or friend, because they know that people will assume that they are intimate with each other. Only when they are married is such behavior socially acceptable.

Despite the importance of marriage as a social institution in Islam, wedding customs vary among classes and regions. The key juridical feature is the drawing up of a marriage contract, but this is embedded in a fluid cycle of ritual observances and transactions based on local traditions. One way of looking at this cycle is as a process for negotiating the movement of the bride from her parents' house to that of the groom. For her especially it is a rite of passage across boundaries in space and status.

Among *baladi* Egyptians, the wedding cycle generally conforms to the following sequence of stages:[19]

1. Informal visits and contacts occur between female members of prospective bride's and groom's families to determine whether the pair has matching characteristics.

2. An agreement *(ittifāq)* is made. Male members of the prospective groom's family, and friends, pay a formal visit to bride's house. A tentative agreement is made with her male relatives on the cost of engagement jewelry *(shabka),* the bride-price *(mahr),* and the trousseau *(gihāz, ʿafsh).*
3. The *Fatḥa* is recited. Contractual confirmation of the marriage agreement is inaugurated by reciting the first chapter of the Quran at the prospective bride's house. The recitation is attended by representatives of both families, as well as the couple.
4. The formal engagement *(khutūba)* period begins. The bride receives *shabka.* Usually held at bride's house, it is marked by a celebration financed by her family. Participants are served sweets and rose water punch.
5. The document is written *(katb ik-kitāb).*[20] Formal signing of marriage contract is conducted by an expert in Islamic marriage law *(maʾzūn)* in the presence of witnesses. The contract specifies bride price and financial obligations of husband in event of divorce. The family of the groom finances the ensuing celebration, which can be held either at the groom's house or at the bride's.
6. The marriage is consummated at the time the bride and groom make entry *(dukhla)* into their new house. The event is accompanied by a great deal of celebration and feasting.

Since this is a fluid cycle of social practices, we can expect to find that it is modified to suit the needs and circumstances of individual couples and their families. For example, one of the chief principles in arranging a marriage is that the pair have roughly equal qualities. This includes equality in family status, wealth, and reputation. In the marriage cycle the bride's family sponsors the first celebrations, and the groom's family the last. If the bride's family is unable to make its home available for its share of the celebrations because it is inadequate, then they might agree to supply refreshments in exchange for use of the groom's residence. Fluidity is also evident in the fact that families may agree to combine two stages of the cycle. Hence, the *Fatḥa* can be combined with the engagement celebration, or the engagement combined with the signing of the contract. In other cases, the signing of the contract and the *dukhla* are combined.

As young people feel that they are freer of parental authority because of the opportunities available to them in the city, they take greater liberties with the cycle. Encounters between the sexes at school, in the work place, and on neighborhood streets make the first stage, informal visits, increasingly unnecessary. Suitors contact the parents of the females they wish to court directly, or they contact the intended without first involving the parents. Young Egyptian couples dispense with expensive gifts, dowries, and wedding arrangements in order to secure a flat and furnishings instead. Despite such trends, young people are well aware of the old norms for courtship and marriage. They usually find it advantageous to keep them, even if it is only a token compliance.

Besides involving organized forms of social action on the level of house and family, four of the stages center on formal speech acts. This is evident in the names Egyptians give to these stages. The *ittifāq* (stage 2) is a preliminary verbal agreement between families. The *Fatḥa* (stage 3) involves a collective recital of the first chapter of the Quran, a short chapter Muslims know by heart from repeated use in their daily lives, including while at prayer. The word *khutūba* (stage 3), which denotes both engagement and the engagement ceremony, is based on the Arabic term for delivering a speech or sermon. The *katb ik-kitāb* (stage 4) focuses on the drawing up and signing of a written contract by male guardians of the bride and groom and witnesses, thus finalizing obligations first discussed in stage 2. Before the contract is signed, however, the marriage official has the parties orally swear that the marriage is being performed in accordance with the Quran and the Sunna of the Prophet.[21] Although the document (or "book") legalizes the marriage relationship, it depends on a series of speech acts; it does not render them unnecessary. Quran chapters, including the *Fatḥa*, are recited prior to the entertainments that will prevail for the rest of the evening.

Wedding customs require the exchange of congratulations using formulaic utterances. "You are blessed!" and "You are a thousand times blessed!" are the most general expressions. During the engagement period, people say, "May our lord bring about a good *(khayr)* conclusion!" "May you see your (other) children married, too!," or similar blessings are common with stages 5 and 6. In keeping with the ideal of balanced reciprocity, the nuptial couple and their families are expected to respond to these congratulations in kind on the spot.

Family and friends fete the couple with songs during celebrations connected with the different stages of the cycle. Participants improvise lyrics to traditional melodies that reflect aspects of their individual hopes and disappointments.[22] These songs are interwoven with others familiar to all celebrants, such as the following:

> Hey coquette! O bride! Come down!
> By God, I'm not coming down, nor leaving my home

Until I get new rings from the jeweler;
Selected by my mother and purchased by my master. (Engagement Song)[23]

You have honored your family, O bride!
You have lifted up your father's head, O bride!
You deserve the earrings, O bride! (Entry Song)[24]

Good for you, O groom! Good for you!
Arising happy in the morn, skull-cap askew,
Good for you! You saw her eyes,
Like those of a gazelle are her eyes, even lovelier!
Good for you! You saw her chest—bath tiles, even lovelier![25]
Good for you! You saw her hair—the plaits of a camel's saddle, even lovelier! (Entry Song)[26]

The marriage cycle involves several forms of speech, from the highly formal to the customary and the poetic. It reflects how Islamic language, particularly selections from the Quran, can become domesticated, that is, embedded in local symbol systems. Through customary and poetic forms of speech, we glimpse values connected with domestic sacrality: blessing, honor, happiness, sex, and prosperity. Some songs celebrate details of the marriage bed. But in general, song lyrics provide a sensuous portrait of the bride; she becomes visible to the celebrants through stereotyped metaphors and similes, especially at the time of her defloration.[27] In a way, the stereotyped nature of this kind of visibility creates a boundary that prevents her private persona from being seen. As Egyptians like to say, "Marriage is a protective covering for girls."[28]

The same idea of guarded visibility holds true for the "interior displays" arranged at the apartment where the celebrations are held. For festivities connected with the last stages of the cycle, people string loops of colorful bright lights on the façade of the apartment building, and in the halls and stairways leading into the flat of the host family. The family leaves its door wide open throughout the festivities, which is something people do not often do in houses located outside of poor city neighborhoods. Guests start coming early in the evening. After they fill the apartment, which has been rearranged to accommodate them, they are directed to the flat of a next-door neighbor (who has volunteered his home for the occasion), or to a colorful pavilion set up in the street or alleyway adjoining the building.

Although men and women intermix during festivities, hosts usually provide a segregated area for women in the center of the house. Men are relegated to seats near the entry or in the street, where they are entertained by bands and belly dancers. The arrival of the bride or groom is announced with the beeping of automobile horns, singing, clapping, and, nowadays, the glare of lights for video cameras.[29] Eventually, the bride and groom are seated together on a gaily decorated dais *(kūsha)* in the apartment's largest room, surrounded by dancing and singing women and children.[30]

Like the bride, the apartment becomes visible to a wide circle of family, friends, and strangers. The creation of this "space of appearance" within the house depends on keeping parts of it "unseen." I do not mean sleeping, cooking, or toilet areas per se, but the normal disposition of the house interior as a whole. During the festivities, outsiders cannot behold it as it normally is, because furnishings have been pushed aside and stored to make room for everyone. Visibility is also controlled by the grouping of women and men in its inner and outer sections respectively. And even though the groom takes a place next to his bride in the midst of all the women in the heart of the apartment, his ability to "see" them is checked by size of the crowd and the excitement of the moment.

The final stage of the marriage cycle is the *dukhla,* a term that denotes both the entry of the groom into the bride, thus ending her virginity, and the entry of the bride into the groom's house. As I pointed out previously, the one ought not to be done without the other. In rural and working-class weddings, the bride is usually led ceremoniously from her parents' house to the groom's, where she is feted with song and dance. At the appropriate time, the groom carries her over the threshold of the nuptial chamber, and then violates her virginity with a gauze-wrapped finger in the presence of close female relatives from both sides of the family. Recalling the moment of her own defloration, one woman states, "Blood has to come out. It stands for honor *(sharaf).* It stands for enormous honor. A girl's honor is worth the world. Her happiness is built on it. It's destroyed without it and can never be repaired."[31] The signs of her "honor," which also stands for the honor of her natal family, are subsequently shown to other close male and female relatives.

An analogous kind of "interior display" occurs during the week prior to the *dukhla,* when the couple's bedding, furniture, carpets, clothes, and kitchen utensils are paraded through neighborhood streets to the nuptial home. The exhibition of household furnishings, which consist in large part of the bride's trousseau, tells people how well she and her family have prepared themselves for her marriage. It can also be understood as an early demonstration of domestic honor and blessing in material form. Hence the furnishings actually serve as a kind of symbolic capital. The correspondence between their exhibition and the *dukhla* is reflected in the fact that the word for the trousseau *(gihāz)* also happens to be a euphemism for the privates.

Mid- and upper-level *baladi* families also celebrate the *dukhla,* but the bride and groom are allowed to be alone after their appearance on the dais. Even though the bride's "honor" remains an important issue, people in these classes consider it poor form to go so far as to display the bloody traces. They are also less likely to parade nuptial furnishings through neighborhood streets.

The family of a retired secondary school teacher in a mid-level *baladi* neighborhood in ʿAbbasiyya (Cairo) married its eldest son to a woman whose father owned an apartment building. The teacher's flat did not have enough space for the couple because it already housed the two parents, their two college-age sons, plus a married daughter, her husband, and their child. Instead, the bride's father promised to add another floor to his building in order to provide them with housing. Their *katb ik-kitāb* was held at the bride's parents' flat, but the couple had to wait two years before holding the *dukhla,* when the new apartment was finally completed. Following custom, the *dukhla* was celebrated at the groom's parents' residence, but then the couple departed together in a car for their new home atop the bride's father's apartment building.

Baladi Muslim couples partly establish their homes in spatial and familial terms by linking themselves to leading local holy places and the family of the Prophet. On the nights of the marriage contract signing and the *dukhla,* they arrange to be taken together by car to the mosques of Sayyida Zaynab or Husayn. These are Cairo's foremost shrines, which contain the holy remains of saints from the household of the Prophet. By going to them, newlyweds hope to acquire saintly *baraka* for their domestic life. The bride in particular wishes for blessing to be manifested in the birth of a son within the first year of marriage, thus securing for her a position in her husband's household.

Photographers take pictures of couples posing in front of these shrines. Later these photos find a place beside other wedding momentos in the home. Although the practice does not have the approval of Islamic law, newlyweds throughout Egypt usually visit a prominent local saint's shrine in the course of wedding ceremonies.

Couples time their weddings to enhance domestic blessing, also. People consider Thursday night *(laylit ig-gumʿa)* to be the best night of the week for marriage, for it precedes the day for communal prayer. It is even more propitious to hold the major stages of the cycle on Thursday nights during Islamic holidays, such as those marking the end of the Ramadan fast, the end of the Hajj rituals, and *mūlid*s (Muslim saints-day celebrations). Consequently every Thursday evening, except in the month of Ramadan when marriage is disapproved, streets and alleys throughout Egypt are filled with joyous clamor from wedding celebrations.

This timing creates a close interrelationship between the establishment of individual households and the cycle of holidays observed in much of the Muslim world. Years later, families can remember important moments in their lifetimes by association with the holiday calendar of the wider collectivity of believers.

Bringing the cycle to a successful conclusion represents a moral victory for the families involved. The display of the bride's honor, of the furnishings, and the establishment of the marital household symbolize this victory. The quality of blessing enhances it, and hopefully sets the foundations for future prosperity.

Nevertheless, the sequence of stages in the marriage cycle is usually fraught with difficulties and dangers for the parties involved. Disputes over the delegation of duties, financial problems, or negative feelings of the prospective bride or groom towards their intended can cut the cycle short at any point. In rural areas, wedding celebrations can turn into deadly staging grounds for the settlement of clan feuds. For the bride, there is the danger of discovering that her hymen is not intact, for whatever reason, during the *dukhla*.[32] For the groom, there is the threat of impotence resulting from tensions and pressures that accompany the festivities. Indeed, as Hamed Ammar observed, "The first year of marriage for both the husband and the wife bristles with difficulties that may lead to divorce."[33]

As Unni Wikan found in her study of the social environment of Egypt's urban poor, the moral victory represented by marriage can be undermined by malicious gossip *(kalām in-nās)* circulated by hostile, jealous relatives and neighbors.[34] They might seek to undermine it by questioning the bride's honor. If her reputation is impeccable, then they can find fault with her family, with the size of the trousseau, or with the quality of the household furnishings.

Egyptians hold that the uncertainties of courtship and marriage, the latent dangers, envy and malicious gossip are manifestations of evil forces. To protect themselves, they marshall the positive forces of blessing stemming from God, the Prophet, the Quran, and the saints. On the other hand, they also attempt to counteract evil forces with curses and threats like the following:

A stick in the eye of the envious!

O people! O evil! End your malicious chatter!

The eye afflicted me, and the Lord of the Throne saved me!

In the name of God, I enchant you to protect you from all harm, from every envious eye!

During the marriage cycle, it is not unusual for people to recite such formulae, along with apotropaic verses from the Quran, for the protection of the bride and groom. Wedding guests sing songs during celebrations for the purpose of repelling the malevolence of envy. At times when women, houses, and belongings are most vulnerable, these devices help to create a supernatural boundary. Indeed, a common word for "amulet" is *ḥigāb,* which also signifies a barrier and the veil worn by women to prevent themselves from being seen by strange men.

"DEATH AND THE DESTRUCTION OF HOUSES"

If marriage is instrumental to transforming a house into a place of sacrality, then there must be events that threaten to end that sacrality. Divorce is one way in which domestic sacrality can be destroyed.[35] For *baladi* Egyptians, as for other people, it is caused by conflicts with relatives, especially between wives and their mothers-in-law, and financial difficulties. Reproduction problems are another prominent cause. If the couple remains childless, or without a son, the wife suffers the blame, and the husband may threaten to repudiate her to acquire a wife who will give him the sons he desires. (He can, according to Islamic law, take other wives without divorcing his first wife, but most Muslims are monogamous.) When divorce occurs, the social fabric within the nuptial household and between the contracting families is rent.

Islamic divorce procedures arc based on spoken utterances delivered by the husband. In the common method of divorce, he merely has to say, "I divorce you," three times and abstain from intercourse with the wife.[36] In contrast to the marriage cycle, however, divorce lacks an elaborate ritual cycle. The wife is obliged to observe a waiting period for up to three months to see if she is pregnant. The husband is legally bound to maintain her during this time and to pay the balance of the bride price, if so stipulated in the marriage contract, when it ends. By law, the divorced woman keeps her trousseau (that is, the house furnishings), a major source of security for supporting herself and her children in difficult times. If she is fortunate, she will return to the folds of her natal family or live with a close relative while anxiously awaiting an opportunity for remarriage.[37] Strong social bias prevents women from living alone. If the husband has the resources, and if his former wife no longer has custody of the children, he may keep the apartment in anticipation of his remarriage, or pocket the rent from subletting it. Otherwise, he, too, may return to his parental household.

When the divorce is final, the principles of domestic sacrality and honor obviously no longer operate for that household. Indeed, divorce acknowledges the absence of blessing in the home. It may also represent the triumph of evil forces that the recitations, songs, and amulets of the marriage cycle were intended to curtail.

Death, because it strikes households repeatedly and inevitably, is a more formidable threat to domestic sacrality than divorce. Contrary to practices dominant in most Euramerican countries, Egyptians are accustomed both to bearing their children at home and dying at home. Egyptian Muslims recognize that death is a force that rests ultimately in God's hands, and they are constantly made aware in sermons and Quran recitations of the rewards that await the blessed in the hereafter. But they also recognize death as an autonomous power that can severely rupture the corporate identity of the family.

The Egyptian adage, "Death and the destruction of houses,"[38] expresses the danger the power of death possesses. Funeral expenses alone can pose a heavy burden upon family budgets, despite charitable gifts received from friends and relatives early in the mourning period. When male heads of household die, widows must struggle to meet the minimal needs of their families. Having little education and perhaps no marketable skills, they may be driven to seek employment outside the home for the first time in their lives. Survivors may have to move out of their apartment and share quarters with relatives, because they can no longer afford to pay rent and utilities on a drastically reduced income. Financial difficulties may force them to sell off valuable furnishings, or accept charity.[39]

The death of a wife means the loss of the family's chief caregiver, the organizer and executor of household chores. The loss of a child, of course, exacts a deep emotional toll on parents and siblings. If it is a son or an only son, the toll is especially hard on the mother, for it is often through her sons that she secures her marriage and enhances her status.[40] With the death of a daughter, she loses a companion and helpmate in her household responsibilities. Arguments over the division of the inheritance is another way in which death works to destroy domestic sacrality. In extreme cases, these arguments can lead to more death in the family.[41]

Death can appear and spread as a direct consequence of human actions, including the evil eye and witchcraft. It can also be caused by different kinds of evil spirits, such as the jinn, *ʿafrīt*s, and spirit-doubles (pl. *aqrān*[42]). In fact, death is the antithesis of domestic blessing, and a threat to the *ḥurma* of the house. This view is expressed in one woman's song of lamentation for her husband from the Delta city of Tanta.

The house *(dār)* is yours—you built it,
  but who told you to go and abandon it?
Whence can I bring you, O lion, to shelter me,
  lest the wild beasts outside throw me down?
Whence can I bring you, O lion, to protect me,
  lest the wild beasts outside devour me?[43]

In funerary rites, the dangerous situation in which the household has been placed by death is expressed publicly, with mixed feelings of grief, loss, guilt, and anger. Concomitantly, these same rites can serve as instruments for healing the breach in the family body, thus regenerating sacrality and blessing. In Egypt, as in many other parts of the world, funerary rites exhibit the importance of maintaining group solidarity. Individuals are discouraged from suffering their grief in private, apart from family, friends, and neighbors. Migrants from rural towns and villages establish special cooperative societies in the city to lend bereaved families moral and financial support.[44] When literate Egyptians pick up the daily paper, they usually turn first to the obituary pages, where death notices and announcements for funerary gatherings are posted. Usually the names of the deceased's relatives and their hometowns are given, so the reader knows to whom condolences should be extended.

Egyptians practice two distinct cycles of funerary rites: the *ganāza* (funeral) cycle, which focuses on the transference of the body of the deceased to the cemetery, and the *ḥidād* cycle (or "time of sorrow" *muddit il-ḥuzn),* which centers on mourning observances. We should bear in mind that the timing of these cycles is very different. Funerals usually take place within twenty-four hours of death, but not after dark. The ritual mourning period continues for up to a year, even longer in extreme cases. Observances take place during daylight and evening hours.[45]

The *ganāza* cycle has four major stages.

1. Ascent of the Soul (*tulūʿ ir-rūḥ*[46]). The dying person attempts minor ablutions, while the bereaved offer water and gather to help recite the testimony of faith *(shahāda)* and Quran verses. When the end comes, death is confirmed, windows in the room are opened, and the family begins to notify relatives, neighbors, friends.
2. Ritual cleansing *(ghusl)*. A washer is summoned. The deceased's body is placed on a mortuary table in a secluded part of the house, with the head tilted to right.[47] The washer, aided by a close relative of the deceased, removes the clothes from the body and

covers it with a sheet. The washer shaves (males) or depilates (females) the body, then gives the body thorough ablution with water (or water mixed with henna). The privates are covered with a white loin cloth *(izār)*, the sheet is removed, and the body is dressed and enshrouded. Testimony of faith and Quran are recited in presence of deceased.

3. Funeral Procession *(kharga* or *ganāza)*. This occurs after stages 1 and 2 are completed. The body is transferred from the house to the mosque on a bier carried by a cohort of men. Funerary prayer is performed at the mosque, with the body, placed in front of participants, facing Mecca. The body is transferred to the cemetery.
4. Burial *(dafna)*. The body is laid in the grave on its right side, facing Mecca. The shroud is loosened and cut or torn and the grave is sealed. The shaykh instructs the deceased in how to answer the angels of the grave (Munkar and Nakir), who will interrogate him that evening. The Quran is recited over the grave. Mourners distribute gifts (food, clothing, and coins) to the poor on behalf of the deceased, perform ablutions, and return home.

The *ḥidād* cycle consists of three chief stages.

1. First Three Days. This is the period of the most intense bereavement at the home of the deceased. The house is open to all condolers, with separate areas for males and females. A temporary pavilion may be set up in the street for male condolers and Quran recitation. The Quran is recited in the home, especially during the morning and evening hours. Taboos are observed with care.
2. Fortieth Day *(il-arbiᶜīn)*. This large gathering marks the end of weekly observances held on Thursdays and Fridays after a death. It is observed at the home of the deceased and in a temporary pavilion, if affordable. It includes Quran recitation, visits to the cemetery, and acts of charity. The bereaved family thanks condolers for their support, and taboos are relaxed.
3. One-Year Anniversary *(sanawiyya)*. This is the formal end of *ḥidād* cycle at the home of the bereaved. It includes Quran recitation, a feast, and visits to the cemetery.

Like the stages of the marriage cycle, the stages of funeral and mourning cycles are rather fluid. Islamic law requires cleansing and shrouding of the body. Cleansing is not performed, however, if the remains have been mutilated, or if the deceased is a martyr, a "denier," or a miscarried fetus. Funeral prayers, prompt burial, and proper decorum among the bereaved are other procedures that should be followed in accordance with religious law. Around these required procedures, however, the local culture has woven a more complex ritual fabric that depends on factors such as the nature of the death, the status of the deceased, and the social class of the bereaved. Obviously a person who dies unexpectedly in the street cannot be offered the same amount of comfort and support as someone who dies surrounded by close family members and friends. The mourning period for an infant is shorter than that of a youth or an adult. Families with moderate and high incomes are able to observe longer and more elaborate mourning periods than poor ones. Rural communities have burial and mourning practices that differ from region to region, and from those of townspeople.[48]

Social actions performed during both cycles profoundly affect the significance of the domestic space of the bereaved, especially in the house of the deceased. For example, in stages 1 and 2 of the *ganāza* cycle, people purify both the body of the deceased and the house. Connected with these actions is the idea that the soul of the deceased hovers near the body, and is reluctant to leave home. A widely circulated pamphlet on death and the afterlife, by the medieval scholar ᶜAbd al-Rahim b. Ahmad al-Qadi (fifth/eleventh century?), clearly expresses this belief.

> When the deceased is placed in the shroud and it is bound around [his feet], his soul exclaims, "By God, O washer! Do not enshroud my head until I see the faces of my family, children, and relatives! This is my last vision until resurrection day." [Then when the deceased is carried from his house *(dār)*, he exclaims, "By God, people, do not hasten with me that I might say good bye to my house, children, family, and property." Then he exclaims, "By God, people, I have left my wife, so do not harm her, and my children are orphans, so do not harm them. Indeed, today I leave my house and will not return to them ever again!"][49]

To help induce the "ascent of the soul," family members open windows in the house, and place the bedding and clothing of the deceased in open air. The room in which the person died then is fumigated with incense and sprinkled with water. On occasion, the family will sacrifice a sheep, goat, or calf when the bier crosses the threshold, and then smear the threshold with its blood. Then they distribute the meat to the needy, saying, "Let there be mercy and light for the soul of PN."[50] The desire of the soul to remain with its loved ones is strong, however, for during the procession to the mosque (stage 3), the pallbearers complain that the bier is pulling them back, or becoming too heavy for them to carry.

In the mourning cycle, the order of objects and behavior in the house are inverted to express the rupture caused by death. Ahmad Amin (1886–1954), an Egyptian intellectual from a conservative *baladi* family, noted the changes brought about by the death of his younger brother. First the house became a total chaos, then it "turned upside down into a place of bereavement *(maḥzana)*." For more than a year, sorrow burned inside him; it was so deep that even "the value of things for me became inverted." He also observed that the death had deeply affected his mother and father.[51]

As with wedding celebrations, the house of bereavement becomes a "space of appearance"; it is rearranged and opened to receive condolers (including strangers) during the mourning period. Some families reverse or remove household furnishings that have a high display value like mirrors, pictures, rugs, mats, and the bed of the deceased. Egyptians express the inverted appearance of the domestic order in songs of lamentation, such as the following one, which is delivered by a bereaved woman.

> I must throw a cloth over you, O house *(dār)* of him who has few heirs.
> You are destroyed, O house—you frighten passersby.
> I overturn the storage jar—that's the bereavement place of him who has few heirs.
> I overturn the storage jar—he has no son to receive condolences from people.
> I overturn the jar—that's the bereavement place of him who has few heirs.
> I overturn the jar—he has no son to receive condolences outside.[52]

This song mourns the loss of a man who has died without a son. It parallels the image of a destroyed house with that of an overturned storage jar, which is another sign of misfortune. The next song is for the loss of a wealthy head of household. Rather than portraying the condition of the whole house, it focuses specifically upon the room where visitors are received.

> The sitting room *(mandara)* mourns for its companions.
> The coffee is poured and its carpets folded up.
> The chair weeps[53] inside the sitting room:
> "O servants of God! He went on a long errand."
> Say, "O sitting room, with your chandelier and water pipe;
> Tomorrow he will come and distribute charitable gifts."[54]

This lamentation depicts the sitting room in a condition opposite to that in which it should normally be found. The master is absent, the room is sorrowful, its colorful floor coverings have been removed. As an expression of consolation, the last lines seem to deny the finality of death. They even suggest the return of the deceased, which conforms to the widely held Egyptian belief in receiving visits from dead relatives.[55] On the other hand, they might be indicating simply that a new master will come to fill the place of the old one.

During the mourning period in *baladi* households, the most common inversions that occur are behavioral. The bereaved should abstain from sexual relations.[56] Female mourners, especially wives and daughters of dead males, should avoid ostentation. Normally, younger women wear colorful clothing at home, but, during the *ḥidād* cycle, they are expected to wear black garments at all times. Men neglect their appearance, especially by not shaving or cutting their hair during the first days of mourning (stage 1). Also in these first days, the immediate family of the deceased is not supposed to prepare meals; their neighbors send plates of food for them. Sweets, which Egyptians love to eat and offer to their guests, are forbidden; instead, the bereaved offer condolers unsweetened black coffee and cigarettes.

All expressions of joy are repressed, entertainments are frowned upon, and televisions and radios should remain turned off, except for Quran recitation programs. Such self-imposed limitations extend to the households of neighbors and relatives on both the husband's and wife's sides of the family, although they are not as strictly observed. Any wedding activities planned by the family of the bereaved are cancelled during the year of mourning. If weddings must be conducted, they occur after the fortieth day, greatly curtailed, and in a hushed atmosphere. Likewise, major Islamic holidays pass without the usual feasting and ostentation. They become days of remembrance.

In sum, when death transgresses the limits of domestic sacrality, Egyptians observe a series of taboos that express their feelings of violation. By doing so, they labor to prevent chaos from reigning in the house. Through the inversion of the domestic order, they exhibit the breach in the corporate identity of the family caused by death. Nonetheless, the corporate solidarity exhibited during the mourning period will hopefully bring about restoration of domestic sacrality and blessing.

Songs of lamentation are but one level of discourse practiced during the *ganāza* and *ḥidād* ritual cycles. As in the cycle of marriage celebrations, death creates a situation where people feel it necessary to recite the Quran, utter religious statements, and engage in formal verbal exchanges with each other. Domestic space provides the chief scene for these recitations and exchanges.[57]

Recitations from the Quran consist of readings of particular chapters (especially the *Fatḥa* and 36 *Yā Sīn*[58]), and of the entire book.[59] Aside from funerary prayers performed in stage 3 of the *ganāza* cycle, none of these recitations is required by religious law. We see instead an example of how a canonical religious text is appropriated and reformulated by the people.

The Quran readings are performed by specialists hired for the occasion, by the washers, and by family members. Since the 1960s, families have simply turned their radio dials to the Cairo Quran station throughout the mourning period. Cassette recordings of famous reciters have been used on such occasions since the 1970s. Sometimes bereaved families place microphones on their balconies so that recitations can be broadcast to the neighborhood during the *ḥidād* cycle.

Ritual expressions such as the testimony of faith, the *basmala,* and the ninety-nine names of God are repeated during both cycles. Ideally, the testimony of faith should be the last words to pass the lips of a dying person. During the *ganāza* cycle, people deliver special invocations for the dead and themselves, which mix quranic statements with extra-quranic ones. The following invocation is recited at the moment of a man's death: "In the name of God and in accordance with the religion of God's Prophet. O God, forgive him, and elevate him among the rightly guided. Let his descendants be victorious. And forgive us and him, O lord of the worlds. Widen his grave for him, and illuminate it."[60] Such declarations at moments of extreme pain and sorrow seek to place the dead and his heirs in the best framework possible. Already, they anticipate the restoration of domestic sacrality.

People also say, "There is no power or strength except through God," a statement usually made in times of distress. In their condolences, they ask that the remainder of the dead person's life be added to that of the survivors. People can say to the bereaved, "Eternity *(dawām)* is God's," "That's the way the world is," or "May God make your reward great." The customary response to these expressions of sympathy is, "May God reward your effort."

In the middle and upper strata of the *baladi* subculture, growing emphasis is being placed on the use of Quran recitation and formulaic sayings at the expense of lamentation songs and ritualized wailing. Men in particular act to displace what they consider to be the excessive emotions of the women with Quran recitation and heavy silence. In part, this gives families a way of representing themselves as superior to other *baladi* and *rīfi* households. On the other hand, it has roots in older ideas, such as those reflected in al-Qadi's collection of accounts about death and the afterlife.

> It is said that when a person dies and crying (people) gather in his house, the angel of death stands at the doorway and says to the criers, "By God, I

have not foreshortened the life or the fortune of a single one of you! I am at (God's) command. If (you weep) because of the dead man, he has been subdued. If it is because of God Almighty, then you are ignorant of God Almighty. By God, I shall surely return to you again and again![61]

At several points in the foregoing discussion, I have suggested that death and mourning ceremonies share certain structural similarities with the cycle of marriage ceremonies. Quran recitations, the exchange of formulaic statements, and the singing of songs are among them. With the removal of body hair, the bathing, and the use of henna, the preparation of the body for burial resembles the preparation of a bride or groom for marriage. During each of the major cycles, houses are opened to nearly everyone, and the internal arrangements are altered to accommodate them. The same pavilions are erected in the streets to accommodate male guests. When a boy or girl dies unmarried, without having "entered a world," the lamentations are replete with references to marriage ceremonies. Furthermore, weddings are aimed at constituting a house; funerals and mourning customs, while acknowledging rupture and grief, are aimed at reconstituting it.

There is a complementarity shared by these cycles, too. Marriage entails "entering a world" *(dukhla),* while death entails "leaving" one *(kharga).* Moreover, marriages should be carefully arranged occasions that look spontaneous; funerals are often spontaneous occasions that should look carefully planned.

We have seen in earlier chapters that in written discourse and in the building of tombs, Muslims, including Egyptian Muslims, have regarded the grave as a kind of domestic space. To what extent do Egyptians today consider graves and cemeteries to be domestic spaces, and for whom?

Egyptians, like other people, have ambiguous feelings toward cemeteries. On the one hand, they designate them with terms such as *turab, qarāfa,* or *gabbāna.* These names convey notions of dirt, loathing, and fear.[62] Egyptian oral traditions are replete with reports and stories about terrible things that have happened to people when they pass by graveyards or dare to go through them at night. In village Egypt, parents warn children against wandering among the tombs. When the government built housing projects near Cairo's southern cemetery in the late 1950s, families were wary about moving in because of the harmful forces to which they feared they would become vulnerable.

On the other hand, the cemeteries of Cairo have traditionally been places for holiday picnics and festivities. Mamluk emirs built religious colleges, hostels, and sufi convents there among the tombs. Today,

Cairo's cemeteries have actually become full-fledged residential neighborhoods (see frontispiece). It is true that many residential neighborhoods in Cairo proper still have shrines containing the remains of saints, but in the case of the cemeteries, the situation is reversed. The quick have taken up residence with the dead in greater numbers than ever before.

Contributing to the growth of this phenomenon in recent centuries has been the practice of building family tombs that resemble old-style houses. Surrounded by high walls, these mausoleums stand one or two stories above ground and contain living quarters, open courts, and gardens. Below ground, the bodies of the dead are laid to rest in common vaults. Reflecting the norms for segregation of the sexes in the mundane world, men are buried together on the right side of the crypt and women on the left. Above ground, the living family gathers on Thursdays, Fridays, and holidays to remember the dead, distribute food to the poor, and share meals together. To a great extent, the family mausoleum functions as a kind of domestic space, where past and present generations can be united. It is called a *ḥūsh*, a term that otherwise refers to a courtyard, or to a kind of tenement building organized around such a courtyard.

In the past, families hired caretakers who lived in the mausoleums. Eventually the caretakers were joined by their own families. When Cairo was faced with severe housing shortages in the 1960s and 1970s due to urban population growth, immigration of people from the countryside, and refugees coming from war-torn settlements near the Suez Canal, the tombs began to serve as houses for squatters who were unable to acquire other quarters. The government failed to curtail this process. The result has been the creation of residential districts among the tombs, with public utilities, schools, shops, and police stations to serve the hundreds of thousands of people who now live there.

If tombs are in fact considered to be a form of domestic space by Egyptians, then we should expect to find people making efforts to relate to the dead in ways analogous to those used to relate to the living. This is most obviously the case with visitation *(ziyāra)* customs. Normally, families, neighbors, and friends establish and maintain relations with each other by exchanging visits and presenting small gifts. This is especially true during holidays. Likewise, people visit and converse with the dead during holiday excursions to the cemeteries. Unless the dead person is a saint who can provide *baraka* to guests, he or she is unable to fulfill the duties of hospitality in the same way as a living person. Instead, members of the dead person's family, especially the women, take gifts of food with them to the cemeteries to distribute to the people they meet there on behalf of the dead. It makes no difference whether their dead are buried in grand mausoleums, or in modest individual graves. The atmosphere among the tombs is quite gay, as it is in most *baladi* Egyptian households during holidays.

Given the importance attached to the principle of reciprocity in Egyptian social relationships, we also find strong evidence for the belief that the dead make return visits to their families. Appearing to relatives in dreams and visions, they usually ask for prayers, or request that food be distributed to the unfortunate on their behalf. The medieval scholar al-Qadi, in a popular pamphlet still sold in Cairo, provides an account of this subject that he attributes to Ibn ʿAbbas, one of the Prophet's companions:

> On a feast day, ʿAshura, the first Friday of Rajab, the eve of the middle of Shaʿban, the Night of Power (at the end of Ramadan), and Thursday evening the souls of the dead leave their graves and stand at the doors of their houses *(buyūt)*. They say, "Have mercy on us this blessed eve by giving charitable gifts [or a bite to eat. We need it. . . .] Remember us by reciting the *Fātiḥa* on this blessed eve.
>
> ["Is there anyone who will ask that God have mercy on us? Will anyone remember our absence? O you who live in our houses (*dūr*)! You who have married our women! You who reside in our roomiest palaces, while we are now in our narrowest graves! O you who have divided our property! You who disparage our orphans! Do any of you remember our absence and poverty? . . . The dead have no recompense in the grave. Do not forget us—(offer) a morsel of your bread or (say) a prayer, for we will always need you."]
>
> If the dead obtain charitable gifts and prayers from them, they return (to their graves) happy and joyful. If they obtain nothing, they return sad and hopeless because of them.[63]

This kind of statement views the situation of the living as more fortunate than that of the dead. Yet, by inventing a discourse of the dead, it ventures to remind the living of their obligations towards them. The implication is that if the living act the right way and say the correct things, they can influence the quality of "life" for the dead in their graves. Just as they can establish sacrality in their own houses through action and speech, they can do the same for the houses of the dead.

Again, al-Qadi's account is instructive on this point:

> [It is said that every day the grave exclaims five times: "I am the house *(bayt)* of solitude,] so let reciting the Quran keep me company. I am the house of darkness, so illuminate me with evening prayers. I am the house of dirt, so put a floor covering on me—that is, righteous deeds. I am the house of vipers, so carry the antidote—that is, (say) "In the name of God, most

سكان المقابر

الزوج ـ زى ما عشنا طول عمرنا فى طربه ..

الاصول لما نموت يدفنونا فى شــــقة ..!

Figure 7. Cemetery Dwellers. Husband: "Since we've lived all our lives in a tomb, it's only proper that they bury us in an apartment when we die" (from *Akhbār al-yawm* [Cairo], 30 December 1978).

compassionate and merciful" [and shed tears]. I am the house of interrogation by Munkar and Nakir, so say often as you walk above me, "There is no god but God, Muhammad is God's messenger."[64]

In this text the grave, speaking on behalf of Islamic norms, advises the living how they can improve the quality of their existence in the afterlife until Judgment Day arrives. They should learn that they can transform the grave into a domestic space by correct speech and action in life. Concomitantly, the text reflects the ambiguities of death; it blurs the distinctions between the grave and the house, the dead and the living. Figure 7 depicts these ambiguities in a light-hearted manner, demonstrating that they are topics of contemporary social commentary in Egypt.

INTERNAL ARRANGEMENTS

In marriage the sacrality of Egyptian Muslim houses is established. With divorce, it is ended. Death brings about its inversion and reconstitution. But sacrality also depends upon the organization of space within the house, space that is filled with furnishings that have qualitative value for its inhabitants. These furnishings are primarily those assembled by husband and wife on the occasion of their marriage, supplemented by religious objects, mementos of holidays, births, and other marriages, and consumer goods acquired since the wedding. Together, these items form the symbolic capital of the house; they are material signs of blessing.

In apartments with three or more rooms, that is, in the apartments of middle- and upper-class Egyptians, the most important space of appearance for these objects is in the sitting room (*ṣalūn*, or *ūdit il-gulūs*[65]). This is the area of the house where outsiders (guests), especially males, are admitted most readily. To get an idea of ways in which this space can be arranged, it is best to consider several concrete examples.

Faruq, a clerk in a foreign oil company, and his family fled to Cairo from Suez City, their hometown, to escape the war of attrition between Egypt and Israel that destroyed the area around the Suez Canal in the years following the 1967 war. They succeeded in finding a new five-room (and one-bath) apartment in Madinat Nasr, a district located in the corridor of new middle-class housing that extends to the northeast of downtown Cairo. Their *ṣalūn* is furnished with a gilded sofa, coffee table, and chairs in the modish (some might say garish) *baladi* adaptation of French rococo furniture *(istīl)*. On the coffee table, in the center of the room, is a copy of the Quran encased in a green velvet box. Behind the sofa on the south wall, the direction of Mecca, Faruq has hung a framed color photograph of the Kaᶜba. He decorated the west wall with a framed calligraphic rendering of the formula "God, mighty and glorious is he!"[66] The east wall has a framed microprint poster of the entire text of the Quran, featuring the Throne Verse (2 *Baqara* 255) in large print along the margins. It is flanked by a wedding photo of Faruq and his wife in European-style dress on the right, and by a portrait of the wife alone on the left. In the northeast corner of the room, the family is keeping large candles for use in their daughter's *dukhla* procession, which is to be held during the next Feast of Sacrifice. A white sheepskin covers part of the floor at the entrance to the room. This is a memento from the sheep the family slaughtered during a previous feast day.

When reconstruction began in the Suez area after the 1973 war, Faruq became qualified for one of the new apartments built in Suez City. The family's main residence in Cairo is being kept because of his job and his two sons' education at ᶜAyn Shams University. But slowly he and his wife have begun to furnish their new unit in Suez. It has a much smaller, more modest sitting room, conjoined to the kitchen. It is furnished in a Euramerican style. Nonetheless, Faruq has already hung a photograph of himself, taken while he was on the Hajj. It shows him dressed in pilgrim's garb, standing before the mosque-tomb of the Prophet in Medina.

Faruq and his wife have fashioned the conventional areas in their houses for receiving guests into places for displaying Euramerican symbols of prosperity and pan-Islamic symbols, together with mementos of key events in their own lives. In doing so, they disclose the sacrality of their domestic spaces, and the blessings of family life to all people invited into their home.

Hasan, a secondary school teacher from al-Azhar University, and his family live in a large, pre-1950s European-style building in ʿAbbasiyya, Cairo. The *ṣalūn* of his six-room (and two-bath) apartment is about the same size as the one in Faruq's Madinat Nasr residence (c. 100–120 square feet). It, too, has rococo-style furniture. The only example of religious decoration, however, is a framed rendering of "God" in Arabic calligraphy. There are also photographs of Hasan from his student days wearing a tarboosh, of his oldest son, and of his oldest daughter and her husband on their wedding day.

Hasan's son-in-law, a young, college-educated government agronomist, uses religious symbols more freely in the sitting room of his apartment in Zaytun, a new lower middle-class suburb north of downtown Cairo. There, on a bookshelf, he has placed a photograph of the Prophet's mosque-tomb, along with a ceramic plate depicting the landmarks of Mecca, a copy of the Quran, and a modern Quran commentary. He has not actually been on the Hajj, but he hopes to. With the help of the Quran commentary, he explores the relation between modern scientific ideas and quranic statements. Concomitantly, he is strongly convinced in the ability of the Quran to overpower malevolent forces.

My fourth example is the sitting room in Fatma's house. Fatma lives together with her father (a house painter), mother (a midwife), sister, and two brothers in a large public housing project built during the late 1950s near Cairo's southern cemetery. Her apartment has three small rooms, a kitchen, and a bath. On holidays and when guests are expected, her teenage brother's bedroom is converted into a sitting room. As such, it is modestly furnished with a gayly colored *baladi*-style couch, a small table, and a few wooden chairs. Photographs of family members are displayed on the walls, but the only item related to their religious belief is a collage of mosque pictures that serves as a background for her brother's portrait. Her parents have placed a talisman against the evil eye on their bedroom door, which can be seen by guests on their way into the sitting room. Outside, in the corner of a balcony, they have hung a braid of garlic for the same purpose.

Fatma's family is not extremely pious in the sense of careful adherence to religious obligations such as performing prescribed prayers and fasting, or memorizing and reciting the Quran. They criticize conservative Muslim groups, whom they call "Sunnis," for being too strict and serious. They express their own religiosity by making weekly visits to saint shrines and attending *mūlid*s in their seasons. Fatma's older brother has a form of epilepsy, and seems to enjoy the therapy provided by the *dhikrs* and dances that occur at the shrines. As a consequence of his affliction, he is considered by some to be a holy man himself. So instead of placing quranic verses or pictures of Mecca and Medina on the walls, the family employs talismans to repel evil. Before noon on Fridays, Fatma and her mother clean and fumigate the apartment with incense to gain God's favor. After all, according to Fatma, Friday midday is when God opens the heavens to hear people's petitions. This is when she feels that her home is most visible to God.

The sitting room arrangements in the houses of Faruq, Hasan, and Hasan's son-in-law on the one hand, and Fatma on the other exemplify the two main varieties found in *baladi* households. The former show the appropriation of symbols of Euramerican material culture together with Islamic symbols and family mementos to make domestic space a quality space. In *afrangi* sitting rooms, Euramerican decor dominates, and Islamic symbols are completely absent. If present in the dwelling at all, they are located in the bedroom or possibly in the family room. With sitting rooms such as Fatma's, order and cleanliness are important, but simplicity is the determining principle in the choice of furnishings and religious symbols. The sacrality of their home is based more on things done than on things shown.

The existence of a space of appearance in the house depends on the presence of spaces that do not normally appear to guests. In apartments with three or more rooms, this non-visible space usually consists of bedrooms, family rooms, bathrooms, and kitchens. Bedrooms are the localities of intimacy, for intercourse between man and wife, childbirth, confinement, rest during illness, and death.[67] Girls store their trousseaus in bedrooms until the *dukhla* can be arranged. If the house has a family room *(maʿīsha)*, it is used by adults and children for informal gatherings and entertainments. Televisions are usually kept in this area.

Of all the rooms in an apartment, the bathroom is the one that has the most negative qualities. Obviously it is a place for cleansing, but it is also connected with bodily functions and substances that produce ritual impurity. It is forbidden to take the Quran or anything else with Arabic writing on it into the bathroom, for fear that it will cause God's name to be sullied. As a sacred text, the Quran must always be honored, and kept away from impurities. Some *baladi* and *rīfi* Egyptians continue to believe that bathing and toilet areas are the favorite haunts of jinn. Since protecting angels will not enter with a person, it is necessary for her or him to take special protective measures to appease the jinn, or at least keep them at bay, before entering.

The kitchen area is one of the chief domestic work places for women. It, too, is normally off-limits to male guests. The family eats their meals here, squatting around a low round table if they are poor, or at a dining table with chairs if they have enough room and can afford it. Male guests, on the other hand, are usually served food and drink in the sitting room. Unless the family wishes a daughter to be seen by a suitor, male members of the family serve male guests from the kitchen. Younger sons usually have this duty.

Many Muslims practice the "remembrance of God" in their homes by reciting the Quran themselves, or listening to it on their cassette players and radios. The melodic chanting, which carries throughout the apartment from the bedroom, is believed to bring blessing and dispel malevolent forces.[68] It also consoles people suffering from illness or the painful loss of a loved one. In rural areas, as in cities prior to the introduction of radios and cassette players, Quran reciters make daily rounds from house to house, earning a small wage for their services.

Prayers, too, are often performed at home. Under normal conditions, Egyptian Muslims pray in non-visible parts of their houses, that is, in bedrooms and family rooms. Sitting rooms are rarely used for this purpose. The home is especially a prayer place for women and small children, in accordance with guidelines set forth in the Quran and Sunna. Some pious householders convert their own apartments into mosques, and require family and guests to remove their shoes at the door.[69] Others reserve an area of their apartment building to serve as a mosque, even going so far as to erect a makeshift minaret on the roof. Under any of these conditions, the bathroom provides the ablution water and a suitable area for purifications.

Islam is experienced intimately as part of a person's domestic life. What she or he knows about it is intertwined with childhood memories of the family and the house. For most Egyptians, the knowledge imparted by formal religious instruction and institutions only comes after a long period of preparation at home. Ahmad Amin's recollections of his early life in an old Cairo *baladi* neighborhood are particularly informative in this regard:

> Religious feeling pervaded the house. My father prayed at the proper times, and often read the Quran mornings and evenings. He would get up at dawn to pray and supplicate, and he often read Quran commentaries and the hadiths. He often mentioned death, and found little to value in mundane life and its enticements. He told stories about the virtuous founders (of Islam), their deeds, and their devotion to the duties of worship. He gave alms, especially to his relatives. My mother joined him in making the Hajj. Moreover, he gave his children a religious upbringing. He would awaken them at dawn to pray, and he monitored their other daily prayers, asking them about when and where they prayed. My mother prayed from time to time. And all of us celebrated Ramadan and its fast. In sum, if you opened the door to our house, you would have smelled the aroma of religion, fragrant and pure.[70]

As we have seen, marriage and death provide ceremonial occasions when the house is open to outsiders. They require special arrangements to be made in the array of objects in the house. At other times, during the normal flow of visitations, the everyday organization of domestic space, with its division into visible and non-visible areas, contributes to the system of controls that regulates the conduct of guests.

Visitors who are not close relatives should knock politely at the door, or ring the bell, then stand back from it. This is a gesture of respect, and safeguards the visitor from obtaining an accidental glimpse of the family inside. Egyptian Muslims are quite aware of quranic rulings and hadiths about the importance of not looking into houses, and asking permission before entering. When they enter, they should do so with the right foot first, especially if it is a first visit.

Once a person is admitted, a system of rules goes into effect to uphold domestic sacrality. Female guests are usually led to non-visible parts of the house. If males are located near the entrance, or in the hallway, women will be sure to avert their faces or veil them to avoid direct eye contact with any men who might be at home. As mentioned earlier, women should never enter another apartment unless a woman is present. Likewise, male guests cannot be admitted unless a male member of the household is present. When males receive permission to enter, they are escorted into the sitting room, which is kept in reserve for such occasions. Prepubescent boys and girls are relatively free to move inside and outside the apartment, and between its visible and non-visible areas. They are governed by rules of respect for adult authorities, rather than by gender-based codes.

Entry into a house should also entail an exchange of formulaic greetings and inquiries about each other's health and kin. When a person serves as host, to maintain the reputation of himself and his house, he is obliged to offer his guests food, drink, and cigarettes. The food offered can range from sweet pastries and fruits to complete meals, depending on the occasion. Drinks include fruit juice, soda, or heavily sugared hot tea. Coffee, because it is expensive, is seldom offered.

The exchanges of verbal formulas between host and guests after the consumption of food and drink, and at the end of the visit express concepts of domestic blessing and honor. For example, when a guest finishes drinking or eating, the host should exclaim, "Good health!" The guest should say, "May your table always be full!" "May God make your house prosperous!" or a similar expression. To this, the host might respond with, "May you live forever!" "Eat with pleasure and good health!" or a simple "Thank you."[71] A host expresses his or her appreciation to guests for their visit by saying, "You have honored *(sharraft)* our house!" "You have illumined our house!" "You have adorned our house!" "You have brought blessing *(baraka)* to the house!" "The Prophet has visited us!" or simply, "You have been good company!" The guest should then choose an appropriate response, depending upon what the host said initially.

Families living in one-room apartments,[72] or crowded into a room with another family, are not able to organize and furnish their domestic spaces as elaborately as those living in larger units. Nevertheless, they still have the capacity to make quality spaces of them. To create a space of appearance within a single room, they can begin by simply setting up a curtain so that one area of the room can remain non-visible. To avoid interaction between the sexes, women can arrange to visit each other while men are at work. Men arrange to meet at the cafe, the mosque, or in a common area on the ground floor of a residential building called the *salāmlik*. To enhance blessing or keep away misfortune, the family purchases inexpensive copies of the Quran, posters and plastic plates imprinted with religious sayings and pictures of religious buildings at local kiosks and shops, especially in the vicinity of popular mosques and shrines. They can also buy amulets for protecting houses and their occupants. Sometimes these are custom-made for them by special shaykhs who claim mastery over the secrets of the spirits. At home, plates, posters, and amulets are placed by doorways, windows, balconies, beds, on shelves, and, as I have noted, on the walls of the sitting room. Together with Quran recitation from the radio or cassette player, these items help sanctify even the humblest dwellings.

ESTRANGEMENTS

What happens when domestic sacrality is violated, or is believed to have been violated? As we have seen, if a serious violation occurs, and it is blamed on the wife, divorce is one possibility. If violation occurs in the form of death, then householders have recourse to funerary and mourning cycles to restore the house to good health. If evil or extreme poverty relentlessly erode domestic sacrality, God, the Prophet, the saints, and apotropaic magic can be called upon to dispel it.

Affronts to domestic sacrality by outsiders of the same social status as the offended family can be rebuffed with verbal insults, curses, and even threats and physical force. For example, when one householder felt that a neighbor who liked to read the newspaper by the window was really trying to ogle his young daughters in the apartment below, he confronted him with warnings and threats. In such instances, greetings, visitations and gift-giving relations between the households usually cease until the violation has been redressed. The violated household can take more forceful measures if it feels that it is of higher status than the offenders. Hence, when a clamorous crowd of poor people, waiting for charitable donations of fabric from a local merchant at the end of Ramadan, loitered in the courtyard of an apartment building in downtown Cairo, the building owners dumped buckets of water on them from their third floor window.

More corrosive affronts to domestic sacrality than these confront Egyptians today. An acute housing shortage means that more and more people have to live in less space. Although government and private interests have undertaken low-income housing projects, these are not enough to assuage the demand for dwelling space. Corrupt dealings among contractors and government officials result in the use of substandard building materials, which too often leads to the collapse of new buildings within several months or years of completion. High demand for fewer units leads owners to demand illegal key money and high monthly rents. Some private sector apartment complexes have gone up in recent years that will only accept hard foreign currency for rent, not Egyptian money. Each of these developments is harmful to all but a few Egyptians. Among the ironies in these developments, however, is that one of the foremost signs of domestic prosperity, having many children, is a leading factor in the deterioration of the quality of life at home and in society at large.

There are also situations where the desires of the government and private investors come into conflict with the desires of ordinary Egyptians for housing and a source of livelihood. When this happens, the government usually has its way, at least in the short run.

Take, for example the confrontation that occurred between the government and the inhabitants of ʿIshash Turguman (Dragoman Shanties) and ᶜArab il-Muhammadi. These were two *baladi* working-class neighborhoods located in the center of Cairo on the east bank of the Nile, near the headquarters of *al-Ahrām*, the semi-official Egyptian daily.

According to a study conducted by the Cairo governorate in the late seventies,[73] ᶜIshash Turguman was inhabited by 5,351 families, comprising 24,000 individuals. The population density of the quarter reached nearly 600,000 per square mile in 1979.[74] (The density for Cairo as a whole is now about 137,255 per square mile.[75]) A full 63 percent of the families lived in one- and two-room apartments. Another 31 percent inhabited shacks in stairwells, basements, and on rooftops. Most households had neither kitchens (75 percent) nor private bathrooms (78 percent). Although ᶜArab il-Muhammadi was smaller in size, it had proportional numbers and similar living arrangements.

Over the objections of local residents and merchants, President Sadat initiated an urban renewal project in October 1979 that was aimed at replacing the two neighborhoods with high-rise office buildings for commercial, touristic, and administrative functions. None of the local people was given a share in the development. Instead, the government promised compensation for the loss of their homes and businesses, which included new housing in iz-Zawiya il-Hamra and ᶜAyn Shams, districts situated about an hour by bus from downtown. The removal of the population from ᶜIshash Turguman and ᶜArab il-Muhammadi was completed early in 1981.

There were at least two major problems with the compensation offered to the people: first, it could not replace the destroyed social and commercial networks that had taken years to develop; and second, not enough new apartments were available for all the families being relocated. By my estimate (admittedly based on partial evidence), 7,000 families from the two neighborhoods were supposed to be housed in some 2,465 new apartments.

For Sadat and the circle of contractors that formed around him, ᶜIshash Turguman and ᶜArab il-Muhammadi were both eyesores that had to be removed and an opportunity for high profit to be seized. Defending himself against critics after touring the new housing project built for the relocated families, Sadat proclaimed, "I was really pleased to see happiness in the faces of the new residents. They had left their shacks and now lived in healthy houses in an area that was rebuilt in accordance with the modern system."[76] Modern system indeed.

Relocated families felt that they had been deprived of their own "native land" and mistreated, that the sacrality of their homes had been violated by the government. In a follow-up study, one Egyptian sociologist has concluded, "The implementation of the relocation program completely disregarded the interests of the people. . . . (It) did not follow a well-defined or organized plan and the consequent situation has been one where the level of crowding is very high in the new environment."[77]

For thirty years or more native Cairenes and immigrants from Upper Egypt had been appropriating houses for themselves in this urban neighborhood on the Nile. Spurred by a rise in urban land values and a policy of pro-Euramerican state capitalism, the Sadat government, in power for only ten years, moved to appropriate this district for the benefit of a comparatively small group of Egyptians and foreign investors. Unfortunately, government appropriation contributed to the estrangement of tens of thousands of *baladi* Egyptians from their homes. Perhaps conditions in their new houses were not much better than they had been in their former ones, but even if they were slightly better, the people still had to live with the memory of the insulting treatment they received from the state, compounded by additional economic hardships. Their relocation was not easily forgotten.

In regard to domestic sacrality, what have Egyptians done when confronted with gross violations caused by deteriorating housing conditions, with critical housing shortages that clash directly with norms requiring young couples to acquire a house before they marry, and with heavy-handed or corrupt state appropriation of their houses? One response has been to continue attributing positive value to domestic space according to the principles of sacrality and the methods for enhancing blessing and fending off misfortune. This implies a somewhat myopic point of view that cannot survive for long under current conditions, except among people who already live under favorable conditions, or who are able to benefit from a declining reserve of opportunities.

Another response involves the adoption of a nihilistic attitude toward society, government, and family life. Unni Wikan has concluded that this is what has been occurring in the poorer sections of Cairo since the late 1960s. Egyptian social scientists have arrived at a similar conclusion as a result of statistical surveys conducted during the 1970s. In 1977, when asked to characterize social life in Egypt, a sample of educated urban dwellers and villagers chose by large margins (85.67 percent among villagers) in favor of dictums such as "each unto himself" and "neither does a brother help his brother, nor a son his father."[78] Students in a school for social workers, interviewed in 1971, agreed by high percentages with "proverbs expressing the attitude that relations with people in general, as well as with relatives, are a source of trouble and that people are hostile and harming to each other."[79]

Statistical surveys are vulnerable to distortions caused by the subjective conditions of the surveyor, the people interviewed, and the interpreter of the results. Another means of discerning feelings of social alienation is to look to contemporary Egyptian literature. In a study of Islamic elements in Egyptian fiction published during the 1970s and early 1980s, Rivka Yadlin draws attention to Salah ʿAbd al-Sayyid's short story, "The Foreigner."[80] The story portrays the sorry fate of a peasant householder who flaunts parochial custom by marrying his daughter off to a wealthy Arab stranger. This marriage leads to the invasion of his house by foreign luxury goods, and an ill-founded material prosperity that alienates the peasant from his land, kin, and neighbors. When he demolishes his traditional village house at his wife's instigation and replaces it with a new one, he realizes how different he has become from other people in the village. Then, when he discovers that his wife has allowed her *ḥurma* to be violated first by a neighbor, then by the stranger (his own son-in-law), instead of avenging family honor, he retreats to the Quran and the village mosque. At the end of the story, the peasant's nude corpse is discovered in the middle of the mosque, the torn leather cover of a Quran clutched in his hand. Had he committed suicide, or had he been murdered? Had God brought him to this end for allowing his domestic order to be violated? Or is the author indicating the futility of seeking refuge in religion in response to the invasion of corrupting foreign goods and ideas? Readers are left to decide the answers for themselves.

Fathi Ghanim's novel, *al-Afyāl,* tells the story of a troubled middle-class Egyptian who evicts his teenage son on the eve of the Feast of Sacrifice, a religious holiday that is supposed to affirm family and communal solidarity.[81] The boy had accused his parents of denying their religion *(kufr).* Father failed to pray, and mother displayed her body immorally. This physical fragmentation of the family, as depicted by Ghanim, had been precipitated by several years of growing disaffection between the parents, which had not escaped their son's notice.

> Hasan lost respect for his father and mother after losing his respect for his school and teachers. In his eyes, they had all failed. They had all declared in no uncertain terms their inability to deal with each other as human beings. Brother intentionally cuts off brother. Classmate intentionally cuts off classmate. Husband and father scolds wife and mother. Mother and wife declares her rejection and lack of respect for father and husband.[82]

Driven from his home, Hasan joins a militant Islamic organization and is imprisoned for plotting against the government. When his father finally locates him and attempts to convince him to come back, the youth decides to remain loyal to his group rather than rejoin his natal family. In fact, Hasan confesses to him, "Prison is dearer to me than that to which you beckon me."

This story points to a third response to the violation of domestic sacrality: the rise of militant Islamic organizations, whose chief goal is to create a morally just society in accordance with Islamic law, the *Shariᶜa*. The key components of their program are the reconstitution of the state on the one hand, and domestic life on the other. As a matter of fact, members of these activist groups, many of whom have *baladi* and *rifi* roots, maintain that the Islamization of one entails the Islamization of the other. The current regime and society are corrupt in their eyes, just as Meccan society was corrupt in the era of ignorance before the historical rise of Islam.[83] They assert that the state's form of Islam is a distortion of true religion; they sometimes refer to it as "American Islam."

The organization of militant Islamic groups is constructed more around the idiom of the family than that of a political party. Following the example of the old Muslim Brotherhood (founded in 1928), they refer to themselves in fictive kinship terms; they are brothers and sisters to each other. They use the term *usra* "family" to designate branches operating on university campuses. These fictive terms tend to be reinforced by actual kinship relations. The groups include members from the same families, and intermarriage is encouraged among members.[84]

The domestic idiom of these groups carries over to their appropriation and use of physical dwelling places. Prior to the eradication of the so-called Renunciation and Emigration Group *(it-takfīr wi'l-higra)* by the Egyptian government in 1977, its youthful male and female members lived as married couples in furnished flats in Cairo. Several couples would crowd together to share a single room in such flats, but they affected privacy by hanging curtains where needed. Furnished flats have comparatively high rents, but require no key money, so they are easier to acquire. To cover the rents, group households relied on contributions from members working abroad in Saudi Arabia and Kuwait. Some hoped that eventually they would be able to migrate to marginal land outside Cairo to create a utopian community of believers, in imitation of the emigration of Muhammad and his followers from Mecca to Medina.[85]

Leading members of another militant group, known as the *Jihad,* appear to have taken the desire to create a pure space for true believers and their women one step further. They covered the windows of their flats with thick curtains, made female relatives conceal themselves from neighbors and the public at large, and obliged them not to watch television. Women could only go outside with the permission of their husbands or close male relatives. To mix with society at large was to become vulnerable to its corruption. Some women avoided drying the laundry in open air like other Egyptians, because this was a form of exposing one's privates to public view, which is condemned by the Quran (24 *Nūr* 30–31). One of the leaders refused to admit outsiders into his home, and wrote outside his door the Quran verse: "O you who believe! Do not enter houses other than your own" (24 *Nūr* 27).[86]

The domestic order created by militant groups such as the *Jihad* is one that stands against relations with the outside world. It signifies a household sacrality that emphasizes internal purity and non-visibility rather than hospitality and a balance between visibility and non-visibility. This attitude may be in conformity with extreme Wahhabi and Orientalist views of Arab Islamic domestic space, but it is contrary to the ideas and practices of most *baladi* Egyptian Muslims.

I should mention one other characteristic of these groups. Because they consider the state to be corrupt, they refuse to attend mosques financed by the state. Instead, they go to small, private mosques, or they use their homes as mosques. House-mosques can evade government surveillance more readily than other kinds. The situation is not unlike that of the first Muslims, who met in private homes in Mecca, then emigrated with Muhammad to Medina, whence they waged their battle against the forces of ignorance, immorality, and false religion.

The contradiction between the desire to achieve or maintain domestic sacrality and the actualities of housing in Egypt have contributed to the growth of the militant groups. Membership in them offers individuals opportunities for finding suitable marriage partners and acquiring places to live. It also gives them the feeling that they are living in an Islamic space, a space governed by the rules of the Quran and the Sunna, where poverty, not material prosperity, is a virtue.

Egypt's desperate housing situation, the violation of domestic sacrality by the state, combined with the rise of militant Muslim groups in the 1970s, precipitated the assassination of President Sadat in 1981. The relocation of the residents of ᶜIshash Turguman and ᶜArab Muhammadi to iz-Zawiya il-Hamra increased social tensions in that neighborhood, which led to a bloody riot between militant Muslim groups and Coptic Christians in June 1981.[87] That riot gave Sadat the pretext he needed to arrest and imprison hundreds of opponents, ranging from Marxists to members of militant Muslim organizations, in early September.

The previous summer, Khalid Islambuli, a young army officer, had joined the militant *Jihad* group. He was recruited by the leader during an excursion to a poor neighborhood of squatter housing on the western edge of Cairo. Islambuli had been looking for affordable vacant apartments to enhance his marriage prospects at the time. The *Jihad* leader advocated, as evidenced in his tract *al-Farīda al-ghā'iba,*[88] the overthrow of corrupt rulers to create a true Islamic society. When Islambuli was not on duty, and not meeting with the group, he stayed with a married sister, who lived in a housing complex near ᶜAyn Shams, where some of the residents from Cairo's urban redevelopment projects were being relocated at the time.

On September 3, 1981, Khalid went to Upper Egypt to help his father and brother build an additional room onto the family house. Instead of a warm family reunion, he found his mother and unmarried sister in great distress. His brother, an outspoken religious opponent to the Sadat regime, had been dragged out of bed the previous night and detained by security police as part of Sadat's crackdown against dissidents. Deeply affected and vowing revenge, Khalid returned to Cairo, where he promptly began plotting with other members of the *Jihad* group. On October 6, he led the attack on the reviewing stands where Sadat and his entourage were seated. It was he who fired the shots that killed Egypt's leader.[89]

When asked during his trial why he killed Sadat, Islambuli answered that he did so because Egypt was not being governed in accordance with Islamic law, to the detriment of Muslims; Sadat had concluded a peace agreement with "the Jews"; and Sadat had arrested and mistreated Muslim leaders *(ᶜulama).*[90] These are rationalizations after the fact. Other groups had called for Islamization, criticized the Egyptian-Israeli treaty, and had members arrested during Sadat's crackdown, but they apparently did not mobilize themselves to assassinate the president. It appears that the affront to Islambuli's family honor, when combined with the other factors I identified, is finally what compelled him to act as he did.

CONCLUSION

From what I have said in this chapter, it would be correct to conclude that the Islamic features of domestic significance come more from the appropriation of key Islamic symbols by the people than from an instituted canon of formal religious requirements. Nonetheless, we should not forget that religious duties such as prayer and Quran recitation have been prominent features of Muslim domestic life since the time of the Prophet. Nor should we overlook the potential influence institutional Islam can have on the domestic sphere. In the past, this would have come by way of the *ᶜulama* to the extent people sought their council in matters of the law and the spirit. Yet the *ᶜulama* were never a closed caste of experts; their values and beliefs were as likely to reflect those of the wider society in which they lived as they would those of the scholarly tradition. In recent decades, the influence of normative Islam upon domestic life may be increasing as radio, television, magazines, newspapers, and books convey its teachings to every house in the country. This could work to suppress local religious beliefs and practices, and impose a more rigid order on Muslim households than had been the case previously.

In the next chapter, I approach this question from a somewhat different perspective. There we shall see how the formal duty of pilgrimage, combined with modern mass transportation and other aspects of modernity, has actually given Egyptians more latitude to appropriate pan-Islamic symbols for their homes, on their own terms.

6

The Metamorphosis of Domestic Space in the Pilgrimage Murals of Egypt

God requires people to perform a Hajj to the house if they are able to do so—
The Quran (3 *Al ʿImrān* 97)

Performing the Hajj to Mecca is a formal ritual duty in Islam. It is required of all Muslims at least once in a lifetime if possible, during the special pilgrimage season, which occurs annually in the last month of the Islamic lunar calendar. The visitation (*ziyāra*) paid to the Prophet Muhammad's mosque-tomb in Medina has, over the centuries, come to be regarded as a comparably important, albeit voluntary, act of devotion. It is usually performed along with the Hajj.

A vast body of literature, ranging from Muslim pilgrimage manuals to historical studies by non-Muslim scholars, has evolved that discusses the ritual practices, traditions, virtues, and histories of the sacred territories of Mecca and Medina, those binary "centers out there." Orientalists have been preoccupied with examining the Hajj in connection with pre-Islamic Arab "paganism," and with its political, economic, and even sanitary aspects. Recent Saudi publications have extended the field of inquiry to include detailed surveys and statistical studies, which are aimed at facilitating the planning and mobilization of modern technologies for the annual event. The Saudi government, after all, must accommodate and control the millions of pilgrims who visit the Islamic holy sites there each year.

Unfortunately this impressive body of literature has overlooked questions concerned with the significance of the Hajj within local Muslim communities beyond the Arabian Peninsula. What status do pilgrims gain in the eyes of family, friends, and neighbors when they return home? How do those who will never be able to travel to the Hijaz (that is, the majority of Muslims) understand and benefit from the accomplishments of their more fortunate peers, the pilgrims?

Any attempt to answer these questions means that the normal priorities in the study of pilgrimage must be inverted. Instead of distant centers, formal ritual rules, and factors creating a global experience of

Islamic *communitas,*[1] the local culture of the pilgrim, together with its indigenous practices and beliefs, becomes the object of scrutiny. Even Mecca and Medina may require being defined anew in terms of regional rather than pan-Islamic discourse. In other words, those who examine pilgrimage phenomena in the history of religions, as well as in the history of Islam, must learn to devote greater consideration to the local, even domestic dimensions of the pilgrimage, and to the continuities and discontinuities between these local dimensions and transregional ones.

Since the Middle Ages, Egypt's governments have been intimately involved with supporting and supervising the Hajj. During the 1970s, the national government organized the sending of an average of 43,000 pilgrims each year for the major pilgrimage, or Hajj proper. The average size of the annual Egyptian contingent increased to 104,000 in the 1980s. Tens of thousands more Egyptians have gone to Mecca for the ᶜUmra, or voluntary pilgrimage, during these decades. If we were to ask about how the Hajj is interpreted within the local Egyptian cultural configuration, our attention would be drawn sooner or later to Egypt's pilgrimage paintings. And here we would discover an instance when the linkage between domestic space and Islamic religion achieves its most manifest expression.

PRAGMATIC DESCRIPTION[2]

Pilgrimage paintings are colorful murals drawn on the walls of houses and apartment buildings when one or more of the occupants inside (male or female) makes the obligatory Hajj to Mecca. Though not endorsed by religious law, the practice is followed by Muslims living on the southern and eastern rims of the Mediterranean basin: west to Libya and east to Syria and Israel-Palestine. Egypt is their heartland, however. There, the paintings are concentrated in villages and neighborhoods of the Saᶜid, the Fayum, the oases, and in the working class and rural-urban sections of Cairo and Suez City. They are noticeably less common in the Delta, the cities of Egypt's Mediterranean coast, and in the Bedouin settlements of the Western Desert. Although this form of art contains obvious Islamic motifs, it is not a pan-Islamic phenomenon.

If the pilgrim lives in his or her own free-standing residence, as is more likely to be the case in village Egypt, the mural is usually drawn on the house façade, around the threshold, and on the inside walls of the *entrée (saqīfa* or *madkhal*) and the formal sitting room (*mandara*). Egyptian pilgrims living in urban flats have their murals drawn on the walls around the building threshold, the stairwell, the balcony, and the most visible part of the flat's façade. Occasionally it may appear that a Hajj mural is being used to decorate a place of business. In this case, the painting is not so much connected with the business as with residents living in the same building, because it is customary in this part of the world for shops and offices to be placed on the ground floors of residential buildings.

The paintings, composed of complexes of figures and Arabic epigraphs, are done during the pilgrim's absence—usually in less than a week—late in the eleventh Islamic month of Dhu'l-Qaᶜda, or early in the twelfth month of Dhu'l-Hijja. It is customary to have them finished in time for the pilgrim's return, and the attendant week of festivities, shortly after the Feast of the Sacrifice (10 Dhu'l-Hijja). The murals are drawn either by an artistically gifted member of the family, or by a contracted artisan, who may make his living as an ordinary house or sign painter, carpenter, art instructor, or even taxi driver during the rest of the year. Though the women of a household customarily decorate house walls with floral designs and framed embroideries, pilgrimage paintings proper are predominantly a male enterprise. The expenses for labor and supplies range between thirty and sixty U.S. dollars. Alone, this may seem to be a modest sum, but given the low per capita income in Egypt ($448 in 1977, $686 in 1983, and $1,357 in 1990), and taken together with the other costs entailed by making the Hajj—travel packages from Egypt in the late 1970s cost between $1,500 and $5,000 per person, excluding tips, gifts, momentos, and homecoming festivities—a mural amounts to a sizeable expenditure. Many maintain that God will generously compensate pilgrims for the sacrifices they have made to travel to Mecca. Of course, when the mural is painted by a member of the family, the labor expense is eliminated.

Creating a Hajj mural is a collective enterprise. If the artist is a member of the pilgrim's family, the content of the paintings is likely to be determined informally. His personal inclinations will be shaped and influenced by suggestions from the pilgrim, other members of the family, and neighbors. Women may also play a role in this process. If the painter is a professional, however, the selection process can be a more formal one. First of all, when he is selected, he is already known for his ability to portray particular subjects (boats, airplanes, the Kaᶜba, flowers, etc.), or for his calligraphy. The family may stipulate that specific subjects be done in a certain manner, and be located on particular parts of the house. Sometimes the two parties involved make a contractual agreement that includes a rough pencil sketch of the proposed mural. Moreover, a contracted artist is just as likely to be influenced by family and community opinions while he is painting, as is his amateur counterpart.

The complexity of the relations between a mural artist, his community, and his work is aptly portrayed in the following recollection by an artist in Port Said:

> When I was a child, I was infatuated with the cinema. I would always frequent movie houses to see the heroic deeds of cowboys and the courage of the silent screen heroes of that time. The images of these heroes made an indelible impression on me. The great fascination I had for them prompted me to make chalk drawings of them on walls. I enjoyed doing this. My talent became known among the kids in the neighborhood, who started calling me by the nickname "Taha the Best of Painters" (*al-rāsim*).
>
> Then, one day my neighbors (*ahl al-ḥayy*) called upon me to engage in a painting competition with a professional painter (*naqqāsh*) that they were bringing in especially from Cairo to paint the house of a well-to-do Hajj, and to decorate its façade with the traditional drawings. At that time there were no professional painters in Port Saᶜid. When my neighbors saw what the painter from Cairo had done, everyone said at once: "I bet little Taha the Best of Painters can paint better than that." So the painter from Cairo asked them to bring this wonder child, that he might meet him.
>
> When I arrived, I took one look at the camels he had drawn, and said, "Are these camels or frogs?" Then I started to draw the camels in my own way. The painter from Cairo was astonished. He went to my father and proposed that I work with him for a monthly wage of thirty pounds. But my father refused, saying that he was preparing me to take over the (sweet) shop, and that he believed that the occupation of picture drawing was a forbidden one (*ḥarām*).[3]

Although painters have opportunities to realize their individual talents and visions, it is important to keep in mind that their work in general draws from, and is shaped by, the consensus of family and local community. Collective involvement may even continue after the mural has been completed. In some cases, after returning from Mecca, a pilgrim may not be satisfied with some aspect of the painting, or objects to one of its elements. In such situations, the desired alterations may be made, or the offending figure erased completely.[4] Since murals last for several years before being washed away by rain or bleached by the sun, artists must anticipate the lasting images their work leaves in the eyes of their patrons and communities.

If another member of a pilgrim's household later performs the Hajj, or if the householder goes again, a new mural may cover the earlier one.[5] In such instances, the commemorative inscription will mention the names of previous pilgrims in the family. For some, therefore, the paintings are never in fact finished. Instead, they are subject to a continuing cultural dynamic analogous to the one that determined the content of the original murals.

Although some would argue that pilgrimage paintings are a dying art form, the weight of empirical evidence contradicts this. A simple reading of commemorative epigraphs indicates that most extant murals have been done since 1974. Area surveys of new housing projects in Cairo and Suez City reveal that the practice is still regarded as legitimate among Egypt's *baladi* working class, which shares affinities with *rīfi* populations in this regard. Buildings in the neighborhoods of Zaynhum and ᶜAyn al-Sira (in Cairo), and in Madinat Faysal (in Suez City), have an average of one mural per apartment building of between fifteen and twenty dwelling units.

I will offer explanations for the vitality of this phenomenon in the following pages. For now, it is worth mentioning that there is little evidence for the practice in residential areas inhabited by Muslim bureaucrats, technocrats, and middle-class businessmen (e.g., in downtown Cairo, Giza, Muhandisin, Madinat Nasr), or in foreign quarters (e.g., in Maᶜadi and Heliopolis). Egypt's Christian communities have no similar practices currently, although there is evidence to suggest that Copts decorated their homes with figures and epigraphs in the past when they made pilgrimages to Jerusalem.[6]

CURIOSITIES AND CONGERIES: THE HISTORY OF INTERPRETATION

The history of the interpretation of the murals can be traced back at least as far as Ibn al-Hajj's juristic condemnations of decorations displayed outside shops during the season when the *maḥmal* (a ceremonial palanquin borne by camel annually on the Hajj from Egypt and Syria to Mecca) was paraded through Cairo's narrow streets in the eighth/fourteenth century. He ruled that women should not be allowed out of the house during this season partly because some of these decorations contained illicit pictures. Such decorations were contrary to the Sunna; they enticed people to commit wicked deeds and they entailed the squandering of wealth.[7]

A remarkably different position was taken two hundred years later by Mustafa ᶜAli, an Ottoman official who wrote a description of Cairo as he found it in 1007/1599. Of its ninth virtue he said:

> This nice custom is also highly praised by wise people that one of the relatives of the person that undertakes the pilgrimage, one who is known to be

> sincerely devoted to him, has the Koran verse on the pilgrimage inscribed with large letters on the wall of his door. Some even decorate it with embellishments and colors. Those who pass through that street will know for sure that the owner of that house has gone on the pilgrimage that year. That noble verse is the following: "God requires people to perform a Hajj to the House if they are able to do so" (3 *Al ᶜImrān* 97).[8]

Mustafa ᶜAli, writing when the custom had become firmly established, clearly attributes to it an integrity and significance that is absent from most other accounts. Later, European travelers to Egypt would also describe the paintings, if only briefly, and include them in their encyclopedic collections of curious information from the Orient. Paul Lucas wrote in 1714 that "the entrances of the houses of those who have returned (from the Hajj) are painted and embellished with various ornaments."[9] A century later, the chief author of the ethnographic volumes of *Description de l'Egypte* refused to discuss any of Egypt's painting and sculpture.[10] However, his British contemporary Edward W. Lane described Hajj murals in Cairo, calling them "rude" and childlike.[11] Others tended to repeat Lane's judgment, sometimes going so far as to characterize the paintings as "bizarre" and "hideous."[12] Europeans thus were inclined to exercise their aesthetic judgments without either attempting to explain the murals, or eliciting native understandings of them. Until the twentieth century, outside observers simply noted that the practice contradicted formal Islamic injunctions against images.

The glimmer of a different orientation emerged after the Second World War. Jacques Jomier, a noted interpreter of Egyptian Islam, called the murals naive, but he also hinted that they are a kind of "poesy" through which people living in urban areas and villages express their sentiments.[13] Unfortunately Jomier did not identify exactly what these sentiments were supposed to be, though he did indicate that they were in great measure apolitical. He felt that "simple people" lacked interest in political matters, a dubious conclusion at best. Such an opinion is based on the premise of a static peasant society and folk culture restricted in outlook to the "simplicities" of subsistence, family life, and "superstition." Nevertheless, Jomier should be credited for recognizing the expressive content of the paintings.

In the early 1960s, the German folklorists Kriss and Kriss-Heinrich showed some interest in the contents of Hajj murals, but they did not offer a very convincing explanation for them. They viewed the murals as congeries of images originating in "memories of things seen on the pilgrimage to Mecca. . . . a soldier, the camel and *maḥmal* from Cairo, a train and a boat—presumably all things the painter had seen somewhere during his pilgrimage to Mecca, and which had made an impression on him.''[14]

This statement, brief as it is, conveys three misleading assumptions: (1) that memories of individual pilgrimages determine mural contents, (2) that the pilgrim is also the artist, and (3) that the pilgrim's mind is a tabula rasa that becomes filled haphazardly with externally derived images that are somehow transferred subsequently to the walls of a building. Some assumptions conflict with empirical fact, and fail to account for the regularities governing the use of figural motifs and epigraphs. They also ignore the fact that pilgrims are not likely to have seen al-Buraq, lions with swords, Ibrahim sacrificing his son, Egyptian political figures, King Sulayman (Solomon), and Israeli bombers during their pilgrimage.

A study of fifty-seven murals executed between 1938 and 1975 in the Saᶜid provides us with a much more detailed picture of the phenomenon.[15] In this study, the Italian folklorist Giovanni Canova describes the ethnographic context of the murals, and attempts to develop a typology of their contents. Though he is not averse to attributing this custom to the culture of the ''simple Muslim,'' he at least posits a semiotic approach to the interpretation of the murals. Moreover, he quite properly shifts emphasis from painters *qua* painters back to pilgrims, their houses, and their communities. ''Even when the representation is the work of an artist, the product remains a collective one by means of a signifier-signified relationship with everything directly experienced. The presence of a single element, the Kaᶜba for example, is sufficient for the 'signified' to emerge in its globality.''[16]

Canova does not pursue the semiotic question further. He does describe, however, the religious and social esteem with which the returning pilgrims are regarded by their families and communities. He also recognizes the existence of ambivalent attitudes towards the murals. The custom of pilgrimage painting may not only be in conflict with formal Islamic aniconic ideals, but is also subject to criticism from other segments of Egyptian society.[17]

More recently, in an analysis of fifty Cairene Hajj murals painted in the early 1970s, the French scholar Jean Michot has provided a detailed exposition of individual motifs and epigraphs.[18] He acknowledges their collective character, but in the end he argues that they reflect especially ''the Islam of the painter,'' an amalgam of mysticism and mundane sentiments.[19]

This review of accounts and interpretations of the Hajj murals shows gradual movement away from their being regarded as mere peculiarities towards an awareness of their semiotic nature. No doubt the maturing of ethnology and cultural studies in the post-colonial era has helped this shift in perspectives to occur. There are still shortcomings. Jomier intimates that the murals have no relation to the spheres of religion and politics. Kriss and Kriss-Heinrich confuse painters with pilgrims, and they make simplistic assumptions about the origins of the representations in personal experience. Canova neglects to analyze the interrelation of epigraphs with figures in specific murals. Michot discusses this last point, but lacking an appropriate schema for defining the rules that operate tacitly to control arrangements of features in the murals, he posits,

> no unity is evident in the frescoes. They are a constellation of scenes distributed indifferently on surfaces unbroken by doors and windows. The façade is the back-drop, a fixed place for the frescoes; it bears little relationship to their signification. For example, floral garlands may delimit its borders, or flowers frame the door, together with some inscriptions to greet the pilgrim. If most façades are saturated with drawings or with inscriptions interwoven with flowers, this is not a general rule. Sometimes there are only large whitewashed surfaces. The drawings alone speak. Since the frescoes have a fragmentary character, one must analyze the different themes that appear in them, rather than the façades as a whole.[20]

A hermeneutic stance such as this means that mural contents must be treated atomistically, or as congeries of figures and inscriptions. Moreover, it rejects the possibility that the semiotics of the murals might be conjoined with the semiotics of domestic space. In the following pages I argue to the contrary that there are regularities governing the relations among elements in the Hajj murals, and that the meanings of the murals are embedded in the meanings of domestic space.

SEMIOTIC ANALYSIS

For many Egyptian Muslims, Hajj murals possess at least some semiotic coherence. One of the most common statements they make about the paintings when asked is that they are "public announcements" (*ʿilānāt*) that someone has succeeded in completing the duty of pilgrimage. But what regularities govern these announcements? What sorts of statements do they proclaim? Since local neighborhood communication networks usually operate quite efficiently, surely there is little need for creating a kind of billboard for announcing that someone has been to Mecca. What other functions are performed by these murals?

The paintings consist of two chief semiotic classes: epigraphic formulae in Arabic and iconic figures.[21] Although murals composed exclusively of one class or the other are encountered occasionally, as a rule both semiotic classes occur together. These two classes appear in four types of complex arrangements: associations (items a, b, c, etc. are related by a single perceptually compelling trait), collections (items a, b, c, etc. differ, but complement each other in a conspicuous way), chains (items a, b, c, etc. are weakly linked by some remote similarity), and oppositions (items a and b, etc. are linked by their opposition to each other).[22] Complexes can combine with other elements to form larger semantic fields, or they can form semantic enclaves within these fields.[23]

For example, in figure 8 the trees and potted plant form an enclave constituted as an associative complex. The Arabic epigraphs comprise another associative complex. Plants and epigraphs, together with birds, the *maḥmal,* the plane, the boat, and the mosque together constitute a collection complex. Within the native symbol system the apparent differences between the elements of this mural are in fact superceded by their tacit complementarity. The figures and epigraphs unite ideas of the long journey with the paradisal goal of the journey itself.

Furthermore, the semantic field of such a mural can be related to the semantic field of the pilgrim's house in several ways. The long epigraph over the boat in the Imbaba mural states, "God requires of people the pilgrimage to the house (*bayt*) if they are able to do so" (3 *Al ᶜImrān* 97). This connotes a chain or collection complex association between the Kaᶜba in Mecca and the pilgrim's home. Moreover, an obvious complementarity exists in Arabic between the phrase *ḥajj al-bayt* "pilgrimage to the house" in the inscription and the phrase *bayt al-ḥājj* "the pilgrim's house," which might be used in common parlance to refer to the residence of the pilgrim. There is also an implicit association between the dwelling and the iconic figure of the mosque, which in this mural is a representation not of the mosque in Mecca, but of the Prophet's mosque in Medina, Muhammad's former house and burial place.

Taken separately as a distinct semiotic class, the epigraphs are strikingly formulaic in character. Drawn from the Quran, hadiths, everyday speech, and from ritual utterances, they are brief, energetic in tone, and sometimes rhyme. That many of them carry quasi-canonical liturgical designations, for example, *basmala, kalima, talbiyya, taṣliyya,* and *takbīr,* underscores their ritual character. Some epigraphs are curtailed forms of lengthier statements found in the Quran and hadith literature. For example, the canonical hadith, "Visiting (Mecca) during the ᶜUmra is a means of atonement; the acceptable Hajj deserves no lesser reward than paradise,"[24] is shortened in the murals to simply: "The acceptable Hajj deserves no lesser reward than paradise." Even long commemorative inscriptions can be reduced to clusters of formulaic units.

The laconic and formulaic character of epigraph contents means that they are not being transposed directly from written sources onto the

Figure 8. Hajj mural on house in Imbaba, western edge of modern Cairo. Shows Prophet's mosque, the *maḥmal*, and modes of transportation. Inscriptions include names of God and Muhammad, and the quranic verse commanding pilgrimage to "the house" (epigraph III.1). Line drawing by Allan Grapard.

walls of pilgrim houses. Rather, they are screened through conventional Arabic speech. Hadiths of the Prophet and verses from the Quran are recited from memory throughout Egypt (which has a large illiterate population) by shaykhs, literate Muslims, the destitute, and handicapped. They are also transmitted by the media, particularly on radios and cassettes. The same material has been incorporated through the centuries into the repertoire of daily conversation to form the content of greetings, blessings, curses, complaints, teachings, advice, and expressions of joy and sorrow.[25] The mural epigraphs, therefore, are based on a popular oral-aural rendering of the canons of the Quran and hadiths. Their selection is first of all based on local Egyptian interpretations of Islam, and only secondarily upon the pan-Islamic written canon.[26]

Iconic figures have their own laconic aspect. They show only the most rudimentary concern for perspective, proportion, and detail. Expression of feeling and immediate communication of meaning appear to be the dominant concerns in this regard.

Epigraphs and icons alike are placed on the upper part of the façade of a house or apartment, with a sensitivity to balance and an awareness of architectural features. They respect the natural limitations of a wall, and frequently are oriented toward openings in it. They cluster around doorways and windows. When a mural extends into a house, it reaches into the reception areas, but not into the most private spaces. The mural can sometimes transgress the opposition between private and public space in a Muslim house, but it does not erase it. The dwelling place itself participates in the semiotic system that gives coherence to a mural in a way that distinguishes it from the semantic vacuum of an artist's sketchbook or canvas. Together with epigraphs and icons, it constitutes an important part of a Hajj mural's semantic field.[27]

Seen semiotically, Hajj murals are three-dimensional, highly metaphoric forms of discourse. Although they are not as fragmentary, bizarre, or offensive as many have claimed, neither are they as precise or abstract as theological, legal, or philosophical discourses. The murals are paratactic in structure; that is, they are built up of limited sets of motifs, formulaic phrases, and principles of composition. In fact, they are remarkably similar to, but not identical with, oral genres of poetry, song, myth, and epic.[28]

SEMANTIC ANALYSES AND TRANSFORMATIONS

The individual elements, or sign units, of each semiotic class can be organized as a lexicon divided into five thematic groupings per class, making ten groups in all. Epigraphic formulae include the following themes, in descending order of frequency:

I. God
II. The Prophet Muhammad
III. Pilgrimage and Holy Places
IV. Divine Blessing
V. Victory over Adversity

The iconic figures, in descending order of frequency, can be classified in terms of the following thematic groups:

A. Pilgrimage and Holy Places
B. General Islamic Religious Motifs
C. Egyptian Culture
D. Plants, Trees, and Animals
E. Designs and Talismanic Figures

Readers should consult Appendixes A and B for a detailed inventory and commentary of individual epigraphic and iconic sign units. Familiarity with this information will facilitate following my close analysis of the murals.

Several important points emerge from these two classifications. One is that they reflect the conjunction of pan-Islamic doctrines and images with local values amidst the semantic fields of the murals and domestic space. Hajj murals interweave statements about God, the Prophet, pilgrimage to Mecca and Medina, and paradise with parochial ideas about family life, chauvinism, and the nature of good and evil. To a certain extent, they are in conformity with the mainstream of Sunni Muslim beliefs. On the other, by their very iconicity, murals tend to be in opposition to them. Nonetheless, they respect traditional Sunni injunctions against figural representations of God and Muhammad; the words "Allah" and "Muhammad," and images of the Kaᶜba and the Prophet's mosque are sufficient.

Another point is that the thematic categories within each class are not absolutely autonomous. For instance, among the epigraphic categories, God (I) can be comprehended as the ultimate agent of blessing (IV) and victory (V). He is the creator of space (sacred and mundane) and the transcendent authority for the institution of pilgrimage rites (III). Muhammad (II) is God's messenger (I), founder of the community and house-mosque at Medina (III), pilgrimage reformer, and conqueror of Mecca.

Taking another example, this time from within the class of iconic figures, we can discern that flowers (D) are linked to talismanic figures (E), to native definitions of femininity and family life (C), and to the symbology of holy places (A), which contain gardens of paradise. This multiplicity of linkages between categories in each semiotic class is a general characteristic of each sign unit contained within them, it is not restricted to statements about God and flower images.

On a higher level of analysis, it is important to bear in mind that even the two chief semiotic classes can be interwoven; seldom is the class of iconic figures independent from that of the epigraphs. For example, depictions of the Kaᶜba, Medina, or a pilgrim are regularly linked to specific formulaic utterances, spoken and written. The fact that iconic images can be identified with words is counterbalanced by the iconicity of the words themselves in Arabic calligraphy.[29] Just as the word *āya* (meaning both "verse" and "sign") links the verses of the Quran with the prose of God's created world, written words in the murals can be identified with God, Muhammad, and holy places. The very interconnection of Arabic letters to form the words "Allah" and "Muhammad" (e.g., over the door in figure 9) tends to convert them into powerful iconic representations.[30] Given Egypt's high rate of illiteracy (55 to 60 percent, especially pronounced in areas where Hajj murals are most common), many Egyptians readily identify such written words as manifestations of divine power without always being able to decipher their literal meanings.

Commenting on the homecoming of Egyptian pilgrims from the Hijaz, one observer has written that, "The happy pilgrim on his return after six to eight months absence, bringing with him the blessings of the holy places to the village, is welcomed like one coming back from the dead."[31] Indeed, according to epigraphs used in the murals, pilgrims have been transformed into special people; they are reborn (see epigraph III.1e in Table 2, Appendix A), free of sin (III.1a and e in Table 2), and deserving of paradise (III.1c in Table 2). Their new status is indicated by the honorable title now attached to their names: *Ḥājj*.[32] The pilgrimage to Mecca thus functions as a transformational rite of passage, as other scholars have noted.

Just as the pilgrimage ideally transforms the faithful Muslim into a near saint, a Hajj mural can transform his or her house into either a center of blessing, like a saint's shrine, or a defensive enclave against evil forces, like a talisman. These transformations can best be demonstrated by a close reading of several actual Hajj murals.

Figure 9. Hajj mural on house in al-Ballas, Upper Egypt. Shows (from left) soldiers, al-Buraq, the Prophet's tomb-mosque standing over a steamboat and a *maḥmal* procession, and the lions-with-swords-versus-serpent figure. The commemoration and related epigraphs are situated over the doorway on the left. Line drawing by Erin Addison.

The following is a schematic representation of a collection complex of epigraphic formulae inscribed over the threshold of a pilgrim's house (figure 9) in the village of al-Ballas, south of Qena (the numbers are coded to epigraphs in Table 2):[33]

	IV.1	
II.1a		I.1d
	Commemorative	
	Epigraph + III.1a	
V.3a (cont.)		V.3a

Herein, the lengthy commemoration proclaims:

> *In the name of God, most compassionate and merciful.* Hajj Saʿd al-Hajj ʿAbd al-Haʾit performed the Hajj and the ʿUmra, circumambulated God's sacred House, and visited the tomb of al-Mustafa (Muhammad), *blessings and peace be upon him.* He made the Hajj in A.D. 1975/A.H. 1395. (Italics added to indicate use of formulae I.1 and II.1a as given in Table 2.)

The commemorative epigraph shows the objectification of the individual pilgrim's experience of the Hajj through the construction of a highly formulaic statement that explicitly links him to the very sacred domestic spaces of Mecca (God's House) and Medina (Muhammad's house-tomb). His name, furthermore, is situated spatially on nearly the same level with those of God and his Prophet. The placement of the names of God and Muhammad again to the upper right and left sides of the commemorative text underscores the importance of what has happened to the pilgrim: few believers have the satisfaction of seeing themselves, represented by name, placed in such august company. The pilgrim's transformation is further substantiated by the hadith formula III.1a (see Table 2), which proclaims that through the performance of the Hajj his sins have been forgiven.

Where is the evidence for the transformation of his house? In part, it is to be found in formula IV.1 (see Table 2), situated immediately above the commemorative epigraph. The pronoun "them" (actually the feminine singular pronomial object suffix *-hā*, which also functions as a non-human plural pronoun) is the key word here. In its familiar quranic context (15 *Ḥijr* 46), this statement refers to entering into the paradisal gardens reserved for the faithful in the hereafter.

In its present context, however, a pun is involved. Read in terms of its semantic field, that is, in relation to its placement over the house threshold, the pronoun *-hā* can also be understood according to its singular meaning: "Enter it (literally 'her') securely, in peace." Read this way, the pronoun denotes the house (fem. *dār*) itself.

Through the use of an ambiguous pronoun in a quranic verse, the pilgrim's house is transformed from a mundane dwelling—meaningful according to the interrelationship of *ḥurma* and *sharaf*—into a paradisal sanctuary. This links it symbolically with the holy sites of the Hijaz, especially with the house-tomb of the Prophet in Medina.

Other key elements in this mural also express the transformation of domestic space into a saintly center of blessing. An iconic figure of the Prophet's mosque dominates the mural as a whole (see figure 9), like it does in the Imbaba Hajj mural (figure 8). The cluster of date palms to the right, the birds alighting on the green dome, and epigraphs inscribed on the mosque itself—"The Noble Garden" and "My garden"—underscore the paradisal associations. The two confronting lions with swords on the right hand side of the mural are based on the symbology of the saint as a warrior-hero, and the tree that separates them is a metonymic sign for a saint's shrine.[34] Birds alight on its verdant branches, just as they do on the green dome of the Prophet's mosque. The snake that slithers beneath this tree connotes, in part, the interrelationship of the saintly with the paradisal. The figures of the armed horsemen and soldiers underscore the militant character of the warrior-saint. The *maḥmal,* plane, boat, train, and horses represent movement across the distances that separate the house of the pilgrim from the houses of God and the Prophet. In fact, they even suggest that such distances have been transcended.

This last interpretation is further supported by the presence of al-Buraq, the miraculous creature that, according to the hadiths, carried Muhammad from Mecca to Jerusalem and from there through the heavens.[35] Some traditions assert that it will convey the Prophet from his tomb to paradise on Judgment Day. Its use in the mural, however, seems to do more than connote instantaneous communication between holy places, heaven, and paradise. The artist has placed it between soldier figures and the threshold's epigraphic enclave on the one hand and the image of the Medina mosque on the other, as if to suggest the direct linkage of house and pilgrim with Medina, paradise, and the Prophet.

An Egyptian pilgrim, having heroically overcome the challenges of the difficult journey to the holy land, returning loaded with *baraka* and gifts from the Hijaz, is now considered to have the "right stuff" for sainthood. Family and friends join to fete male pilgrims in the same manner as they honor a saint during his *mūlid;* there are communal processions, feasts, singing and dancing, Quran recitations, and *dhikrs*. It is even customary to hold a "big night" a week after his return, not unlike the "big night" that culminates the week of *mūlid* festivities. Pilgrim houses, cleansed and newly decorated with brightly colored figures and epigraphs organized into semiotic complexes, now resemble only one other kind of building in the Egyptian landscape: the saint's shrine.

These shrines, in contrast to shrines and mosques in Mecca and Medina, are local pilgrimage centers and focal points for blessing. They contain the relics of holy personages who in death still live. Many saints had themselves fulfilled the Hajj requirements. People visit their domed tombs seeking relief from illness and family problems, or to obtain a benefit such as success in marriage, at school, or at work. If their petitions are answered, people may return with placards containing ornate renderings of the names of God and Muhammad, or of verses from the Quran. They also bring rugs and framed photographs that contain representations of the Kaʿba and the Prophet's mosque. In Upper Egypt, it is customary to whitewash the shrine and decorate it with epigraphs and figures nearly identical to those used in the Hajj paintings.[36]

Figure 10. Hajj mural on front of house near Qurna, Upper Egypt. Shows (from left) Kaʿba, *maḥmal* caravan under attack, the Prophet's tomb-mosque, and apotropaic figures. The commemorative epigraph above the doorway states that householder made the Hajj with his wife (*ḥaram*) in 1395/1975. The other epigraphs (from right) are III.1a, III.2, and III.1b.

The organization of iconic figures and epigraphs in Hajj murals such as those shown in figures 8, 9, and 10 into semiotic complexes, coupled with the conjoining of the semantic fields of the houses with those of the murals, transforms pilgrim houses into shrine-like places. They partake of the divine qualities of a saint's tomb, Medina, Mecca, and paradise itself. Moreover, by the rules of sympathetic magic (i.e., like produces like, and the idea of contagion), decorated pilgrim houses produce additional blessing for their inhabitants, visitors, and neighbors. As one Saᶜidi muralist put it, "People receive blessing (*yitbarku*) from these paintings."

Actually the murals operate bidirectionally. They objectify the individual life experiences of pilgrims by building associations between them and their houses with saints, prophets, Mecca, Medina, and paradise using religious epigraphs and images as bricks and mortar. The symbols, or sign units, they contain are partly transregional, recognized widely by people in both Arab and non-Arab Islamic cultures. Concomitantly murals subjectify the blessing powers attributed to holy personages and localities by creating a place for them within the domestic spaces of pilgrims and their families. In other words, pilgrimage to Mecca and Medina, and the hope of attaining paradise, are appropriated by Muslims at home in terms of the local configurations of meaning. We might well posit, in light of this phenomenon, that the persistence of pilgrimage depends partly upon maintaining the bidirectionality of its symbolism.[37]

As I mentioned earlier, however, there is another kind of transformation of domestic space that the murals may accomplish. Instead of becoming paradisal centers of blessing, houses can become talismanic defensive enclaves, architectural amulets.

In Egypt, a talisman (*ṭalsam*) or amulet (*ḥijāb*) is employed to protect the body or valuable property from the dangers of envy, the evil eye, and the jinn. Thanks to the studies of Kriss and Kriss-Heinrich, and of Schienerl,[38] it is possible to identify the epigraphs and figures that amulets and Hajj paintings have in common. They share epigraphs (I.1), (I.1a), (I.1b) + (II.2), (I.1e), (I.6), and (IV.2a). (See Table 2 for the specific epigraphs cited here.) Notably, these are some of the most frequently used epigraphs in the murals. Shared figural motifs include mosques and *maḥmal*s (Appendix B, Table 4, figural category B); male and female figures standing alone or in pairs, soldiers, and mermaids (category C); camels, birds, scorpions, snakes, fish, flowers, palms and trees (category D); stars, crescent moons, hands, and eyes (category E).

Egyptian tattoo art is another talismanic genre that shares similarities with pilgrimage paintings.[39] Tattoos combine therapeutic with apotropaic functions: al-Buraq brings strength and virility; a bird on the temple relieves a person of migraine headaches; a fish on the arm keeps evil spirits away. Field studies, conducted during the first half of this century, and contemporary tattoo parlor screens, show that figural tattoo motifs include mosques, *maḥmals*, crescent moons and stars, and water pitchers (Table 4, category B); Arab warriors, women holding flowers, food, jars, birds, and even swords (category C); plants, flowers, palm trees, birds (especially the hoopoe), fish, lions with swords, and snakes (category D); and diverse geometric designs (category E). Writing is used occasionally for personal names only; formulaic expressions do not appear to be employed in tattoo art.

The most explicit talismanic elements in the al-Ballas mural (figure 9) are epigraph V.3a (see Table 2), the two rosettes over the threshold, the fish and serpent under the boat, and the lions-with-swords-versus-serpent figure on the far right hand side of the mural. The epigraph connotes triumph over hardship, the rosettes, fish, and serpent deflect the evil glances of the envious, and the lions represent the subjugation of demonic forces.

In another Hajj mural (see figure 10), from the vicinity of Qurna (near the Valley of the Kings), apotropaic functions are served by an unusual rendering of the confronting lions-and-tree motif on the right and the crocodile over the heads of the pilgrim's wife and daughter.[40] As if to underscore the idea of the triumph over evil, the muralist has portrayed the chief pilgrim as an officer in the act of shooting the leg off of an Israeli paratrooper who threatens the *maḥmal* caravan with a bomb. Like such warrior-saint archetypes as ᶜAntar, ᶜAli, Abu Zayd, and even the Prophet Muhammad, the pilgrim appears as a defender of his people, homeland, and religion. The distinctions between time, space, and human identities are collapsed, as they frequently are in the other murals.

Why would Egyptians use apotropaic figures in their pilgrimage paintings, or desire that their houses be transformed into talismans? On one side, talismanic figures often are part of the symbolism of sainthood. People believe that saints are both bringers of blessing and conquerors of demonic beings. On the other side, with the marked rise of a pilgrim's status in the eyes of the local community, the surplus *baraka* obtained from Mecca and Medina, and the celebrations following his or her return, the sacrality of the household becomes exposed to the dangers of human envy (*ḥasad*).

Pilgrims acquire extraordinary blessing from transgressing the limits of distant holy places according to ritual rules. Much of this acquired blessing is transmitted to pilgrim households. People flock to meet pilgrims when they return, some offering congratulations, others hoping to acquire a momento or blessing for themselves. As in wedding ceremonies and funerals, pilgrims' houses become open to the collectivity. Therefore, along with bringing blessing home and enhancing domestic sacrality, returning pilgrims also make their households extremely vulnerable to misfortune. The fulfillment of the desires of pilgrims and their families finds its "space of appearance" in the murals, where it comes face-to-face with the unfulfilled desires of their neighbors.[41] Talismanic figures, as well as the latent apotropaic aspects of epigraphs invoking God and his Prophet, of iconic figures of Mecca, Medina, the *maḥmal,* and so forth counteract the dangerous forces pilgrimage unleashes in the pilgrim's community. If evil is in the eye of the beholder, the epigraphs and icons function to keep it there.

COMPARISONS, CONTEXTS, EXPLANATIONS

Hajj murals are iconographic modalities of expression in an Islamic society. I have argued that they have meaning and coherence when other observers (Europeans and some Muslims) have been inclined to conclude that they have little or none. In order to do this, I have reduced the varieties of their contents to a "treasury" of two semiotic classes and ten semantic categories of sign units. This has made it possible to show how sign units combine to form semiotic complexes, semantic fields, and enclaves in the murals that become integrated with physical features of houses. The conjunction of the semantic field of a mural and that of domestic space leads to the transformation of the pilgrim's dwelling into a shrine-like center of blessing or into an amulet.

Given this analytical framework, it becomes possible to further classify murals according to whether epigraphs or iconic figures predominate. Or distinctions may be drawn between murals stressing shrine symbolism and those stressing talismanic ideas. Most either stress positive values, like figure 8, or seek to balance the positive with the negative, as in figures 9 and 10. Murals where apotropaic figures and epigraphs predominate suggest a distrustful attitude to neighbors and the outside world.

The classificatory schema for murals and their contents also allows comparisons to be made among murals in different regions of the country, urban and rural murals, and the work of different artists. For example, pharaonic figures are most likely to be encountered in murals of the Luxor region. Murals in Cairo and Suez City tend to be less elaborate and more conservative than those in upper Egyptian villages. As for individual artists, Taha of Port Said seems to have excelled in horsemen, camels and mermaids. ᶜAli Sayyid ᶜAli likes to use lion figures and al-Buraq in his work. Other artists take pride in their calligraphic skills.

Questions concerning such variations, as well as the variety of native interpretations about individual figures and epigraphs are best held for another occasion. Now a more pressing pair of issues must be addressed: How can the occurrence of Hajj murals as a general and persistent phenomenon in Egypt be explained? What is the status of these murals in relation to other Islamic discourses in Egypt?

One of the leading premises of structuralism is that "meaning is the effect of non-meaning."[42] In the study of religious phenomena, non-meaning need not be taken simply as an a priori "clearing," or as a semantically neutral space from which meaning emerges. Rather, non-meaning entails the humanly conceived threat of meaninglessness. For Egyptian pilgrims, their families, and neighbors, this threat appears in several guises: as death, illness, or personal misfortune occurring in relation to the Hajj itself; or in the concern that the sheer number of pilgrims, combined with the passage of time, will diminish the value of the experience.

Meaninglessness might even appear in the form of disenchantment whenever the experience of the journey and of the holy sites becomes trivialized by governmental bureaucracies and unabashed materialism. After describing the Hajj in glowing terms, some pilgrims grumble about the incompetence of their guides and price-gouging by pilgrimage entrepreneurs. A sixteenth-century pilgrim wrote, "The rich pilgrimage for pleasure, the middle classes for trade, the readers of the Quran from hypocrisy (to be heard and seen), the poor in order to beg, and thieves in order to steal."[43] Ahmad Amin expressed dissatisfaction with aspects of the Hajj when he went in 1937, and proposed remedies for them, but the government discouraged him from publicizing his views.[44] Thus, for all the positive accounts about the Hajj that have been written, there is also a small, but noteworthy, body of negative statements about it.

Among the frankest expressions of disenchantment in recent times can be found in the 1964 Hajj journal of Jalal Al-e Ahmad, a modern Iranian writer.

> I'm now sitting on the second level of the outer corridor, writing. From up here the Kaᶜba is just half the size I had imagined. The devotee of God who was the architect of this new outer corridor was evidently unaware of the fact

> that when you destroy proportion you change the architecture. The Kaᶜba is still the same size, but they've made the outer corridor twice as wide, and twice as high. How about destroying the Kaᶜba itself and making it higher and larger? Out of reinforced concrete, no doubt? . . .
>
> Neon fills the streets everywhere. It's even on top of the House's minarets and the Kaᶜba itself. When it pleased God to have a house built on the surface of the land, he should have realized that the land would one day fall into the hands of the Saudi government, and that its door and walls would be covered with neon because of the exigencies of oil exportation. . . . Why shouldn't they order specially designed lamps from these companies that would be worthy of such grandeur, and not have even the House of God become a common consumer for Pennsylvania? Doing things this way means tainting even the world of the unseen for company profits.[45]

Lastly, the threat of meaninglessness can be encountered in the guise of developments witnessed by Egyptians in their recent history: the failures of revolutionary Arab nationalism; the loss of wars and land to Israel; a crisis in moral leadership on the national and local levels; the weaknesses of the national infrastructure in the spheres of housing, jobs, and education, complicated by a phenomenal population growth rate (nearly 3 percent annually) and severe crowding in cities and the Nile agricultural zones. Thus, while the Hajj murals strive to represent coherent visions of reality using authentic Islamic symbols, they are born in a decentered practical reality that they seek to mask or convert.

In addition to the problem of meaninglessness, there are other factors that have contributed to the occurrence and spread of Hajj murals in recent times. These include the numerical growth and patterns of urban migration among sectors of the Egyptian population that assign greatest validity to the practice. The widespread availability of paint in a panoply of colors and an increase in the number of painter-artisans resulting from the government's promotion of commercialism and tourism also have been contributing factors.

Historical factors that have contributed to the practice of making Hajj murals include the painting of landscapes, flowers, and palms on the walls of the sitting rooms and halls in the great Ottoman palaces of Cairo in the twelfth/eighteenth and thirteenth/nineteenth centuries. Sometimes, as I have mentioned, these murals included depictions of Mecca and Medina.[46] In the Anatolian and European reaches of the Ottoman Empire it became the fashion for upper class families to decorate their homes with murals, probably under European influence.[47]

This evidence suggests that Muslim ruling class fashions gave impetus to the practice, but the relation of Hajj murals to Egypt's Coptic heritage should also be kept in mind. Coptic beliefs and forms of worship have tended for centuries to conjoin the veneration of warrior-saints with religious iconography, pilgrimage (*ziyāra*) to Jerusalem, and with the use of talismans. Although current political conditions are prohibitive, Copts used to organize annual pilgrimages to Jerusalem for Easter. A Christian pilgrim would thereupon gain the title *muqaddis* (that is, Jerusalem pilgrim), an appellation based on the same Arabic root used for referring to Jerusalem (*al-Quds*) and to a Christian saint (*qadīs*). *Muqaddis*, like the term Hajj for Muslims, is used in everyday speech when addressing older Coptic Christians with respect.

Coptic informants say that in the past a Christian pilgrim's home was decorated with a picture of the cross, or the Eucharist, and a commemorative inscription. There are no extant Coptic pilgrimage paintings in Egypt, although Canova has discovered a commemorative epigraph, accompanied by the sign of the cross, over a pilgrim's doorway: "God is love, God is one. In the name of the Father, the Son, and the Holy Spirit, Amen. 'I rejoiced when they told me that we would go to God's house. Our feet stand at your gates O Jerusalem!' The *Muqaddis* PN visited the House of God, Jerusalem, on April 9, 1961/Barmuda 1, 1677.'"[48] Other evidence for Coptic pilgrimage painting is not very strong.[49] Tattooing the body, rather than marking the house, seems to have been a more popular method for Christian pilgrims to commemorate their visit to Jerusalem. A number of Coptic tattoo motifs are identical to those appearing in Hajj murals.[50]

Historically pilgrimages to regional Egyptian monasteries and shrines have been more popular among Copts than the pilgrimage to Jerusalem.[51] These holy places house the relics and iconic images of ascetics and martyrs like St. Barsumas the Naked (Mari Anba Barsumas al-ᶜAryan) and St. Onouphrios (Appa Nafr al-Sayah). Icons of the former show him subduing a snake near his tomb, while those of St. Onouphrios depict him standing next to a date palm and spring. Other holy men are depicted as mounted warrior-saints.[52] Like the paintings on the tombs of Muslim holy men, these saintly images are commissioned and presented to the shrines as votive gifts. Copts take pictures and images of the saints home with them for blessing and protection after visiting a shrine to this day.[53]

Coptic religious iconography also includes murals. Archaeological discoveries in upper Egypt and Nubia reveal that Copts painted them inside their holy places between the sixth and eleventh centuries C.E. The murals contain portraits of holy men, warrior-saints, scenes from sacred history, and apocalyptic visions.[54] Murals are still used inside Coptic churches today to depict saints and important events in ecclesiastical history. Both the ancient and contemporary varieties of Coptic wall-painting bear remarkable resemblance in style and content to Muslim pilgrimage paintings.

It is no accident that Egyptian Hajj paintings and Coptic iconography are similar. Coptic iconography flourished during the centuries after the Muslim conquest in 21/642. Indeed, for some two hundred years, Muslim rulers authorized church-building activities; later they controlled it. Concomitantly, Coptic artisans played an important role in mosque-building and decoration. Also, they controlled textile production, which employed floral, geometric, and figural motifs.

The interplay of Coptic and Islamic iconography must be seen against a background of complex religious, social, political, and economic relations between the two communities. When relatively benign conditions changed in the wake of a series of popular revolts that were suppressed harshly by Muslim rulers, Copts began to convert to Islam in large numbers. Around the fourth/ninth century, Islam became nominally the religion of most of Egypt's populace. Copts remained a sizeable minority in the country until the Mamluk era.[55] Ira Lapidus has posited that, due to the nature of their conversion, converts maintained close links with their Christian relatives.[56] Religious conversion did not entail completely renouncing one's religious or cultural heritage; it had a cumulative character. Hence, while some Christian saint shrines may have been destroyed or converted into Islamic ones, a significant part of Egypt's new non-Arab Muslim population felt that it was permissible and beneficial to continue attending festivities at Christian shrines and monasteries. Even in the modern era, it is possible to find Muslims visiting Coptic *mūlid*s, or seeking the aid of a priest or saint at a church.

The holy man and the warrior-saint are figures common to the heritage of both Islam and Christianity. This shared feature has proven to be a significant one, because the Islamization of Egypt's populace, especially during the Mamluk era and thereafter, was intensified by devotional forms of piety centered on human figures. Popular Sufi orders, the cult of Muslim saints, and the veneration of the Prophet gained widespread support and acceptance among Muslims, in the palace and out,[57] with the exception of a few conservative legists like Ibn Taymiyya (d. 728/1328).[58] In this context, Copts found it possible to continue some of their former religious attitudes and practices as Muslim converts. Consequently the use of figural images to represent beliefs associated with warrior-saints and their shrines endured, as did the popular practice of using them as amulets for blessing and protection. Eventually the Christian warrior-saints became Islamic ones.

Two overall factors have combined to produce the murals—synchronic and diachronic. The former is based on the human concern for appropriating symbols of pilgrimage and paradise to enhance if not transform the meanings of everyday existence in the world of the house. The diachronic factor is rooted in the history of religions in Egypt, and the place of religious icongraphy within that history. Obviously, connections might also be made with aspects of ancient Egyptian monumental and funerary art. The ideals expressed therein of making a long journey to attain the blessings of paradise were combined with domestic imagery. The pharaonic tomb after all was a house of the dead. Furthermore, as archaeological evidence demonstrates, some ancient Egyptian houses contained murals depicting deities and other figures.[59]

It would be erroneous, however, for us to conclude that Egyptians draw Hajj murals today because ancient Egyptians or Copts used the walls of their edifices to portray religious beliefs in the past. It would also be incorrect to see the murals as unadulterated products of Islam, of laws promulgated in the Quran and Sunna. On the other hand, to ignore history and conclude that the impulse to make life meaningful alone explains them would be equally untrue. Both sets of factors need to be considered in order to offer a valid explanation for the phenomenon.

What is the status of Hajj murals in relation to other Islamic discourses in Egypt today?

Sunni jurists like Ibn al-Hajj have considered them illicit, even provocations to sin.[60] A similar view is reflected in Taha the Painter's testimony that his father considered figural art *ḥarām* (that is, illicit with respect to Islamic law). This also happens to be the judgment of members of Egypt's militant Muslim organizations, many of whom come from the same *baladi* and *rīfi* areas where the murals are most prevalent.[61] Did not the Prophet declare, "Angels do not enter houses containing figural images. Whoever makes a figural image is tortured on the Day of Resurrection?"[62] From formal Sunni textualist and reformist standpoints alike, therefore, Hajj murals are not only forbidden, they are also a scandalous innovation (*bidᶜa*) in religion. Their perpetrators will be punished in the hereafter.

This perspective even enters into discourse among pilgrims themselves. Those whose murals are composed strictly of epigraphs will sometimes point out that they are being true to Islamic aniconic norms, in contrast to their peers who have allowed the use of figural representations to "corrupt" their murals. Most Egyptian pilgrims today are happy with holding a *fantaziyya* upon their return, and placing photos, posters, quranic verses, and images of Mecca and Medina on the inside walls of their reception rooms.

Criticism and condemnation of Hajj murals within specific sectors of Egypt's Muslim population does not necessarily entail wholesale rejection of the use of figural art in connection with religion, however. When a very popular Egyptian shaykh was asked about the practice of painting pictures and epigraphs on pilgrim houses, he pronounced it to be legally reprehensible (*makrūh*). Yet, a casual look around his office, which is situated in an annex of his mosque, reveals to the visitor walls covered with framed pictures of Mecca and Medina, and with ornate renderings of verses from the Quran and the like.

With the propagation of printing, photography, the cinema, and television in this century, Islam has become as much a religion of the image as of the book. In 1951, al-Azhar University published a series of articles in its journal that frankly criticized traditional aniconic juridical views, especially those espoused by members of the al-Azhar Committee on *Fatwa*s.[63] The editors of the journal called for further debate on the question. Religious iconism, within limits, has since become the de facto winner of the debate. Although popular books and magazines on Islamic topics dare not depict God, Muhammad, or his companions in figural form, they are replete with figures of animals and human beings, including prominent Muslim jurists and scholars. The leading magazine of Egypt's right-wing Muslim activists, *al-Daʿwa* (published in Cairo from 1975 to 1981), is an outstanding example of this phenomenon.

Although rulers and officials like Mustafa ʿAli in former times no doubt recognized the virtues of Hajj murals, the present Egyptian national government has little to say about them. A campaign waged since 1985 to ban the use of religious symbols on motor vehicles in order to limit sectarian conflict in the country has not yet affected the murals. Some members of Egypt's *afrangi* Muslim elite criticize pilgrimage paintings and related practices; but because their familiarity with life in *rīfi* and *baladi* residential areas is minimal, they are more likely to claim that these things are no longer done. Alternately, they say that Hajj paintings are merely quaint ways that members of the "popular" classes (*al-shaʿb*) have devised for saying that they have made the pilgrimage. A few even profess complete ignorance of the phenomenon.

Hajj murals are a reflection of the quest for authenticity and integrity in the modern era.[64] They have a place alongside other contemporary

Islamic discourses, such as those of rulers and militant opposition groups. Unlike the Islam of the rulers, the Islam of the murals does not have as its main purpose the legitimation of the political power of elites who, in actuality, seek the material and ideological comforts of Euramerican life at the expense of the masses. Unlike the Islam of militant opposition groups, the Islam of the murals, despite its use of the warrior-saint image, does not struggle to overthrow corrupt rulers and unify the world under a firmament of divine law by force of will or arms. Nor does it usually signify a retreat away from an outside world, which is impure, into the confined world of a house, which is pure.[65]

The Islam of the murals is concerned with explicitly linking the familial world of the house with communal symbols of sacred power and space. In other words, it embodies a metamorphosis of the domestic religion of Egypt's *rīfi* and *baladi* majorities. By its very nature, it underlies the Islams of ruling and moralistic elites. But it also retains the capacity for restraining the secularizing excesses of the government and the millennialistic extremes of the militant groups.

Epilogue

Knowing how people endeavor to organize and attribute meaning to their domestic spaces is a mandatory part of the study not only of sacred space, but of religious systems of belief and practice in general. At least this is what the study of Islamic discourses of domestic space has taught us. Moreover, Islam as a complex configuration of religious thought and practice cannot begin to be really known or recognized until the variety of ways in which its adherents have claimed and attributed meaning to space, especially domestic space, has been understood.

The study of the religious meanings of domestic space in Islam has also shown that they have histories, that they are subject to the dynamics of change and continuity in time. Mosques have been transformed from intrinsic parts of ordinary houses into monumental places of worship, yet some Muslims have continued to use their own homes as mosques. The Prophet's simple house in Medina became the paradigm for the mosque-palace complexes and mosque-tombs that dominated premodern Muslim cities and towns. Once the Kaᶜba ceased to be regarded as an enceinte for multiple deities, and became God Almighty's house, it was associated with the beginning of the world, with the lives of prophets. When imperial Islam had fully emerged in history, the Kaᶜba was identified with both a heavenly temple and the heart of the Sufi. Egyptian Hajj murals, moreover, show that it can even be appropriated to the believer's own house.

The code of house rules conveyed by the Quran and the authoritative hadiths contain perhaps the most stable of domestic discourses in Islam. They have guided the conduct of Muslims for centuries; stipulating visitation practices, affirming hospitality customs, and securing the collective privacy of their homes. There is little doubt that with the creation of new Muslim settlements from north Africa to India, and the cycles of non-Arab conversion to Islam during the Middle Ages, such rules operated to facilitate the cohesion of the society in its everyday relations. They allowed a space for privacy within a heterogeneous collectivity. In the modern era, as more and more Muslims adapt themselves to alien buildings and cities, these same rules provide a way for Islamizing their own lives and dwellings. Moreover, because they are the rules of God and his Prophet, and part of a soteriological vision of time, they endow the conventions of house life with a transcendent value. Not only can they bring blessing to the home, but they also can promise the attainment of paradise.

Houses and idealized aspects of house life assumed a prominent place in Islamic notions of paradise. On the one hand, they provided believers a set of domestic and bodily images about what lay in store for them in the afterlife. On the other, believers could use such paradisal images as part of a discourse of superordination, thus ascribing significance of their dwellings and themselves in this world. The first mode, as expressed in the Quran and hadiths, sanctioned emigration, homelessness, and sacrifice in this life with the promise of eternal reward. The latter, however, often served as a discourse of princely power and status. Hence, we frequently find the monuments of Medina, Damascus, and Baghdad, the houses of premodern Cairene elites, the royal compounds of Persian, Ottoman, and Mughal rulers, and the tombs of Muslim saints and princes imbued, through design and inscriptions, with the attributes of paradise. Even the somewhat more modest homes of Egyptian pilgrims exemplify the use of this variety of paradisal symbolism.

Many have remarked how rapid and far-reaching the pace of social change in Muslim countries has been since the beginning of this century. This change has entailed a series of displacements caused first by direct contact with European colonizing powers, then by the incorporation of colonized and formerly colonized peoples into the global economic system. Among the basic spatial displacements that have occurred are the eradication of the premodern quarters of towns and cities, and the resettlement of town dwellers in European and American-style buildings and neighborhoods. Another kind of displacement has been the internal migration of rural populations to cities, where they seek new and better opportunities, but often end up living in slum conditions. Many of these people in Egypt, as I pointed out, have taken up new quarters in Cairo's cemeteries.

On the basis of evidence submitted in the foregoing chapters, I have reached the conclusion that the ability to domesticate Islam through social action, speech, and interior display has assuaged the effects of displacement. People endeavor to attribute meaning to all but the most dire living conditions by observing Islamic house rules, or by placing religious objects and talismans by their doors, windows, or in their rooms. They also do so in the ways they inaugurate their new houses, and through cycles of observances such as those surrounding marriage and death. The on-going practice of painting Hajj murals on apartment buildings in working-class *baladi* neighborhoods and in the countryside supports this conclusion.

Since the attribution of religious significance to domestic space is a corporate project, I expect that the negative effects of displacement have been felt most strongly by abused or divorced women who, for a variety of reasons, have no family to whom they can turn for support, and young, single men who do not have the resources for marriage. Islamic activist groups have something to offer such people. They attract members by offering both housing and marriage partners. I have already noted how such groups can assume fictive kinship identities and redefine domestic sacrality for their members. In the past, religious colleges and Sufi convents may have played an analogous role.

Under severe crisis conditions with respect to housing and the economy, just how long the sacralization of domestic space can ameliorate living conditions is difficult to answer. Despite famines, plagues, earthquakes, invasions, and wars, Muslims have for centuries been able to collectively adapt to radically new conditions. Their homes have often been the loci of adaptation. Whether the modern era represents a radical break with the past in this regard is debatable.

If we turn briefly to Iran, where rural-urban migration and deteriorating living conditions were factors that contributed to the downfall of the Shah, we find that the Constitution of the Islamic Republic states: "Since the family is the fundamental unit of Islamic society, all pertinent laws, regulations, and programs must tend to facilitate the foundation of a family and to protect the sanctity and stability of family relations on the basis of the law and the ethics of Islam" (Article 11).[1] What this may indicate is that Iranians have decided to assert the sacrality of the home even more strongly than in the past as a response to the tyrannical imposition of modernization by the Shah's government in the 1960s and 1970s. What the effects of the policies of both the Shah's regime and the Islamic Republic on Iranian Muslim definitions of domestic space have actually been is a question that requires empirical research. Other possible contexts for examining the fate of Islamic definitions of domestic space in the modern period would be among Afghani refugee populations, Kurdish peoples who have suffered oppression in Iraq and Turkey, Palestinian Muslims who have been forced to leave their homes, or whose homes have been dynamited by Israeli Defense Forces, Muslim refugees driven from Kuwait by the Iraqi invasion, and among Muslim immigrants in Europe, the United States, and Canada.

The question of how Muslims attribute religious significance to their houses in the modern era is but one of an array of questions. For example, in Islamic contexts, we ask whether Muslims in sub-Saharan Africa, Turkey, Pakistan, India, or southeast Asia attribute the same kinds of meanings to their houses as do Muslims in the Arabic-speaking world. What happens to God's house, the mosque of the Prophet, the hereafter, and house rules in Bangladesh or Indonesia? To what extent has domestic discourse in these regions been affected by non-Islamic culture and non-Arabic modes of speech? Even within the Arabic-speaking world, how does the domestication of Islam in Egypt differ from its domestication in Morocco, Syria, or Saudi Arabia? How have oil revenues affected the structure and symbolism of domestic space in Saudi Arabia, Kuwait, or the United Arab Emirates? How have Islamic domestic orders affected those of non-Muslim Arabic-speaking minorities such as Copts, Orthodox Christians, and Jews?

In non-Islamic contexts, historians of religion must begin to ask about the representations of domestic space in canonical religious texts and study their relation to the history and society of the peoples who have fashioned them. To what degree are they inscribed with a language of superordination? To what degree do they serve as a basis for challenging or circumventing existing political orders? Do members of particular religious communities attribute religious significance to their own dwellings? How do they do this? If not, why not?

In seeking answers to these questions, scholars of Islam and historians of religion will, I believe, find themselves in territory that is both familiar and different. This book is an initial attempt to map and explore that territory in order to further our understandings of human efforts to imagine worlds of meaning and to live within them.

Appendix A
Epigraphic Formulae Used in Hajj Murals: Index and Commentary

Hajj mural epigraphs are presented in this appendix in three ways. First, Table 2 provides an index of epigraphs arranged by semantic category and subcategory. The categories are organized in descending order, depending upon the total number of epigraph exemplars they represent. Subcategories are organized according to the same principle. I have assigned each type of epigraph a reference number to facilitate discussion and analysis in Chapter 6. Second, Table 2 epigraphs are discussed and explained individually in the form of a commentary. Third, I have compiled an inventory of epigraphs in Table 3 so that readers can quickly distinguish the popular epigraphs from rarer ones. The figures provided in Table 3 are based on a count of individual examples. They do not reflect the number of houses on which they occur. It is possible, though unusual, for a house to contain two or more examples of the same epigraph. The distortion that this manner of counting the epigraphs imposes on the data is minimal. Mural artists operated according to the principle of nonredundancy in selecting the specific elements they wanted the murals to contain.

Table 2. Index of Semantic Categories and Epigraphic Formulae Used in Egyptian Hajj Murals

I. Allah

1. In the name of Allah, most compassionate and merciful (1 *Fātiḥa* 1, etc.)[a]
   a. Allah is most great!
   b. There is no god but Allah.
   c. Praise be to Allah! (1 *Fātiḥa* 2)
   d. Allah, mighty and glorious is He!
   e. Allah.

a. Quranic references are provided for convenience. They do not appear in the actual epigraphs.

f. O Lord!

g. Allah be with us![b]

2. Light upon light. (24 *Nūr* 35)
3. At your service, O Allah, at your service!
4. Allah the almighty has spoken the truth.
5. Remember your Lord, you dimwit!
6. Whatever Allah wills. (18 *Kahf* 39)[c]

II. The Prophet

1. Bless the Prophet!

a. Muhammad (or God's messenger), may God bless him and grant him peace.

b. Truly Allah and his angels bless the Prophet. (33 *Aḥzāb* 56)

2. Muhammad is Allah's messenger.

a. Allah's messenger has spoken the truth.

3. We have not sent you except as a mercy for sentient beings. (21 *Anbiyā*ʾ 107)
4. O light of the Prophet (or Muhammad)!
5. O my beloved Muhammad![d]

III. Pilgrimage and Holy Places

1. God requires people to perform a Hajj to the house if they are able to do so. (3 *Al ʿImrān* 97)

a. (Let it be) an acceptable pilgrimage, (may your) sins be forgiven, and a worthy effort.

b. Proclaim the pilgrimage to the people! They will come to you by even the most treacherous of mountain roads, on foot and on camels made lean by the journey. (22 *Ḥajj* 27)

c. The acceptable pilgrimage deserves no lesser reward than paradise.

d. Truly, the first house established for people is in Bakka (i.e., Mecca), blessed and a guidance for the world. (3 *Al ʿImrān* 96)

e. Whoever performs the pilgrimage, and is neither obscene nor wicked, has left his sins behind, and is as he was on the day his mother gave birth to him.

f. Islam is built on five things: the testimony that there is no god but God and Muhammad is God's messenger; the performance of

---

b. Recorded in Canova, "Nota sulle raffigurazioni popolari del pellegrinaggio in Egitto." *Annali della Facoltà di Lingue e Letterature Straniere di Ca'Foscari* 14 (1975): 90.

c. Recorded in Michot, "Les fresques du pèlerinage au Caire." *Art and Archaeology Research Papers* 13 (1978): 17.

d. Recorded in ibid., p. 18.

prayers; almsgiving; the Ramadan fast; and the pilgrimage to the house for those able to do so.[e]

g. On the way of Allah to Mina and ʿArafat.[f]

h. Turn your face towards the Sacred Mosque! (2 *Baqara* 144)[g]

2. Whoever visits my tomb (i.e., the Prophet's) deserves my intercession.

 a. What lies between my tomb and my pulpit is one of the gardens of paradise.

 b. No one stands by my tomb wretched.

 c. For anyone that prays forty times by my mosque without missing once, it is written that there will be immunity from hell, immunity from affliction, and immunity from hypocrisy.

 d. The green dome: that dome contains Muhammad, whose light illumines the darkness. The Protector watches over it at all times.

 e. Whoever performs the Hajj without visiting me, treats me harshly.[h]

IV. Divine Blessing

1. Enter it securely, in peace! (15 *Ḥijr* 46)

2. I have no prosperity except through God. (11 *Hūd* 88)

 a. I trusted in God. (11 *Hūd* 56, 88)

 b. The King of kings: if he grants something, don't ask why. Truly, God gives to whomever he pleases.

 c. This is by the grace of my Lord. (27 *Naml* 40)[i]

3. Eat from among the good things we have bestowed upon you. (2 *Baqara* 172)

 a. Shake the palm by its trunk towards yourself, so that dates fresh and ripe tumble down to you. (19 *Maryam* 25)[j]

4. Truly the most honorable of you in Allah's eyes are the most Godfearing. (49 *Ḥujurāt* 13)

V. Victory over Adversity

1. Truly we have granted you a manifest victory. (48 *Fatḥ* 1)

 a. If God makes you victorious, no one can overcome you. (3 *Al ʿImrān* 160)

 b. (Allah) kept his promise by making his servant victorious, and by making Islam strong alone.[k]

2. O Lord, your protection!

---

e. Recorded in Canova, "Raffigurazioni popolari," p. 89.

f. Recorded in ibid.

g. Recorded in Michot, "Fresques du pèlerinage," p. 17.

h. Recorded in Canova, "Raffigurazioni popolari," p. 89.

i. Recorded in ibid.; and in Michot, "Fresques du pèlerinage," p. 18.

j. Recorded in Michot, "Fresques du pèlerinage," p. 17.

k. Recorded in Canova, "Raffigurazioni popolari," p. 89.

3. Patience is beautiful.
   a. Patience is the key to relief.
4. Haven't we laid your heart open to you, and relieved you of the burden that weighed you down? And haven't we given you a good reputation? Truly, with difficulty comes ease. Yes, with difficulty comes ease. If you are idle, work hard, and seek our Lord. (94 *Sharḥ*)
   a. Lord, lay my heart open to me! (20 *Tāhā* 25)[l]
5. To the envious—no![m]

Table 2 Commentary

I. Allah

I.1. This formula is known technically either as the *basmala* or the *tasmiyya*. It precedes all suras of the Quran but one, and it is used by Muslims at the beginning of most of their books, essays, treatises, documents, and letters. It is pronounced orally prior to public speeches, and on numerous occasions in daily life. This formula can also have apotropaic functions, because of its prominence in the Quran, and because it contains the name of God. In pilgrimage paintings, it was joined to other inscriptions in eighteen cases, and occurred six times alone, over doorways.[1]

I.1a. This is another common formula, known as the *takbīr*. It is used frequently in Muslim worship. Pronouncing the *takbīr* at the beginning of prayer is considered one of the pillars of this rite. Known as *takbīr al-iḥrām*, it is analogous to the *talbiyya* in pilgrimage (see I.3 below), putting the worshipper in a sacred condition for the duration of the ritual. Outside of formal ritual usage, the formula functions as a vocative exclamation of praise.

I.1b. Known as the *tahlīl* or *kalima*, this formula constitutes the first half of the *shahāda*, or testimony of faith. It is meant to affirm the absolute oneness of God. In the paintings, it occurred most frequently with the second half of the *shahāda* (see II.2).

I.1c. Muslims recite this formula in praise of God on many occasions, both good and bad. In contrast to the *basmala*, which initiates activities, the *taḥmīd* is often used to conclude activities, such as journeys or meals. It is also repeated in answer to questions about one's health, in which context it means "fine."[2]

I.1d. *Allāh jall jalāluh.*[3] This phrase frequently occurs in posters and framed religious inscriptions that are hung in reception rooms and businesses, often in juxtaposition with invocations for blessing the Prophet (see II.1a).

I.1e. Muslims hold this to be the great name of God. It is an extremely common element in daily speech and in writing. Depending on context, it can function as an exclamation, as part of an oath, a curse, a blessing, or an invocation for protection against evil.

l. Recorded in Michot, "Fresques du pèlerinage," p. 17.
m. Recorded in ibid., p. 18.

I.1f. *Yā rabb!* This phrase is often used in everyday speech when calling for God's help or protection (see V.2).

I.1g. *Allāh maʿna!* This utterance is both a proclamation that God has demonstrated his support in the past and that he will demonstrate it in the near future through his protection or blessing.[4]

I.2. The interpretation of this phrase, as with the entire Light Verse itself, has been the object of much speculation in Islamic tradition, especially in Sufi and theosophical circles. Besides being an aspect of God, light has also been identified with the perfect man, Muhammad (see II.4, and cf. the phrase "Illumined Medina").

I.3. *Labbayka Allāhumma labbayk!* Reciting the *talbiyya* is one of the requisite steps for entering into the state of consecration (*iḥrām*) for the pilgrimage. Pilgrims are to recite this formula throughout their stay in the *ḥaram* of Mecca, until they re-enter the mundane world at the end of the Hajj. Outside of Mecca, Muslims recite it after they perform prayers connected with the Feast of Sacrifice, which celebrates the end of the pilgrimage rites. Remarkably, the *talbiyya* occurred only three times in the paintings surveyed. In only one example was it written in its entirety. In two other cases, it appeared in abbreviated form, as cited here.

I.4. *Ṣadaqa Allāhu 'l-ʿaẓīm.* This formula is most commonly pronounced after recitations of quranic verses, and is analogous in use to II.2a, which follows prophetic hadiths (see below). It rarely occurs in Hajj murals.

I.5. *(U)zkur rabbak yā ghaflān! Dhikr (zikr* in Egyptian colloquial), or the act of remembering God and his name, is a widely recognized form of devotion in Islam. It is prescribed by the Quran, and has acquired liturgical significance. *Dhikr* is known in Egypt and elsewhere as the name for Sufi rites in which the name of God is recited repeatedly in various ways to achieve a mystical state of transcendence. In the context of this epigraph, the command to remember God is expressed in a scolding manner.

I.6. Like other formulae in this category, this one ostensibly refers to God's omnipotence. In Egyptian usage, both written and oral, it is believed to have magical properties that protect one from evil powers and misfortune.

II. The Prophet

II.1 and II.1a. *Ṣallī ʿalā 'l-nabī!* Epigraphs II.1 and II.1a (the *taṣliyya*), occurred frequently with numerous variations in the murals. Variants based on the *taṣliyya* included the following: "O ye who enter this house, bless the chosen Prophet!"[5] "Break the fast, and bless the Prophet!" "Drink and bless the Prophet!" "Bless the beauty of the Prophet!" "By the life of the Prophet, bless the Prophet!" Muslims customarily invoke blessings on Muhammad whenever reference is made to him in speech or in writing.[6] In Egyptian usage, phrase II.1 can function as an exclamation of delight, or as a preface for a piece of advice.[7]

The *taṣliyya* also has widely recognized apotropaic properties. Adults protect children and valuable property with it. They recite it at the onset of marriage negotiations to alleviate disputes between the contracting families prior to and after the actual marriage. Similarly, the formula is repeated during discussions of family problems and of dilemmas encountered in daily life. Although the verb *ṣallā* means "to pray," it assumes the meaning "to bless" when combined with the preposition *ʿalā* in reference to Muhammad and other holy personages.

II.1b. This verse is the quranic authority for invoking blessings on the Prophet.

II.2. As the second part of the *shahāda*, this formula occurs in the murals most frequently with the first part (I.1b).

II.2a. *Ṣadaqa rasūl Allāh.* Usually Muslims recite this formula after quoting hadiths attributed to the Prophet. In one of the murals, however, it was used independently (cf. I.4).

II.3. The beneficent nature of the Prophet suggested by this verse has become a key feature in Muslim devotionalism, particularly since the seventh/thirteenth century. As "a mercy" (*raḥma*), some Muslims understand Muhammad to be closely associated with Allah, the "most compassionate and merciful," *al-Raḥmān al-Raḥīm.*[8] This verse was often written on *ḥilya*s, ornately embellished pages of calligraphy that listed Muhammad's qualities. Ottoman Turks placed *ḥilya*s in their homes for blessing.[9]

II.4. *Ya nūr al-nabī!* In Egyptian oral discourse, this is an exclamation of delight.[10] The doctrine of the divine light of the Prophet is a major feature of Muslim devotionalism. It is another way of expressing the closeness of Muhammad's relation to Allah and the cosmos.[11]

II.5. Expressions of love for the Prophet and friendship with holy men are common to Islamic devotionalism. A similar statement found in the murals exclaims, "O he whom I love and adore, I will never forget you!."[12] Both of these statements address Muhammad in the second person, as a living being.

III. Pilgrimage and Holy Places

III.1 This is a quranic verse that authorizes the duty of pilgrimage. In keeping with the brief formulaic style of Hajj mural epigraphs, it contains only one-third of the complete verse. "House" (*bayt*) is a reference to the sanctuary in Mecca.[13]

III.1a. *Ḥajj mabrūr wa-dhanb maghfūr wa-saʿy mashkūr.* This formula, with its concise rhyming structure, is customarily addressed to returning pilgrims by well-wishers.[14] Muslim lexicographers usually take "acceptable" (*mabrūr*) to mean "sinlessly performed."[15] The first two phrases are recorded in Ibn Hanbal's hadith collection.[16] The last phrase (*wa-saʿy mashkūr*) does not occur in hadiths; it is not used in murals and daily speech as often as the first two.

III.1b. In its quranic context, this verse comprises part of the divine commandment given to Ibrahim for instituting the first rites of pilgrimage.

III.1c. This is part of a canonical hadith found in the collections of Muslim[17] and al-Bukhari.[18] The full hadith states, "Visiting (Mecca) during the ʿUmra (lesser pilgrimage) is a means of atonement; the acceptable Hajj deserves no lesser reward than paradise."

III.1d. Traditional Muslim exegetes have interpreted "house" in this verse as referring specifically to a place of worship, God's house in Mecca. Other Muslims have interpreted *bayt* generically, making the Meccan mosque-temple the paradigmatic model for all houses: habitations as well as places of worship.[19]

III.1e. The two variants of this epigraph found in my survey differed with respect to verbs used in describing the pilgrim's release from sin: one has the verb "to come out, leave" (*kharaja*); the other employs the verb "to return" (*rajaʿa*). These inscriptions are interpolations of canonical hadiths found both in al-Bukhari[20] and Muslim.[21] Even in these collections, however, the hadiths vary in wording. Interestingly, none of these authoritative variants makes explicit reference to sins. They state that the pilgrim "returns as on the day his mother gave him birth." Rebirth is clear, but expiation must be inferred.

It seems, therefore, that mural artists have drawn upon Egyptian oral (or perhaps written) traditions that conflate classical hadiths with each other (e.g., III.1c and 1e) and with later statements (e.g., III.1a and 1e) to make the pilgrim's sinlessness more explicit. I should add here that these canonical hadiths themselves stand as interpolations to verses from the Quran, such as 2 *Baqara* 197ff., which make only indirect reference to forgiveness resulting from the proper performance of the pilgrimage.

III.1f. This is a canonical hadith found in the collections of al-Bukhari[22] and Muslim.[23] It is a succinct statement of the religious duties demanded of all Muslims.

III.1g. This statement refers to two of the major pilgrimage sites in the *ḥaram* of Mecca.

III.1h. This verse from the Quran is connected with the change of the prayer direction from Jerusalem to Mecca, where Muslims should face in prayer no matter where they reside. Since the attention of pilgrims and their co-religionists is ideally focussed on Mecca during the Hajj season, this is a fitting verse to put on the murals.

III.2, 2b, c, e. This is a group of noncanonical hadiths concerned with extolling the benefits of visiting the mosque-tomb of Muhammad in Medina. Arguments over their authenticity became part of an ongoing controversy among Muslim legists in the ninth/thirteenth and tenth/fourteenth centuries, when popular devotionalism for the Prophet and Muslim holy men was on the rise. The Egyptian jurist Taqiyy al-Din al-Subki (d. 756/1355) defended the correctness of such hadiths in *Shifāʾ al-saqām fī ziyārat khayr al-anām*.[24] Muhammad b. Ahmad Ibn Qudama al-Maqdisi (d. 745/1344), a student of Ibn Taymiyya, condemned his views in *al-Sārim al-munkī fī'l-radd ʿalā 'l-Subkī*. Such Hanbalite opinions have been in the minority through the centuries.[25] The devotionalist conceptions of Muhammad have predominated in most of the Muslim world, including Egypt.

III.2. Despite its questionable authority, this epigraph was used during the first half of this century on official pilgrimage certificates issued in Mecca.[26] The notion of Muhammad's intercession on behalf of the faithful, however, dates back to the early Muslim hadith collections. Along with belief in the intercession of saints, it remains a very popular notion in Muslim communities today.[27]

III.2a. This formula represents another interpolation of a canonical hadith found in al-Bukhari,[28] Muslim,[29] and Malik.[30] In the versions cited by these collections, the word "house" (*bayt*) is attested more frequently than "tomb" (*qabr*). Tradition has given preference to the use of "tomb" instead of "house" however, particularly on the authority of Ibn Hanbal.[31]

III.2c. Although this is a spurious hadith, it nonetheless highlights the conviction in Muhammad's ability to intercede for the faithful. This statement also expresses the idea of protection from evil forces.

III.2d. This epigraph functions as a caption for depictions of the Medina mosque-tomb in some murals. The mosque's dome is renowned for the light that is said to radiate from it, a manifestation of the light of the Prophet himself (see Table 2, epigraph II.4).

III.2e. Some jurists consider this to be a spurious hadith. It usually occurs in hadith compilations together with the statement, "Whoever visits me after my death is like one who visited me while I was alive."[32]

IV. Divine Blessing

IV.1. This verse is written over doorways. Since the pronoun refers to either the house or paradise, it may be interpreted as a formula that invokes the blessings of paradise on all who enter the house.

IV.2a. *Tawakkaltu ʿalā Allāh.* This formula and variations of it occur frequently in the Quran. *Tawakkul,* complete trust in God, was elevated to doctrinal status by Sufis, who regarded it as a stage on the path to integration with the supreme being. Theoretically, complete surrender to divine providence leads to proof of God's loving-kindness for the faithful in the form of a gift, *rizq.*[33] In everyday Egyptian practice, this statement is exhibited on signs at the entrances to businesses and workshops. There is clearly a complicated line of historical transmission from Quran to Sufism to pilgrims' houses, commercial vehicles, shops, and cafes evident here. Probably the display of such a formula on a house, vehicle, or shop is a way of saying that one's mundane success or prosperity is attributable to steadfast faith in the one God, despite any obstacle. It is also statement of hope for future success.[34]

IV.2b. This epigraph implies the idea of *tawakkul.* It was written on the sitting room wall of a pilgrim's house in Qurna. Unfortunately, I was not able to obtain the complete inscription.

IV.2c. This verse is also displayed in commercial quarters. As with *tawakkul,* "grace" (*faḍl*) here connotes the idea of a gift from God.[35]

IV.3. This verse is part of the Quran's dietary laws. In the murals, it is probably connected with the feasting that occurs at the end of the Hajj and during celebrations held by Egyptians for returning pilgrims.

IV.3a. In its quranic context, this verse forms part of the narrative about the miraculous birth of Jesus. In the murals, it may be associated either with pilgrimage festivities or with the fulfillment of a vow. Just as Mary conceived Jesus, journeyed to "a far place," and was cared for by God, so might a childless or barren woman hope to conceive and successfully bring a child to term as a result of fulfilling her vow of going to Mecca on the pilgrimage.[36]

IV.4. The root for "honorable" (*k-r-m*) is a semantically loaded one in Egyptian culture. It can connote the charismatic gifts and grace acts of a saint,[37] or human hospitality and generosity. This verse, therefore, serves as a compliment for the returning pilgrim, perhaps associating him or her with the saints. It may also be an admonition for others to fulfill their pilgrimage duty so that their piety will enhance their esteem.

V. Victory over Adversity

V.1. In one example among the murals, verses 1 and 2 from this chapter of the Quran were conjoined. While the first verse proclaims God's gift of victory, the second speaks of his forgiveness for past and future sins. According to Islamic tradition, these verses were first revealed as Muhammad returned from al-Hudaybiyya, two years before the conquest of Mecca. In the Hajj murals, however, victory serves as a metaphor for the successfully completed pilgrimage. Pilgrims and their kinfolk thus become linked to Muhammad, to whom the pronoun "you" refers in the verse's original context. The verse also connotes triumph over misfortune.

V.1b. As in V.1, the pilgrim and Muhammad are tacitly linked to each other by the use of this statement in the murals.

V.2. *Yā rabb satrak!* This formula is among the more explicitly apotropaic invocations used in the paintings. Egyptian colloquial speech has several other versions, all based on forms of the root *s-t-r* "to cover, shield, protect": *Yā sātir! "O Protector!" Rabbina yusturhā maʿāna!* "May our Lord protect all of us!," or simply *Rabbina yustur!* In spoken or written form, these formulae are directed against misfortune and evil, and are examples of refuge-taking with God. *Yā sātir!* is also uttered when entering another's house, so that the women inside are not caught unawares.[38]

V.3, 3a. *Al-ṣabr jamīl. Al-ṣabr muftāḥ al-faraj.* The justification for placing these formulae in Category V lies partly in what they connote: namely that difficult times will improve with patience and the grace of God. This contention is supported by the fact that *faraj* "relief" or "relief from suffering" is related to "patience" in V.3a.[39]

V.4. This chapter from the Quran is usually associated with the Opening of the Breast incident in Muhammad's youth that prepared him for prophethood.[40]

Here, as in other Hajj mural epigraphs, the Prophet and the pilgrim are tacitly being linked. The purification of Muhammad's body at the hands of the angels is subtly associated with the purification achieved by individuals who have successfully overcome the difficulties of making the pilgrimage to Mecca. In Egyptian discourse, the opening verse can be taken to mean, "Haven't we given you great delight?"[41] The general idea contained in these verses is that God will provide the righteous blissful relief from hardship.

V.4a. In the Quran, this invocation is spoken by Moses in connection with his difficulty in speaking. It is joined with a request for God to make his situation easier. From this, and from the similarity of this verse to V.4, freedom from adversity seems to be implied.

V.5. This is another apotropaic formula (see V.2). It suggests that evil will be overcome and that the object of envy can escape the threats directed against it. One can compare it with the quranic verse that declares, "I seek refuge in the lord of daybreak from the evil of the envious when he envies" (113 *Falaq* 5). This verse is also used in Hajj murals. On the house of one Cairene pilgrim, it was written around the depiction of a human eye pierced by an arrow.[42]

Table 3. Inventory of Epigraphic Formulae Used in Egyptian Hajj Murals

Category	Ref. No.	Occurrences[a]	Ref. No.	Occurrences[a]
I	1	24	1g	—
	1a	23	2	3
	1b	8	3	3
	1c	6	4	2
	1d	5	5	1
	1e	3	6	—
	1f	2		
II	1	14	3	6
	1a	10	4	2
	1b	1		
	2	8		
	2a	2		
III	1	14	1h	—
	1a	13	2	8
	1b	5	2a	6
	1c	5	2b	3
	1d	3	2c	3
	1e	2	2d	1
	1f	—	2e	—
	1g	—		
IV	1	10	3	1
	2	2	3a	—
	2a	1	4	1
	2b	1		
	2c	—		
V	1	4	3a	1
	1a	1	4	1
	1b	—	4a	—
	2	4	5	—
	3	2		

[a] If no figure is shown, the epigraph was obtained from Canova or Michot, neither of whom provided epigraphic counts.

Appendix B
Iconic Figures Used in Hajj Murals: Index and Commentary

Table 4. Index of Iconic Figures Used in Egyptian Hajj Murals

A. Pilgrimage and Holy Places
  1. Transport Vehicles (68.4, 160.0, 119.4)
  2. Kaᶜba (75.4, 72.0, 63.9)
    a. Mecca's Mosque Area & Kaᶜba (47.3, 36.0, 30.6)
  3. Medina Mosque (40.3, 44.0, 66.7)
  4. *Maḥmal* (29.8, 12.0, 36.1)
  5. Pilgrims (33.3, 2.0, 16.7)
  6. Prophet's *Minbar* (-, -, 19.4)
  7. Water sellers (12.2, 20.0, 0)
  8. Ibrahim's Sacrifice (0, 8.0, 2.8)

B. General Islamic Religious Motifs
  1. New Moon (-, -, 58.3)
  2. Mosques (-, -, 19.4)
  3. Al-Buraq (0, 6.0, 16.7)
  4. Supplicants (0, 2.0, 5.5)
  5. King Sulayman (0, 0, 2.8)
  6. Quran (1.7, 0, 0)[a]

C. Egyptian Culture
  1. Musicians and Dancers (31.6, 6.0, 8.3)
  2. Horsemen & Warriors (-, -, 50)
  3. Women (-, -, 27.7)
  4. Family Scenes (-, -, 19.4)

Note: The numbers enclosed in parentheses represent the ratio of occurrences for each type of figure per total number of houses surveyed. The three numbers correspond to the findings of Canova (out of fifty-seven houses), Michot (out of fifty houses), and myself (out of thirty-six houses), respectively. The dash (-) means that Canova or Michot did not explicitly mention this figural type, but that they may have included it in another category instead. The zero means that no exemplars of a particular figure were found.

a. Recorded in Canova, "Raffigurazione popolari," p. 87.

5. Rulers (0, 0, 2.8)
6. General National Symbols (8.8, 20.0, 2.8)

D. Plants, Trees, and Animals
1. Flowers (66.6, 58.0, 83.3)
2. Trees (-, -, 13.9)
   a. Palm Trees (-, -, 25)
3. Camels (31.6, 28.0, 5.6)
4. Birds (12.3, 12.0, 25.0)[b]
5. Facing Lions with Swords (3.5, 0, 19.4)
6. Snakes (0, 0, 8.3)
7. Scorpions (0, 0, 5.6)
8. Foxes (0, 0, 5.6)
9. Fish (0, 0, 5.6)
10. Crocodiles (0, 0, 2.8)

E. Designs and Talismanic Figures
1. Geometric Patterns (-, -, 30.5)
2. Pharaonic Motifs (8.8, 0, 27.8)
3. Hands (7.0, 4.0, 5.6)
4. Anthropomorphic Statuettes (0, 0, 2.8)

Table 4 Commentary

A. Pilgrimage and Holy Places

A.1. Examples of this group of motifs occur in figures 8, 9, and 10. The most popular forms of mechanical transportation in the murals are planes and boats. Automobiles, busses, trains, and even helicopters are also depicted. Most Egyptians today travel to Saudi Arabia either by boat or plane. Murals do not always represent the forms of transport actually used by pilgrims, however, since many murals show boats and planes together. An Egyptian pilgrim is not likely to take both on his journey. The array of vehicles murals display conveys the notion of movement to and from the houses of God and his Prophet. They also proclaim the enhanced status of the pilgrim, since relatively few Egyptians would otherwise have had an opportunity to travel either by sea or air.[1]

A.2, 2a, and A.3. A full discussion of the symbolism of the mosques of Mecca and Medina, the chief figures contained in the murals, would require a separate study.[2] Generally both sites are considered *ḥarām:* sacred and forbidden. Only Muslims are permitted to visit and reside near them. The Mecca mosque, with its Kaᶜba, and the route to the plain of ᶜArafat comprise the official loci of Hajj

b. These are the figures for the bird class as a whole, without distinguishing between individual species.

rites. For Muslims everywhere, the Kaᶜba (shown in figure 10) is the center towards which they direct their daily prayers. The Medina mosque (shown in figures 8, 9, and 10) contains the tomb of the Prophet, and is believed to be graced with a paradisal garden. Together, these two holy cities have obtained complementary symbolic statuses in Islamic tradition and myth: Mecca is associated with early cosmogony and sacred history, Abrahamic traditions and motifs of return and restoration; Medina is associated with the creation of a specifically Islamic society, the Prophet and his family, and emigration. Millions of Muslims have traveled to both of these sites through the centuries to fulfill the Hajj duty and to acquire blessings from God and the Prophet.

A.4. The *maḥmal* (shown in figures 8, 9, and 10) played a significant role in state pilgrimage processions from Egypt and Syria to Mecca between the seventh/thirteenth and fourteenth/twentieth centuries.[3] Although these processions were discontinued in 1347/1927, and occurred only periodically within Egypt as local parades until 1957, the decorated camel-borne palanquin remains a common feature in Hajj paintings today.

The interpretation of this motif in Egypt, however, appears to have changed since the 1340s/1920s. Pilgrims, painters, and their neighbors express only vague familiarity with the *maḥmal* per se, and prefer to interpret the motif as the Prophet's funerary palanquin *(tābūt al-rasūl),* as the she-camel that located the site of the first mosque in Medina during the Hijra, or as the palanquin *(hawdaj)* that bears a bride to her new home in rural wedding ceremonies.[4] Pulp prints of ᶜAntar and Abu Zayd al-Hilali include depictions of their brides in these camel-borne palanquins.[5] Also, in actual practice, decorated palanquins representing local Muslim holy men are included in parades during *mūlid*s in Upper Egypt.[6] *Rīfi* and *baladi* Egyptians are inclined to view it as a symbol of blessing and festivity. They also believe that the *maḥmal* figure can have apotropaic functions, since it is used on Zar amulets and vestments.[7] Moreover, the camels are symbols of male control (see commentary for figure D.3).

A.5. The murals often show men dressed in pilgrim garb assembled around the Kaᶜba, at ᶜArafat, or in procession to the holy sites. In a few instances, especially on indoor murals, female pilgrims are depicted praying towards the Kaᶜba.

A.6. The Prophet's *minbar,* or pulpit, is a relic preserved in the Medina mosque. It signifies the Muhammad's authority, and defines one of the limits to his paradisal garden (see epigraph III.2a). During the Ottoman era, it was a standard feature in illustrations of the Medina mosque,[8] and remains so in Hajj murals today.

A.7. Water sellers were recorded in the mural surveys done by Canova and Michot, but were not found during my fieldwork in 1977 and after. Supplying water has been an essential aspect of pilgrimage through the centuries. Moreover, obtaining flasks of water from the well of Zamzam next to the Kaᶜba is among the most important practices observed by pilgrims, and has required the establishment of a special guild to control the distribution of Zamzam water. As Michot has noted, this water is believed to be charged with *baraka*. Water sellers depicted in the murals are not necessarily connected with Zamzam, however, since in several instances they are shown next to the Prophet's mosque in Medina, together with the epigraph, "Drink and bless the Prophet!"[9]

A.8. In Islamic sacred history, Ibrahim and his son are understood to be the builders of the Meccan shrines, and institutors of the Hajj rites.[10] Ibrahim's sacrifice is the precedent for the Feast of Sacrifice, the celebration that marks the end of the official pilgrimage. Posters and paintings of Ibrahim's sacrifice are placed in the guest rooms, sitting rooms, and entryways of peasant houses.

B. General Islamic Religious Motifs[11]

B.1. The appearance of the new moon signals the beginning of months and years in the Islamic calendar. Egyptians bless each other when they first spot it in the evening sky. As a figure, the crescent moon adorns the pinnacles of mosque domes and minarets. In former times, it was depicted on Egyptian national flags; it can still be found on the flags of some Muslim countries. It is also one of the images commonly used on amulets in Egypt and west Asia.[12]

B.2. This group is comprised of generic mosque images, excluding those of Mecca and Medina. Representations of mosques are ubiquitous in television graphics and the print media. They occur on book and magazine covers, calendars, postcards, and even advertisements for banks and businesses. They constitute part of the cultural iconography with which Muslims prefer to identify themselves. They are popular public symbols during Ramadan and major holidays, including the Feast of Sacrifice. Mosque images contribute in a general way to the expression of positive religious ideals in the Hajj murals.

B.3. Al-Buraq (shown in figure 9) is a fantastic animal with the body of a horse, wings of a bird, and face of a woman. From early times, Muslims have considered it to be the steed of the prophets. It is said to have been the prophet Muhammad's mount during the Night Journey and Ascension. This event is connected with Muhammad's miraculous journey from Mecca to Jerusalem and up to the seventh heaven with the speed of light, not with the Hajj.[13] Other traditions state that Ibrahim rode al-Buraq whenever he made a pilgrimage to Mecca.[14]

Al-Buraq is a popular iconographic figure in Turkey and eastern parts of the Islamic world. It has also been depicted on posters for display at home. In the Hajj murals of southern Egypt it represents a miraculous form of transportation. According to popular eschatological beliefs, al-Buraq will carry Muhammad from his grave in Medina to paradise on the day of resurrection.[15] As a tattoo figure, some Egyptians believe that the figure of al-Buraq can enhance their virility.

B.4. A modest number of scenes that show individual Muslims at prayer constitutes this group. Except for the fact that they occur in Hajj murals, there is nothing to indicate that this class of figures has a direct association with pilgrimage. Prayers, after all, can be performed almost anywhere. Like generic mosque representations, prayer figures connote piety more than anything else.

B.5. Mural portraits of King Sulayman appear to have been based on that of a king in a deck of playing cards. Sulayman has long been held by peoples in the west Asian and Mediterranean regions, including Muslims, to possess secret powers for communicating with animals and commanding the spirits.[16] His appearance in Hajj murals, therefore, may be connected with the belief in his power to protect houses from demonic forces. In one mural, he was depicted beside the hoopoe. According to the Quran, this is the bird that informed Sulayman about the existence of Sheba and its queen (27 *Naml* 20–26). In al-Thaᶜlabi's *Tales of the Prophets,* the hoopoe was once dispatched by King Sulayman to look for water when he was traveling in Yemen after having performed the pilgrimage to Mecca.[17]

B.6. In addition to phrases from the Quran (listed in Table 2, Appendix A), some murals also depict the Quran in its book form. This image, like mosques and new moons, is a part of popular Islamic religious iconography. As I pointed out in chapter 5, a copy of the Quran in the house is intended to promote domestic blessing and protect the inhabitants from malevolent forces. The same function is served by representing it in Hajj murals. Quran reciters were depicted in one mural, as recorded by Canova.[18]

C. Egyptian Culture

C.1. Processions with musicians and dancers are part of neighborhood celebrations that accompany the departure and arrival of pilgrims. Their depiction in the murals commemorates these festivities and enhances the joyful atmosphere surrounding the return of the pilgrims. Similar parades also occur during *mūlid*s and wedding festivities in rural areas and *baladi* quarters throughout the year.

C.2. This group is comprised of horsemen, armed soldiers (see figures 9 and 10) and hunters. These figures represent the combination of male patriarchal ideals with images of Islamic warrior-saints. Some murals contain captions that specifically identify a figure with the pilgrim, or with male members of his family. In a few instances, a warrior figure is identified with a Muslim folk hero such as Abu Zayd al-Hilali, or with Imam ᶜAli, the fourth caliph.[19] Prior to World War II, depictions of horsemen and soldiers in Hajj murals were inspired by the procession of the *maḥmal* from Egypt to Arabia. Between 1967 and the late 1970s, however, this type of figure was sometimes shown doing battle with Israeli soldiers and aircraft, which indicates that mural motifs can sometimes be tied to specific events in Egyptian history (see figure 10).

Hunters, instead of contending with human enemies, are depicted in countryside murals in the act of shooting at birds and predatory animals. Hunting is a popular male sport in Egypt, but hunting scenes might also characterize patriarchal norms in a society where males claim to be the chief providers and protectors of the home, and where a gun can serve as a symbol of authority. This is especially so in regions of upper Egypt, where the hunting motif is most likely to be represented in murals.

C.3. Females, like males, are stereotypically represented in Hajj murals, but not always as one would expect. True, there are instances where they are portrayed standing behind or next to their husbands and fathers, usually in a smaller scale, wearing the traditional *milāya* and veil, or balancing water jars on their heads (see figure 10). But in many cases, murals depict females with their heads uncovered, in western-style dress, offering food and drink. This way of portraying them is paradoxical in view of the religious and cultural concern for making women the most protected and hidden individuals in society.

Nevertheless, images of women as figures of beauty are widespread in Egypt. These images are based partly upon the traditional figure of the *ᶜarūsa,* which in colloquial Egyptian discourse can be a gaily dressed bride, a remarkably beautiful female, or a young girl. A bride holds ambivalent status; she offers but cannot fully give; she is ideally a virgin, but being a bride requires the loss of that virginity. She collapses the oppositions of inside and outside. During a wedding feast, she is intentionally exposed to the public eye, but ideally must be protected from it both before and after the ceremonies. The image of the bride conveys the emotion of joy through marriage,[20] a notion reflected in the garish female sugar dolls that fiancés give to their prospective brides at the time of the Prophet's *mūlid.*[21] On the other hand, the bride can be a threat to the family honor, which would be severely damaged were it to be demonstrated that she was not a virgin on her wedding night.[22]

Egyptian ideas of the *ᶜarūsa* can also be connected with magic and spirit possession. In Zar rites, she is the possessed woman who must celebrate her marriage to a demon in order to appease him. *ᶜArūsa* figures made of brick are embedded in the earthen façades of rural houses, or placed along the parapets to drive away malevolent forces. The *ᶜarūsa* has also been a popular motif in Egyptian tattoo art, where she functions to bring men strength and virility. Finally, I should note that embroidered portraits of belly dancers, pictures of beautiful women, and nudes are hung in the reception rooms and bedrooms of *baladi* houses from Alexandria to Nubia. Like tattoo images, these too are often intended to enhance male virility and female fertility.[23]

In summary, images of women in the Hajj paintings range from the submissive wife to the enchanting coquette, or bride. They can be used to publicly enhance the honor of a male pilgrim, convey the emotions of joy felt when the pilgrim returns (as in a wedding), or appease and repel malevolent entities.

C.4. Family scenes showing the pilgrim, his wife, and children together are sometimes included in the murals, as in figure 10. In some cases the artist shows them traveling in procession to Mecca or Medina, in others he situates them next to the Kaᶜba.

C.5. Egyptian rulers have traditionally had a vested interest in promoting the pilgrimage and caring for the shrines of Mecca and Medina. The sending of an official pilgrim caravan with the *maḥmal* was one of their annual responsibilities. Since the establishment of the Saudi dynasty, this role has been curtailed to a strictly Egyptian field of action. The portraits that occasionally occur in Hajj murals of national leaders such as ʿAbd al-Nasir and Sadat in military uniform or in pilgrim garb reflect recognition of the active role government takes in organizing and sponsoring Egyptian pilgrimage groups. Moreover, these portraits are in harmony with warrior-hero images and patriarchal symbolism.

C.6. These include representations of the pyramids of Giza, Egyptian flags, the national eagle, and even Nile River scenes. Such subjects enjoy wide dissemination in Egyptian print and broadcast media, as well as on coinage and currency.

D. Plants, Trees, and Animals

D.1. Depictions of flowers in the murals are often highly stylized, and seemingly serve decorative functions. In some cases the flower is distinguishable as a rose, or as a pharaonic-style lotus. The lotus motif is common to the Luxor-Qurna area, where it is also used in the tourist craft industry upon which this region is economically dependent. Historically floral motifs have been a popular element in both Coptic and Islamic decorative arts. Today gaudy flower prints are popular in female fashions (especially for *baladi* and *rīfi* groups) and the upholstery of household furnishings. Even with this group of figures, however, it is possible to delineate wide fields of cultural significance.

The rose is the ideal flower in Islamic tradition. In Arabic usage, the word for rose *(ward)* even serves as the generic taxon for all flowers. According to a hadith of doubtful canonical authenticity, Muhammad is reported to have declared, "When I ascended into the heavens, some of my sweat fell to earth, where a rose sprouted from it. Let whoever wishes to smell my scent smell the rose."[24] Lane notes that in thirteenth-/nineteenth-century Cairo roses were sold by the cry, "The rose was a thorn; from the sweat of the Prophet it blossomed!"[25] The same phrase is sung during rural wedding processions, as the groom makes his way to claim his bride.[26]

Egyptians conjoin flowers, weddings, and the Prophet Muhammad in several ways. They refer to brides metaphorically as flowers in their wedding songs during the henna-night, the bridal procession, and *dukhla*. Bouquets of flowers typically decorate the platform erected for the bride and groom at weddings. Women participating in Zar rites and Sufis in their *dhikr*s sing devotional hymns that either compare Muhammad to a rose, or describe how roses bloom in his presence. I have already mentioned that men present candy figurines dressed as brides, and decorated with flowers, to their fiancées during the Prophet's *mūlid* (see commentary C.3). These figures are kept in a prominent place at home as tokens of good fortune for the couple's relationship, and are paraded during *rīfi* and *baladi* Egyptian wedding festivities.[27] Finally, rose water is the preferred flavoring for sherbets served to guests at weddings, and for candies sold during the Prophet's *mūlid*.[28]

The frequent use of flower motifs in the Hajj murals draws upon a wide semantic field. At its heart is the concern for expressing the emotions of happiness and joy. Related to this, however, are ideas that link the Hajj with weddings, feminine beauty, and the Prophet Muhammad. Flowers can also symbolize paradisal ideals.

D.2 and 2a. Depictions of large branching trees and palms occur often in Hajj murals (shown in figures 8, 9, and 10), especially in upper Egypt. A cluster of three palms is often pictured next to the Prophet's mosque. They represent his garden (cf. epigraph III.2a), or the famed date groves outside Medina. Customarily, dates were brought back from Medina by pilgrims to be distributed to family and friends as gifts. In village contexts, palms and acacias typically grow over the tombs of holy men and convey their blessing. Fronds are used in wedding festivities and to decorate family tombs.

Islamic plant lore has assigned a place of prominence to the palm among other plants. Indeed, Muhammad is reported to have said that the date palm resembles the Muslim believer.[29] Another hadith maintains that God created the date palm from the same soil used in the formation of Adam. This idea occurs both in canonical Islamic texts and in contemporary Egyptian folk traditions.[30]

D.3. Camels without palanquins are an extremely popular motif in pilgrimage paintings. Often they are depicted in a desert setting, led by a Bedouin or peasant. In the past, camels were the leading mode of transport for pilgrims (cf. figural category A.1). Now they are one of the chief animals sacrificed at the end of the Hajj. In Egypt they are an inexpensive source of meat and they are still used as beasts of burden in the countryside.

The camel can also serve as a metaphor for the paterfamilias, who is conceived as the person upon whose shoulders the chief family responsibilities rest.[31] Furthermore, because camels are known to be such ornery beasts, they serve as apt metaphors for male domination, especially so when murals depict them being led docilely by men.[32] This notion may explain the use of camel images in Zar amulets, where they are associated with the demons Sultan al-ʿArabi and Baba Amir al-Hajj (i.e., Baba, Emir of the Pilgrimage).[33] By wearing the amulet, the possessed victim is exercising control over malicious beings.

D.4. The murals depict birds, except for hoopoes,[34] in pairs or flocks perched on trees and flowering plants, and in the vicinity of the Medina and Mecca mosques (see figures 8 and 9). As iconic signs bird figures are readily intelligible, because of their obvious connection with everyday nature, and because it is well-known that pigeons congregate in large numbers within the *ḥarams* of Mecca and Medina, where they and other animals are protected by religious sanction.

Such motifs, however, are not adequately accounted for until conventional complexes of meanings associated with them are examined. For example, birds (especially pigeons) are recognized as message bearers. When described in connection with Mecca and Medina, they are believed to be carriers of divine blessing from the sacred precincts to Muslims in outlying areas. Egyptian folklore expresses the belief that such birds serve as messengers for "dead" holy men. They can either convey messages from the shaykh to the faithful, or carry offerings from the faithful to the shaykh's tomb. During the late 1970s, the Egyptian government promoted the symbol of the white dove as the harbinger of peace in newspapers and billboards.

In Egyptian versions of the *Sīrat Banī Hilāl,* women from the tribe make a pilgrimage to a river, and wish for sons like the birds they see flocking there. In this context, birds represent the heroes of the epic and also are involved in their procreation.[35]

Many Egyptians have maintained that individual species of birds carry formulaic praises to God on their tongues, as well as admonitions to the faithful. The hoopoe, known for its piety, cries, "There is no mercy for him who shows no mercy!" Swallows, known as "birds of paradise," call the faithful to do good deeds and glorify God. Domestic pigeons coo, "Glory be to God, the most high, who pervades his heaven and earth"; while wild pigeons cry out, "Proclaim that there is no god but God!" Turtledoves say, "Glory to the living God who never dies!" Seeing or hearing these birds is taken as a good omen, especially if they happen to roost in one's home.[36]

In Islamic tradition, gregarious species of birds have also come to be identified as the transformed souls of the faithful. A well-known canonical hadith teaches that, "The spirit of the faithful is a bird perched in the trees of paradise until the appointed day, when it will return to its body." Similar hadiths describe the souls more specifically as being inside green birds that drink from the waters of paradise and eat of its fruits.[37] Specifically with regard to Egypt, Blackman has noted that peasants of the Saᶜid believe green birds seen in the vicinity of tombs represent the souls of the dead who lie buried there.[38]

D.5. Pilgrimage paintings of the Qena governorate show two lions with human faces and swords confronting each other from either side of a palm or sycamore (shown in figure 9). In some exemplars a snake lies at their feet. Nubian versions show lions with swords drawn, attacking crocodiles, or standing on serpentine geometrical designs, swords in hand.[39] The facing lions-with-swords motif obviously cannot be explained on a strictly iconic basis. Conventionally peoples of the Nile Valley interpret it as part of the iconography of the holy man and warrior-saint.

Variants of the lion-snake-tree pattern can be found in Cairo pulp posters, printed early this century, which were once displayed in houses and shrines. In these posters, lions are depicted entwined by snakes, standing on either side of the tomb of the Sufi saint Ahmad al-Rifaᶜi.[40] Thus, the Hajj mural version of this motif substitutes a tree for the saint's tomb, but maintains the same symbolism. As noted previously, trees are a common feature of saint shrines throughout Egypt, especially in rural areas. Other Cairo pulp posters show holy man ᶜAbd al-Qadir al-Jilani with a lion familiar that he himself had tamed, according to Sufi legends. Both al-Rifaᶜi and ᶜAbd al-Qadir, therefore, are associated with lions, and in popular Egyptian cosmology, each is identified as a pole *(qutb)* in the cosmic hierarchy of saints who intercede to relieve misfortunes of the faithful.[41]

Two other Islamic folk heroes also happen to be known as lions in Egypt: ᶜAli ibn Abi Talib and ᶜAntar. Occasionally, these warrior-saints are central characters in Egyptian oral narratives. In posters, they are portrayed alike, mounted on horses, doing battle with the enemies of Islam and with demons.[42] It is in Egyptian tattoo art, however, where lion and warrior-saint motifs are most clearly conjoined. In this medium, lions are depicted as warrior-saints, attacking serpents, or serving as the mounts for warrior-saints.[43]

In quotidian speech, the Arabic terms for lion *(asad* and *sabaᶜ*) are used metaphorically by women when referring to husbands and other important males in the family. Former Egyptian president ᶜAbd al-Nasir is still popularly remembered as an *asad.* Egyptians therefore use lions as metaphors to convey cultural notions of masculinity, strength, power, and authority.

Theories about the origins of the lion/warrior motif usually invoke some form of the diffusionist argument. In her work on Nubian house decoration, Wenzel speculates that it originated in Shiᶜa contexts, and was brought to Egypt during the Fatimid era (357/969–566/1171).[44] Others have speculated that the motif was transferred to Egypt by Gypsies from India and Persia.

In addition to overlooking the significance the lion/warrior symbol might hold for native Egyptians at any given time, such explanations overlook its possible indigenous origins. The iconography of hellenistic Egypt includes several versions of the lion/warrior motif. The household god Bes appears as a grotesque human figure with lion's mane, brandishing a sword, and mastering serpents in some late reliefs. A fresco has been uncovered at Karanis (c. 50–170 C.E.) that shows young Horus (Harpocrates) flanked by a lion-sphinx holding a dagger in each paw, while snakes entwine themselves around each leg (cf. iconography of the Muslim saint al-Rifaᶜi).[45] A well-known relief, now housed in the Louvre, shows falcon-headed Horus as a Roman warrior, slaying a crocodile (cf. iconography of ᶜAli, ᶜAntar, etc.). Such iconographic motifs became popular not only in Christian Egypt, but subsequently in Islamic Egypt as well.

D.6–10. Depictions of snakes, scorpions, canines, and crocodiles should generally be regarded as apotropaic figures, although such animals (crocodiles excepted) occur naturally in the daily life of rural Egyptians. In some areas of upper Egypt, people maintain that saints have the power to transform themselves into snakes, and that in this form they can heal the sick and make women fertile.[46] Nonetheless, as Kriss, Kriss-Heinrich, and Wenzel have affirmed, figures of creatures such as these more likely serve to combat sinister forces threatening houses and their occupants.[47] Similarly, protective amulets can be made in the form of a fish to ward off water demons.[48] In their contemporary Egyptian Islamic cultural milieu, there is no connection between any of these figures and astrological symbolism.

E. Designs and Talismanic Figures

E.1. Geometric patterns used in Hajj murals include circles, rosettes, triangles, and parallelograms. They can be used to define the borders of a mural, doorways (figure 9), and windows (figure 8). Such embellishments have long been a key feature of Islamic decorative arts. Besides their aesthetic qualities, they also can function to deflect the evil eye.

E.2. The pharaonic motifs include temple portals, the eye of Horus, and figures of ancient Egyptian men. As a rule, these occur on Hajj murals in areas of upper Egypt that are situated near spectacular archaeological sites, where local residents benefit from tourism. This is especially so in the vicinity of Luxor and Qurna. The artists and patrons who employ such motifs are involved either in the manufacture of ancient Egyptian curios, the sale of "antiquities," or some other aspect of the tourist industry.

On the other hand, within the upper Egyptian belief system, pharaonic figures are used to promote female fertility. Women inscribe them on amulets, and go out on nighttime journeys to tombs, temples, and pyramids, where they perform Hajj-like rituals in hopes of conceiving children.[49]

E.3–4. Hand prints made with the blood of sacrificed animals are left on house walls, especially around entrances. This is done both in urban and rural settings as a sign of celebration and to repel evil. The anthropomorphic statuettes *(ʿarāʾis)* are made of sun-dried brick and placed on house parapets to deflect the evil eye, according to informants in upper Egypt.

Notes

Abbreviations Used

Baladhuri, *Futūḥ*	Ahmad b. Yahya b. Jabir al-Baladhuri. *Futūḥ al-buldān,* edited by M. J. de Goeje. Leiden: E. J. Brill, 1866.
Bukhari, *Ṣaḥīḥ*	Muhammad b. Ismaʿil al-Bukhari. *Ṣaḥīḥ.* 9 vols. Cairo: Dar Matabiʿ al-Shaʿb, n.d.
DEA	Martin Hinds and El-Said Badawi, *A Dictionary of Egyptian Arabic: Arabic-English.* Beirut: Librairie du Liban, 1986.
EI1	*Encyclopaedia of Islam,* edited by M. T. Houtsma et al. 4 vols. 1st ed. Leiden: E. J. Brill, 1913–1934. Supplement, 1938.
EI2	*Encyclopaedia of Islam,* edited by H. A. R. Gibb et al. 2d ed. Leiden: E. J. Brill, 1960–.
Ibn Hanbal, *Musnad*	Ahmad Ibn Hanbal. *Musnad.* 6 vols. Boulaq: al-Matbaʿa al-Kubra al-Amiriyya, 1895.
Ibn Saʿd, *Ṭabaqāt*	Abu ʿAbd Allah Muhammad Ibn Saʿd. *al-Ṭabaqāt al-kubrā.* 9 vols. Beirut: Dar Sadir, [1957–1960].
IFAO	Institut Français d'Archaéologie Orientale.
IJMES	*International Journal of Middle East Studies*
Muslim, *Ṣaḥīḥ*	*Muslim b. al-Hajjaj. Ṣaḥīḥ.* 8 vols. Cairo: Dar al-Tahrir li'l-Tabʿ wa'l-Nashr, 1963.
Palais et maisons	Jean-Claude Garcin, Bernard Maury, Jacques Revault, Mona Zakariya, André Raymond. *Palais et maisons du Caire.* 2 vols. Paris: Centre Nationale de la Recherche Scientific, 1982–1983.
Tabari, *Taʾrīkh*	Muhammad b. Jarir al-Tabari. *Taʾrīkh al-rusul wa'l-mulūk,* edited by M. J. de Goeje. 15 vols. Leiden: E. J. Brill, 1879–1901.

Tirmidhi, *Jāmiᶜ al-ṣaḥīḥ*	Muhammad b. ᶜIsa al-Tirmidhi. *Jāmiᶜ al-ṣaḥīḥ*. 13 vols. Beirut: Dar al-Kitab al-ᶜArabi, n.d.

Introduction

1. Numa Denis Fustel de Coulanges, *The Ancient City: A Study on the Religion, Laws, and Institutions of Greece and Rome*, trans. W. Small (1864, revised ed. 1875; English trans., New York: Doubleday, 1956).

2. Gerardus van der Leeuw, *Religion in Essence and Manifestation: A Study in Phenomenology*, trans. J. E. Turner, 2 vols. (1938; English trans., New York: Harper & Row, 1963), vol. 2, pp. 393–402; idem., *Sacred and Profane Beauty: The Holy in Art*, trans. D. E. Green (New York: Holt, Rinehart and Winston, 1963), part 5.

3. Eliade's major statements on sacred space can be found in *Patterns in Comparative Religion*, trans. R. Sheed (1949; Cleveland: World Publishing, 1958); *The Myth of the Eternal Return*, trans. W. Trask (1949; New York: Bollingen Foundation, 1954), chap. 1; *Images and Symbols: Studies in Religious Symbolism*, trans. P. Mairet (1952; New York: Sheed & Ward, 1969), chap. 1; *The Sacred and the Profane: The Nature of Religion*, trans. W. Trask (1956; New York: Harcourt, Brace & World, 1959), chap. 1; and "The World, the City, the House," in *Occultism, Witchcraft, and Cultural Fashions: Essays in Comparative Religions* (Chicago: University of Chicago Press, 1976), chap. 2.

4. Colleen McDannell, *The Christian Home in Victorian America, 1840–1900* (Bloomington: Indiana University Press, 1986). Religious aspects of domestic life in Europe are taken up in the volumes by Philippe Ariès and Georges Duby, gen. eds., *Histoire de la vie privée*, 3 vols. (Paris: Seuil, 1985).

5. For example, Clarke E. Cunningham, "Order in the Atoni House," *Bijdragen tot de Taal-, Land- en Volkenkunde* 120 (1964), pp. 34–38; revised version in *Right and Left: Essays in Dual Symbolic Classification*, ed. Rodney Needham (Chicago: University of Chicago Press, 1973), pp. 204–38; Stanley J. Tambiah, "Animals Are Good to Think and Good to Prohibit," *Ethnology* 8 (1969): 423–59; Jerome A. Feldman, "The House as World in Bawömataluo, South Nias," in *Art, Ritual and Society in Indonesia*, ed. E. M. Bruner and J. O. Becker (Athens, OH: Ohio University Center for International Studies, 1979).

6. The original version of Pierre Bourdieu's study is to be found in, "La Maison Kabyle ou le monde renversé," in *Echanges et communications: Mélanges offerts à Claude Lévi-Strauss à l'occasion de son 60ème anniversaire*, ed. J. Pouillon and P. Maranda, 2 vols. (The Hague: Mouton, 1970), vol. 2, pp. 739–58. An English translation has been published in Bourdieu, *Algeria 1960* (Cambridge: Cambridge University Press, 1979), pp. 133–53.

7. Jean-Paul Lebeuf, *L'Habitation des Fali, montagnards du Cameroun septentrional: technologie, sociologie, mythologie, symbolisme* (Paris: Librairie Hachette, 1961). See also the distinguished monograph by Suzanne Preston Blier, *The Anatomy of Architecture: Ontology and Metaphor in Batammaliba Architectural Expression* (Cambridge: Cambridge University Press, 1987).

8. For exact references, see chap. 4 and the bibliography under Jacques Revault and Bernard Maury.

9. Oleg Grabar, *The Formation of Islamic Art*, 2d ed. (New Haven: Yale University Press, 1987), chap. 6; idem., "The Architecture of Power: Palaces, Citadels, and Fortifi-

cations," in *Architecture of the Islamic World: Its History and Social Meaning*, ed. G. Mitchell (New York: William Morrow, 1978), pp. 48–79; and idem., "Architecture," in *The Legacy of Islam*, 2d ed., ed. by J. Schacht and C. E. Bosworth (Oxford: Oxford University Press, 1979), pp. 261–69.

10. Mohamed Boughali, *La représentation de l'espace chez le marocain illettré: Mythes et tradition orale* (Paris: Editions Anthropos, 1974); and Besim Selim Hakim, *Arabic-Islamic Cities: Building and Planning Principles* (London: KPI Limited, 1986). Hakim's study deals mainly with Tunisia, and is not as comprehensive as its title would indicate. Hasan Fathy's writings, for example, *Architecture for the Poor: An Experiment in Rural Egypt* (Chicago: University of Chicago, 1973), though they occasionally reflect a quasi-religious perspective, emphasize the relations of vernacular architecture with the natural environment and local climate. Paul Wheatley's oft-cited essay, "Levels of Spatial Awareness in the Traditional Islamic City," *Ekistics* 253 (1977), does not deal specifically with domestic space.

11. In the English language, the word "home" usually has stronger affective connotations than does "house." A thorough study would have to examine the history of the meanings of both terms in English usage. I prefer to treat them as synonymous in this book, because many other languages, including Arabic, do not make the same distinction among their primary house terms. A house/home can be a physical habitation, a kin group, or a center of affections. Under certain conditions it may be all three simultaneously.

12. Religious studies, including the subfield of the history of religions, still has not attained the level of academic consensus with respect to theory, method, and subject matter that would qualify it for being classed as a full-fledged discipline. It takes little more than a review of articles published in in-house journals such as *History of Religions*, *Journal of Religion*, and *Journal of the American Academy of Religion* to verify this claim. Religious studies, however, is not alone among the humanities and social sciences in this regard. The notion of "would-be discipline" was devised by Stephen Toulmin, and is discussed in relation to religious studies by Jonathan Z. Smith, in "Religion and Religious Studies: No Difference at All," *Soundings* 71 (1988): 235–36.

Chapter 1: Images of Domestic Space in the Quran

1. Fully vocalized versions of the Quran are widely attested after the fourth/tenth century only. For a recent discussion of the development of the quranic canon, and a summary of some of the controversial views advanced by Euramerican scholars, see *EI2*, s.v. "*Ḳurʾān*," by Alford Welch, pp. 404–9.

2. Quranic house terms are distributed as follows:

bayt	65 occurrences	28 *suras*
dār	48 "	23 "
maʾwā	22 "	16 "
mathwā	13 "	9 "
maskin	12 "	11 "
ghurfa	4 "	4 "

3. I have found two instances where house terms do not fall easily within any of the four main semantic categories. These are references to the houses of bees (16 *Naḥl* 68), and the spider (29 *ʿAnkabūt* 41).

4. The Quran does not explicitly state the location of either the Kaʿba or the regions of the hereafter. Of course, other sources state that the Kaʿba is in the Arabian city of Mecca, a view with which Muslims have been in general agreement for centuries. No such consensus has been reached with respect to the locations of paradise and hell. It is sufficient for Muslims to acknowledge their existence.

5. This rendering is tentative, since the word *ʿatīq* can also mean excellent or freed.

6. All translations from the Quran are the author's.

7. See chap. 6.

8. Here, I have combined verses from two different parts of the Quran: 7 *Aʿrāf* 74 and 27 *Naml* 52.

9. The term *dār* used in this context can stand both for Korah's dwelling place and his family. Quranic accounts of the flood (71 *Nūḥ* 26–28) and the Babylonian capture of Jerusalem (17 *Isrāʾ* 4–8) may involve a similar theme.

10. This sura also promotes the idea that those who have previously entered "the house *(dār)* and the faith" should regard poor emigrants more highly than themselves, and help provide for them (59 *Ḥashr* 9). Commentators usually treat *dār* in this context as a reference to the city of Medina. But it might just as well be intended to connote paradise.

11. For example, the Sumerian and biblical lamentation texts, the Gilgamesh epic, and the Babylonian Exile of the Judeans.

12. See, for example, the gospels of Matthew (10:12–15, 34–37) and Luke (14:26).

13. The reference to *qibla*, the direction of prayer, is an anachronism here. The Jerusalem temple did not exist in the time of Moses. The text reflects later Jewish, perhaps even Muslim practices. If this is the case, is the *qibla* Jerusalem or the Kaʿba? Traditionally, commentators preferred the latter. For example, Muhammad b. ʿUmar al-Zamakhshari (d. 539/1144) wrote, "Moses and his followers used to pray facing the Kaʿba. Initially they were commanded to pray in their homes in concealment from deniers, lest they come to harm them and tempt them to leave their religion. *This is also the way it was for the believers in Mecca in the early days of Islam.*" (Italics added; *al-Kashshāf ʿan haqāʾiq al-tanzīl wa-ʿuyūn al-aqāwīl fī wujūh al-taʾwīl*, 4 vols. [Cairo: Mustafa al-Babi al-Halabi wa-Awladuhu, 1972], vol. 2, p. 248).

14. Here I have rendered the term *ṣidq* as "righteousness" in accordance with the meaning of the Hebrew term. The Hebrew Bible used *ṣedeq* in construct phrases relating to place, especially to Jerusalem (see, e.g., Isaiah 1:26, Jeremiah 31:23, 50:7, and Ecclesiastes 3:16).

15. The exact context for this sura is unknown, although the accepted view is that it was revealed in Mecca shortly before the Hijra. The story about emigration of the Israelites may well have served two purposes: to motivate Muhammad's followers before the Hijra, and to validate it afterwards.

16. The Arabic phrase *ahl al-bayt* was probably first used to describe a kin group occupying the same dwelling place. *Ahl* occurs frequently in the Quran in construct phrases with places, such as towns and cities, including Yathrib (the name of Medina before the Hijra). In earlier Semitic languages, the Akkadian cognate *ālu* usually meant "city," while the Hebrew *ohel* usually meant "tent."

17. See further, *EI2*, s.v., *"Ahl al-Bayt"* by I. Goldziher et al., and Rudi Paret, *Der Koran: Kommentar und Konkordanz* (Stuttgart: W. Kohlhammer, 1971), p. 239.

18. As is often the case, the wider historical context for such rules is lacking. Muslim commentators suggest that commensality became an issue for believers left behind when Muhammad and his supporters went off to battle; see for example, al-Zamakhshari, *al-Kashshāf*, vol. 3, pp. 76–78; and Ignaz Goldziher, *Introduction to Islamic Theology and Law*, trans. A. and R. Hamori (Princeton: Princeton University Press, 1981), p. 28n.37. On the other hand, is it possible that these rules were originally intended to relax prohibitions against sharing food with the disabled, or with non-Muslim relatives and friends?

19. The identification of God with light in the heavens and in houses, together with the idea of houses being "raised up," has gnostic overtones. It is especially reminiscent of Mandaean discourses about the "house of life" and the ascent of Adam to the celestial dwellings and his place of origin with the Father.

20. See also, Muhammad b. ʿAbd Allah b. Ahmad al-Azraqi (d. c. 244/858), *Kitāb akhbār Makka*, (Beirut: Maktabat Khayat, 1964), p. 123–24; and A. Guillaume, *The Life of Muhammad* (London: Oxford University Press, 1955), p. 89. Nonetheless, this verse was cited in a late hadith wherein the Caliph ʿUmar is reprimanded for sneaking into a man's house; see chap. 2.

21. A later quranic ruling required that both the male and female adulterers be punished with the whip instead of confinement (24 *Nūr* 2).

22. The word for "making completely pure" in verse 33 is based on the root *ṭ-h-r*, which also appears in verse 53. This root forms the basis for the word *ṭahāra*, which is the technical term for "ritual purity" in Islam. *Ṭahāra* is a necessary requirement for prayer.

23. For a general discussion of quranic ideas about the hereafter, see Soubhi el-Saleh, *La vie future selon le Coran* (Paris: Librairie Philosophique J. Vrin, 1971), pp. 15–22.

24. For example, 6 *Anʿām* 135; 13 *Raʿd* 22, 24.

25. 35 *Fāṭir* 35.

26. 40 *Ghāfir* 39.

27. 16 *Naḥl* 30.

28. For example, 2 *Baqara* 94; 6 *Anʿām* 32.

29. 6 *Anʿām* 127; 10 *Yūnus* 25. Muslim commentators note that *salām* is one of God's names, hence this phrase could be rendered into English as "house of God as peace."

30. See Colleen McDannell and Bernhard Lang, *Heaven: A History* (New Haven: Yale University Press, 1988). The Quran also contains evidence for "theocentric" afterlife concepts, wherein the beatific vision of God predominates. In fact, the passage from 13 *Raʿd* quoted above contains an allusion to this. See further, Jane Smith and Yvonne Haddad, *The Islamic Understanding of Death and Resurrection* (Albany: State University of New York Press, 1981), pp. 95–97.

31. In his commentary on this verse, al-Zamakhshari cites a hadith on the authority of Abu'l-Dardaʾ, wherein the Prophet declares that Eden is the *dār* of God, unseen by humans, and inhabited by prophets, martyrs, and the righteous; *al-Kashshāf*, 2:202.

32. See, for example, Thomas G. Allen, trans., *The Book of the Dead, or Going Forth by Day: Ideas of the Ancient Egyptians Concerning the Hereafter As Expressed in Their Own Terms*, Studies in Ancient Oriental Civilization, No. 37 (Chicago: University of Chicago Press, 1974), index, s.v., "*pr*" and "*ht;*" and Samuel J. Fox, *Hell in Jewish Literature* (Northbrook, IL: Whitehall, 1972), pp. 37–38.

33. 13 *Raʿd* 25; 40 *Ghāfir* 52.

34. 14 *Ibrāhīm* 28.

35. 41 *Fuṣṣilat* 28. Another reference to hell may be the phrase "the house of the transgressors" *(dār al-fāsiqīn)*, which occurs in a narrative about Moses in the wilderness (7 *Aʿrāf* 145).

36. My interpretation of these two terms as denotations for domestic space is supported by Muslim Quran commentators such as al-Tabari, al-Zamakhshari, and Baydawi, who gloss them with synonymous words for "dwelling place," such as *manzil* and *dār al-iqāma*. Although *manzil* itself does not occur in the Quran, it is attested in later hadith compilations.

37. 7 *Aʿrāf* 44–46.

38. For example, 15 *Ḥijr* 43–44; 38 *Ṣad* 50; 40 *Ghāfir* 76.

39. For example, 15 *Ḥijr* 47.

Chapter 2: The Houses of the Hadiths

Note: Hadith collections are notorious for lacking standard scholarly editions, which means that specific page references alone are not always helpful to the reader who wishes to check the original Arabic. In this book, consequently, I use three kinds of citations for hadiths so that readers can locate them more easily in whatever editions they have at hand. Hadiths from the collections of al-Bukhari, Muslim, al-Tirmidhi, and Malik are cited according to chapter name and division number. Hadiths from the collections of Ibn Maja and Abu Dawud are cited by chapter name and hadith number. For Ibn Hanbal's *Musnad*, I provide the volume and page number.

1. Recent Muslim accounts of this history are to be found in Fazlur Rahman, *Islam*, 2d ed. (Chicago: University of Chicago Press, 1979), chap. 3; and Muhammad Abdul Rauf, "Hadith Literature I: The Development of the Science of Hadith," in *The Cambridge History of Arabic Literature*, gen. eds. A. F. L. Beeston, T. M. Johnstone, J. D. Latham, et al., vol. 1: *Arabic Literature to the End of the Umayyad Period*, eds. A. F. L. Beeston, T. M. Johnstone, R. B. Serjeant, et al. (Cambridge: Cambridge University Press, 1983), pp. 271–79. Leading non-Muslim scholarly works on the history of the hadith literature include Ignaz Goldziher, *Muslim Studies*, ed. S. M. Stern, 2 vols. (London: George Allen & Unwin, 1971), vol. 2, pp. 17–251; and Joseph Schacht, *The Origins of Muhammadan Jurisprudence* (Oxford: Oxford University Press, 1950). My own views acknowledge Muslim concern with the authenticity of the hadiths, but are closer to those of Goldziher in seeing their compilation in written form as primarily a third/ninth century phenomenon.

2. See Marshall G. S. Hodgson's notion of "pristine Medina" and "the Medina ideal," in his discussion of the development of Islamic legal thinking in the early ʿAbbasid period: *The Venture of Islam: Conscience and History in a World Civilization*, vol. 1: *The Classical Age of Islam* (Chicago: University of Chicago Press, 1974), pp. 318–26.

3. This does not mean, however, that I subscribe to the view that the ideas and practices of Muslims have remained static since the first/seventh century. Once rulers and literati agreed upon a written canon, Muslim understandings of its meanings and applications continued to change as their institutions and social configurations developed in history. What Sufis and the Shiʿa, Africans and Asians, or modern traditionists and reformers have

made of the Quran and the hadiths differs from what the first Muslims or partisans of the early caliphate made of them.

4. Goldziher, *Muslim Studies*, vol. 2, pp. 240–43.

5. The reference that has been of greatest assistance to me in identifying house terms and their use in the classical hadith collections is A. J. Wensinck et al., *Concordance et indices de la tradition musulmane*, 8 vols. (Leiden: E. J. Brill, 1927–1988).

6. Edward W. Lane, *An Arabic-English Lexicon*, 8 vols. (London: Williams and Norgate, 1863–1893), supplement, p. 3031.

7. Muslim, *Ṣaḥīḥ*, *Ḥajj* 67.

8. Muslim, *Ṣaḥīḥ*, *Ḥajj* 81. Ibn ʿAbbas's version actually states that the *idhkhir*-reed was used for their "smith" and houses. Two other variants cited by Muslim mention "graves" instead of "smith." The latter may well be an erroneous reading of the word for "graves," which is similar in appearance and appears more extensively in the hadith literature.

9. See, for example, Muslim, *Ṣaḥīḥ*, *al-Jihād wa'l-siyar* 32. More detail is of course provided in Ibn Ishaq, *Sīra*, pp. 411–18.

10. See, for example, Muslim, *Ṣaḥīḥ*, *al-Fitan wa-ashrāt al-sāʿa* 2. Glosses on these traditions identify the events they mention with Ibn al-Zubayr's attempt to establish himself as caliph in Mecca after 64/683. According to hadiths and other Islamic sources, the Kaʿba was demolished and rebuilt by Ibn al-Zubayr, then returned to its pre-Islamic form when Marwani forces captured the city in 72/692. See Muslim, *Ṣaḥīḥ*, *Ḥajj* 69; and *EI2*, s.v. "ʿAbd Allah Ibn al-Zubayr" by H. A. R. Gibb.

11. The verb *ʿamara*, from which the passive participle *maʿmūr* is obtained, means "to become inhabited" or "to make well peopled"—"to make in a state of good repair"—in discussions about houses and built environments. It is opposed to the idea of making a place desolate. In some contexts, the participle can be used to describe a house haunted by the jinn. This last sense does not appear to apply in the present context, except that "the flourishing house" reportedly is visited by thousands of angels daily. See Lane, *Arabic-English Lexicon*, pp. 2153–56.

12. Bukhari, *Ṣaḥīḥ*, *Badʾ al-khalq*, p. 6 and Ibn Hanbal, *Musnad*, vol. 4, p. 207. Cf. Bukhari, *Ṣaḥīḥ*, *Manāqib al-anṣār*, 40; Muslim, *Ṣaḥīḥ*, *Imān*, 259; Nasaʾi, *Sunan*, *Ṣalāh* 1; Ibn Hanbal, *Musnad*, vol. 3, pp. 149, 153; vol. 4, pp. 209, 210; and the versions related in Ibn Ishaq, *Sīra*, vol. 1/2: pp. 396–408.

13. For example, Bukhari, *Ṣaḥīḥ*, *Manāqib al-anṣār* 40; Ibn Hanbal, *Musnad*, vol. 4, pp. 208–210.

14. See Muslim, *Ṣaḥīḥ*, *Imān* 259; and Ibn Hanbal, *Musnad*, vol. 3, p. 149. There are striking parallels between early accounts of Muhammad's ascent and Jewish heavenly ascents in apocalyptic texts of the hellenistic and late-antique eras, some of which are known to have been translated into Arabic. See, for example, the testaments of Abraham and Isaac, as edited and translated by E. P. Sanders and W. F. Stinespring, in *The Old Testament Pseudepigrapha*, vol. 1, *Apocalyptic Literature and Testaments*, ed. J. H. Charlesworth (Garden City, NY: Doubleday, 1983), pp. 869–912.

15. This subject is taken up again in chapter 3.

16. Muslim, *Ṣaḥīḥ*, *Masājid* 1; and Bukhari, *Ṣaḥīḥ*, *Ṣalāh* 57.

17. The three hadiths cited above are from Muslim, *Ṣaḥīḥ, Ṣalāt al-musāfirīn* 29; cf. Malik, *al-Muwaṭṭa', Qaṣr al-ṣalāh fī'l-safar* 73, which states simply, "Perform some of your prayers in your homes!"

18. Ibn Maja, *Kitāb al-sunan, Iqāma* 186.

19. For example, Muslim, *Ṣaḥīḥ, Masājid* 49.

20. For example, Muslim, *Ṣaḥīḥ, Ṣalāt al-musāfirīn* 3.

21. I understand the phrase *ahl al-dār* in this hadith as a way of designating kin who live together in the same domestic compound or quarter. ʿItban's *bayt*, therefore, occupies one part of this compound.

22. Bukhari, *Ṣaḥīḥ, Ṣalāh* 47; with emendations from variants in ibid., *Taṭawwuʿ* 49 and Muslim, *Ṣaḥīḥ, Masājid* 48. See also Wensinck et al., *Concordance*, vol. 1, p. 328 for other references to this hadith.

23. Bukhari, *Ṣaḥīḥ, Ṣalāh* 47.

24. Ibn Hanbal, *Musnad*, vol. 5, p. 371. Cf. ibid., vol. 5, p. 17; Tirmidhi, *Jāmiʿ al-ṣaḥīḥ, Safar* 27; and other citations listed in Wensinck et al., *Concordance*, vol. 2, p. 159.

25. See M. J. Kister, " 'A Booth Like the Booth of Moses . . . ': A Study of an Early Hadith," *Bulletin of the School of Oriental and African Studies* 25 (1962):155; and my discussion of Muhammad's house-mosque in Medina below.

26. Bukhari, *Ṣaḥīḥ, Ṣalāh* 88, cf. ibid., *Manāqib al-anṣār 43;* and Ibn Ishaq, *Sīra*, vols. 1–2, pp. 373–74.

27. Bukhari, *Ṣaḥīḥ, Mawaqīt al-ṣalāh* 123.

28. Bukhari, *Ṣaḥīḥ, Ṣalāh* 89; and Muslim, *Ṣaḥīḥ, Masājid* 50. Cf. Muslim, *Ṣaḥīḥ, Masājid* 43.

29. Muslim, *Ṣaḥīḥ, Masājid* 51.

30. Ibid., *Masājid* 52.

31. Ibid., *Masājid* 36, 43.

32. More information on this subject is provided in the next two chapters.

33. For example, Muslim, *Ṣaḥīḥ, Ṣalāh* 30.

34. Ibn Hanbal, *Musnad*, vol. 2, pp. 76f.; Abu Dawud, *Sunan, Ṣalāh* 567.

35. The term *ḥujra* is commonly taken to mean "room" and "chamber." In some contexts it denotes an enclosure for camels; see Lane, *Arabic-English Lexicon*, p. 518. As it stands, these definitions make little sense in this context. My own translation of the word is based on the connection of its root meaning with the notion of forming a protective enclosure next to or around a house. A walled area adjoining the Kaʿba is known as the *Ḥijr*. Hadiths mention that the Prophet performed some of his prayers at home in a *ḥujra*, which was probably located outside his living quarters (see, e.g., Bukhari, *Ṣaḥīḥ, Mawāqīt al-ṣalāh*, 123). A translation similar to my own is offered by ʿAbd al-Hamid Siddiqi in his English edition of *Ṣaḥīḥ Muslim*, 4 vols. (Lahore: Sh. Muhammad Ashraf, 1972), vol. 1, p. 241n.668.

36. Ibn Hanbal, *Musnad*, vol. 6, p. 371. Cf. Abu Dawud, *Sunan, Ṣalāh* 570; and the tenth/sixteenth-century compendium of al-Muttaqi al-Hindi, *Muntakhab kanz al-ʿummāl fī sunan al-aqwāl wa'l-afʿāl*, in the margins of the Bulaq edition of Ibn Hanbal's *Musnad*, vol. 3, p. 268.

37. Hadiths concerning family relations and behavior toward others are usually assembled in the chapters on "good behavior" *(adab)* in the topically organized hadith collections. An anthology of such hadiths is provided by Muhammad b. ʿAbd Allah al-Khatib al-Tabrizi, *Mishkāt al-Maṣābīḥ*, trans. James Robson, 2 vols. (Lahore: Sh. Muhammad Ashraf, 1975), pp. 969–1065.

38. Bukhari, *Ṣaḥīḥ, Istiʾdhān* 9.

39. Ibid., *Adab* 85. Another tradition, one that gives priority to the neighbor over the stranger, states, "The neighbor of the house *(dār)* is worthier of the house than anyone else;" Ibn Hanbal, vol. 5, pp. 5, 18. This hadith has achieved proverbial status in the Muslim world, particularly in the form, "The neighbor (comes) before the house" *(al-jār qabla 'l-dār)*. Sufi interpretations of this maxim are discussed in the next chapter.

40. See, for example, Bukhari, *Ṣaḥīḥ, Istiʾdhān* 2.

41. Abu Dawud, *Sunan, Adab* 5176; Tirmidhi, *Jāmiʿ al-ṣaḥīḥ, Istiʾdhān* 18. Other hadiths support the quranic instruction to go away if permission is not received by visitors, for example, Abu Dawud, *Sunan, Adab* 5180–81. Quranic verses, hadiths, and rulings of the major Sunni legal schools concerning greetings and seeking permission are conveniently collected in the seventh/thirteenth-century work of Abu Zakariya Yahya b. Sharaf al-Din al-Nawawi, *al-Adhkār* (Beirut, n.d.), pp. 206–30.

42. Abu Dawud, *Sunan, Adab* 5186.

43. See, for example, Muslim, *Ṣaḥīḥ, Aqḍiya* 4, as well as accompanying commentary.

44. Ibn Hanbal, *Musnad*, vol. 5, p. 326.

45. For example, Bukhari, *Ṣaḥīḥ, Istiʾdhān* 11; Muslim, *Ṣaḥīḥ, Adab* 9; and Tirmidhi, *Jāmiʿ al-ṣaḥīḥ, Istiʾdhān* 18.

46. Bukhari, *Ṣaḥīḥ, Istiʾdhān* 12.

47. Muslim, *Ṣaḥīḥ, Salām* 8.

48. Tirmidhi, *Jāmiʿ al-ṣaḥīḥ, Istiʾdhān* 10.

49. Muslim, *Ṣaḥīḥ, Ashriba* 13. Variants are cited in Abu Dawud, Ibn Maja, and Ibn Hanbal.

50. These hadiths are cited in the collections of Abu Dawud, al-Tirmidhi, al-Nasaʾi, and Ibn Maja; see further al-Nawawi, *al-Adhkār*, pp. 18–19.

51. Muslim, *Ṣaḥīḥ, Ashriba* 13; Bukhari, *Ṣaḥīḥ, Badʾ al-khalq* 14, *Ashriba* 22.

52. Bukhari, *Ṣaḥīḥ, Istiʾdhān* 16; Muslim, *Ṣaḥīḥ, Faḍāʾil* 13.

53. Based on Quran verse 32 *Sajda* 11, Muslims hold that one angel in particular has the power of death: Izraʿil. Cf. 4 *Nisāʾ* 97, which indicates that more than one angel has this power.

54. For example, Muslim, *Ṣaḥīḥ, Libās* 25.

55. For example, Malik, *Muwaṭṭaʾ, Istiʾdhān* 12; Muslim, *Ṣaḥīḥ, Qatl al-ḥayyāt;* Bukhari, *Ṣaḥīḥ, Badʾ al-khalq* 14. See further Wensinck et al., *Concordance*, vol. 1, p. 239.

56. A related rule is expressed in a hadith conveyed on the authority of Abu Saʿid al-Khudri: "Haste is not proper when (a man) sets out for a mosque. . . . And it is not proper for a woman who has entered Islam to leave her house (*bayt*) on a journey, unless she is with her husband, or a man with whom marriage is impermissible *(maḥram)*" (Ibn Hanbal, *Musnad*, vol. 3, p. 64).

57. Muslim, *Ṣaḥīḥ, Imāra* 5; Bukhari, *Ṣaḥīḥ, Istiqrāḍ* 22. Ibn Hanbal (*Musnad*, vol. 6, p. 68) cites a hadith on the authority of ʿAʾisha that tells women, "You are obligated (to look after) the house. It is your *jihād*."

58. Muslim, *Ṣaḥīḥ, Ḥajj* 19. Ibn Ishaq's version of these statements makes the subordinate position of women to men in domestic life even more explicit. He quotes Muhammad as saying, "Look after women. They are your captives, and do not possess for themselves anything;" *Sīra*, vols. 3–4, p. 604. See further R. B. Sergeant, "Early Arabic Prose," in *Cambridge History of Arabic Literature*, gen. eds. A. F. L. Beeston, et al., vol. 1, pp. 119–22.

59. Cited in Abu Hamid al-Ghazali, *Iḥyāʾ ʿulūm al-dīn*, 4 vols. (Cairo: ʿIsa al-Babi al-Halabi, 1957), vol. 2, p. 199.

60. According to another account, however, ʿUmar was dissuaded from even entering a house where he suspected people were drinking; ibid., vol. 2, p. 198.

61. One reform that has been proposed, and legislated in a few cases, would give a divorced woman the right to a home until she remarries, or until she no longer has custody of her children. This means that a court can order her former husband to seek lodging elsewhere. Formerly, under the regime of traditional Islamic law, she would only be allowed to stay legally until her waiting period had ended (for about three months), whereupon her former husband would have the right to evict her if the house was not originally hers. See further Norman Anderson, *Law Reform in the Muslim World* (London: Athlone, 1976), pp. 100–162; John L. Esposito, *Women in Muslim Family Law* (Syracuse: Syracuse University Press, 1982). On the woman's right to housing in the event of divorce, see Aziza Hussein, "Recent Amendments to Egypt's Personal Status Law," in *Women and Family in the Middle East: New Voices of Change*, ed. Elizabeth W. Fernea (Austin: University of Texas Press, 1985), p. 231.

62. Ibn Hanbal, *Musnad*, vol. 6, p. 71.

63. Muslim, *Ṣaḥīḥ, Zuhd* 1.

64. For example, Bukhari, *Ṣaḥīḥ, Nikāḥ* 18; and Muslim, *Ṣaḥīḥ, Salām*, p. 35. See further Wensinck et al., *Concordance*, vol. 2, p. 159. *Maskin* replaces *dār* in some versions of this tradition.

65. Some hadith scholars consider this hadith to be a weak one, because of ʿAʾisha's reported objection to it. See further G. H. A. Juynboll, *The Authenticity of the Tradition Literature: Discussions in Modern Egypt* (Leiden: E. J. Brill, 1969), pp. 83–86.

66. For a general discussion of the portrayal of the hereafter in the hadiths, see El-Saleh, *La vie future*, pp. 25–43.

67. Likewise for the rarer word *maʾwā*, which refers to the place of the Prophet in paradise. See Bukhari, *Ṣaḥīḥ, Maghāzī* 83; Ibn Maja, *Sunan, Janāʾiz* 65.

68. This term, from the Arabic *shahīd*, is an Islamized rendering of the Christian notion of a martyr, that is, one who is killed for his or her faith. The hadiths, however, extend the term to include a much wider range of the faithful, as pointed out by Goldziher in *Muslim Studies*, vol. 2, pp. 350–54.

69. Bukhari, *Ṣaḥīḥ, Janāʾiz* 92. One version of this hadith refers to the Prophet's paradisal house as a *dār* instead of a *manzil;* see Ibn Hanbal, *Musnad*, vol. 5, pp. 14–15; al-Muttaqi al-Hindi, *Muntakhab kanz al-ʿummāl*, vol. 6, p. 96. Cf. Ibn Hanbal, *Musnad*, vol. 5, pp. 8–9.

70. See, for example, 3 Enoch 17:3 in P. Alexander, trans., "3 (Hebrew Apocalypse of) Enoch," in *The Old Testament Pseudepigrapha*, ed. J. H. Charlesworth, vol. 1, pp. 223–

315. Also *b. Mo^ced Qatan* 9 and *Midrash Tehillim*, vol. 11, pp. 1–2.; extract nos. 1625 and 1643 in C. G. Montefiore and H. Loewe, *A Rabbinic Anthology* (New York: Schocken Books, 1974), pp. 588, 597–98.; and Louis Ginzberg, *Legends of the Jews*, 7 vols. (Philadelphia: Jewish Publication Society of America, 1955), vol. 1, pp. 21–23, 5:30ff.

71. For example, Bukhari, *Ṣaḥīḥ, Badʾ al-khalq* 8; Muslim, *Ṣaḥīḥ, Janna* 3; Ibn Hanbal, *Musnad*, vol. 1, p. 400, vol. 5, pp. 287, 348; Tirmidhi, *Jāmiʿ al-ṣaḥīḥ, Ṣifat al-janna* 19.

72. Some traditions state that the *ghuraf* appear like stars, others that their occupants do so.

73. Ibn Hanbal, *Musnad*, vol. 5, p. 343; Tirmidhi, *Jāmiʿ al-ṣaḥīḥ, Ṣifat al-janna* 3.

74. For example, Muslim, *Ṣaḥīḥ, Masājid* 5, *Zuhd* 4; Ibn Hanbal, *Musnad*, vol. 6, pp. 326–27. Cf. Bukhari, *Ṣaḥīḥ, Ṣalāh* 66; and the lengthy list of similar traditions assembled in al-Muttaqi al-Hindi, *Muntakhab kanz al-ʿummāl*, vol. 3, pp. 258–60.

75. For example, Bukhari, *Ṣaḥīḥ, Badʾ al-khalq* 8; Muslim, *Ṣaḥīḥ, Janna* 9.

76. For example, Muslim, *Ṣaḥīḥ, Imān* 62.

77. Bukhari, *Ṣaḥīḥ, Badʾ al-khalq* 8; Muslim, *Ṣaḥīḥ, Janna* 6–7.

78. See Ibn Maja, *Sunan, Zuhd* 4337; and Tirmidhi, *Jāmiʿ al-ṣaḥīḥ, Ṣifat al-janna* 23. According to Ibn Maja, the blessed can also inherit in paradise houses lost to the damned; *Sunan, Zuhd* 4341. Comparable traditions are conveniently collected in al-Muttaqi al-Hindi, *Muntakhab kanz al-ʿummāl*, vol. 6, pp. 109, 117–18. Neither Bukhari nor Muslim contains hadiths expressly supporting such ideas.

79. For example, Tirmidhi, *Jāmiʿ al-Ṣaḥīḥ, Ṣifat al-janna* 6.

80. Ibid., *Ṣifat al-janna* 23; Ibn Maja, *Sunan, Zuhd* 4338.

81. For example, Muslim, *Ṣaḥīḥ, Ṣalāt al-musāfirīn* 29.

82. Muslim, *Ṣaḥīḥ, Buyūʿ* 51.

83. Ibn Maja, *Sunan, Janāʾiz* 36, and *Zuhd* 36. Cf. Muslim, *Ṣaḥīḥ, Janāʾiz* 35, where the dead are addressed both as *dār* and *diyār.*

84. Tirmidhi, *Jāmiʿ al-ṣaḥīḥ, Ṣifat al-qiyāma* 26.

85. The punishment of the dead in the grave is mentioned in a number of hadiths, and became a feature of early Islamic creedal statements. See, for example, Bukhari, *Ṣaḥīḥ, Janāʾiz* 85; Tirmidhi, *Jāmiʿ al-ṣaḥīḥ, Janāʾiz* 71; and Arent Jan Wensinck, *The Muslim Creed: Its Genesis and Historical Development* (London: F. Cass, 1965), pp. 117–21.

86. Tirmidhi, *Jāmiʿ al-ṣaḥīḥ, Ṣifat al-qiyāma* 26.

87. Ibid., *Amthāl* 1; and Muhammad Ibn Saʿd (d. 230/845), *al-Ṭabaqāt al-kubrā*, 9 vols. (Beirut: Dar Sadir, [1957]), vol. 1, p. 172. Cf. Bukh., *Iʿtiṣām* 2; al-Darimi, *Sunan, Muqaddima* 2; and the late version contained in Muhammad b. Yusuf al-Salihi (d. 942/1535), *Subul al-hudā wa'l-rashād fī sīrat khayr al-ʿibād*, 7 vols. to date (Cairo: al-Majlis al-Aʿla li'l-Shuʾun al-Islamiyya, 1972–) vol. 2, pp. 374, 382–83. Al-Bukhari's version, which is probably earlier than al-Tirmidhi's, identifies *dār* with paradise, not with Islam; it identifies God with a man rather than a king. Al-Salihi's later version associates a fortified building or palace *(qaṣr* instead of a *dār)* with Islam, and the meal with paradise.

88. See further, Goldziher, *Muslim Studies*, vol. 2, pp. 346–62.

89. Tirmidhi, *Jāmiʿ al-ṣaḥīḥ, Amthāl* 2, with emendations from Muslim, *Ṣaḥīḥ, Faḍāʾil* 7. Some versions refer to the structure as a building, a *bayt*, or as a collection of smaller

houses or rooms *(buyūt)*. For further references, see Wensinck et al., *Concordance*, vol. 2, p. 159; cf. al-Salihi, *Subul al-hudā*, vol. 2, pp. 389–90.

Chapter 3: The Birth of the House of Submission

1. For a discussion of the continuities shared by Jewish, Christian, and Islamic traditions about Alexander, see further, Friedrich Pfister, "Alexander der Grosse in den Offenbarungen der Griechen, Juden, Mohammedaner und Christen," in *Kleine Schriften zum Alexanderroman* (Meissenheim am Glan: Anton Hain, 1976), pp. 301–47.

2. The term for darkness used in the story is *ẓulma*. This word connotes the ideas both of tyranny and transgression. The story suggests that darkness is an appropriate weapon in the struggle against infidels. Alexander's use of it, however, is mitigated by his use of light also to subdue his opponents. According to the story, God promised him, "I will make light and darkness subservient to you, and I will make the two of them as armies of your armies;" trans. Gordon D. Newby, *The Making of the Last Prophet: A Reconstruction of the Earliest Biography of Muhammad* (Columbia: University of South Carolina Press, 1989), p. 195.

3. Some of the basic features of this narrative are contained in the Quran (18 *Kahf* 84–101). The fuller version is related to al-Tabari's *Jāmiʿ al-bayān fī tafsīr al-Quʾrān*, 30 vols. (Cairo: Mustafa al-Halabi wa'wladuhu, 1954), vol. 16, pp. 9, 17–21. Al-Tabari obtained it from the first part of Ibn Ishaq's biography of the Prophet Muhammad, which was written during the first half of the second/eighth century. The whole first part of Ibn Ishaq's text was lost centuries ago, but it has been partially reconstructed and translated by Newby, in *The Making of the Last Prophet*. The Alexander story can be found on pp. 193–200.

4. Newby, *The Making of the Last Prophet*, pp. 7, 194. Ibn Ishaq was not the first Muslim to use the Alexandrian Romance for princely instruction. A scribe to the Umayyad caliph Hisham (reigned 105/724–125/743) had prepared a collection of letters between Alexander and Aristotle, based on the Romance, containing advice for rulers. See further, J. D. Latham, "The Beginnings of Arabic Prose Literature: The Epistolary Genre," in *Cambridge History of Arabic Literature*, gen. eds. A. F. L. Beeston, et al., vol. 1, pp. 155–64.

5. Abu'l-ʿAbbas Ahmad b. Yahya b. Jabir al-Baladhuri (d. 279/892), *Futūḥ al-buldān*, ed. M. J. de Goeje (Leiden: E. J. Brill, 1866).

6. Abu Jaʿfar Muhammad b. Jarir al-Tabari (d. 310/923), *Taʾrīkh al-rusūl wa'l-mulūk*, ed. M. J. Goeje, 15 vols. (Leiden: E. J. Brill, 1879–1901).

7. Orientalists and Euramerican scholars of religion misrepresent the significance of the term *hijra* when they translate it as "flight." Muslims tend to view their *hijra* as a planned, self-conscious movement away from a world of corruption to one of moral virtue. It lacks the negative connotations borne by the English term, which suggests an animal-like hasty departure out of fear.

8. Muslim accounts usually refer to this site as the Prophet's mosque, rather than house. It may have included houses for him and his wives, but it is in their eyes primarily a mosque site. Oleg Grabar has argued that the site was actually designed to be Muhammad's house, with a large courtyard suited for religious and nonreligious activities; *The Formation of Islamic Art*, 2d ed. (New Haven: Yale University Press, 1987), pp. 102–5.

My review of quranic and hadith statements about prayer in houses supports this view, because, aside from the area around the Kaʿba in Mecca, it was more common for mosques in the lifetime of Muhammad to be erected within domestic compounds, not the other way around. Given the new situation for Muhammad and his followers brought about by the Hijra, however, it may well be that Muhammad intended the structure to serve both as a residence and as a place for congregational prayer from the outset. This is the position of Salih Lamʿi Mustafa, *al-Madīna al-munawwara: Taṭawwuruhā al-ʿumrānī wa-turāthuhā al-miʿmārī* (Beirut: Dar al-Nahda al-ʿArabiyya, 1981), pp. 53–55. Maintaining that references to the location of the Prophet's quarters are ambiguous, others maintain that the site was intended to function exclusively as a mosque; see, for example, Ghazi Izzeddin Bisheh, "The Mosque of the Prophet at Madinah throughout the First Century A. H. with Special Emphasis on the Umayyad Mosque" (Ph.D. dissertation, University of Michigan, 1979), p. 143.

9. Members of the Banu Najjar were among the first to negotiate to bring Muhammad and his Meccan followers to Medina. They are remembered in the hadiths as the best of the Ansar.

10. Ibn Ishaq, *Sīra*, vols. 1–2:494–96; Bukhari, *Ṣaḥīḥ, Manāqib al-anṣār* 43; Baladhuri, *Futūḥ*, pp. 5–6; Ibn Saʿd, *Ṭabaqāt*, vol. 1, p. 239; Tabari, *Taʾrīkh*, vol. 1, pp. 1258–59.

11. Ibn Khaldun, *Kitāb al-ʿibar*, 3d ed., 7 vols. (Beirut: Matbaʿat al-Madrasa wa-Dar al-Kitab al-Lubnani, 1967), vol. 1, p. 634. Cf. idem., *The Muqaddima*, trans. F. Rosenthal, vol. 2, pp. 264–65.

12. Ibn Saʿd, *Ṭabaqāt*, vol. 1, p. 240; al-Salihi, *Subul al-hudā*, vol. 3, p. 486; and Kister, " 'A Booth Like the Booth of Moses'," pp. 150–55.

13. See discussion in Mustafa, *al-Madīna al-munawwara*, p. 57; cf. al-Salihi, *Subul al-hudā*, vol. 3, pp. 506–508. A courtyard enclosure *(ḥujra)* was added to four of the houses. Although small by north American standards, Muhammad's quarters appear to have been considerably more spacious than other dwellings at the time. The area of rooms excavated at the early Islamic Arabian site of al-Rabadha range between 21.5 and 32.5 square feet. (six to nine square meters); Saʿd b. ʿAbd al-ʿAziz al-Rashid, *Al-Rabadhah: A Portrait of Early Islamic Civilization in Saudi Arabia* (Riyad: King Saud University, [1986]), pp. 26, 39.

14. Ibn Saʿd, *Ṭabaqāt*, vol. 1, pp. 499–500. Further details on the building of the Prophet's house-mosque can be found in K. A. C. Creswell, *Early Muslim Architecture*, 2 vols. (Oxford: Oxford University Press, 1932–1940), vol. 1, pp. 1ff.; and most recently in Mustafa, *al-Madīna al-munawwara*, pp. 47–62.

15. Ibn Ishaq, *Sīra*, vols. 1–2, p. 496. Cf. Ibn Saʿd, *Ṭabaqāt*, vol. 1, p. 240; and Bukhari, *Ṣaḥīḥ, Manāqib al-anṣār*, p. 43. Ibn Ishaq and others took pains to point out that the Prophet broke the rhyme and meter of this verse so as to avoid being accused of reciting poetry. His opponents used to undermine his claim to prophethood, and thus the divine origin of the Quran, by leveling this accusation against him.

16. This agreement, now known as the "Constitution of Medina," is regarded by modern scholars as one of the most authentic early Islamic documents. The extant text is probably a compilation of articles promulgated on different occasions in the years after the Hijra, but Ibn Ishaq clearly associates it with the first year of the Hijra and the building of the house-mosque; *Sīra*, vols. 1–2, pp. 501–4. See further, R. B. Serjeant, "The 'Consti-

tution' of Medina," *Islamic Quarterly* 8 (1964):3–16; and idem., "Early Arabic Prose," in *The Cambridge History of Arabic Literature*, gen. eds. A. F. L. Beeston, et al., vol. 1, pp. 133–47.

17. Ibn Ishaq, *Sīra*, vols. 1–2, p. 508; the Quran verse is from 59 *Ḥashr* 9.

18. They were known as *ahl al-ṣuffa* "people of the portico." See, for example, Ibn Saᶜd, *Ṭabaqāt*, vol. 1, pp. 255–56; *EI2*, s.v. "*Ahl al-Ṣuffa*" by W. Montgomery Watt.

19. Al-Salihi, *Subul al-hudā*, vol. 4, p. 488.

20. Baladhuri, *Futūḥ*, p. 6.

21. Ibid., pp. 6–7; and Jean Sauvaget, *La mosquée omeyyade de Médine: Etude sur les origines architecturales de la mosquée et de la basilique* (Paris: Vanoest, 1947), pp. 10–21, and chap. 4.

22. Ibn Saᶜd, *Ṭabaqāt*, vol. 1, p. 499.

23. See, for example, the hadiths and arguments cited in Muhammad b. ᶜAbd Allah al-Zarkashi (d. 794/1392), *Iᶜlām al-sājid bi-aḥkām al-masājid* (Cairo: al-Majlis al-Aᶜla li'l-Shu'un al-Islamiyya, 1384/1964), pp. 115–19, 186–93.

24. See further, M. J. Kister, " 'You Shall Only Set Out for Three Mosques': A Study of an Early Tradition," *Le muséon* 82 (1969):173–96.

25. These hadiths are cited in Bukhari, *Ṣaḥīḥ*, *Ḥaram Madīna;* and Muslim, *Ṣaḥīḥ*, *Ḥajj* 84ff.

26. On traditions about the station *(maqām)* of Ibrahim, see M. J. Kister, "*Maqām Ibrāhīm:* A Stone with an Inscription," *Le muséon* 84 (1971):477–91; and G. R. Hawting, "The Origins of the Muslim Sanctuary at Mecca," in *Studies on the First Century of Islamic Society*, ed. G. H. A. Juynboll (Carbondale and Edwardsville: Southern Illinois University Press, 1982), pp. 30–33.

27. See further Hawting, "Muslim Sanctuary," pp. 33–34.

28. It is sometimes stated that Muhammad is buried in ᶜA'isha's *ḥujra*, but the early sources all use the term *bayt* instead (e.g., Bukhari, *Ṣaḥīḥ*, *Kitāb al-nabī ilā kisrā wa-qayṣar* 2; and Ibn Saᶜd, *Ṭabaqāt*, vol. 2, pp. 232–33). According to traditional accounts, there was some discussion after the Prophet's death among his followers as to where his remains should be laid to rest. Medina's main cemetery and the mosque itself were both proposed, but they were ruled out partly because the Prophet is said to have condemned Jews and Christians for making graves into mosques. Then Abu Bakr mentioned a tradition that prophets should be buried where they die, which meant that Muhammad should be buried in ᶜA'isha's quarters (e.g., Ibn Saᶜd, *Ṭabaqāt*, vol. 2, pp. 240–41, 292–94). This area was incorporated into the mosque proper, however, under al-Walid. Traditions about Muhammad's burial therefore appear to criticize later caliphal building projects in Medina.

29. See further, ᶜAli b. ᶜAbd Allah al-Samhudi (d. 912/1506), *Kitāb wafā' al-wafa bi-akhbār dār al-Muṣṭafā*, 2 vols. (Cairo: Matbaᶜat al-Adab wa'l-Mu'ayyid, 1909), vol. 2, pp. 394–458.

30. See, for example, al-Zarkashi, *Iᶜlām al-sājid*, pp. 186–93; al-Salihi, *Subul al-hudā*, vol. 3, pp. 451–55, 459–65.

31. See chap. 6.

32. This is a widely attested hadith; see, for example, Bukhari, *Ṣaḥīḥ*, *Ḥaram al-Madīna* 13; Muslim, *Ṣaḥīḥ*, *Ḥajj* 84; Malik, *al-Muwaṭṭā'*, *Qibla* 5. Further citations in

Wensinck et al., *Concordance*, vol. 1, p. 237. It is also used frequently today in Egyptian Hajj murals (see chap. 6 and appendix A). Variants use *qabr* "grave" and *ḥujra* instead of *bayt*. The former is obviously an anachronism.

33. Bukhari, *Ṣaḥīḥ*, *Riqāq* 53; Ibn Saʿd, *Ṭabaqāt*, vol. 1, p. 250. See further, *EI2*, s.v. "*Ḥawḍ* (1)" by A. J. Wensinck.

34. *EI2*, s.v. "*Ḥawḍ* (2)" by A. B. M. Husain. Archaeological excavations in Arabia indicate that courtyard reservoirs in the early Islamic period could be covered with stone, with a hole left for drawing water. Conceivably, therefore, objects could be placed on top of these stone pavements, as may have been the case with the Prophet's *minbar*.

35. For example, Ibn Hanbal, *Musnad*, vol. 1, pp. 307, 329, 373; Tirmidhi, *Jāmiʿ al-ṣaḥiḥ*, *Ḥajj* 50. One of these traditions mentions that "the station" (of Ibrahim?) was from paradise also.

36. Ibn al-Najjar, quoted in Sauvaget, *Mosquée omeyyade*, p. 81.

37. See further, Richard Ettinghausen and Oleg Grabar, *The Art and Architecture of Islam 650–1250*, Pelican History of Art (New York: Viking Penguin, 1987), pp. 30–33, 40–44.

38. That is, Muhammad, the most praised.

39. That is Muhammad, the chosen.

40. Ibn Ishaq, *Sīra*, vols. 3–4, pp. 666–69, lines 1–6, 11–13, 42–46; cf. the translation rendered by A. Guillaume, *The Life of Muhammad: A Translation of Ishaq's "Sīrat Rasūl Allāh"* (Karachi: Oxford University Press), pp. 795–98. The poem is attributed to Hassan b. Thabit, the Prophet's poet. The anachronisms it contains indicate that it was composed much later by someone else, perhaps for Ibn Ishaq himself. See further, Guillaume's discussion in ibid., pp. xxv–xxx.

41. See, for example, Michael G. Morony, "Conquerors and Conquered: Iran," in *Studies*, ed. G. H. A. Juynboll, pp. 73–87; and idem., *Iraq after the Muslim Conquest* (Princeton: Princeton University Press, 1984).

42. Fred McGraw Donner, *The Early Islamic Conquests* (Princeton: Princeton University Press, 1981), p. 245. Donner provides citations to the original documents.

43. Ibid., p. 246.

44. Baladhuri *Futūḥ*, p. 392; and Morony, "Conquerors and Conquered: Iran," p. 78.

45. Abu Bakr Muhammad b. Jaʿfar al-Narshakhi (c. 332/943), *The History of Bukhara*, trans. Richard N. Frye (Cambridge, MA: Mediaeval Academy of America, 1954), p. 48.

46. See further Donner, *Islamic Conquests*, pp. 240–41.

47. Tabari, *Taʾrīkh*, vol. 1, p. 2360.

48. Ibid., vol. 1, p. 2484.

49. Although part of Kufa has been excavated, we have to rely on historical texts to reconstruct its development. My discussion is based largely on the most complete account, that of Sayf b. ʿUmar, which is contained in Tabari's history, *Taʾrīkh*, vol. 1, pp. 2481–95. For a thorough analysis of the sources and of Kufa's organization and growth, see Hichem Djait, *Al-Kūfa: Naissance de la ville islamique*, Islam d'hier et d'aujourd'hui, no. 29 (Paris: G.-P. Maissoneuve et Larose, 1986).

50. See Djait's reconstructions in *Al-Kūfa*, pp. 112 and 124.

51. Ibid., pp. 114–15.

52. Donner, *Islamic Conquests*, pp. 229–36; Djait, *Al-Kūfa*, pp. 268–70.

53. Djait, *Al-Kūfa*, pp. 212–22, 302.

54. Accounts about the founding of Baghdad can be found in Tabari's history, *Ta'rīkh*, vol. 3, pp. 271–82, and 319–26; and in al-Khatib al-Baghdadi, *Ta'rīkh Baghdād aw madīnat al-salām*, 14 vols. (Beirut: Dar al-Kitab al-ʿArabi, [1966?–1986]), vol. 1, pp. 66–78; and Jacob Lassner, *The Topography of Baghdad in the Early Middle Ages* (Detroit: Wayne State University Press, 1970). Modern scholarship on the founding of Baghdad has sometimes overlooked both the religious and domestic elements involved. See further the discussion and citations of Lassner, *The Shaping of ʿAbbasid Rule* (Princeton: Princeton University Press, 1980), chaps. 6–8 passim.

55. Tabari, *Ta'rīkh*, vol. 3, p. 274.

56. Lassner, *ʿAbbasid Rule*, pp. 185–88.

57. Grabar, *Formation of Islamic Art*, p. 68.

58. Lassner, *ʿAbbasid Rule*, pp. 230–8.

59. Bear in mind that the legitimacy of the rulers at this time depended partly on their ability to convince their Muslim subjects that they were truly among "the people of the house" *(ahl al-bayt)*.

60. On Baghdad's etymology and epithets, see further al-Baghdadi, *Ta'rīkh*, vol. 1, pp. 58–62; Abu ʿAbd Allah Yaqut, *Muʿjam al-buldān*, ed. F. Wüstenfeld, 6 vols. (Leipzig: F. A. Brockhaus, 1866–1873), vol. 1, pp. 677–80; and Lassner, *Topography*, p. 231n.3.

61. Al-Baghdadi, *Ta'rīkh*, vol. 1, pp. 101–4.

62. Ibid., vol. 1, p. 68; attributed to a third-/ninth-century poet of the ʿAbbasid court. A later variant opens with the lines:

> Have you see in the length and breadth of the earth
> A house like Baghdad *with a dwelling (maskin) of ease*?
> Life in Baghdad is pure, its wood is verdant
> Life outside of it is uncomfortable and stale. . . .
> (italics added; Yaqut, *Muʿjam*, 1:685)

This variant reveals that a paradisal image can be replaced by a domestic one.

63. Al-Baghdadi, *Ta'rīkh*, vol. 1, pp. 101–5.

64. Ibid., vol. 1, p. 46.

65. A hypothetical account of the development of this concept is provided by Monoucher Parvin and Maurie Sommer, "Dār al-Islām: The Evolution of Muslim Territoriality and Its Implications for Conflict Resolution in the Middle East," *IJMES* 11 (1980):1–21. The authors, however, do not discuss the use of concept in Islamic legal texts in detail. See also, Majid Khadduri, *War and Peace in the Law of Islam* (Baltimore: Johns Hopkins University Press, 1955), pp. 141–296; and Ann K. S. Lambton, *State and Government in Medieval Islam, an Introduction to the Study of Islamic Political Theory: The Jurists* (Oxford: Oxford University Press, 1981), chap. 12, passim.

66. Zakaria Bashier, *Hijra: Story and Significance* (Leicester, England: The Islamic Foundation, 1983), p. 91.

67. See further, Parvin and Sommer, "Dār al-Islām," pp. 4–5.

68. Al-Azraqi, *Kitāb akhbār Makka*, p. 6; cf. p. 355. See also Arent J. Wensinck, *The Ideas of the Western Semites Concerning the Navel of the Earth* (Amsterdam: Johannes Muller, 1916), chap. 3.

69. Courtly writers continued to extoll the virtues of Baghdad long after it was founded nevertheless. The fifth-/eleventh-century scholar Abu Mansur ʿAbd al-Malik b. Muhammad b. Ismaʿil al-Thaʿalibi said of Baghdad, "It is called the earthly paradise, the meeting-place of the two rivers, i.e., the Tigris and Euphrates, the center of the world, the city of peace, the dome of Islam; for it is the shining light of the land, the seat of the caliphate, the place where all rare and choice things are found together" (*Laṭāʾif al-maʿārif*, trans. C. E. Bosworth, Edinburgh: Edinburgh University Press, 1968, p. 124).

70. Tabari, *Taʾrīkh*, vol. 3, p. 197.

71. Louis Massignon, *The Passion of al-Ḥallāj: Mystic and Martyr of Islam*, vol. 1: *The Life of al-Ḥallāj*, trans. H. Mason, Bollingen Series 98 (Princeton: Princeton University Press, 1982), pp. 485, 541.

72. See *EI2*, s.v. "Makka (4), As the Center of the World" by David A. King.

73. Baladhuri, *Futūḥ*, p. 412; al-Narshakhi, *History of Bukhara*, pp. 40–41.

74. W. Montgomery Watt, *Islamic Philosophy and Theology* (Edinburgh: University of Edinburgh Press, 1962), pp. 13–19.

75. From Ibn Qawlawayh al-Qummi, *Kāmil al-ziyāra;* quoted in Muhammad Mahdi Shams al-Din, *The Rising of al-Husayn: Its Impact on the Consciousness of Muslim Society*, trans. I. K. A. Howard (London: The Muhammadi Trust, 1985), p. 150.

76. Al-Hujwiri said, "Sufism is founded on celibacy;" see the discussion in Margaret Smith, *Rabiʿa the Mystic and Her Fellow-Saints in Islam* (Cambridge: Cambridge University Press, 1928), chap. 13.

77. ʿAli b. ʿUthman al-Jullabi al-Hujwiri, *Kashf al-muḥjūb*, ed. V. A. Zukovskij (Leningrad, 1926), p. 121f.; and idem., *The* "Kashf al-Mahjūb": *The Oldest Persian Treatise on Sufism*, trans. R. Nicholson, E. J. W. Gibb Memorial Series, o.s. 17 (London: Luzac, 1959), p. 327.

78. See Paul Nywia, *Exegèse coranique et langage mystique: Nouvel essai sur le lexique technique des mystiques musulmans* (Beirut: Dar El-Machreq, 1970), pp. 325–34.

79. Muhammad b. ʿAbd al-Jabbar al-Niffari, *The* Mawāqif *and* Mukhātabāt *of Muhammad ibn ʿAbdi 'l-Jabbar al-Niffari with Other Fragments*, ed. A. J. Arberry, E. J. W. Gibb Memorial Series, n.s. 9 (London: Luzac, 1935), Arabic text, p. 41; cf. Arberry's translation, p. 56.

80. Al-Khatib al-Baghdadi, *Taʾrīkh*, vol. 8, p. 138; see further Massignon, *Passion of al-Ḥallāj*, vol. 1, pp. 540, 546–51.

81. Massignon concluded that such rulings were what finally led to al-Ḥallāj's execution, after a long prison term; *Passion of al-Ḥallāj*, vol. 1, pp. 539–40; and *EI2*, s.v. "al-Ḥallāj," by L. Massignon and L. Gardet. Nevertheless, al-Ḥallāj's rulings offered pilgrims a safe alternative to performing the Hajj in troubled times. In 281/894, the Qarmatians established an extremist Shīʿi state in the eastern part of the Arabian Peninsula, and began attacking pilgrim caravans. Eight years after al-Ḥallāj's execution, they raided Mecca, slaughtered the pilgrims, and stole the Black Stone from the Kaʿba (317/930). Pilgrim traffic decreased as a result.

82. Smith, *Rabiᶜa the Mystic*, p. 25. Once, when offered a house in good repair and decorated with paintings, she refused it on account of her fear that it would distract her attention from the affairs of the hereafter; ibid., p. 86.

83. Farid al-Din Attar, *Muslim Saints and Mystics*, trans. A. J. Arberry, Persian Heritage Series No. 1 (London: Routledge & Kegan Paul, 1966), pp. 66–70.

84. Sufis circulated a legend that recounts that when Ibrahim eventually reached Mecca, he did not see the Kaᶜba. He was quite perturbed when he discovered that it had actually gone to meet Rabiᶜa, who was still mid-way in her journey to Mecca for the Hajj. In some circles, therefore, Rabiᶜa's piety was considered to be superior to Ibrahim's. See Smith, *Rabiᶜa the Mystic*, p. 9.

85. Al-Ghazali, *Iḥyāʾ*, vol. 4, p. 305; and Smith, *Rabiᶜa the Mystic*, p. 71f.

Chapter 4: Muslim Dwellings in Urban Egypt, Past and Present

1. See Wladyslaw B. Kubiak, *Al-Fusṭāṭ: Foundation and Early Development* (Cairo: American University in Cairo Press, 1987), p. 56; and J.-C. Garcin, "Habitat médiéval et histoire urbaine à Fustat et au Caire," in *Palais et maisons du Caire*, 2 vols., eds. J.-C. Garcin, B. Maury, J. Revault et al. (Paris: Centre Nationale de la Recherche Scientific, 1982–1983), Vol. 1, p. 149.

2. Kubiak, *Fusṭāṭ*, p. 83 and n. 46. In subsequent centuries, the population decreased by half. When Napoleon's troops occupied Cairo, its population was estimated to be 263,000. See André Raymond, "Le Caire sous les Ottomans (1517–1798)," in *Palais et maisons*, vol. 2, pp. 15–19, 25.

3. Taqiyy al-Din Ahmad al-Maqrizi (c. 842/1438), *Kitāb al-mawāᶜiẓ wa'l-iᶜtibār bi-dhikr al-khiṭaṭ wa'l-athār*, 2 vols. (Bulaq: al-Matbaᶜa al-Amiriyya, 1270/1853), vol. 2, pp. 246–47; Kubiak, *Fusṭāṭ*, p. 129 and Plan 4.

4. Garcin, "Habitat médiéval," in *Palais et maisons*, vol. 1, pp. 150–51, 154–55; cf. Kubiak, *Fusṭāṭ*, pp. 125–27.

5. Kubiak, *Fusṭāṭ*, pp. 80–81. That Muslim houses were indistinguishable from those of the local populace is implied by the fact that in times of persecution, Christians were obliged to hang wooden images of demons on the doors of their houses (al-Maqrizi, *Khiṭaṭ*, vol. 2, p. 494).

6. Al-Maqrizi, *Khiṭaṭ*, vol. 2, pp. 247–49; Estelle Whelan, "The Origins of the *Miḥrāb Mujawwaf:* A Reinterpretation," *IJMES* 18 (1986): 209–11.

7. Ettinghausen and Grabar, *Art and Architecture*, pp. 45–71.

8. Al-Maqrizi, *Khiṭaṭ*, vol. 1, pp. 209, 302. Al-Maqrizi's sources do not mention a bath, but I infer that ᶜAbd al-ᶜAziz's compound had one from the fact that it was built on top of the mineral spring located there.

9. A sizeable minority remained Coptic until the ninth/fifteenth century. See further, Ira M. Lapidus, "The Conversion of Egypt to Islam," *Israel Oriental Studies* 2 (1969): 260–62.

10. Naser-e Khosraw, *Book of Travels (Safarnama)*, trans. W. M. Thackston, Jr., Persian Heritage Series no. 26 (Albany: State University of New York Press, 1986), pp. 47, 52. Al-Maqrizi reports that at about this time, Fustat's dwellings were between five and seven stories tall, and that perhaps 200 people could live in a single house (*dār*); *Khiṭaṭ*, vol. 1, p. 334.

11. Solomon D. Goitein, *A Mediterranean Society: The Jewish Communities of the Arab World as Portrayed in the Documents of the Cairo Geniza*, vol. 4: *Daily Life* (Berkeley: University of California Press, 1983), pp. 21–24, 59, 77.

12. Goitein writes, "The strict division of a home into male and female sections perhaps became common under the influence of the Mamluk and Turkish military aristocracies, who kept real harems and were imitated in this custom by the high bourgeoisie;" ibid., p. 64. See also Garcin, "Habitat médiéval," in *Palais et maisons*, vol. 1, p. 157.

13. See further, Goitein, *Mediterranean Society*, vol. 4, pp. 82–97.

14. Ibid., pp. 15–21.

15. Raymond, "Le Caire sous les Ottomans," in *Palais et maisons*, vol. 2, pp. 21–22, 77–89; idem., *The Great Arab Cities in the 16th and 18th Centuries*, Hagop Kevorkian Series on Near Eastern Art and Civilization (New York: New York University Press, 1984), pp. 58–69.

16. Raymond, "Le Caire sous les Ottomans," in *Palais et maisons*, vol. 2, pp. 86–87.

17. For example, al-Maqrizi, *Khiṭaṭ*, vol. 2, pp. 51–78; see also his descriptions of palaces and *madrasas*. *Waqf* documents are another valuable written source for this subject. See, for example, Laila ʿAli Ibrahim, "Middle Class Living Units in Mamluk Cairo: Architecture and Terminology," *Art and Archaeology Research Papers* 14 (1978): 24–30; and Garcin, "Habitat médiéval," in *Palais et maisons*, vol. 1, pp. 197, 202, 205, 211.

18. The wooden screens, known as *mashrabiyya*, may not have been widely used until after the ninth/fourteenth century.

19. Describing a visit to one of these houses, Lane-Poole stated that there was "no sign of life" in the courtyard, "doors are jealously closed, the windows shrouded . . . nothing of the domestic life of the inhabitants" is to be seen. Of course he was there as a stranger, when the British were governing Egypt directly. Aside from not noticing the "display" of privacy that was being made for him, would he have made the same observations if he had been there for a holiday feast, wedding, circumcision, or funeral? Why did he not describe courtyards in collective housing complexes, which might have offered him a different image of domestic life? See Stanley Lane-Poole, *The Story of Cairo* (London: J. M. Dent & Sons, 1902), pp. 12–17.

20. In less affluent houses, where formal reception rooms may be absent, male visitors were invited into the *ḥarīm* area itself. Women as a rule would retire to another room, or wear a veil. See Edward W. Lane, *An Account of the Manners and Customs of the Modern Egyptians*, 5th ed. (London: John Murray, 1860; reprint ed. New York: Dover, 1973), pp. 177–78.

21. Evidence for an economy of design in early Islamic architecture was presented above in our discussions of the development of the Prophet's house-mosque, and of the placement of mosques within tribal residential areas in the early garrison cities. See also, Grabar, *Formation*, p. 117.

22. J. Revault, "L'Architecture domestique au Caire à l'époque mamlouke (XIIIe–XVIe siècles)," in *Palais et maisons*, vol. 1, pp. 73–74. There were obvious differences as well: houses lacked minarets and large domes; religious colleges and Sufi monasteries lacked the irregularities of interior layout required in houses for security and privacy. Collective housing complexes were more like religious buildings in this last respect.

23. Alexandre Lezine, *Trois palais d'époque ottomane au Caire*, Memoires de IFAO No. 93 (Cairo: IFAO, 1972), p. 11, pl.11A.

24. I have reached this conclusion after investigating the plans of surviving Mamluk and Ottoman houses (e.g., Bayt al-Razzaz, Bayt al-Suhaymi, and the Musafirkhana) published by the Institut Français d'Archéologie Orientale du Caire. See plans in ibid.; Jacques Revault and Bernard Maury, *Palais et maisons du Caire du XIV e au XVIII e siècle*, 3 vols., Memoires de IFAO nos. 96, 100, 102 (Cairo: IFAO, 1975–1979); and the two-volume CNRS edition of *Palais et maisons* cited in note 1 in this chapter. One exception is the Mamluk *qāʿa* of Ahmad Quhya's house, which faces due east, but which had a southeast-oriented prayer niche added in one corner when it was converted into a mosque; A. Lézine, "Les salles nobles des palais mamlouks," *Annales islamologiques* 10 (1972): 86–89.

25. Two different *qibla* directions were used in Cairo in the medieval period, which resulted in orientational variations among the layouts of the Fatimid city and of the Mamluk Northern Cemetery. See David King, "Architecture and Astronomy: The Ventilators of Cairo and Their Secrets," *Journal of the American Oriental Society* 104 (1984): 116–18.

26. Ibid., pp. 120–22.

27. K. A. C. Creswell, *Muslim Architecture of Egypt*, 2 vols. (Oxford: Oxford University Press, 1952–1959) vol. 2, pp. 129–31; Revault, "Architecture domestique (mamlouke)," in *Palais et Maisons*, vol. 1, p. 40; see also, al-Maqrizi, *Khiṭaṭ*, vol. 2, pp. 63, 364, 374, 378. There were also instances when influential men destroyed mosques in order to build their palaces; for example al-Maqrizi, *Khiṭaṭ*, vol. 2, p. 70.

28. Garcin, "Habitat médiéval," in *Palais et maisons*, vol. 1, p. 177; see also al-Maqrizi, *Khiṭaṭ*, vol. 2, pp. 64, 365–66, 368, 372.

29. André Raymond, "Les grands waqfs et l'organisation de l'espace urbain à Alep et au Caire à l'époque ottomane (XVIe–XVIIe siècles)," *Bulletin des études orientales* 31 (1980): 122–23; J. Revault, "L'Architecture domestique au Caire à l'époque ottomane (XVIe–XVIIIe siècles)," in *Palais et maisons*, vol. 2, pp. 119–20.

30. Of course, houses were not the only source of *waqf* revenue. Nearly any perpetual income-producing property could be so used. In addition to houses, this included agricultural lands, hostels, caravanserais, baths, warehouses, workshops, ovens, slaves, cattle, and beasts of burden. In sixth/twelfth and seventh/thirteenth centuries, houses were among the most common *waqf* properties in Cairo, if the Geniza documents are representative for the Muslim as well as the Jewish populace; Goitein, *Mediterranean Society*, vol. 2, pp. 112–13, 413–37. See also Muhammad M. Amin, *al-Awqāf wa'l-ḥāyāh al-ijtimāʿiyya fī Miṣr 648–923 A.H./1200–1517 A.D.* (Cairo: Dar al-Nahda al-ʿArabiyya, 1980), pp. 100–101.

In the absence of a comprehensive study of later *waqf* properties in Cairo, Abraham Marcus's study of charitable trusts in Aleppo provides us with some idea about the relative size of *waqf* revenues derived from houses during the Ottoman era. Between 1164/1751 and 1167/1753, residential properties represented 13 percent of *waqf* holdings that provided 98 charitable foundations with 19 percent of their endowments (*The Middle East on the Eve of Modernity: Aleppo in the Eighteenth Century*, New York: Columbia University Press, 1989), pp. 306–307. For Egypt, see Janet Abu-Lughod, *Cairo: 1001 Years of the City Victorious*, Princeton Studies on the Near East (Princeton: Princeton University Press, 1971), pp. 76–79.

31. See further, Marcus, *Aleppo in the Eighteenth Century*, pp. 311–312.

32. The physician was Fath Allah b. Muʿtasim al-Tabrizi (d. 816/1413), the grandson of a Persian Jewish convert to Islam; al-Maqrizi, *Khiṭaṭ*, vol. 2, p. 62.

33. Amin, *Awqāf*, chaps. 3–5.

34. Such murals can still be seen in the palaces of ʿAli Katkhuda, Sitt Wasila, and Qayt Bey. See Lézine, *Trois palais*, pp. 25–30, 41–42, pls. 24B, 25, 26, 31B, 32; and Revault and Maury, *Palais et maisons*, 1: 28, pl. 15B. Cf. Lane, *Modern Egyptians*, p. 18; and chap. 6 in this volume.

35. Recorded by the author in a field survey of the Musafirkhana in Cairo's Gamaliyya quarter; inscription dated 1203/1789. The palace is described in Revault, "Architecture domestique (époque ottomane)," in *Palais et maisons*, vol. 2, pp. 223–36. Another inscription likens this "illustrious and sublime" house to the *ḥaram* of Mecca; ibid., p. 231 n.10.

36. Raymond, *Great Arab Cities*, p. 56.

37. See John R. Weeks, *The Demography of Islamic Nations*, Population Bulletin vol. 43 (Washington, D.C.: Population Reference Bureau, 1988), pp. 8–9, 13.

38. See further, ibid., pp. 33–34; and Saad Eddin Ibrahim, "Urbanization in the Arab World: The Need for an Urban Strategy," in *Arab Society: Social Science Perspectives*, eds. Nicholas S. Hopkins and Saad Eddin Ibrahim (Cairo: American University in Cairo Press, 1985), pp. 123–47.

39. These are 1990 unofficial estimates; cf. Weeks, *Demography*, pp. 33–34; Mark S. Hoffman, ed., *The World Almanac and Book of Facts 1990* (New York: Pharos Books, 1989), p. 774.

40. See, for example, al-Maqrizi, *Khiṭaṭ*, vol. 2, pp. 362–404. Al-Maqrizi lists at least seventy-three religious colleges for Cairo in this chapter.

41. Abu-Lughod, *Cairo*, p. 158.

42. Ibid., p. 223.

43. This typology of class-based residential areas is based on a schema developed in Abu-Lughod, *Cairo*, chap. 12 and fig. 17.

44. See Sawsan el-Messeri, *Ibn al-Balad: A Concept of Egyptian Identity* (Leiden: E. J. Brill, 1978); and Laila Shukry El-Hamamsy, "The Assertion of Egyptian Identity," in *Arab Society*, eds., N. S. Hopkins and S. E. Ibrahim, pp. 56–58. Actually *baladi* can describe something of either the town or the country, in the sense of "native Egyptian" more than "rural." The term *zawāti* "aristocratic" is synonymous with *afrangi; fellāḥi* "peasant-like" occurs more often in common parlance than *rīfi*. Such labels may also be used to chide members of one's own group. Of course, members of the *afrangi* and *rīfi* populations use this three-fold classification in a different manner, but exactly how they do so is a topic demanding further empirical research.

45. *Ṣaʿīdi* is used by *afrangi* and *baladi* Egyptians to convey the most negative qualities of the *rīfi* subculture; Upper Egyptians are usually made the butt of Cairene jokes. Zamalik is linked with the *afrangi* subculture; Shubra with lower-middle class off-shoots of the *baladi* subculture; Sayyida Zaynab, Zaynhum, and Gamaliyya with the soul of the *baladi* subculture; and Khalifa and Imbaba are associated with the *rīfi* subculture.

46. Premodern Egyptian house terms were mentioned earlier in this chapter. See further, Goitein, *Mediterranean Society*, vol. 4, pp. 56–78; Ibrahim, "Middle Class Living Units in Mamluk Cairo"; and Raymond, *Great Arab Cities*, pp. 58–85.

47. *DEA*, p. 114. Hinds and Badawi include in their entry for this word the saying, "Egypt is one house." This expression, however, does not enjoy wide circulation in Egypt, although it reflects the familial tone of governmental rhetoric.

48. This connotation originated in the medieval period; see Goitein, *Mediterranean Society*, vol. 4, pp. 26–29.

49. *DEA*, p. 142.

50. In technical parlance, the Arabic equivalent for the house as a "dwelling unit" is now *wiḥda sakaniyya*.

51. Medieval Arabic lexicographers maintained that a *bayt* and a *maskan* were permanent dwelling places, whereas a *manzil* was a form of transient housing; Ibrahim, "Middle Class Living Units," p. 30n.11. The late medieval meaning of *manzil* may have contributed to its infrequent use in modern Egyptian oral discourse.

52. The use of *ūda* for designating an ordinary room in Egyptian vernacular is obviously due to the Ottoman presence between the tenth/sixteenth century and the fourteenth/twentieth century. Since it became a common word for rooms in Turkish town houses in the late tenth/sixteenth century, it probably did not enter Egyptian domestic vocabulary until later. See Suraiya Faroqhi, *Men of Modest Substance: House Owners and House Property in Seventeenth-Century Ankara and Kayseri* (Cambridge: Cambridge University Press, 1987), chap. 2. So far I have been unable to find evidence for the term in Mamluk *waqf* documents, nor in al-Maqrizi's notes on Cairene houses; idem., *Khiṭaṭ*, vol. 2, pp. 51–79. The word *ūda* does occur in eleventh-/seventeenth-century Ottoman *waqf* documents from Damascus; see Antoine Abdel Nour, "Types architeturaux et vocabulaire de l'habitat en Syrie aux XVIe et XVIIe siècle," in *L'Espace social de la ville arabe*, ed. Dominique Chevalier (Paris: G.-P. Maisonneuve et Larose, 1979), p. 68.

53. Muhammad Galal, "Essai d'observations sur les rites funéraires en Egypte actuelle relevées dans certaines régions compagnardes," *Revue des études islamiques* 11 (1937): 204.

54. *DEA*, pp. 471–72; for premodern meanings of this root, which do not include the equivalent of "apartment," see Lane, *Arabic-English Lexicon*, pp. 1576–79.

55. Nawal al-Messiri Nadim, "Family Relationships in a 'Ḥārah' in Cairo," in *Arab Society*, N. S. Hopkins and S. E. Ibrahim, eds., pp. 214–16; and Nadim, "The Concept of the *Ḥāra:* A Historical and Sociological Study of al-Sukkariyya," *Annales islamologiques* 15 (1979):324–34.

56. *Al-iskān al-mushawwah;* Milad Hanna, *Urīdu maskanan: Mushkila lahā ḥall* (Cairo: Maktabat Ruz al-Yusuf, 1978), pp. 61–62; and Parliamentary Committee on Housing, Public Utilities, and Reconstruction, *Dirāsāt wa'wrāq ʿamal ḥawl qaḍāyā al-iskān fī Miṣr, marḥala ūlā* (Cairo, 1985), p. 30. Hanna explains that this phrase is meant to draw attention to the way this kind of housing deforms the "human souls" of its inhabitants, at the same time that it deforms the visage of the entire society.

57. Milad Hanna, *"Ishkāliyyat al-iskān: Manāhij al-baḥth,"* lecture delivered at the Center for Arabic Studies Abroad, American University in Cairo, July 1985; and Parliamentary Committee on Housing, *Dirāsāt wa'wrāq*, pp. 98–100. John A. Williams (personal communication, 1990) states that the number of people living under such conditions is actually between one and two million.

58. "The (Arab) house, closed to the outside, is . . . totally open to its courtyard, and from there to heaven. The (heavenly) courtyard . . . thus accomplishes communication, not with other men, but with the universe;" Antoine Abdel Nour, "Types architeturaux," p. 83.

59. See further, Oswald Ducrot and Tzevetan Todorov, *Encyclopedic Dictionary of the Sciences of Language*, trans. C. Porter (Baltimore: Johns Hopkins University Press, 1979), pp. 61–67, 118–19, 333–45.

60. Hannah Arendt, *The Human Condition* (New York: Doubleday, 1959), pp. 178–79.

61. Defining boundary crossing as transgression, Bataille writes, "It opens the door into what lies beyond the limits usually observed, but it maintains these limits just the same. Transgression is complementary to the profane world, exceeding its limits but not destroying it. Human society is not only a world of work. Simultaneously—or successively—it is made up of the profane and the sacred, its two complementary forms. The profane world is the world of taboos. The sacred world depends on limited acts of transgression" (Georges Bataille, *Death and Sensuality: A Study of Eroticism and the Taboo*. New York: Walker and Co., 1962, pp. 67–68). See also, Mary Douglas, *Purity and Danger* (Baltimore: Penguin Books, 1970); Victor Turner, "Betwixt and Between: The Liminal Period in *Rites de Passage*," in Turner, *The Forest of Symbols: Aspects of Ndembu Ritual* (Ithaca, NY: Cornell University Press, 1967), pp. 93–111. Cf. the insightful introductory remarks of Fredrik Barth in his *Ethnic Groups and Boundaries: The Social Organization of Culture Difference* (Boston: Little, Brown and Co., 1969), pp. 9–18.

Chapter 5: Domestications of Islam in Modern Egypt: A Cultural Analysis

1. *Kull bayt luh ḥurmituh*. The variant, "Houses have their sacrality" (*al-buyūt laha ḥurma*) is also attested; *DEA*, p. 201.

2. Likewise, *ḥarīm*, from which the word "harem" has been derived, once referred both to women's quarters in large mansions or palaces and to women as a collectivity. In Egypt today, only the latter significance is common, because most Egyptians neither have the inclination nor the ability to maintain separate quarters for women in the home.

3. In contemporary Egyptian discourse, *ḥurma* has been employed by students and intellectuals to signify the inviolability of public university campuses, particularly during student demonstrations. By doing so, they attribute a positive moral value to their own words and deeds, while defending themselves and their campuses against attack by government troops.

4. *Sharaf* is synonymous with *ʿirḍ*, which emphasizes the public display of honor. See further, Peter C. Dodd, "Family Honor and the Forces of Change in Arab Society," *IJMES* 4 (1973): 40–54.

5. Dale F. Eickelman, *The Middle East: An Anthropological Approach* (Englewood Cliffs, N.J.: Prentice-Hall, 1981), p. 86.

6. Ahmad Amin, based on his own experience, maintains that the patriarchal order of the Egyptian household is being replaced by a more democratic one where women and children also hold sway. He takes a dim view of this development (Ahmad Amin, *Ḥayātī*, 2d ed. Cairo: Maktabat al-Nahda al-Misriyya, 1966, pp. 24–25).

7. Because it is a kind of hidden economy, Egypt's domestic economy cannot be easily quantified. With price inflation, population growth, a low per capita income, and a decline of revenues from emigrant labor, domestic production must be a crucial source of support for the social infrastructure.

8. Andrea Rugh, *Family in Contemporary Egypt* (Syracuse, NY: Syracuse University Press, 1984), pp. 262–270.

9. See, for example, Edward Westermarck, *Ritual and Belief in Morocco*, 2 vols. (London: Macmillan, 1926), vol. 1, chaps. 2 and 3; Clifford Geertz, *Islam Observed: Religious Development in Morocco and Indonesia* (Chicago: University of Chicago Press, 1968), pp. 32–33, 44–45, 50–56; *EI2*, s.v. "*baraka*" by G. S. Colin; and Raymond Jamous, *Honneur et baraka: Les structures sociales traditionelles dans le Rif* (Cambridge: Cambridge University Press, 1981), chap. 10. Ahmad Amin called *baraka* "the secret of God, the prophets, and the saints found in things," (Ahmad Amin, *Qāmūs al-ʿādāt wa'l-taqālīd wa'l-taʿābīr al-miṣriyya*, Cairo: Lajnat al-Taʾlif wa'l-Tarjama wa'l-Nashr, 1953, p. 86).

10. A fatalistic outlook, which outside observers used to say dominated the outlook of Muslims in Egypt and elsewhere, arises only in situations where alternative measures appear to be ineffective, such as when a woman has actually been divorced, or when death really strikes. Then people say, "It is written;" or, "Everything is a matter of fate" (*qisma wa-naṣīb*). Rather than ending efforts to enhance blessing and repel evil, however, even such "fatal" events in the life cycle as divorce and death provoke the afflicted, or their associates, into continuing the struggle to ameliorate their condition.

11. The data on this subject was obtained from interviews with residents of Upper Egypt, as well as from Canaan, "Palestinian Arab House" (1933), pp. 61–67; Hans Winkler, *Bauern zwischen Wasser und Wüste: Volkskundliches aus dem Dorfe Kimān in Oberägypten* (Stuttgart: W. Kohlhammer, 1934), p. 63; Westermarck, *Ritual and Belief in Morocco*, vol. 1, pp. 315–18; Bourdieu, "Maison Kabyle," pp. 751–53.

12. *DEA*, p. 830f.

13. See further, Amin, *Qāmūs*, p. 124; and Moshe Piamenta, *Islam in Everyday Arabic Speech* (Leiden: E. J. Brill, 1979), pp. 90, 165, 215. Lane mentions the custom of stepping over chard in connection with marriage ceremonies. (Lane, *Modern Egyptians*, p. 172). The expression "*mabrūk!*" is an all-purpose way of conveying congratulations.

14. Comparable procedures are followed in many parts of the world, including the United States. See, for example, Newbell N. Puckett, *Popular Beliefs and Superstitions: A Compendium of American Folklore* (Boston: G. K. Hall, 1981), vol. 1, pp. 687–702.

15. *DEA*, p. 425. In the Cairene dialect, however, *q* is pronounced as a glottal stop, which makes the words sound less similar.

16. Ibid., p. 432.

17. Ibid., p. 613.

18. Marriage in rural Egypt does not always entail patrilocal residence. In parts of Upper Egypt, it is customary for the couple to reside with the bride's family for the first years of the marriage. See, for example, Hamed Ammar, *Growing Up in an Egyptian Village: Silwa, Province of Aswan* (London: Routledge & Kegan Paul, 1954), pp. 194, 198.

19. See further, Unni Wikan, *Life among the Poor in Cairo*, trans. A. Henning (London: Tavistock, 1980), chap. 6; Janet Abu Lughod and Lucy Amin, "Egyptian Marriage Advertisements: Microcosm of a Changing Society," *Marriage and Family Living* 23 (1961): 127–36. Cf. Lane, *Modern Egyptians*, pp. 155–75 for an account of marriage practices among wealthy classes in Cairo more than one hundred years ago; Ammar, *Growing Up*, pp. 193–200; and Samiha al-Katsha, "Changes in Nubian Wedding Ceremonies," in J. G. Kennedy, ed., *Nubian Ceremonial Life: Studies in Islamic Syncretism and Cultural Change* (Berkeley: University of California Press, 1978), pp. 171–202.

20. The Islamic legal phrase for this act is *ʿaqd al-nikāḥ*. Egyptians will use *ʿaqd qarān* in formal speech instead.

21. Ammar, *Growing Up*, p. 194; cf. Lane, *Modern Egyptians*, p. 160.

22. See, for example, Nayra Atiya, *Khul-Khaal: Five Egyptian Women Tell Their Stories* (Syracuse, N.Y.: Syracuse University Press, 1982), pp. 115–16.

23. ʿAbd al-Ghani al-Nabawi al-Shal, *ʿArūsat al-mawlid* (Cairo: Dar al-Katib al-ʿArabi li'l-Tibaʿa wa'l-Nashr, 1967), p. 132.

24. Amin, *Qāmūs*, p. 350; cf. Atiya, *Khul-Khaal*, p. 114.

25. Bath tiles are a metaphor for the pure, radiant smoothness of her skin.

26. Al-Shal, *ʿArūsat al-mawlid*, p. 132. Cf. the rural wedding songs recorded in Gaston Maspero, "Chansons populaires recueillies dans la Haute-Egypte, de 1900 à 1914, pendant les inspections du Service des Antiquités," *Annales du Service des Antiquités de l'Egypte* 14 (1914): 123.

27. See, for example, al-Shal, *ʿArūsat al-mawlid*, pp. 120–22; and Atiya, *Khul-Khaal*, p. 114.

28. *Gawāz il-banāt sutra.*

29. Since the early 1980s, it has become customary for *baladi* and *afrangi* Egyptians to have their wedding celebrations recorded on video tape.

30. Wealthier families use private clubs for weddings, reserving their homes for intimate gatherings of family and friends only. The wealthiest make use of facilities offered by foreign-owned hotels, like the Hilton, Sheraton, and Oberoi. Most Egyptians, however, make their homes the center of wedding celebrations. Copts follow similar patterns, but go to churches to perform the formal vows.

31. Om Gad, quoted in Atiya, *Khul-Khaal*, p. 14.

32. See the comments of Nawal El Saadawi in *The Hidden Face of Eve: Women in the Arab World*, trans. S. Hetata (Boston: Beacon Press, 1982), chap. 5.

33. Ammar, *Growing Up*, p. 199.

34. Wikan, *Life among the Poor*, p. 137.

35. The Egyptian divorce rate in recent decades has been around 2 percent of the total population, with urban rates reaching as high as 2.9 percent; Rugh, *Family in Contemporary Egypt*, p. 177; El Saadawi, *Hidden Face of Eve*, p. 204.

36. According to Islamic law, there are several divorce methods. Reforms of Egyptian personal status laws have given women more rights and protections de jure in such matters, but they are not strictly enforced. See, for example, Esposito, *Women in Muslim Family Law*, pp. 30–37, 53–63; and El Saadawi, *Hidden Face of Eve*, pp. 198–99.

37. The terrible plight of divorced women who are not so fortunate is discussed in El Saadawi, *Hidden Face of Eve*, p. 200. See also Wikan, *Life among the Poor*, pp. 103–8.

38. *Mūt wi-kharāb diyār.*

39. Andrea Rugh, *Coping with Poverty in a Cairo Community*, Cairo Papers in Social Science No. 2.1 (Cairo: American University Press, 1979), pp. 67–72.

40. Of course, the death of any beloved child can affect the parents for the rest of their lives. See the comments of Om Gad about the death of her teenage son in Atiya, *Khul-Khaal*, pp. 7–9, 26–27.

41. See further, Rugh, *Family in Contemporary Egypt*, pp. 185–87.

42. See, for example, Winifred S. Blackman, *The Fellāḥīn of Upper Egypt: Their Religious, Social and Industrial Life with Special Reference to Survivals from Ancient Times* (London: George G. Harrap, 1927), pp. 69–72.

43. Recorded in Tanta during the early 1900s; Paul Kahle, *Die Totenklage im heutigen Ägypten: Arabische Texte mit Übersetzung und Erläuterungen* (Göttingen: Vandenhoed & Ruprecht, 1923), p. 33f.; cf. Galal, "Rites funéraires en Egypt." p. 269.

44. Sayyid ʿUways, *al-Khulūd fī ḥayāt al-Miṣriyyīn al-muʿāṣirīn* (Cairo: al-Hayʾa al-Misriyya al-ʿAmma li'l-Kitab, 1972), p. 79.

45. We are sorely in need of detailed studies of contemporary *baladi* funerary practices. Here, I rely chiefly on my field research in Cairo, and on these publications: Galal, "Rites funéraires en Egypte," pp. 131–299; Amin, *Qāmūs*, pp. 124–25, 139–40; ʿUways, *al-Khulūd fī ḥayāt al-Miṣriyyīn;* ʿAlya Shukri, *al-Turāth al-shaʿbī al-miṣrī fī'l-maktaba al-urūbiyya* (Cairo: Dar al-Jayl li'l-Tibaʿa, 1979). Funeral practices are also alluded to in Egyptian works of fiction; see, for example, Alifa Rifaat, "At the Time of the Jasmine," in *Distant View of a Minaret and Other Stories*, trans. Denys Johnson-Davies (London: Heinemann, 1983). Lane, *Modern Egyptians*, chap. 28, provides the most thorough account of Cairene funerary practices in the last century.

46. Another name for this stage is *khurūg ir-rūḥ* "departure of the soul." Euphemisms for a person's death itself are related to this phrase: *is-sirr il-ilāhi kharag/ṭiliʿ* "the divine mystery departed/ascended"; *igguhara kharagit* "the jewel departed"; Galal, "Rites funéraires en Egypte," p. 158.

47. The head may also be turned to the west, or toward Mecca (south/southeast).

48. Galal's account of Egyptian funeral practices is helpful for its comparative scope; "Rites funéraires en Egypte." He was a student of Marcel Mauss and Louis Massignon.

49. ʿAbd al-Rahim b. Ahmad al-Qadi, *Kitāb daqāʾiq al-akhbār fī dhikr al-janna wa'l-nār* (Cairo: Maktabat al-Jumhuriyya al-ʿArabiyya, n.d.), p. 14; with substantial emendations from an older manuscript edited and published by Monitz Wolfe, *Muhammedanische Eschatologie (Kitāb aḥwāl al-qiyāma)* (Leipzig: F. A. Brockhaus, 1872), pp. 26–27. Cf. the conflated English version, Aʾisha ʿAbd ar-Rahman at-Tarjumana, trans., *Islamic Book of the Dead: A Collection of Hadiths on the Fire and the Garden* (San Francisco: Diwan Press, 1977).

50. Galal, "Rites funéraires en Egypte," p. 191.

51. Amin, *Ḥayātī*, pp. 123–25.

52. Recorded by Galal, "Rites funéraires en Egypte," p. 264.

53. Thus according to Galal's transcription. The phrase *ʿayyāt il-kursi*, however, sounds very similar to the phrase *ayāt il-kursi;* that is, the Throne Verse from the Quran (2 *Baqara* 255) that is used to repel misfortune.

54. Galal, "Rites funéraires en Egypte," p. 272.

55. See, for example, ʿUways, *al-Khulūd fī ḥayāt al-Miṣriyyīn*, pp. 151–59. ʿUways provides figures based on a limited survey of Cairene university students during the mid-1960s; nevertheless, it casts light upon modern *baladi* attitudes toward death and the dead. See also Jane I. Smith, "Concourse between the Living and the Dead in Islamic Eschatological Literature," *History of Religions* 19 (1980): 232.

56. In Upper Egypt, married women who become pregnant during the mourning period are shunned. They are even obliged to abort the fetus in extreme cases. Pregnancy is regarded as an affront to the family of the deceased. Also, parents fear that the child born

during this time will be destined to a life of misfortune. See Galal, "Rites funéraires en Egypte," p. 234. Ahmad Amin wonders if the sadness of his life was the result of his being a fetus at the time his sister burned to death in a household accident. He writes, "I was nurtured on sad blood, and, after my birth, I nursed on sad milk. I was welcomed with sadness when I was born" (Amin, *Ḥayātī*, p. 19).

57. If the family can afford it, formal receptions with Quran recitation and the exchange of condolences are held for men in temporary pavilions erected in the street next to the apartment building, or at a mosque. This is especially so for the third day, fortieth day, and one-year anniversaries of the death. As is the case with weddings, these pavilions are an extension of domestic space. Moreover, they have not yet replaced receptions and recitations at home, which is where women can appropriately suffer their grief, and where condolers can come if they are not able to attend the formal receptions.

58. *Yā Sīn* contains succinct statements about life, death, and the hereafter. The bereaved may have it read over and over again, believing that it will bring mercy for the dead and assuage their own grief (Amin, *Qāmūs*, p. 284).

59. Amin (*Qāmūs*, p. 120) states that in his time, at both funerals and weddings, selections were read from 2 *Baqara* in the afternoon, and from 10 *Yūnus*, 11 *Hūd*, 12 *Yūsuf*, 13 *Raʿd*, 15 *Ḥijr*, 16 *Naḥl*, 17 *Isrāʾ* and the last chapters of the Quran in the evening. Galal indicates that 36 *Yā Sīn* is recited before the body is carried from the house. He also states that 41 *Fuṣṣilat*, 36 *Yā Sīn*, or 18 *Kahf* are read in the room where the last breath was taken during stage 1 of the mourning cycle. See Galal, "Rites funéraires en Egypte," pp. 166, 190. For details on Quran passages recited at Cairene funerals over a century ago, see Lane, *Modern Egyptians*, pp. 517, 525f.

60. Galal, "Rites funéraires en Egypte," p. 157.

61. Al-Qadi, *Kitāb daqāʾiq al-akhbār*, p. 15.

62. If *turab* is pronounced with an unemphatic "*t*," it is related to the idea of dirt; with an emphatic "*ṭ*," however, it suggests fright; *DEA*, pp. 124, 534. Most Egyptians use the emphatic form, as exemplified by the Arabic caption for figure 7.

63. Al-Qadi, *Kitāb daqāʾiq al-akhbār*, p. 22, with emendations from *Kitāb aḥwāl al-qiyāma*, edited by Wolfe, pp. 44–45.

64. Al-Qadi, *Kitāb daqāʾiq al-akhbār*, p. 13, with emendations from *Kitāb aḥwāl al-qiyāma*, edited by Wolfe, pp. 24–25. Note that the text advises the use of the *basmala* and the *shahāda* to deflect harmful beings. See my discussion of this subject in the next chapter and in Appendix A.

65. *Mandara* designated the formal reception hall in Mamluk and Ottoman palaces. It is now mainly used to designate a sitting room in a *rīfī* house.

66. This formula is also used in Hajj murals; see Appendix A, I.1d.

67. Males who are not closely related to the husband or wife under special circumstances are invited to rest or spend the night in the bedroom. In such a situation, the wife retreats to another part of the apartment, or to a relative's house if this is not possible. Similar adjustments are made when adult males come to visit a man who is bedridden. The general principle remains in effect, however: when the bedroom is transformed into a space of appearance, other sections of the apartment serve as non-visible spaces.

68. Some believe that having a copy of the Quran in the house prevents the house from being robbed or destroyed by fire (Amin, *Qāmūs*, p. 370).

69. In Egypt today, people do not usually remove their shoes when they pay someone a visit. If a member of the household plans to spend an extended period of time in the house, however, they will usually change into house slippers.

70. Amin, *Ḥayātī*, pp. 23–24.

71. For further examples of this sort of exchange, see *DEA*, pp. 314, 914–15.

72. According to a reliable 1976 survey, more than 241,000 Cairene families, consisting of nearly one million people, lived in one-bedroom apartments. For all of Egypt, the count was nearly 600,000 families with more than 2.5 million members. See further, Parliamentary Committee on Housing, *Dirāsāt wa'wrāq*, pp. 102–4.

73. The results of this study were published in *Akhbār al-yawm* (Cairo), 8 November 1979, p. 5. The reliability of these figures has been questioned in some quarters. Apparently distrusting the government, some families inflated their membership, hoping to be relocated to larger flats in public housing projects. Some underestimated their size, thinking that they could fool the government into relocating one family into several apartments if some members registered separately. If both strategies were used by families in the survey, it is possible that one cancelled out the other, thus leading me to conclude that the government figures are reasonable. Moreover, we know that other Cairo districts had larger densities at the time. See further, *al-Akhbār* (Cairo), 12 October 1978, p. 14; and Madiha al-Safty, "Sociological Perspectives on Urban Housing," in *Urban Research Strategies for Egypt*, ed. Richard Lobban, Cairo Papers in Social Science 6 (Cairo: American University in Cairo, 1983), p. 3.

74. or 230,000 per square kilometer.

75. This is my estimate, assuming a 1990 population of fourteen million and a metropolitan area of 102 square miles. Compare with the 1987 densities of New York City and Chicago: 14,168 and 10,696 per square mile respectively (Hoffman, ed., *World Almanac 1990*, pp. 556, 774).

76. *Mayo* (Cairo), 22 June 1981, quoted in Hamied Ansari, *Egypt: The Stalled Society* (Albany: State University of New York Press, 1986), p. 226.

77. al-Safty, "Sociological Perspectives," p. 3. Andrea Rugh takes a more favorable view of the relocation scheme, perhaps reflecting the attitudes of people living in adjacent neighborhoods in Bulaq. Nonetheless, she too notes the disruption it caused; Rugh, *Family in Contemporary Egypt*, p. 23.

78. See Rivka Yadlin, "Militant Islam in Egypt: Some Sociocultural Aspects," in *Islam, Nationalism, and Radicalism in Egypt and the Sudan*, ed. G. R. Warburg and U. M. Kupferschmidt (New York: Praeger, 1983), p. 178n.4. Yadlin's assumption that these views are part of the traditional Egyptian value system is debatable.

79. Ibid.

80. Summarized in ibid., p. 172; originally published in 1974; reprinted in Salah ʿAbd al-Sayyid, *al-Juththa* (Cairo: al-Hayʾa al-Misriyya al-ʿAmma li'l-Kitab, 1981), pp. 15–28.

81. Fathi Ghanim, *al-Afyāl* (Cairo: Ruz al-Yusuf, 1981), chaps. 9–10; summarized in Yadlin, "Militant Islam," pp. 168–170.

82. Ghanim, *Afyāl*, p. 166.

83. See Saad Eddin Ibrahim, "Egypt's Islamic Militants," in *Arab Society*, ed. Ibrahim and Hopkins, p. 498.

84. On Muslim Brotherhood families, see for example, Sami Jawhar, *al-Mawtā yatakallamūn*, 2d ed. (Cairo: al-Maktab al-Misri al-Hadith, 1977), pp. 105–106. See also Fadwa el-Guindi, "Veiling Infitah with Islamic Ethic: Egypt's Contemporary Islamic Movement," *Social Problems* 28 (1981): 475n.12. In Egyptian colloquial, *usra* usually refers to the natal family living under one roof, as opposed to the *ᶜayla*, which is a patrilineage composed of several households.

85. See Gilles Kepel, *The Prophet and Pharaoh: Muslim Extremism in Egypt*, trans. J. Rothschild (London: Al Saqi Books, 1985), pp. 88–89; and Saad Eddin Ibrahim, "Anatomy of Egypt's Militant Islamic Groups: Methodological Note and Preliminary Findings," *IJMES* 12 (1980): 442.

86. Yadlin, "Militant Islam," p. 169. Members seem to have chosen not to consider the remaining part of this verse, which states, "until you have asked permission and greeted the family within."

87. Ansari, *Egypt*, pp. 225–28.

88. This document is translated and contextualized in Johannes J. G. Jansen, *The Neglected Duty: The Creed of Sadat's Assassins and Islamic Resurgence in the Middle East* (New York: Macmillan, 1986).

89. I assembled this account based on information given in Muhammad Hasanayn Haykal, *Kharīf al-ghadab* (Beirut: Sharikat al-Matbuᶜat li'l-Tawziᶜ wa'l-Nashr, 1983), pp. 500–506; Kepel, *Prophet and Pharaoh*, pp. 210–11; and Ansari, *Egypt*, pp. 224–25.

90. Haykal, *Kharīf al-ghadab*, p. 499.

Chapter 6: The Metamorphosis of Domestic Space in the Pilgrimage Murals of Egypt

1. The classic statement on pilgrimages as ritual processes that entail the creation of *communitas* remains Victory Turner's "The Center Out There: The Pilgrim's Goal," *History of Religions* 12 (1973): 191–230.

2. The ensuing discussion relies heavily upon fieldwork data I collected during several visits to Egypt between 1976 and 1985. This entailed photographing and analyzing carefully thirty-six murals, located mostly in the Qena Governorate in upper Egypt, as well as meetings with pilgrims, their families and friends, painters, and Egyptians from different walks of life. I also conducted regional surveys in Greater Cairo, Suez City, and the Fayum to establish a firmer basis for comparison. An early version of this chapter appeared as "Shrines and Talismans: Domestic Islam in the Pilgrimage Paintings of Egypt," *Journal of the American Academy of Religion* 55 (1987): 285–305.

3. *Al-Akhbār* (Cairo), 7 September 1979, p. 12.

4. For example, a scorpion was drawn over the entrance to the guest room of a house in Najᶜ al-ᶜAtiyat (near the Valley of the Kings in Upper Egypt), but was removed at the request of the pilgrim shortly after his return.

5. In Yahya al-Tahir ᶜAbd Allah's vignette, "Pilgrim's Return," a pilgrim's wife instructs the painter to completely remove old drawings and inscriptions with whitewash before redecorating the front wall of their house (*The Mountain of Green Tea*, trans. D. Johnson-Davies, London: Heineman, 1983, pp. 35–38).

6. This topic is discussed further at the end of this chapter.

7. Ibn al-Hajj, *al-Madkhal*, 4 vols. (Cairo: Dar al-Hadith, 1401/1981), vol. 1, pp. 272–75.

8. Mustafa ᶜAli, *Mustafa Ali's Description of Cairo of 1599*, trans. Andreas Tietze (Vienna: Verlag der Österreichischen Akademie der Wissenschaften, 1975), p. 33.

9. Paul Lucas, *Voyage fait en 1714 par ordre de Louis XIV dans la Turquie, l'Asie, Sourie, Haute et Basse Egypt, 1720*, vol. 1, p. 393. Quoted in Giovanni Canova, "Nota sulle raffigurazioni popolari del pellegrinaggio in Egitto," *Annalli della Facoltà di Lingue et Letterature Straniere di Ca'Foscari* 14 (1975): 92n.1.

10. M. de Chabrol, "Essai sur les moeurs des habitants modernes de l'Egypte," in *Description de l'Egypte, ou recueil des observations et des recherches qui ont été faite en Egypte pendant l'expédition de l'armée français, publié par les ordres de sa majesté l'empereur Napoléon le grand*, ed. Edme-François Jomard, 23 vols. (Paris: Imprimerie Impériale, 1809–1828), vol. 14, *Etat moderne*, pt. 2, p. 395.

11. Lane, *Modern Egyptians*, pp. 308, 438.

12. Karl B. Klunzinger, *Upper Egypt: Its People and Its Products* (New York: Scribner, Armstrong, & Co., 1878), pp. 4–5. See also James A. St. John, *Egypt and Nubia* (London: Chapman & Hall, 1845), pp. 106–7; Bayle St. John, *Village Life in Egypt with Sketches of the Said*, 2 vols. (London: Chapman & Hall, 1852; reprint ed., New York: Arno Press, 1973), vol. 1, pp. 157–58; Georg Moritz Ebers, *Egypt: Descriptive, Historical, Picturesque*, 2 vols., trans. C. Bell (London: Cassell, Petter, Galpin & Co., 1881–1882), vol. 1, pp. 68fig., 70, and vol. 2, p. 223; Robert T. Kelly, *Egypt Painted and Described* (London: A. & C. Black, 1912), p. 21; S. H. Leeder, *Modern Sons of the Pharaohs: A Study of the Manners and Customs of the Copts of Egypt* (London: Hodder & Stoughton, 1918), p. 16; Winkler, *Reitenden Geister*, pp. 116–20, pls. 11–14.

13. Jacques Jomier, *Le maḥmal et la caravane égyptienne des pèlerins de la Mecque (XIIIe–XXe siècles)* (Cairo: IFAO, 1953), p. 207, pl. 6.

14. Rudolf Kriss and Hubert Kriss-Heinrich, *Volksglaube im Bereich des Islams*, 2 vols. (Wiesbaden: Otto Harrassowitz, 1960), vol. 1, pp. 112–13.

15. Canova, "Raffigurazioni popolari," pp. 83–94.

16. Ibid., p. 91.

17. Ibid., p. 91 f.

18. Jean Michot, "Les fresques du pèlerinage au Caire," *Art and Archeology Research Papers* 13 (1978): 7–21.

19. Ibid., p. 18.

20. Ibid., p. 8.

21. An iconic figure or sign is one that represents the same features as the denoted object. See further, Ducrot and Todorov, *Encyclopedic Dictionary of the Sciences of Language*, p. 86.

22. In seeking adequate categories for describing regularities in the murals, I have adopted Vygotsky's idea of the complex, a mode of human thought that lies between thinking in terms of congeries on the one hand and concepts on the other. See Lem Semenovitch Vygotsky, *Thought and Language*, trans. E. Hanfmann and G. Vakar (Cambridge: Massachusetts Institute of Technology Press, 1963), chap. 5. Bärbel Inhelder and Jean Piaget's concept of the place of the collection in the development of logical thought is analogous

(*The Early Growth of Logic in the Child* New York: W. W. Norton, 1969, chap. 1). Lévi-Strauss's use of the term bricolage to describe aspects of mythical thought and art is illuminating, but he does not develop a useful typology of relations; see *The Savage Mind* (Chicago: University of Chicago Press, 1966), pp. 16–33.

23. The terms "semantic field" and "semantic enclave" were originally proposed by art historian Mieczylaw Wallis in connection with the semiotic analysis of painting; *Arts and Signs,* Studies in Semiotics no. 2 (Bloomington: Indiana University Press, 1975), pp. 22–23, 27, 59–60.

24. Muslim, *Ṣaḥīḥ, Ḥajj* 78.

25. See, for example, Piamenta, *Islam in Everyday Arabic Speech.*

26. There is actually a complex reciprocity between the oral and written canons, for the written Quran and the hadith collections alike are recognized to have their origins in speech. Moreover, in Islamic schools, learning the Quran and hadiths has been based on oral-aural interaction between teacher and student.

27. The colors used in murals also have a semiotic function. White signifies ritual purity and sinlessness, and green stands for the Prophet, abundance, and the gardens of paradise. Red is linked to marriage and fertility. Blue is believed to deflect evil and misfortune.

28. Of course, oral genres are primarily acoustic ones, which embody verbal images for performers and listeners alike. The murals, by contrast, are primarily visual images that embody and generate speech.

29. See, for example, Anthony Welch, "Epigraphs as Icons: The Role of the Written Word in Islamic Art," in *The Image and the Word: Confrontations in Judaism, Christianity, and Islam,* ed. Joseph Gutman, American Academy of Religion and Society of Biblical Literature, Religion and Arts Series No. 4 (Missoula, MT: Scholars Press, 1977), pp. 63–74; Anthony Welch, *Calligraphy in the Arts of the Muslim World* (Austin: University of Texas Press, 1979).

30. This idea is supported by the fact that short verbal descriptions of the Prophet have been rendered in calligraphic form to be placed in Turkish and north African Muslim houses for blessing since the eleventh/seventeenth century. Gazing at one of these *ḥilyas* is said to be like beholding the Prophet himself. See Annemarie Schimmel, *And Muhammad Is His Prophet: The Veneration of the Prophet in Islamic Piety* (Chapel Hill: University of North Carolina Press, 1985), p. 36.

31. Henry Habib Ayrout, *The Egyptian Peasant,* trans. J. A. Williams (Boston: Beacon Press, 1963), p. 92. Since the 1970s, most pilgrims are absent for weeks rather than months.

32. In the eyes of some, this new status could be a mixed blessing. Critchfield records a conversation in which a peasant from a village near Luxor mocks his mother's desire to perform the Hajj saying, "If you went to Mecca . . . you would come back a very pious Moslem. There would be no more drinking or cursing in the house. You would keep us to a narrow path. Who could live with you?" From *Shahhat, an Egyptian* (Syracuse: Syracuse University Press, 1978), p. 3. I should also point out that in Egypt the title *Ḥājj* (or *Ḥājja* for females) is used as a respectful form of address for any elderly Muslim. Some commentators have complained that it is abused for business purposes and by Egyptian politicians in elections as a ploy for getting more votes. Anwar al-Sadat, Egypt's late "believing president," reputedly went by the assumed name "Hajj Muhammad Nur al-Din" as

a young adult, without actually having performed the pilgrimage, in order to impress his peers. See further, Haykal, *Kharīf al-ghadab*, p. 39; and *al-Ahrām* (Cairo), 11 July 1988, p. 2.

33. This is from one of several remarkable Hajj murals that decorate the façades of houses in al-Ballas and its environs. The most recent ones were done by one artist, ᶜAli Sayyid ᶜAli, beginning circa 1974.

34. See further, Appendix B commentaries for figures D.2 and D.5.

35. See further, Appendix B commentary on figure B.3. Kriss and Kriss-Heinrich have reproduced a pulp poster from Cairo of al-Buraq flying over what appears to be the Medina mosque and its gardens; *Volksglaube*, vol. 1, pl. 9.

36. See, for example, Kriss and Kriss-Heinrich, *Volksglaube*, vol. 1, pls. 35–36, 48–55; and George Castel and Mahmoud ᶜAly, "Mausolées des Cheikhs ᶜUmar et Kahil près d'Esna," *Annales Islamologiques* 15 (1979): 441–68.

37. See also Nancy Munn's insightful analysis in "The Transformation of Subjects into Objects in Walbiri and Pitjantjatjara Myth," in *Australian Aboriginal Anthropology: Modern Studies in the Social Anthropology of the Australian Aborigines*, ed. Ronald M. Berndt (Nedlands: University of Western Australia Press, 1970), pp. 141–63.

38. Kriss and Kriss-Heinrich, *Volksglaube*, vol. 2, chap. 1, and pp. 149–55; Peter W. Schienerl, "Kameldarstellungen im ägyptischen Schmuck- und Amulettwesen," *Archiv für Völkerkunde*, 33 (1979): 137–56.

39. See Charles S. Meyers, "Contributions to Egyptian Anthropology: Tatuing," *Journal of the Anthropological Institute of Great Britain and Ireland* 33 (1903): 82–89; M. Coloyanni, "Etude des tatouages sur les criminels d'Egypt," *Bulletin de l'Institut d'Egypte* 4 (1923): 115–28; Blackman, *Fellāḥin*, pp. 50–54; Louis Keimer, *Remarques sur le tatouage dans l'Egypte ancienne, Memoirs présentés à l'Institut d'Egypte* no. 53 (Cairo: IFAO, 1948), pp. 73–96; Henry Field, *Body-Marking in Southwestern Asia* (Cambridge: Peabody Museum, 1958), pp. 59–60; John Carswell, *Coptic Tattoo Designs* (Beirut: American University of Beirut Press, 1958); and Nadia Kossiakov, "Un répertoire modèle de tatouage egyptien," *Objets et mondes*, 6 (1966): 263–78.

40. Dried bodies of crocodiles and monitor lizards have been placed traditionally over entrances to houses in Upper Egypt and Nubia for apotropaic purposes.

41. Bridget Connelly sheds light on the social logic of envy in Upper Egypt. She writes: "In a world where upward mobility is potential and status in the village hierarchy can change according to fluctuations in material wealth, much jostling for property occurs and much enmity arises out of jealousy upon seeing close relatives or neighbors prosper. . . . Peasant societies (are based on) a zero-sum game wherein there exists only so much bounty and any change in material wealth upsets the balance." (*Arabic Folk Epic*, pp. 154–55). In such an environment, the act of pilgrimage and the murals are demonstrations of prosperity.

42. Vincent Descombes, *Modern French Philosophy* (London: Cambridge University Press, 1980), p. 95.

43. Aqhisari, *Majālis al-abrār*, folio 74; quoted in Goldziher, "The Veneration of Saints in Islam," in *Muslim Studies*, vol. 2, p. 288.

44. Amin, *Ḥayātī*, pp. 268–71.

45. Jalal Al-e Ahmad, *Lost in the Crowd*, trans. John Green (Washington, D.C.: Three Continents Press, 1985), pp. 58–59.

46. See discussion in chap. 4.

47. See further Guensel Renda, "Wall Paintings in Turkish Houses," in the *Fifth International Congress of Turkish Art*, ed. G. Feher (Budapest: Akademiai Kiado, 1978), pp. 711–34, compare pp. 64–68. Renda attributes the origins of this trend to the confluence of Turkish miniature painting and European styles, beginning at the court in Istanbul in the 1750s, and spreading to provincial areas. I would suggest that for Egypt, however, there was already an indigenous impetus for depicting religious subjects on house walls. The complexity of the interrelationship between Ottoman art and Egyptian pilgrimage paintings is further exemplified when one of the earliest published renditions of a Hajj mural (Ebers, *Egypt*, vol. 1, p. 68) is compared with a still extant mural on the façade of an Ottoman house in Albania (Jacque Millot, "Vacances albanaises," *Objets et mondes*, 5 [1966]: fig. 17). In all probability both date from the thirteenth/nineteenth century, and both have stylistically similar versions of the confronting lions-and-tree motif.

48. Canova, "Raffigurazioni popolari," p. 93n.27. This epigraph contains a quote from Psalm 122, thus paralleling the use of quranic verses and hadiths in Hajj mural commemorative epigraphs. The similarities are even more striking if the reader bears in mind that this epigraph also implies the collapsing of distinctions between pilgrim's house and pilgrim's goal. Furthermore, the statement, "God is love" and the quotation from Psalms suggest apotropaic functions for the inscription. The first proclamation, like "Bless the Prophet" is uttered when conflict arises, in order to resolve the conflict. The magical function of Psalms in Coptic Egypt is thoroughly discussed in Nessim Henry Henein and Thierry Bianquis, *La magie par les Psaumes: Edition et traduction d'un manuscrit arabe chrétien d'Egypte*, Bibliothèque d'Etudes Coptes no. 12 (Cairo: IFAO, 1975).

49. In the nineteenth century, Ebers described the house of a Coptic merchant in Qena, saying, "The façade is covered with a perfect menagerie of beasts in red, orange, and yellow. . . . It excites the most ardent admiration, and the Nile boatmen, and camel drivers talk of it with rapture as they rest and gossip" (*Egypt*, vol. 2, p. 223). Cf. Leeder, *Modern Sons*, p. 16. But can these truly be descriptions of Coptic pilgrimage paintings?

50. For example, Ibrahim's sacrifice, angels, mermaids, lions, birds-in-tree, flowers, churches, and shrines. The figure of St. George corresponds to that of the Muslim warrior-saint. See Carswell, *Coptic Tattoo Designs*.

51. Pilgrimages to Coptic shrines are performed either on a saint's holy day, or during a church feast. These visits tend to share a number of features with the *mūlid*s of Muslim saints. Christian and Muslim pilgrims alike make vows and votive offerings. Whereas Muslims prefer to have their sons circumcised on these occasions, Copts will have theirs circumcised and baptised. Tattooing is also done. See Otto Meinardus, "Some Theological and Sociological Aspects of the Coptic Mulid," *Bulletin de l'Institut d'Egypte* 44 (1962–1963): 7–25; and Jacob Muyser and Gerard Viand, *Les pèlerinages coptes en Egypte*, Bibliothèque d'Etudes Coptes no. 15 (Cairo: IFAO, 1979). Muyser lists at least sixty-two active pilgrimage sites in Upper and Lower Egypt. Muslim shrines are even more numerous, of course.

52. Coptic warrior-saints with similar characteristics include St. George (Mari Girgis), St. Mercurius (Abu Sayfayn), St. Theodore (Mari Tadros), and St. Menas (Mari Mina al-Amin).

53. See further, Otto F. A. Meinardus, *Christian Egypt: Faith and Life* (Cairo: American University Press, 1970), pp. 269–79; and Cawthra Mulock and Martin T. Langdon,

The Icons of Yuhana and Ibrahim the Scribe (London: Nicholson & Watson, 1946). Meinardus's generalizations on Coptic iconography should be viewed with caution.

54. See, for example, Sirarpie Der Nersessian, "Some Aspects of Coptic Painting," in *Coptic Egypt*, ed. John D. Cooney (New York: Brooklyn Museum, 1941), pp. 43–50; Pierre du Bourguet, "La peinture murale copte: Quelques problemes devant la peinture murale nubienne," in *Kunst und Geschichte Nubiens in Christlicher Zeit: Ergebnisse und Probleme auf Grund der jüngsten Ausgrabungen*, ed. Erich Dinkler (Recklinghausen: Verlag Aurel Bongers, 1970), pp. 303–12; and C. C. Walters, *Monastic Archaeology in Egypt* (Warminster, U.K.: Aris & Phillips, 1974), chap. 4, appendix B, and pls. 36–37.

55. The conversion of Egypt's Coptic population to Islam is described in Lapidus, "The Conversion of Egypt to Islam;" and Richard W. Bulliet, *Conversion to Islam in the Medieval Period: An Essay in Quantitative History* (Cambridge: Harvard University Press, 1979), chap. 8.

56. Lapidus, "Conversion," p. 248.

57. See, for example, Fazlur Rahman, *Islam*, chap. 9; Annemarie Schimmel, *Mystical Dimensions of Islam* (Chapel Hill: University of North Carolina Press, 1975), pp. 216, 249–50.

58. See Taqi al-Din Ibn Taymiyya, *Ibn Taimiya's Struggle against Popular Religion*, trans. and ed. Muhammad Umar Memon (The Hague: Mouton, 1976).

59. Barry J. Kemp, "Wall Paintings from the Workmen's Village at El-ᶜAmarna," *Journal of Egyptian Archaeology* 65 (1979): 47–53. For evidence from Greco-Roman Egypt, see Elinor Husselman, *Karanis Excavations of the University of Michigan in Egypt 1928–1935: Topography and Architecture* (Ann Arbor: University of Michigan Press, 1979), pp. 61–62, pl. 102 a.

60. See, for example, Rudi Paret, "Textbelege zum islamischen Bilderverbot," in *Das Werk des Künstlers*, ed. Hans Fegers (Stuttgart: W. Kohlhammer, 1960), pp. 36–48. Iranian Shiᶜa jurists have a much more relaxed stance on this subject; see, for example, Paret, "Das islamische Bilderverbot und die Schia," in *Festschrift Werner Caskel*, ed. Erwin Gräf (Leiden: E. J. Brill, 1968), pp. 224–32.

61. For the social origins of members of Egypt's militant Islamic groups, see, for example, Ibrahim, "Anatomy of Egypt's Militant Islamic Groups," pp. 438–40; Ansari, *Egypt*, pp. 220–23; and Kepel, *Prophet and Pharaoh*, pp. 215–19.

62. For example, Bukhari, *Ṣaḥīḥ*, *Badᵓ al-khalq* 7, and *Maghāzī* 12. See also the discussion in chap. 4.

63. Ahmad Muhammad ᶜIsa, "Muslims and taṣwīr," trans. H. Glidden, *Muslim World* 45 (1955): 250–68.

64. The issue of the search for authenticity in modern Arabo-Islamic societies is explored in Fouad Ajami, *The Arab Predicament: Arabic Political Thought and Practice since 1967* (Cambridge: Cambridge University Press, 1981), pp. 50–75, 116–19, 164–200.

65. Compare with my discussion of militant Muslim organizations and their formations of domestic space in the previous chapter. For their ideology in general, see Ibrahim, "Anatomy of Egypt's Militant Islamic Groups," pp. 423–53; Ansari, *Egypt*, chap. 10; Kepel, *Prophet and Pharaoh*, chaps. 3, 5, 7, passim; and Jansen, *Neglected Duty*, chap. 1, passim.

Epilogue

1. *Constitution of the Islamic Republic of Iran*, trans. Hamid Algar (Berkeley: Mizan Press, 1980), p. 32.

Appendix A: Epigraphic Formulae Used in Hajj Murals: Index and Commentary

1. See, for example, "On the Excellence of the Basmala" from ʿAbd al-Majid ʿAli's *al-Tuḥfa al-mardiyya fī'l-akhbār al-qudsiyya*, in Arthur Jeffrey, *A Reader on Islam* (New York: Humanities Press, 1962), pp. 556–59; Constance E. Padwick, *Muslim Devotions: A Study of Prayer-Manuals in Common Use* (London: Society for Promotion of Christian Knowledge, 1961), pp. 94–102; and Piamenta, *Islam in Everyday Arabic Speech*, pp. 32–39.

2. See Piamenta, *Islam in Everyday Arabic Speech*, pp. 176, 193–95.

3. *DEA*, p. 167.

4. See further Piamenta, *Islam in Everyday Arabic Speech*, pp. 46–48.

5. Compare with the variant, "O ye who enter this place (*makān*), bless the Prophet of the ʿAdnan." An inscription used in a saint's shrine said, "O ye who enter this shrine-place (*maqām*), bless the Prophet of the ʿAdnan;" see Kriss and Kriss-Heinrich, *Volksglaube*, vol. 1, pl. 49.

6. See Lane, *Arabic-English Lexicon*, p. 1720; Ignaz Goldziher, "Über die Eulogien der Muhammedaner," *Zeitschrift der Deutschen Morgenlandischen Gesellschaft* 50 (1896): 97–128, reprinted in *Gesammelte Schriften*, ed. Joseph De Somogyi (Hildesheim: Georg Olms, 1970), vol. 4, pp. 37–68; and Chadwick, *Muslim Devotions*, pp. 152–66.

7. *DEA*, p. 509.

8. See epigraph I.1; Schimmel, *Mystical Dimensions*, pp. 217, 225; and idem., *And Muhammad Is His Messenger*, p. 81.

9. Schimmel, *And Muhammad Is His Messenger*, pp. 36–38.

10. *DEA*, p. 890.

11. See, for example, al-Qadi, *Daqaʾiq al-akhbār*, pp. 2–3; Schimmel, *Mystical Dimensions*, pp. 214–27, passim; and *And Muhammad Is His Messenger*, chap. 7. Compare with epigraph I.2.

12. Recorded in Michot, "Fresques du pèlerinage," p. 18.

13. See epigraph III.1d and the discussion in chap. 4.

14. See also Piamenta, *Islam in Everyday Arabic Speech*, p. 132. Compare with epigraph III.1c and 1e.

15. Lane, *Arabic-English Lexicon*, p. 177.

16. Ibn Hanbal, *Musnad*, vol. 1, p. 426.

17. Muslim, *Ṣaḥīḥ*, *Ḥajj* 78.

18. Bukhari, *Ṣaḥīḥ*, *Ṭawāf al-wadāʿ* 9.

19. See the discussion of this subject in chap. 3.

20. Bukhari, *Saḥīḥ*, *Ḥajj* 4, and *al-Muḥsar wa-jazāʾ al-ṣayd* 10.

21. Muslim, *Ṣaḥīḥ*, *Ḥajj* 78.

22. Bukhari, *Ṣaḥīḥ*, *Imān* 2.

23. Muslim, *Ṣaḥīḥ*, *Imān* 6.

24. See also al-Samhudi, *Kitāb wafā' al-wafā*, vol. 2, pp. 394–403.

25. See further Memon, *Ibn Taimiya's Struggle against Popular Religion.*

26. Samuel M. Zwemer, *Arabia: The Cradle of Islam* (New York: F. H. Revell, [1900]), insert after p. 40.

27. See Schimmel, *And Muhammad Is His Messenger*, chap. 5; and Smith and Haddad, *The Islamic Understanding of Death and Resurrection*, pp. 25–27, 141–43, 183–91.

28. For example, Bukhari, *Ṣaḥīḥ*, *Jumʿa* 14, and *Riqāq* 53.

29. Muslim, *Ṣaḥīḥ*, *Ḥajj* 91.

30. Malik, *Muwaṭṭa'*, *Qibla* 5.

31. Ibn Hanbal, *Musnad*, vol. 3, p. 64.

32. See further, al-Samhudi, *Kitāb wafā' al-wafā*, vol. 2, pp. 397–98.

33. Schimmel, *Mystical Dimensions*, p. 117–18.

34. See further Piamenta, *Islam in Everyday Arabic Speech*, pp. 26–32.

35. See Lane, *Arabic-English Lexicon*, p. 2412.

36. I am unable to ascertain the exact significance of this epigraph, since Michot lists it out of context.

37. See Michael Gilsenan, *Saint and Sufi in Modern Egypt: An Essay in the Sociology of Religion* (London: Oxford University Press, 1973), pp. 20–35.

38. *DEA*, pp. 398–99. Compare with Padwick, *Muslim Devotions*, pp. 83–93; and Piamenta, *Islam in Everyday Arabic Speech*, pp. 101–13, passim.

39. *DEA*, p. 494; and Piamenta, *Islam in Everyday Arabic Speech*, pp. 87–89.

40. Schimmel, *And Muhammad Is His Messenger*, pp. 67–69.

41. See *sharaḥ iṣ-ṣidr* in *DEA*, p. 458.

42. Schienerl, "Kameldarstellungen," fig. 4.

Appendix B: Iconic Figures Used in Hajj Murals: Index and Commentary

1. Horses and camels, other than the *maḥmal* figure, might also be mentioned here, but they are discussed in figural categories C and D.

2. Michot gives a detailed discussion of depictions of the Kaʿba and Medina in Hajj murals in "Fresques du pèlerinage," pp. 8–13.

3. Jomier, *Le maḥmal;* and *EI2*, s.v. "*Maḥmal*." See also Lane, *Modern Egyptians*, pp. 438–42; and Kriss and Kriss-Heinrich, *Volksglaube*, 1: 25–29.

4. See, for example, Ayrout, *Egyptian Peasant*, pp. 105–6.

5. See Bridget Connelly, *Arab Folk Epic and Arab Identity* (Berkeley: University of California Press, 1986), pls. 13–16 and 18.

6. See Joseph W. McPherson, *The Moulids of Egypt* (Cairo: N. M. Press, 1941), p. 132 (with photo); and Kriss and Kriss-Heinrich, *Volksglaube*, vol. 1, pp. 70–74, 104–5.

McPherson suggests that there are distinct terms for each kind of palanquin: *tub* for that of the most honored saint, *tabūt* for that of other local saints, and the *takhtarawān* for brides. Kriss and Kriss-Heinrich do not make these distinctions, but identify all with the term "*maḥmal*."

7. Schienerl, "Kameldarstellungen," pp. 145–46, 151. See also my commentary on figure D.3.

8. See, for example, Sauvaget, *Mosquée omeyyade de Médine*, plate following p. 142.

9. See Michot, "Fresques du pèlerinage," pp. 8, 14.

10. *EI2*, s.v. "Ibrāhīm," by Rudi Paret; and "Ismāʿīl," by A. J. Wensinck. See also my discussion in chap. 1.

11. Other figures in this category that are recorded by Michot, but are not discussed here include angels and "Sufis." See Michot, "Fresques du pèlerinage," pp. 13 and 19.

12. Kriss and Kriss-Heinrich, *Volksglaube*, vol. 2, pp. 36–38, pls. 32, 36–39.

13. *EI2*, s.v. "*al-Burāḳ*," by Rudi Paret. The celebration of the Night Journey and Ascension is observed on the 27th of Rajab, about four months before the actual pilgrimage.

14. Newby, *Making of the Last Prophet*, p. 76.

15. al-Qadi, *Daqāʾiq al-akhbār*, pp. 27–28.

16. *EI1*, s.v. "Sulaimān b. Dawud," by J. Walker. For information on pre-Islamic ideas about Sulayman's magic powers, see D. C. Duling's edition of the "Testament of Solomon," in *Old Testament Pseudepigrapha*, ed. J. H. Charlesworth, vol. 1, pp. 935–87.

17. *EI2*, s.v. "*Hudhud*," by A. J. Wensinck; and Ibn Ishaq Ahmad b. Muhammad al-Thaʿlabi, *Qiṣaṣ al-anbiyāʾ (ʿArāʾis al-majālis)*, (Beirut: al-Maktaba al-Thiqafiyya, n.d.), pp. 276–77.

18. Canova, "Raffigurazioni popolari," p. 87.

19. Ibid., p. 87.

20. In fact, the popular word for a wedding in Egypt is "joy" *faraḥ*.

21. See al-Shal, *ʿArūsat al-mawlid*, p. 63.

22. The figure of the bride is a highly ambivalent one not only in Egypt, but elsewhere in north Africa as well.

23. In parts of Tunisia paintings of Zaziya the bride, a heroine of the *Sīrat Banī Hilāl*, decorate bedroom walls. An offspring of a marriage between a prince and the daughter of a jinn, she is, according to Bridget Connelly, "an all-powerful generating force, the protector of the tribe who bears children and grinds grain like all tribal women, but who also girds herself for battle to do man-to-man combat" (*Arab Folk Epic*, p. 199). Similar images are evident in Egyptian tattoos.

24. According to another hadith, Muhammad once said, "The white rose was created from my sweat on the night of my ascent, the red rose was created from the sweat of Gabriel, and the yellow rose was created from the sweat of al-Buraq." See further, Jalal al-Din al-Suyuti, *Ḥusn al-muḥāḍara fī taʾrīkh Miṣr wa'l-Qāhira*, 2 vols. (Cairo: Dar Ihyaʾ al-Kutub al-ʿArabiyya, 1967–1968), vol. 2, pp. 401–8; Schimmel, *And Muhammad Is His Messenger*, p. 35.

25. See Lane, *The Thousand and One Nights, Commonly Called in England the Arabian Nights Entertainments*, 3 vols. (London: Chatto & Windus, 1889), vol. 1, pp. 197–200.

26. See Winkler, *Reitenden Geister*, p. 45.

27. See al-Shal, *ʿArūsat al-mawlid*, pp. 63, 78.

28. More generally in Egypt, women are named after flowers; for example, *Zahra* "Flower," *Warda* "Rose," *Yasmīna* or *Fulla* "Jasmine," and *Nargis* "Narcissus." In the exchange of greetings, flower terminology is used to wish someone a particularly pleasant morning or evening (*full* and *ward* are most common). The expression "A rose upon you!" (*warda ʿaleek*) is a way of saying "How wonderful you are!" (*DEA*, p. 932). Egyptians use *full* metaphorically when referring to something pleasing or well done (*DEA*, p. 671). In a devotional context, actual flowers are sometimes used to decorate the tombs of Muslim holy men.

29. For example, Muslim, *Ṣaḥīḥ*, *Ṣifat al-qiyāma wa'l-janna wa'l-nār* 15. Also found in the hadith collections of al-Bukhari, Ibn Hanbal, and al-Tirmidhi.

30. See further, Richard Burton, *Personal Narrative of a Pilgrimage to al-Madina and Mecca*, 2 vols. (London: George Bell & Sons, 1907), vol. 1, pp. 400–403; Winckler, *Bauern zwischen Wasser und Wüste*, p. 46; and Amin, *Qāmūs*, p. 95.

31. When the male head of household dies, his widow may cry out, "O my camel!"

32. See also Yahya al-Tahir ʿAbdallah, *Mountain of Green Tea*, pp. 37–38.

33. Schienerl, "Kameldarstellungen," pp. 145–51 passim.

34. Egyptians consider the hoopoe to be a solitary creature. They do not usually portray it with other birds. In some areas of the country, people hang dead hoopoes over the entrances to their dwellings as talismans.

35. Susan Slyomovics, *The Merchant of Art: An Egyptian Hilali Oral Epic Poet in Performance* (Berkeley: University of California Press, 1987), p. 49.

36. See Lane's list of bird cries in Arabian Society in *The Middle Ages: Studies from the "Thousand and One Nights"* (London: Curzon, 1971), p. 133. Also see Kamal al-Din al-Damiri (d. 808/1405), *Ḥayāt al-ḥayawān al-kubrā* (Beirut: al-Maktaba al-Islamiyya, [1353?/1934?]), s.v. "*ḥamām*" (pigeon), "*khuṭṭāf*" (swallow), "*qumrī*" (turtledove), and "*hudhud*" (hoopoe). Useful notes on bird lore in contemporary Egypt can be obtained from Muhammad al-Jawhari, *al-Dirāsa al-ʿilmiyya li'l-muʿtaqidāt al-shaʿbiyya*, 2 vols. (Cairo: Dar al-Kitab li'l-Tawziʿ, 1978), vol. 1, p. 183.

37. Ibn Maja, *Sunan*, *Zuhd* 32, and *Janāʾiz* 4. See also Muslim *Ṣaḥīḥ*, *Imāra* 33: "Their souls are in the bellies of green birds that nest in candelabra attached to God's throne. They leave paradise, roaming wherever they will, and then return to nest in the candelabra. Their lord reveals all things to them." Compare this with the version recorded in Abu Dawud (*Sunan*, *Jihād* 27), where the birds are said to contain the souls of those who have been slain while furthering God's cause. Other references to pertinent hadiths can be found in Wensinck et al., *Concordance*, s.v. "*ṭīr*." See also Ignaz Goldziher, "Der Seelenvogel im islamischem Volksglauben," *Globus* 83 (1902): 301–4.

38. Blackman, *Fellāḥīn of Upper Egypt*, p. 121.

39. Marian Wenzel, *House Decoration in Nubia* (Toronto: University of Toronto Press, 1972), pls. 46–49, 77, fig. 47. The Nubian examples are not connected with the pilgrimage to Mecca. The serpentine design in some cases resembles the dome of a saint's tomb, or a rising sun.

40. Members of the Rifaʿi order claim the power to ride lions, and to keep snakes and scorpions away from houses; Kriss and Kriss-Heinrich, *Volksglaube*, vol. 1, p. 47, pl. 10.

These posters were also found in Nubian homes; Wenzel, *House Decoration in Nubia*, p. 44.

41. An ʿAbd al-Qadir print is reproduced in Kriss and Kriss-Heinrich, *Volksglaube*, vol. 1, p. 46, pl. 7. Legends concerning the four "poles" are still told in Egyptian oral narratives; see Hasan El-Shamy, *Folktales of Egypt* (Chicago: University of Chicago Press, 1980), pp. 150–53. Compare Lane, *Modern Egyptians*, pp. 229–34. Like al-Jilani, other "poles" also have animal familiars. Ahmad al-Badawi is associated with a green bird, al-Rifaʿi with a rooster, and al-Dasuqi with a small black bird; Kriss and Kriss-Heinrich, *Volksglaube*, vol. 1, p. 8.

42. A portrait of ʿAli as an ʿAntar-like hero is reproduced in Winkler, *Reitenden Geister*, p. 125, pl. 15. There, he is shown slaying a demon and a snake. Similar depictions of ʿAntar, ʿAli, and Diyab al-Ghanim are reproduced in Saʿd al-Khadim, *Taṣwīrunā al-shaʿbī khilāl al-ʿuṣūr* (Cairo: Dar al-Qalam, 1963), figs. 21, 22, 24. Such posters were placed on the walls of saint shrines, as well as in houses; see, for example, Kriss and Kriss-Heinrich, *Volksglaube*, vol. 1, fig. 48, which shows a poster of Abu Zayd al-Hilali in the shrine of Shaykh Tayyib at Qurna. El-Shamy includes several Imamu ʿAli legends in *Folktales of Egypt*, pp. 153–58, 278–79. The version of the ʿAli/ʿAntar tale recorded by El-Shamy was told to him as recently as 1969 by an informant who said that he had heard it recited often in his Saʿidi village (p. 154). But ʿAli is not the only Islamic holy man to be associated with ʿAntar. Goldziher has noted striking parallels between legends of Ahmad al-Badawi and ʿAntar; *Muslim Studies*, vol. 2, p. 266.

43. Keimer, *Remarques sur le tatouage*, figs. 67–68; and Kossiakov, "Répertoire-modèle," figs. 3–4. Warrior-saint and lion motifs, not surprisingly, are among the tattoo designs requested by Coptic Christians as proof of their pilgrimage to Jerusalem. Coptic informants, however, interpret the lion as a representation of Jesus, the Lion of Judah (Rev. 5:5); Carswell, *Coptic Tattoo Designs*. These motifs are also important in the religious iconography of the Ethiopian Church; see Sven Rubenson, "The Lion of the Tribe of Judah: Christian Symbol and/or Imperial Title," *Journal of Ethiopian Studies* 3 (1965): 75–85; and S. Chojnacki, "The Iconography of Saint George in Ethiopia," *Journal of Ethiopian Studies* 11 (1973): 57–73.

44. Wenzel, *House Decoration in Nubia*, p. 161.

45. Elinor Husselman, *Karanis Excavations of the University of Michigan in Egypt 1928–1935: Topography and Architecture* (Ann Arbor: University of Michigan Press, 1979), pp. 61–62, pl. 102a. The site of Karanis is on the northern edge of the Fayum.

46. See, for example, Kriss and Kriss-Heinrich, *Volksglaube*, vol. 1, pp. 88–96.

47. Kriss and Kriss-Heinrich, *Volksglaube*, vol. 2, pp. 29–30; Wenzel, *House Decoration in Nubia*, pp. 159–160.

48. Kriss and Kriss-Heinrich, *Volksglaube*, vol. 2, pp. 30–32.

49. See further, Blackman, *Fellāḥīn of Upper Egypt*, pp. 97–100; Critchfield, *Shahhat*, pp. 7–9.

Select Bibliography

Abu Dawud, Sulayman b. al-Ashʿath. *Sunan,* edited by Muhammad Muhyi al-Din ʿAbd al-Hamid. 4 vols. Cairo: Dar al-Fikr, 1935.

Abu-Lughod, Janet. *Cairo: 1001 Years of the City Victorious.* Princeton: Princeton University Press, 1971.

Amin, Ahmad. *Qāmūs al-ʿādāt wa'l-taqālīd wa'l-taʿābīr al-miṣriyya.* Cairo: Lajnat al-Ta'lif wa'l-Tarjama wa'l-Nashr, 1953.

———. *Ḥayātī.* 2d ed. Cairo: Maktabat al-Nahda al-Misriyya, 1966.

Ammar, Hamed. *Growing Up in an Egyptian Village: Silwa, Province of Aswan.* London: Routledge & Kegan Paul, 1954.

Ansari, Hamied. *Egypt: The Stalled Society.* Albany: State University of New York Press, 1986.

Arendt, Hannah. *The Human Condition.* New York: Doubleday, 1959.

Ariès, Philippe, and Georges Duby, general editors. *Histoire de la vie privée.* 3 vols. Paris: Seuil, 1985.

Atiya, Nayra. *Khul-Khaal: Five Egyptian Women Tell Their Stories.* Syracuse: Syracuse University Press, 1982.

Ayrout, Habib. *The Egyptian Peasant,* translated by J. Alden Williams. Boston: Beacon Press, 1963.

Beeston, A. F. L., T. M. Johnstone, R. B. Serjeant, and G. R. Smith, gen. eds. *The Cambridge History of Arabic Literature,* vol. 1, *Arabic Literature to the End of the Umayyad Period.* Cambridge: Cambridge University Press, 1983.

Betaille, Georges. *Death and Sensuality: A Study of Eroticism and the Taboo.* New York: Walker and Co., 1962.

Bourdieu, Pierre. "La maison Kabyle ou le monde renversé." In *Echanges et communications: Mélanges offerts à Claude Lévi-Strauss à l'occasion de son 60ème anniversaire,* vol. 2, pp. 739–58, edited by J. Pouillon and P. Maranda. The Hague: Mouton, 1970.

Bukhari, Muhammad b. Isma^cil al-. *Ṣaḥīḥ*. 9 vols. Cairo: Dar Matabi^c al-Sha^cb, n.d.

Bulliet, Richard W. *Conversion to Islam in the Medieval Period: An Essay in Quantitative History*. Cambridge: Harvard University Press, 1979.

Canova, Giovanni. "Nota sulle raffigurazioni popolari del pellegrinaggio in Egitto." *Annali della Facoltà di Lingue e Letterature Straniere di Ca'Foscari* 14 (1975): 83–94.

Creswell, K.A.C. *Early Muslim Architecture*. 2 vols. Oxford: Clarendon Press, 1932–1940.

Cunningham, Clarke E. "Order in the Atoni House." In *Bijdragen tot de Taal-, Land- en Volkenkunde* 120 (1964): 34–38. Revised version in *Right and Left: Essays on Dual Symbolic Classification*, edited by Rodney Needham, pp. 204–38. Chicago: University of Chicago Press, 1973.

Djait, Hichem. *Al-Kūfa: Naissance de la ville islamique*. Islam d'hier et d'aujourd'hui, no. 29. Paris: G.-P. Maissoneuve et Larose, 1986.

Dodd, Peter C. "Family Honor and the Forces of Change in Arab Society." *IJMES* 4 (1973): 40–54.

Donner, Fred McGraw. *The Early Islamic Conquests*. Princeton: Princeton University Press, 1981.

Eliade, Mircea. *Patterns in Comparative Religion*. Translated by R. Sheed. Cleveland: World Publishing, 1958.

———. *The Sacred and the Profane: The Nature of Religion*. Translated by W. Trask. New York: Harcourt, Brace & World, 1959.

———. "The World, the City, the House." In *Occultism, Witchcraft, and Cultural Fashions: Essays in Comparative Religions*, pp. 18–31. Chicago: University of Chicago, 1976.

Encyclopaedia of Islam, edited by M. T. Houtsma et al., 4 vols. Leiden: E. J. Brill, 1913–1934. Supplement, 1938. 2d ed., edited by H.A.R. Gibb et al., 6 vols. to date. Leiden: E. J. Brill, 1954– . S.v. "*Ahl al-Bayt*" by I. Goldziher et al.; "*Ahl al-Ṣuffa*" by W. Montgomery Watt; "*Dār*" by George Marçais; "*Ḳur'ān*," by Alford Welch; "*Maḥmal*" by Jacques Jomier; "Makka (4), As the Center of the World" by David A. King.

Ettinghausen, Richard, and Oleg Grabar. *The Art and Architecture of Islam 650–1250*. Pelican History of Art. New York: Viking Penguin, 1987.

Fustel de Coulanges, Numa Denis. *The Ancient City: A Study on the Religion, Laws, and Institutions of Greece and Rome*. Translated by W. Small. New York: Doubleday, 1956.

Galal, Muhammad. "Essai d'observations sur les rites funeraires en Egypte actuelle releveés dans certaines regions compagnardes." *Revue des études islamiques* 11 (1937): 131–299.

Garcin, Jean-Claude, Bernard Maury, Jacques Revault, Mona Zakariya, André Raymond. *Palais et maisons du Caire*. 2 vols. Paris: Centre Nationale de la Recherche Scientific, 1982–1983.

Gilsenan, Michael. *Recognizing Islam: Religion and Society in the Modern Arab World*. New York: Random House, 1982.

Goitein, Solomon D. *A Mediterranean Society: The Jewish Communities of the Arab World as Portrayed in the Documents of the Cairo Geniza*. 5 vols. Berkeley: University of California Press, 1967–1986.

Goldziher, Ignaz. *Muslim Studies*, translated by S. Stern. 2 vols. Chicago: Aldine, 1971.

Grabar, Oleg. *The Formation of Islamic Art*. 2d ed. New Haven: Yale University Press, 1987.

———. "Architecture." In *The Legacy of Islam*, pp. 244–73, edited by J. Schacht and C. E. Bosworth. 2d ed. Oxford: Oxford University, 1979.

Hinds, Martin and El-Said Badawi, *A Dictionary of Egyptian Arabic: Arabic-English*. Beirut: Librairie du Liban, 1986.

Hodgson, Marshall G. S. *The Venture of Islam: Conscience and History in a World Civilization*. 3 vols. Chicago: University of Chicago Press, 1974.

Ibn Hanbal, Ahmad. *al-Musnad*. 6 vols. Boulaq: al-Matbaᶜa al-Kubra al-Amiriyya, 1895.

Ibn Ishaq, Muhammad. *al-Sīra al-nabawiyya*. 4 vols, 2d ed. Cairo: Mustafa al-Baqi al-Halabi wa-Awladuhu, 1955.

Ibn Maja, Abu ᶜAbd Allah Muhammad b. Yazid. *Sunan*, edited by Muhammad Fuʾad ᶜAbd al-Baqi, 2 vols. Cairo: ᶜIsa al-Babi al-Halabi, 1951.

Ibn Saᶜd, Abu ᶜAbd Allah Muhammad. *al-Ṭabaqāt al-kubrā*. 9 vols. Beirut: Dar Sadir, [1957–1960].

Ibrahim, Laila ᶜAli. "Middle Class Living Units in Mamluk Cairo: Architecture and Terminology." *Art and Archaeology Research Papers* 14 (1978): 24–30.

Ibrahim, Saad Eddin. "Anatomy of Egypt's Militant Islamic Groups: Methodological Note and Preliminary Findings." *IJMES* 12 (1980): 423–53.

Jomard, Edme-François, editor. *Description de l'Egypte, ou recueil des observations et des recherches qui ont été faite en Egypte pendant l'expédition de l'armée français, publié par les ordres de sa majesté l'empereur Napoléon le grand*, 23 vols. Paris: Imprimerie Impériale, 1809–1828.

Jomier, Jacques. *Le maḥmal et la caravane égyptienne des pèlerins de la Mecque (XIIIe–XXe siècles)*. Cairo: IFAO, 1953.

Kepel, Gilles. *The Prophet and Pharaoh: Muslim Extremism in Egypt*. Translated by J. Rothschild. London: Al Saqi Books, 1985.

Khadduri, Majid. *War and Peace in the Law of Islam*. Baltimore: Johns Hopkins University Press, 1955.

Khatib al-Baghdadi, Abu Bakr Ahmad al-. *Taʾrīkh Baghdād aw madīnat al-salām*. 14 vols. Beirut: Dar al-Kitab al-ᶜArabi, [1966?–1986].

Kister, Meir J. " 'A Booth Like the Booth of Moses': A Study of an Early Hadith." *Bulletin of the School of Oriental and African Studies* 25 (1962): 150–55.

———. " 'You Shall Only Set Out for Three Mosques': A Study of an Early Tradition." *Le muséon* 82 (1969): 173–96.

Kriss, Rudolf, and H. Kriss-Heinrich. *Volksglaube im Bereich des Islam*. 2 vols. Wiesbaden: Harrassowitz, 1960.

Kubiak, Wladyslaw B. *Al-Fusṭāṭ: Foundation and Early Development*. Cairo: American University in Cairo Press, 1987.

Lambton, Ann K. S. *State and Government in Medieval Islam, an Introduction to the Study of Islamic Political Theory: The Jurists*. Oxford: Oxford University Press, 1981.

Lane, Edward W. *An Account of the Manners and Customs of the Modern Egyptians.* 5th ed. London: John Murray, 1860; reprint ed. New York: Dover, 1973.

———. *An Arabic-English Lexicon.* 8 vols. London: Williams and Norgate, 1863–1893.

Lane-Poole, Stanley. *Cairo: Sketches of Its History, Monuments, and Social Life.* 3d ed. London: J. S. Virtue, 1898; reprint ed., New York: Arno Press, 1973.

Lapidus, Ira M. "The Conversion of Egypt to Islam." *Israel Oriental Studies* 2 (1969): 248–62.

Lassner, Jacob. *The Topography of Baghdad in the Early Middle Ages.* Detroit: Wayne State University Press, 1970.

———. *The Shaping of Abbasid Rule.* Princeton: Princeton University Press, 1980.

Lebeuf, Jean-Paul. *L'Habitation des Fali, montagnards du Cameroun septentrional: technologie, sociologie, mythologie, symbolisme.* Paris: Librairie Hachette, 1961.

Leeuw, Gerardus van der. *Religion in Essence and Manifestation: A Study in Phenomenology.* Translated by J. E. Turner. 2 vols. New York: Harper & Row, 1963.

Lézine, Alexandre. *Trois palais d'époque ottomane au Caire.* Memoires de IFAO, vol. 93. Cairo: IFAO, 1972.

Malik b. Anas. *al-Muwaṭṭa'*, edited by Muhammad Fu'ad ʿAbd al-Baqi. 2 vols. Cairo: Dar Ihya' al-Kutub al-ʿArabiyya, 1951.

Maqrizi, Taqiyy al-Din Ahmad al-. *Kitāb al-mawāʿiẓ wa'l-iʿtibār bi-dhikr al-khiṭaṭ wa'l-athār.* 2 vols. Bulaq: al-Matbaʿa al-Amiriyya, 1270/1853.

Meinardus, Otto. *Christian Egypt: Faith and Life.* Cairo: American University Press, 1970.

Messeri, Sawsan el-. *Ibn al-Balad: A Concept of Egyptian Identity.* Leiden: E. J. Brill, 1978.

Michot, Jean. "Les fresques du pèlerinage au Caire." *Art and Archaeology Research Papers* 13 (1978): 7–21.

Morony, Michael G. *Iraq after the Muslim Conquest.* Princeton: Princeton University Press, 1984.

Munn, Nancy. "The Transformation of Subjects into Objects in Walbiri and Pitjantjatjara Myth." In *Australian Aboriginal Anthropology: Modern Studies in the Social Anthropology of the Australian Aborigines*, pp. 141–63, edited by Ronald M. Berndt. Nedlands: University of Western Australia Press, 1970.

Muslim b. al-Hajjaj. *Ṣaḥīḥ.* 8 vols. Cairo: Dar al-Tahrir li'l-Tabʿ wa'l-Nashr, 1963. Translated by ʿAbd al-Hamid Siddiqi, *Ṣaḥīḥ Muslim*, 4 vols. Lahore: Sh. Muhammad Ashraf, 1972.

Mustafa, Salih Lamʿi. *al-Madīna al-munawwara: Taṭawwuruhā al-ʿumrānī wa-turāthuhā al-miʿmārī.* Beirut: Dar al-Nahda al-ʿArabiyya, 1981.

Muttaqi al-Hindi, al-. *Muntakhab kanz al-ʿummāl fī sunan al-aqwāl wa'l-afʿāl.* In the margins of Ibn Hanbal, *al-Musnad*, 6 vols. Boulaq: al-Matbaʿa al-Kubra al-Amiriyya, 1895.

Nadim, Nawal al-Messiri. "The Concept of the *Ḥāra:* A Historical and Sociological Study of al-Sukkariyya." *Annales islamologiques* 15 (1979): 313–48.

Paret, Rudi. "Textbelege zum islamischen Bilderverbot." In *Das Werk des Künstlers*, pp. 36–48, edited by Hans Fegers. Stuttgart: W. Kohlhammer, 1960.

Parvin, Monoucher, and Maurie Sommer. "Dar al-Islam: The Evolution of Muslim Territoriality and Its Implications for Conflict Resolution in the Middle East." *IJMES* 11 (1980): 1–21.

Piamenta, Moshe. *Islam in Everyday Arabic Speech*. Leiden: E. J. Brill, 1979.

Qadi, ʿAbd al-Rahim b. Ahmad al-. *Kitāb daqāʾiq al-akhbār fī dhikr al-janna wa'l-nār*. Cairo: Maktaba al-Jumhuriyya al-ʿArabiyya, n.d. Translated by ʿAʾisha ʿAbd ar-Rahman at-Tarjumana. *Islamic Book of the Dead: A Collection of Hadiths on the Fire and the Garden*. San Francisco: Diwan Press, 1977.

Rahman, Fazlur. *Islam*. 2d ed. Chicago: University of Chicago Press, 1979.

Raymond, André. "Les grands waqfs et l'organisation de l'espace urbain à Alep et au Caire à l'époque ottomane (XVIᵉ–XVIIᵉ siècles)." *Bulletin des études orientales* 31 (1980): 113–28.

———. *The Great Arab Cities in the 16th–18th Centuries: An Introduction*. Hagop Kevorkian Series on Near Eastern Art and Civilization. New York: New York University, 1984.

Revault, Jacques, and Bernard Maury. *Palais et maisons du Caire du XIVᵉ au XVIIIᵉ siècle*. 3 vols. Memoires de IFAO, nos. 96, 100, 102. Cairo: IFAO, 1975–79.

Rugh, Andrea. *Coping with Poverty in a Cairo Community*. Cairo Papers in Social Science, no. 2.1. Cairo: American University Press, 1979.

———. *Family in Contemporary Egypt*. Syracuse: Syracuse University Press, 1984.

Said, Edward W. *Orientalism*. New York: Random House, 1978.

Saleh, Soubhi el-. *La vie future selon le Coran*. Paris: Librairie Philosophique J. Vrin, 1971.

Salihi, Muhammad b. Yusuf al-. *Subul al-hudā wa'l-rashād fī sīrat khayr al-ʿibād*. 7 vols. to date. Cairo: al-Majlis al-Aʿla li'l-Shuʾun al-Islamiyya, 1972– .

Samhudi, ʿAli b. ʿAbd Allah al-. *Kitāb wafāʾ al-wafā bi-akhbār dār al-Muṣṭafā*. 2 vols. Cairo: Matbaʿat al-Adab wa'l-Muʾayyid, 1909.

Sauvaget, Jean. *La mosquée omeyyade de Médine: Etude sur les origines architecturales de la mosquée et de la basilique*. Paris: Vanoest, 1947.

Schimmel, Annemarie. *And Muhammad Is His Messenger: The Veneration of the Prophet in Islamic Piety*. Chapel Hill: University of North Carolina Press, 1985.

Serjeant, R. B. "Ḥaram and Ḥawtah; the Sacred Enclave in Arabia." In *Mélanges Taha Husain*, pp. 41–58, edited by ʿAbd al-Rahman Badawi. Cairo: Dar al-Maʿarif, 1962.

Shal, ʿAbd al-Ghani al-Nabawi al-. *ʿArūṣat al-mawlid*. Cairo: Dar al-Katib al-ʿArabi li'l-Tibaʿa wa'l-Nashr, 1967.

Shamy, Hasan M. el-. *Folktales of Egypt*. Chicago: University of Chicago Press, 1980.

Smith, Jane I. "Concourse between the Living and the Dead in Islamic Eschatological Literature." *History of Religions* 19 (1980): 224–36.

Smith, Jane I. and Yvonne Y. Haddad. *The Islamic Understanding of Death and Resurrection*. Albany: State University of New York Press, 1981.

Smith, Margaret. *Rabiʿa the Mystic and Her Fellow-Saints in Islam*. Cambridge: Cambridge University Press, 1928.

Tabari, Muhammad b. Jarir al-. *Ta'rīkh al-rusul wa'l-mulūk*, edited by M. J. de Goeje. 15 vols. Leiden: E. J. Brill, 1879–1901. Egyptian version edited by Muhammad Abu'l-Fadl Ibrahim. 11 vols., 2d ed. Cairo: Dar al-Maʿarif, 1967–1977. English translation appearing under general editorship of Ehsan Yar-Shater. Albany: State University of New York, 1985– .

Tabrizi, Muhammad b. ʿAbd Allah al-Khatib al-. *Mishkāt al-maṣābīḥ*, translated by James Robson. 2 vols. Lahore: Sh. Muhammad Ashraf, 1975.

Tirmidhi, Muhammad b. ʿIsa al-. *Jāmiʿ al-ṣaḥīḥ*. 13 vols. Beirut: Dar al-Kitab al-ʿArabi, n.d.

Turner, Victor. "The Center Out There: The Pilgrim's Goal." *History of Religions* 12 (1973): 191–230.

Vygotsky, Lem Semenovitch. *Thought and Language*, translated by E. Hanfmann and G. Vakar. Cambridge, Mass.: M.I.T. Press, 1962.

Wallis, Mieczylaw. *Arts and Signs*. Studies in Semiotics no. 2. Bloomington: Indiana University Press, 1975.

Wensinck, Arent Jan et al., eds. *Concordance et indices de la tradition musulmane*. 8 vols. Leiden: E. J. Brill, 1927–1988.

Wenzel, Marian. *House Decoration in Nubia*. Toronto: University of Toronto Press, 1972.

Wikan, Unni. *Life among the Poor in Cairo*. Translated by A. Henning. London: Tavistock, 1980.

Yadlin, Rivka. "Militant Islam in Egypt: Some Sociocultural Aspects." In *Islam, Nationalism, and Radicalism in Egypt and the Sudan*, pp. 159–82, edited by G. R. Warburg and U. M. Kupferschmidt. New York: Praeger, 1983.

Yaqut, Abu ʿAbd Allah al-Hamawi. *Muʿjam al-buldān*, edited by F. Wüstenfeld, 6 vols. Leipzig: F. A. Brockhaus, 1866–1873.

Subject Index

ᶜAbbasid dynasty, 19, 60–63, 67
ᶜAbbasiyya (Cairo), 111, 126
ᶜAbd al-Nasir, Jamal, 187, 190
Abraham. *See* Ibrahim
Abu Bakr (caliph), 33–34, 53
Abu Zayd al-Hilali, 183, 185
ᶜAʾisha (Muhammad's wife), 33, 38–39, 54
Al-e Ahmad, Jalal, 159–60
Alexander the Great, Romance of, 48–49, 68, 203 n.4
ᶜAli ibn Abi Talib (caliph), 60, 185, 230 n.42
Amin, Ahmad, 128–29, 159, 214 n.6, 217 n.56
Amulets, 113, 126–27, 130, 151, 156–58, 178–79, 182–83, 186, 188, 190–91, 223 n.40
Angels, 17, 38, 116; Gabriel, 31, 38, 42, 45; Michael, 42, 45
Ansar, 50, 52–54
ᶜAntar, 183, 230 n.42
Apartments. *See* Houses, apartments
Appropriation, 17, 51, 57–58, 68; 94–98, 104–6, 131–33, 137–38, 166
Arabic language. *See* Hadiths; Hajj murals, epigraphs; Houses; Epigraphs; Literature; Quran
ᶜArab il-Muhammadi (Cairo), 132, 136
Architecture, Islamic, 3, 51–53, 55, 58–62, 75–86, 88, 94
Arendt, Hannah, 95
Authenticity, 164–65
Azhar University, al-, 88, 164
Azraqi, Ahmad ibn ᶜAbd Allah ibn Muhammad al-, 66–67

Baghdad, 60–63, 67, 207 n.54, 207 n.62, 208 n.69
Ballas, al- (Upper Egypt), 153, 157, 223 n.33
Banu Nadir (tribe), 57
Banu Najjar (tribe), 16, 51, 204 n.9
Baraka. *See* Blessing
Basmala, 173
Bataille, Georges, 214 n.61
Bathrooms, 127–28
Bayt. *See* Flourishing House; Houses; Kaᶜba
Beatific vision, 196 n.30
Bedrooms, 127, 186, 218 n.67
Bes (ancient Egyptian god), 190
Bible, 18, 45
Birds, 229 n.37; images of, 154, 188–89. *See also* Hoopoe
Bistami, Abu Yazid al-, 70
Blackman, Winifred S., 189
Black Stone, 46, 55, 208 n.81
Blessing, 102–3, 111–12, 119, 127, 130, 150, 154–56, 157–58, 172, 177–78; marriage, 108
Boundaries, 95–96
Bourdieu, Pierre, 2
Brides, 106–13, 186, 215 n.18
Bukhara, 58, 68
Bukhari, Muhammad ibn Ismaᶜil al-, 29, 36, 176–77
Buraq, al-, 152 fig.9, 154, 184, 223 n.35
Burial, 116–17
Busiri, Sharaf al-Din Muhammad al-, 85

Cairo, 87; cemeteries of, 121–24, 126–27; contemporary houses, 88–91, 130–33; Euramerican influence in, 88–90, 93–96; founding of, 74; Hajj murals in, 140, 143–44, 158–59; modern layout, 88; orientation, 82–83, 88; population, 74, 132, 219 n.72, 219 n.75; residential patterns, 75, 77–78, 83–84, 86, 89–91, 121–22; shrines, 111; slums and squatter housing, 89–90, 130–33; subcultures, 90–91, 96–97; traditional houses, 74–87; urban renewal, 131–33
Camels, 51; images of, 188. *See also* *Maḥmal*
Canova, Giovanni, 145–46
Cartography, 67
Cemeteries. *See* Cairo, cemeteries of; Tombs
Children, 128–29, 134–35, 216 n.40, 217 n.56; in paradise, 43

Christians, 8, 25, 57, 78; Copts, 74, 76, 91, 136, 143, 160–63, 224 n.48; pilgrimage paintings and, 143
Companions of the Prophet, 59, 75
Complex (mode of thought), 221 n.22
Conquest, 48–49, 56–58, 67–68, 74–76; legends of, 48–49
Conversion, 48–49, 57–58, 68; in Egypt, 76, 162
Copts. *See* Christians, Copts
Courtyards. *See* Houses, with courtyards
Crocodiles, 223 n.40

Dajjal (false messiah), 54
Dār. See House of . . . ; Houses
Dār al-Islām. See House of Islam
Daʿwa, al- (Egyptian Islamic magazine), 164
Death, 114–24, 216 n.40, 217 n.55; mourning, 217 n.56, 218 n.57. *See also* Hell; Paradise; Tombs
Deniers (unbelievers), 12–13, 17, 26, 69; as guests, 36–37; *see also* Muslims, and deniers
Description de l'Egypte, 81 fig.3, 82 fig.4, 144
Dhahabi, Jamal al-Din al-, mansion of, 85 fig.5
Dhikr, 128, 174
Displacement, 57–58, 68, 131–33, 167–69
Divorce, 22, 113, 216 n.35, 216 n.36
Djait, Hichem, 60
Domestic space, 68, 90, 106; defined, 5–6; inversions of, 118–19; meaning of, 94–96, 98–103, 117–19, 124–25, 146, 166–68; transgression of, 119, 130–37. *See also* Houses; Hajj murals
Dukhla (marriage consummation), 107, 110–11, 125, 127

Egypt, 5; ancient, 25, 163, 190–91; funerals in, 115–21; government corruption in, 131–33; government support for pilgrimage, 140; Islamization of, 74–76, 162–63; literacy rate, 151; population, 87; social values, 133–35; subcultures of, 212 n.44, 212 n.45; Upper Egypt, 140, 145. *See also* Hajj murals; Houses
Eickelman, Dale, 100
Eliade, Mircea, 1, 15
Emigrants, 52, 54
Emigration (Hijra), 13, 15, 17–18, 27, 50–51, 57, 64, 135–36, 195 n.15, 203 n.7
Endowments. *See* Trusts
Engagement. *See* Marriage ceremonies
Envy, 102–3, 104, 112–13, 157, 179, 190–91, 223 n.41
Epigraphs, 84–86, 146–54, 156–57, 161, 170–80, 222 n.30
Estrangements, 68–69, 130–37
Evil, 85–86, 102–4, 112–13, 114–15, 126–27, 130, 156–58, 178–79

Fali (Cameroon), 2
Families, 20–21, 77–80, 100–2, 106–19, 122–37, 185–86, 215 n.18, 218 n.57; in Egyptian literature, 134–35; militant Islamic groups as, 135–36; of pilgrims, 141–43, 154–56. *See also* People of the House
Fatalism, 215 n.10
Fatimid dynasty, 74, 76–79
Flourishing House, 31–32, 66–67, 198 n.11
Flowers, 228 n.24, 229 n.28; images of, 187
Funerals, 115–21; compared with marriage ceremonies, 121
Fustat, 74–76, 78; houses of, 76, 209 n.10
Fustel de Coulanges, Numa Denis, 1

Garden. *See* Paradise
Ghanem, Fathy, 134
Ghazali, Abu Hamid al-, 70
God, 54, 62–63, 69–72, 85–86, 101–4, 112, 120–21, 150–51, 153, 170–71, 173–74, 177–78; in hadiths, 28, 30, 37–38, 43–46; in the Quran, 9, 12–18, 20–25
Gossip, 112
Grabar, Oleg, 3, 62
Grooms, 106–11

Hadiths, 3–4, 28–29, 102–3, 147–49, 176–77, 189; collections of, 7, 29, 47, 55, 63, 197
Hajar, 54
Hajj (Pilgrimage to Mecca), 71, 84, 126, 139–40, 171–72, 174–76, 208 n.81; Egyptian government support of, 186–87; expenses, 141; in the hadiths, 54–55; meaning of, 159–60; and paradise, 147; in the Quran, 12–13, 19–20; transportation, 182
Hajj murals, 166–67; ancient Egyptian motifs, 191; as amulets, 156–58; in Cairo, 145–46; of cities and villages

compared, 158–59; classification of, 158–59; colors, 222 n.27; and Coptic iconography, 161–62; distribution of, 140, 143; epigraphs, 142–43, 146–54, 156–58, 163–64, 170–80, 224 n.48; history of, 160–63; iconic figures, 146–52, 154–58, 181–91; interpretations of, 143–46; location in houses, 140–41; meaning of, 159–60, 164–65; Muslim views of, 163–65; organization of contents, 146–49; painters, 141–42, 144–46, 160, 176; painting of, 141–43; and paradise, 151, 153–54, 156; semantics, 149–58, 170–79; semiotics, 145–49; transformations in, 151, 153–54
Hallaj, Mansur al-, 71–72, 208 n.81
Ḥaram. *See* Mecca, *ḥaram* of; Medina, *ḥaram* of; Sacrality
Harems, 77, 79, 210 n.12, 214 n.2
Ḥasad. *See* Envy
Hasan ibn Thabit, 206 n.40
Hasan Kashif (Mamluk emir), mansion of, 81–82
Hell (the Fire): in the hadiths, 41–42, 44; as a house, 46; people of, 69; in the Quran, 12–13, 15–16, 26;
Helwan (Egypt), 76
Ḥijāb (barrier, veil), 23, 26, 113, 156
History of religions, 1–6
Holidays, 111–12
Homelessness, 17–18, 27, 41, 53, 69, 71
Honor, 99–100, 102–3, 110, 112, 134, 137, 154, 178
Hoopoe, 185, 229 n.34
Horus (ancient Egyptian god), 190
Hospitality. *See* Visitation and hospitality
Houris, 41
House of Denial, 69
House of Dissimulation, 69
House of Faith, 69
House of Islam, 45, 49–50, 63–67
House of War, 64–65, 69
Houses: angels in, 38; apartments, 92, 104–5, 109–11, 125–28, 130–33, 135–37, 140–41, 143, 219 n.72; of believers, 48–49; and blessing, 102–3; in cemeteries, 121–22, 124 fig.7; centers of productivity, 101–2; of common people, 87–91, 93–94, 122, 130–33; control of, 39–41; with courtyards, 76–77, 79–82, 94, 210 n.19, 213 n.58; death in, 115–19; decoration, 79–80, 84–85, 95, 110, 118, 124–27, 130, 135–36, 154, 160, 224 n.47; defined, 5–6; of deniers and polytheists, 15–17, 48–49; destruction of, 15–17, 113–14, 131–33; dogs in, 38; as evil omens, 41; furnishings, 118, 125–28; of government, 59; of the heart, 70; of hell, 17, 26, 46; inauguration ceremonies, 104–5; layouts, 77, 80–83, 93, 110, 118–19, 125–28, 130, 135; and mosques, 75–76, 83–84; as mosques, 18, 32–35, 128, 136, 166; murals in, 84; orientation, 82–83; Ottoman, 74–84, 160, 224 n.47; ownership, 77, 83–84; and paradise, 85, 153–54, 167; in paradise, 24–26, 41–43, 83, 167; pictures in, 38; pilgrimage to, 71; posters in, 105, 125–26, 228 n.23; in proverbs, 41; religious feelings in, 129; ritual activities in, 4–5; similar to religious buildings, 80, 82–83; symbolism, 1–5; terminology, Arabic, 8–9, 24–26, 29, 41, 59, 76, 91–94, 176, 194 n.2, 199 n.35, 213 n.51; terminology, English, 5–6, 194 n.11; terminology, Turkish, 213 n.52; as tombs, 43–44. *See also* Appropriation; Flourishing House; Kaʿba; Hajj murals; Muhammad, house-mosque of; Sacrality; Visitation and hospitality
Ḥurma. *See* Sacrality
Husayn ibn ʿAli, 69
Husayn Mosque, 111

Ibn al-Hajj, 143, 163
Ibn Hanbal, Ahmad, 29, 37, 55
Ibn Hisham, ʿAbd al-Malik, 56
Ibn Ishaq, Muhammad, 34, 49–50, 52, 56, 203 n.3, 204 n.15
Ibn Khaldun, 51
Ibn Qudama, 176
Ibrahim (Abraham), 12, 19, 30–31, 46, 54, 175, 181, 184
Ibrahim Agha (Mamluk emir), mansion of, 83
Ibrahim ibn Adham, 71–72
Institut Français d'Archéologie Orientale (Cairo), 3
Interior display, 94–95, 109–10
Iran, 57–58; Islamic Republic of, 168
Iraq, 58–63
ʿIshash Turguman (Cairo), 131–32, 136
Islam (Submission), 7–8, 53, 59–60, 67–69, 96, 103; aniconism in, 163–64; domestication of, 75–87, 96, 167; of Hajj murals, 145; in the Quran, 14–15, 27; study of, 2. *See also* House of Islam; Muslims

Islambuli, Khalid, 137
Islamic Law. *See* Shariᶜa; ᶜUlama
Islamic militant groups, 135–37, 165, 168
Ismaᶜil (Ishmael), 54
Ismaᶜil, Khedive, 88
ᶜItban ibn Malik, 33, 35–36

Jerusalem, 161, 230 n.43; temple of, 14, 31–32, 195 n.13
Jesus, 45–46, 178
Jews, 8, 16–18, 25, 52, 57, 65, 68, 78, 91
Jihad, 64
Jihad group (Egypt), 135–37
Jinn. *See* Spirits
Jomier, Jacques, 144
Judgment Day, 15, 51, 54, 58, 124, 154, 177
Jurists. *See* ᶜUlama

Kaᶜba (God's house), 53–55, 59–60, 70–72, 82–84, 92, 125, 147, 150–51, 153, 159–60, 166, 181–83, 195 n.13, 208 n.81, 209 n.84; in hadiths, 30–32; 46, 54–55, 66–67; in the Quran, 9–14, 19–20, 176, 195 n.4. *See also* Mecca; *Qibla*
Kabyle (Berber), 2
Karbala (Iraq), 69
Kharijites, 69
Kirman (Iran), 57–58
Kitchens, 128
Kriss, Rudolf, and H. Kriss-Heinrich, 144–46
Kufa (Iraq), 58–62, 75, 206 n.49

Lane, Edward W., 144
Lane-Poole, Stanley, 79
Lapidus, Ira, 162
Lassner, Jacob, 61
Lebeuf, Jean-Paul, 2
Leeuw, Gerardus van der, 1
Lions-with-swords motif, 152 fig.9, 154, 182, 189–90
Literature: Arabic, 48–50, 56, 63, 66, 117, 164, 228 n.23; modern Egyptian, 134–35; pilgrimage, 139. *See also* Hadiths; Quran
Lucas, Paul, 144

Madinat Nasr (Cairo), 125
Maḥmal (camel-borne Hajj palanquin), 143, 148 fig.8, 152 fig.9, 157, 181, 183, 185–86
Malik ibn Anas, 54
Mamluks, 77–80, 83–84, 88
Mansur, al- (caliph), 60–62, 67
Marriage ceremonies, 105–12, 125, 186–87, 216 n.29, 216 n.30; compared to funerals, 118; engagement, 107–8
Mary (mother of Jesus), 178
Mecca, 8, 20, 30–32, 99, 103, 126, 136, 182–84, 188; compared with Medina, 54–55; conquest of, 47; *ḥaram* of, 30, 65–67, 103; orientation to, 116. *See also* Kaᶜba; *Qibla*
Medina, 28, 34–35, 46–47, 50–56, 68, 99, 135–36, 188; "constitution" of, 204 n.16; *ḥaram* of, 54, 65, 67; and paradise, 62–63; pilgrimage to, 54–55, 139, 150–56. *See also* Muhammad, house-mosque of
Men, 130; domestic status of, 99–101; images of, 185. *See also* Grooms; Vistation and hospitality; Warrior-saints; Women
Michot, Jean, 145–46, 183–84
Moses, 18, 46, 51, 179, 195 n.15
Mosque-palace complex. *See* Palaces
Mosques, 32, 43, 99, 181, 184, 210 n.21; in Baghdad, 61–62; in houses, 50–56; in Kufa, 59. *See also* Houses, as mosques; Kaᶜba; Muhammad, house-mosque of; *Qibla;* Saint shrines
Mourning rites, 115–21
Movement, 4. *See also* Emigration; Hajj; Pilgrims
Muhammad (the Prophet), 7–8, 13, 20, 30–37, 46, 171, 178–79, 204 n.15; sees angels, 45; blessings for, 174–75, 222 n.30; burial, 205 n.28; companions of, 59, 75; farewell pilgrimage, 39–40; in Hajj murals, 150; house of, 23; house-mosque of, 50–56, 59, 62, 166, 203 n.8, 204 n.13; intercession of, 177; light of, 175; mosque-tomb of, 54, 139, 147–48, 150, 152 fig.9, 154–55, 172, 176–77, 182–83, 188; Night Journey and Ascension, 154, 184, 187, 198 n.14; parables of, 44–46; sees paradise and hell, 41–43; pulpit of, 183; veneration, 85, 175–77; women of, 23–24, 35, 39, 53. *See also* Medina; People of the House
Mūlids (saint days), 154–55, 162, 183, 187, 224 n.51
Musicians, 185
Muslim Brotherhood (Egypt), 135
Muslim ibn al-Hajjaj, 29, 35, 176–77

Muslims (believers), 8, 12–14, 17; and deniers, 20; and non-Muslims, 12–14, 46, 57, 60, 64–66, 68–69, 74–76, 78, 162–63
Mustafa ʿAli, 143–44
Muʿtasim, al- (caliph), 67
Mysticism. *See* Sufism

Nadim, Nawal al-Messiri, 93
Nasir-e Khosraw, 76–77
New moon, 184
New Testament, 45
Niffari, Muhammad ibn ʿAbd al-Jabbar al-, 70, 72
Nubia, 189

Ottomans, 77–80, 160, 213 n.52

Palaces, 59–60, 61–62, 68–69, 86, 93; in Cairo, 76–86; Mamluk and Ottoman, 77–84, 160; Musafirkhana (Cairo), 85;
Parables, 44–46
Paradise, 62–63, 72, 85, depiction of, 147; in the hadiths, 41–45; houses in, 24–26, 41–43, 83, 167; Jewish and Christian notions of, 55; and Mecca, 55; Muhammad's house-mosque as, 55–56; people of, 69; in the Quran, 16, 24–25; tents in, 41, 43. *See also* Hajj murals
People of the House, 18–19, 69, 72, 195 n.16
Pharaoh, 18; in Hajj murals, 191
Photographs, 111, 125–27
Pilgrimage. *See* Hajj; Medina; Pilgrims; Saint shrines
Pilgrimage paintings. *See* Hajj murals
Pilgrims, 139–43, 151–53, 159–60; Coptic, 160–61, 224 n.51, 230 n.43; European views of, 144–46; processions, 183, 185–86; return, 141, 151, 154–55, 157–58, 164, 178, 222 n.32; status, 151, 153, 157–58, 222 n.32; transformation of, 175–76; vows, 178; water for, 183–84
Polytheists, of Mecca, 34–35
Port Said (Egypt), 142
Prayer, 32–35, 53, 116, 128–29, 184–85
Privacy, 21, 39–41, 77, 86, 127–31, 135–36, 149, 210 n.20, 218 n.67; public and private space, 79–80, 95–96, 109–10

Qāʿa (hall), 77, 80–82, 85
Qadi, ʿAbd al-Rahim ibn Ahmad al-, 117, 120–21, 123–24
Qasim Bey (Mamluk emir), mansion of, 82 fig.4
Qena (Upper Egypt), 189
Qibla (prayer direction), 18, 51, 54, 59–61, 67, 83, 195 n.13, 211 n.25
Quran, 3–4, 7–8, 28, 53, 55, 57, 63, 65–66, 103–5, 107–9, 112–13, 125–26, 128, 130, 147, 149, 176, 178–79, 185, 194 n.1, 218 n.68, 222 n.26; compared with hadiths, 46; Euramerican study of, 2; as motif in Hajj murals, 151; houses in, 7–27, 33; inscribed on house walls, 85–86, 144; recitation of, 115–16, 119–21, 123, 128, 218 n.59; status of women in, 40. *See also* Hajj murals, epigraphs; Hajj murals, Quran in; Visitation and hospitality
Quraysh (tribe), 8–9
Qurna (Upper Egypt), 157
Qutayba ibn Muslim, 58

Rabiʿa al-ʿAdawiyya, 71–72, 209 n.84
Ramadan, 111
Religion, study of, 1–2, 194 n.12
Resurrection Day. *See* Judgment Day

Sacrality, 98–103; of domestic space, 37, 119, 123, 136, 154; threats to, 37, 113–14
Sacred history, 9, 14–19, 46
Sacrifice, 19–20, 104, 117, 184
Sadat, Anwar al-, 132–33, 187, 222 n.32; assassination of, 136–37
Saints, 151, 154–55, 188; Christian, 161–63; veneration of, 72
Saint shrines, 111, 127, 154–56, 188–89; Coptic, 161–63
Satan, 37–38, 103
Saudi Arabia, 53, 139, 186
Sayyid, Salah ʿAbd al-, 134
Sayyida Zaynab Mosque, 111
Sex, 105–6, 109–10, 119
Shahāda. *See* Testimony of faith
Shame, 100
Sharaf. *See* Honor
Shariʿa (Islamic law), 7, 64–66, 96, 135, 201 n.61, 216 n.36
Shiʿa, 19, 67, 69, 72, 190, 208 n.81
Sitting rooms, 118, 125–27, 160, 218 n.65
Snakes, 38–39, 154, 157, 182, 189–90
Social action, 94, 117
Songs, 108–9, 114–15, 118–19
Souls, 115, 117, 123, 217 n.46, 229 n.37
Space of appearance, 118, 127, 130, 158

Speech, 94–95, 112–13, 130, 149, 222 n.26; during funerary observances, 119–21; at marriage ceremonies, 108–9. *See also* Hadiths; Quran, recitation of; Songs
Spirits, 104, 114
Subki, Taqiyy al-Din al-, 176
Submission. *See* House of Islam; Islam
Suez City, 125–26
Sufis, 53, 69–72, 162, 177, 187, 209 n.84; study of, 2
Sulayman (King Solomon), 185
Syria, 57

Takbīr, 173
Takfīr wa'l-Hijra group (Egypt), 135
Talbiyya, 174
Talismans. *See* Amulets
Tattoos, 156–57, 184, 186, 190
Testimony of faith, 120, 173, 175
Tirmidhi, Muhammad ibn ᶜIsa al-, 29, 44–46, 55
Tombs, 43–44, 84, 121–24, 155–56, 191, 205 n.28; in Cairo, 90, 93. *See also* Muhammad, mosque-tomb of
Transgression, 119, 130–37; 214 n.61
Trees, images of, 188
Trusts (*waqfs*), 83–84, 88, 211 n.30

ᶜUlama, 28–29, 40–41, 71, 86, 96, 138, 143, 163, 176
ᶜUmar ibn al-Khattab (caliph), 40, 53, 58–59
Umayyad dynasty, 76
Urban renewal. *See* Cairo
ᶜUthman ibn ᶜAffan (caliph), 8, 52 fig.1, 53

Victory (theme in Hajj murals), 150, 172–73, 178–79
Visibility, 109–10
Visitation and hospitality, 20–21, 36–38, 79–80, 99, 122–23, 127, 129–30, 219 n.69
Vygotsky, Lem Semenovitch, 221 n.22

Walid ibn ᶜAbd al-Malik al- (caliph), 53, 55, 58
Waqfs. *See* Trusts
Warrior-saints, 154, 157, 161–62, 185, 189–90, 224 n.52, 230 n.42
Wikan, Unni, 112, 133
Women: attending mosques, 200 n.56; effects of displacement upon, 168; domestic quarters, 79–80; and domestic sacrality, 98–99; fertility rites, 191; and Hajj, 178; images of, 186, 228 n.23; in Islamic militant groups, 135–36; names, 229 n.28; in paradise, 43; power of, 101; and prayer, 35; in the Quran, 22–24; relations with men, 100–101, 105–6, 113–14, 129–30; sacrality of, 37; seclusion of, 143, 210 n.12, 210 n.20; status of, 39–40, 201 n.58, 201 n.61; Sufis, 71–72

Yadlin, Rivka, 134

Zamzam, 183–84
Zar (spirit possession cult), 183, 186, 187–88
Zawiya il-Hamra, iz- (Cairo), 132, 136
Zaytun (Cairo), 126

Index of Quran Citations

1 *Fatiḥa;* 107–8
1:1; 170
1:2; 170

2 *Baqara*
2:125–28; 12
2:144; 172
2:172; 172
2:189; 22, 40
2:196–203; 19
2:197; 176
2:255, 85–86, 125, 217 n.53

3 *Al ʿImrān*
3:96; 9, 171
3:97; 19, 139, 144, 147, 171
3:96–97; 12
3:151; 26
3:160; 172
3:195; 27
3:196–97; 26

4 *Nisāʾ*
4:15; 22
4:34; 22, 39
4:95–100; 17
4:97; 200 n.53

5 *Maʾida*
5:2; 9, 20
5:94–96; 19–20
5:97; 9, 12

7 *Aʿrāf*
7:40–41; 26
7:44–46; 26
7:74; 15
7:91; 15
7:128; 60
7:145; 197 n.35

8 *Anfāl*
8:34–35; 9
8:34–36; 13

9 *Tawba*
9:17, 18, 28; 14, 20
9:72; 25

10 *Yūnus*
10:25; 24, 62
10:87; 18
10:93; 18

11 *Hūd*
11:56; 172
11:73; 19
11:88; 172
11:94–95; 15

13 *Raʿd;* 196 n.30
13:20–24; 25
13:25; 26

14 *Ibrāhīm*
14:28; 26

15 *Ḥijr*
15:46; 153, 172

16 *Naḥl*
16:26; 15
16:30; 24
16:68; 194 n.3
16:80–83; 14, 16

17 *Isrāʾ*
17:4–8; 195 n.9

18 *Kahf*
18:39; 171
18:84–101; 203 n.3

19 *Maryam*
19:25; 172

20 *Ṭāhā*
20:25; 173

21 *Anbiyāʾ*
21:107; 171

22 *Ḥajj*
22:26; 19
22:27; 171

24 *Nūr;* 22
24:2; 196 n.21
24:2–26; 21
24:27–29; 20, 21, 23, 36, 40, 136
24:30–31; 21, 36, 136
24:35; 171
24:35–37; 21
24:61; 20–21, 37

25 *Furqān*
25:10; 85 fig.5
25:15; 62–63

27 *Naml*
27:20–26; 185
27:40; 172
27:52; 15

28 *Qaṣaṣ*
28:12; 19
28:79–82; 15

29 *ʿAnkabūt*
29:41; 194 n.3
29:58; 25

32 *Sajda*
32:11; 200 n.53

33 *Aḥzāb*
33:32–34; 23
33:33; 19, 196 n.22
33:33–34; 35
33:53; 23, 196 n.22
33:56; 171
33:59; 23–24

34 *Saba*
34:15; 15

35 *Fāṭir*
35:35; 24

36 *Yā Sīn;* 218 n.58

39 *Zumar*
39:60; 26

40 *Ghāfir*
40:39; 24
40:52; 26

41 *Fuṣṣilat*
41:28; 26

43 *Zukhruf*
43:33–35; 16
43:68–73; 16

46 *Aḥqāf*
46:25; 15

48 *Fatḥ*
48:1; 172
49 *Ḥujurāt*
49:12; 40
49:13; 172
52 *Ṭūr*
52:4; 31
52:17–26; 25
55 *Raḥmān*
55:46–78; 25
55:72; 41
59 *Ḥashr*
59:2–4; 16
59:7–9; 17, 53, 195 n.10
65 *Ṭalāq*
65:1, 6; 22
66 *Taḥrīm*
66:11; 25
71 *Nūḥ*
71:26–28; 195 n.9
79 *Nāziʿāt*
79:41; 25
94 *Sharḥ;* 173
106 *Quraysh;* 9
113 *Falaq;* 103
113:5; 179
114 *Nās;* 103

Index of Hadith Citations

Abu Bakr saw fit to build a mosque, 33–34
The acceptable pilgrimage deserves no lesser reward than paradise, 171, 176
Angels do not enter houses containing figural images, 163
As for a man's prayer, it is light, 32

The best prayers are those performed in one's home, 34

The day of conquest, the conquest of Mecca, 30
Do not forbid women from going to mosques, 35

Each of you is a shepherd, 39
The earth is a mosque for you, 32
The earth was made a pleasant place, 32
Every day the grave speaks, 43–44

For anyone who prays forty times by my mosque, 172

Haste is not proper when (a man) sets out for a mosque, 200 n.56
The house is a sacred area, 37

If a man goes into his house mentioning God, 37
In my sleep I thought I saw Gabriel, 45
Islam is built on five things, 171–72, 176

(Let it be) an acceptable pilgrimage, 171, 175
Let whoever wishes to smell my scent smell the rose, 187
Look after women, 201 n.58

The most evil thing on which the wealth of Muslims is spent is building, 53
My parable . . . is like the man who built the house, 45

The neighbor of the house is worthier of the house than anyone else, 200 n.39
No one stands by my tomb wretched, 172

O enemy of God, did you think that God would shield you while you were disobeying him?, 40

Peace be upon you, O house of believing people!, 43
Perform some of your prayers in your homes!, 32, 199 n.17
(The pilgrim) returns as on the day his mother gave him birth, 176
Prayer in your quarters is better for you, 35

Satan does not open a closed door, 38
The spirit of the faithful is a bird, 189

Their souls are in the bellies of green birds, 229 n.37

There is no life but the life of the hereafter, 52
This is the fifth of fifteen houses, 66

Visiting (Mecca) during the ʿUmra is a means of atonement, 147, 176

We went on until we reached a green garden, 42
Whatever believer's eyes shed tears for the death of al-Husayn, 69
What is between my house and my pulpit is one of the gardens of paradise, 55; cf. 172, 177
When a believer desires a child in paradise, 43
Whereabouts in your house would you like me to pray?, 33
The white rose was created from my sweat, 228 n.24
Whoever believes in God and the Last Day should not harm his neighbor, 36
Whoever performs the pilgrimage, and is neither obscene nor wicked, 171, 176
Whoever performs the pilgrimage without visiting me, 172, 176–77
Whoever visits me after my death, 177
Whoever visits my tomb deserves my intercession, 172, 176–77
The world is the house of those who have no house, 41
The world is a prison for believers, 41

You are obligated (to look after) the house, 201 n.57
You should provide food and recite the greeting, 36